CHILE 1970-73:
ECONOMIC DEVELOPMENT AND ITS INTERNATIONAL SETTING

INSTITUTE OF SOCIAL STUDIES

SERIES ON THE DEVELOPMENT
OF SOCIETIES

VOLUME IV

INTERNATIONAAL INSTITUUT
VOOR SOCIALE STUDIËN - 'S GRAVENHAGE

CHILE 1970-73: ECONOMIC DEVELOPMENT AND ITS INTERNATIONAL SETTING

Self-criticism of the *Unidad Popular* Government's Policies

Edited by

S. SIDERI

In collaboration with

B. EVERS

1979

MARTINUS NIJHOFF

THE HAGUE/BOSTON/LONDON

ISBN 90 247 2198 9

PRINTED IN THE NETHERLANDS

FOREWORD

One of the main objectives of the *Unidad Popular* ('Popular Unity') Government was to attain Chile's evolution towards more advanced forms of social organization within the framework of strictly respected democracy.

This objective, which is deeply inherent in every human being and consequently present under all conditions and in all parts of the world, is not weakened by temporary defeats or transient retreats. History proves this, and current events in many parts of the world fully confirm it.

One of the areas in which this struggle for progress takes place most intensively is economics. Here, clashes take place between the forces which work towards social progress, and those which oppose it and aim to maintain a system of intolerable priveleges. The ideological and material resources available to the forces which attempt to restrain social progress are not small, and under given circumstances they overcome the forces by which the majority tries to realize a better future.

This is expressed very clearly in the relationships which link the internal dynamics of social development with the great economic and political forces operating at the international level. Consequently, analysis of the social transformation process in such countries as Chile, in the context of the political and economic reactions these processes unleach at the international level, is of key importance.

The chapters in this book are intended to contribute to the much-needed reflection that nations and movements which aspire to emancipation must scientifically undertake in order to devise political strategies which are viable in the different and changing conditions under which this great social struggle progresses.

This book aims to be a self-critical analysis of certain aspects of one particular experience – the Chilean experience – which was of brief duration and took place in the extreme south of the Western hemisphere. Undoubtedly, because this experience has many peculiarities and limitations, one cannot extract conclusions from it which are automatically applicable to other countries. Nonetheless, I believe that analysis of this experience, which is absolutely imperative to carrying on the process of re-establishing democracy in Chile, may offer some lessons which can be used creatively by the nations which, each in its particular way, face the same internal and external enemies as those whose actions are described in the following chapters.

The above becomes more relevant if one considers that those who contributed to this book have been important in creating the economic policies of Salvador Allende's Government. However, they have not shied away from carrying out the most thorough self-critical analysis of the actions they took. This constitutes proof of their honesty and their desire to contribute to searching scientifically to discover the truth.

I believe that those governments which, like that of the Netherlands, implement policies of supporting the Third World countries in their fight for emancipation are likely to find some guidelines in this book for making their technical assistance and international cooperation programmes more directly effective and relevant in fostering the social transformation processes which will continue to take place in these countries.

The experience studied in this book was shattered. Those who came into power by shattering a legitimate government sacrificed democracy for the sake of a minority's priveleges. The events in Chile during the last few years more than confirm the validity and justness of the proposals of all those social and political forces for whom the key objective is attaining an advanced democracy. What the Chilean nation has experienced and suffered has not been in vain, for an increasingly large number of people, with a greater awareness and a stronger spirit of unity, are preparing themselves to obtain the return and development of new forms of democracy which will uproot Chilean fascism forever. It is in this perspective that the studies presented in this book have been written.

Mexico City
March 1978

Hortensia Bussi de Allende

CONTENTS

PARTICIPANTS IN THE SEMINARS

Clodomiro Almeyda	Former Minister of Foreign Affairs and of Defence
Mireya Baltra	Former Minister of Labour and Social Affairs
Alejandro Bell	Former member of the National Congress
Sergio Bitar	Former Minister of Mining
Otto Boye	Former political adviser to the Ministry of Foreign Affairs
David Baytelman	Former Vice-President of the Corporation for Agrarian Reform (CORA)
Anna Corossacs	Former staff member of the Documentation Center of the Central Bank
Ben Evers	Staff member of the Development and Research Institute of Tilburg University (IVO)
Fernando Fajnzylber	Former executive of the Foreign Trade Department of the Central Bank (SEREX)
Hugo Fazio	Former Vice-President of the Central Bank
Edgardo Floto	Former economic adviser to the Ministry of Foreign Affairs
Carlos Fortin	Former Head of the European Office of the Copper Corporation (CODELCO)
Alexis Guardia	Former economic adviser to the President of the Republic
Agustín Gumicio	Former member of the National Congress
Peter van Ginneken	Staff member of the Dutch Ministry of Foreign Affairs
Claudio Huepe	Former member of the National Congress
Alfonso Inostroza	Former President of the Central Bank
Leon Jansen	Staff member of the Development and Research Institute of Tilburg University (IVO)
Orlando Letelier	Former Minister of Foreign Affairs and of Defence
Alberto Martínez	Former Director of the Industry and Trade Department of the Ministry of Economics (DIRINCO)
Orlando Millas	Former Minister of Economics
Hugo Miranda	Former member of the National Congress
Carlos Morales	Former member of the National Congress

Carlos Parra	Former legal adviser to the Chilean Embassy in London
Hernán Ramírez	Former Dean of the Faculty of Philosophy and Education, University of Chile
Pedro Felipe Ramírez	Former Minister of Mining
Sergio Ramos	Former Secretary of the Economic Committee of Ministers
Anselmo Sule	Former Senator
Sandro Sideri	Staff member of the Institute of Social Studies, The Hague
Johan Wolfs	Staff member of the Dutch Ministry of Foreign Affairs
José Zalaquett	Former chief attorney of the Corporation for Agrarian Reform (CORA)

INTRODUCTION

This volume is a collective effort to examine the economic policies of the Government of the *Unidad Popular* ('Popular Unity', hereafter UP), which was in office in Chile from September 1970 to September 1973. The analysis presented here is the work of the very leaders who created the Chilean experience and were responsible for formulating and implementing important parts of the UP Government's policy, for they have contributed the chapters which make up this volume (excepting chapter 10). The profound inside knowledge which these contributors have is an essential element of the volume and is augmented by the fact that the years which have lapsed since the UP Government's demise have enabled the contributors to gain the perspective which is needed to analyze their policies successfully.

This volume is the result of two seminars which were held at the Institute of Social Studies in The Hague, the Netherlands, in April and July 1976. The chapters it contains were originally written as papers to be presented for discussion at the first seminar. The papers were collectively analyzed, evaluated and criticized at the seminar, and thereafter the writers reconsidered and rewrote them in the light of the realizations, consensus, conclusions and deepened understanding which they had reached through the discussions. The papers were then presented for final discussion at the second seminar.

Two points should be emphasized about these seminars: the seminar in April 1976 was the first time that many of the participants had seen each other since the tragic days immediately following the *coup d'état* in September 1973; furthermore, the two seminars together gave the participants their first opportunity to freely consider, discuss and criticize the UP policies in retrospect, not only with fellow party members but also with members of other Chilean parties, particularly with Christian Democrats.

From the start, the political significance of this volume and the political impact which it might have on Chile's future were quite apparent. The contributors have therefore tried to avoid any semblance of apologia, while incessantly stressing the need for sincere self-criticism. It is their conviction that only such an evaluation of the 1970-73 period could help to re-establish progressive democracy in Chile.

This self-critical attitude does not imply that the criteria used in evaluating the Allende Government's economic policies derives from an abstract, supposedly neutral, analysis of the development process. On the contrary, these criteria logically and necessarily originated in the UP strategy's fundamental objectives and in its policy for a structural transformation of the Chilean society. More explicitly, the criteria for evaluation were related to the basic questions of the degree to which the UP Government had succeeded in structurally changing Chilean society and in generating a new economic dynamism through this process of change.

Since all the contributors, except myself, are from the top ranks of the UP, it was felt that their analyses should be scrutinized and criticized at the seminars by a wider group of high-level experts and politicians, including those not connected to the UP and members of the Christian Democratic Party. This means that a wider and more general political dimension was given to what otherwise might have become a mere academic exercise, for the overall analyses given here, together with the conclusions reached in the specific chapters, seems relevant both to other developing countries which are undertaking a process of accelerated social transformation, and to any assessment of the role of international development cooperation.

1. THE CENTRAL THEME IN THE ANALYSES

The theme which unites the chapters is the interaction between the international economic and power system and the domestic economic, social and political structures of developing countries during a process of accelerated social change; Chile is taken as a specific example. The various analyses concentrate on the problem of formulating and executing economic policy during such a process, while at the same time maintaining or even increasing democratic participation.

Many studies of the UP's economic development strategy and policies have tried to explain the ultimate demise in terms of the continual and consistent destructive activities of the hegemonic powers in the international economic system of which Chile is part. Although such studies provide valuable information, most of them fail because they do not make adequate allowance for the fact that the so-called external obstacles and constraints are neither completely external nor exogenous: they are external only initially; very soon they are expressed principally through internal or endogenous variables. Other studies have concentrated on these internal variables, either emphasizing the shortcomings in the UP economic policy or accentuating the impossibility of carrying out a consistent economic policy in the face of such economic and political obstructions as those created by the social forces that opposed the Allende Government. Many studies in the latter category fail to deal adequately with the interaction between, on the one hand, these internal variables and the workings of the present international system and, on the other hand, between these variables and the final objectives and inner logic of the process of accelerated transformation set in train by the UP Government.

In fact, the structure of dominance in the international power system has become internalized in the developing countries. This gives rise to a very complex interaction between the external and internal variables, particularly in countries which are undergoing a rapid social transformation process. Such transformations are conditioned and affected by changes in the production level. A negative evolution in the variables that directly influence this production level may have different causes. For instance, it may be generated by unfavourable developments on the world market (e.g. a fall in the prices for raw material exports); it may be caused by conscious action by a dominant group in the international power system (e.g. an economic blockade); or it may be the result of activities of domestic groups with or without foreign support who oppose the changes (e.g. flights of capital from the country, strikes, etc.). Unsound policy measures may also result in a negative evolution, while governments may sometimes consciously give higher priority to measures that accelerate the process of change, even though this may imply accepting a temporary deterioration in the production pattern. On the other hand, if the production pattern is not negatively affected during a process of change, this may give some indication of the efficiency of Government actions.

Knowledge of the mechanisms of the interaction between the international economic and power system and the structural changes in developing countries is thus necessary for understanding the development process. It is even more important for establishing the conditions for success of similar development strategies in other underdeveloped countries, or in Chile in the future. This point reinforced the decision to concentrate the analyses in this volume on these problems; however, the lessons that can be drawn from the Chilean case are not necessarily and directly applicable to other developing countries. Domestic socioeconomic structures tend to differ and the process by which the dependence structure becomes internalized certainly differs in each case. In addition, the international system is itself still in a process of constant evolution. However, a better understanding of the Chilean case, based on an analytical approach, may provide a valuable lesson to those developing countries that are trying to re-arrange their position within the international economic and power system and at the same time pursue a democratic road to socialism.

The nature of the interaction described above leads to the formulation of three basic questions: (1) how did the system of interaction between the domestic and international economic orders operate in Chile during the 1970-73 period? (2) how was the system perceived by the responsible Chilean policy-makers? (3) how did the UP Government try to deal with it in terms of economic policy?

In order to get a reasonably complete picture of the situation, it was felt that the analyses should deal with different levels and different areas of interaction. Taking into account certain limitations of time and resources, it was decided that at least the following subjects should be included: (1) a general analysis of the domestic (in a broad sense) structural transformations in Chile and the international economic system; (2) a description of how the interaction was perceived by the Chilean policy-makers and the kind of international policy they consequently formulated and executed; (3) a critical examination of the function of the foreign trade sector's in the Chilean economy and of foreign trade policy; (4) a discussion of the mechanics of interaction from a domestic viewpoint, which would complement the analyses above. On one hand it seemed necessary to analyze how and to what degree the domestic structure of production and consumption was geared towards and determined by the international economic system, thus imposing structural limitations on a process of accelerated change. On the other hand, the degree to which the short-term economic policy was or was not in contradiction with the UP strategy of accelerated structural transformation was also an important area for investigation, in which particular attention was to be given to inflation. Also included is (5) an explanation of the mechanics of interaction in terms of more detailed analyses of the structural transformation process. Preference was given to analyzing the nationalizations in the industrial sector, the copper industry and the banking system, because these nationalizations interacted most directly with the international system.

These approaches constitute the basic structure of the volume. However, as was the case during the seminars, additional subjects were touched upon when necessary.

2. THE MAIN RESULTS

The following general conclusions have emerged from the seminars and from this volume.

The *first* and most important conclusion is that the programme of structural transformation with which the UP came to power was an adequate and consistent answer to the Chilean economy's structural problems. Many of the changes proposed and initiated by the UP have a solid basis in modern development theory; moreover, more than two thirds of the Chilean voters favoured parties, programmes and candidates that had explicitly rejected capitalism as a viable and desirable road to development and proposed more or less advanced forms of socialization.

In analyzing why the process of accelerated social change was halted by a military *coup d'état*, it is necessary to look primarily at the implementation of the UP's programme and the conditions under which it was carried out.

While the first point refers basically to the policy-making aspect, the second refers to the question of the viability or non-viability of the Chilean experiment.

The problem of viability has an internal and external dimension, as well as political and economic aspects – apart, of course, from complications that are exogenous to the process of change itself. The analyses in this volume shows that economically and politically the process was viable, at least as regards the external dimension. The UP Government not only successfully frustrated the United States' efforts to isolate Chile economically and politically, but also succeeded in building positive relations with Latin American, socialist, Third World, and Western European countries.

This affirmation of the external viability does not imply any underestimation of the very serious negative impact on the Chilean society and economy of external obstructions and constraints. In fact, it is shown that the discrepancies between Chile's productive structure and its pattern of demand made it extremely vulnerable to external pressure. Detailed analysis of Chile's external sector illustrates the strategic importance of trade with the United States and of the traditional short-term foreign credit lines, both aptly utilized by the United States in what has become known as the 'invisible blockade'. However, while the blockade certainly contributed to the overthrow of the UP Government, the facts do not support the thesis that the Government was doomed unless it gave in to U.S. demands.

This conclusion about the external viability of the Chilean process of structural change should not be too easily generalized and extended to other developing countries. While it can be assumed that any process of structural transformation in a developing country, especially if it aims at constructing a social society, will be severely opposed by the dominant power in the international system by the various means at its disposal, the specific reactions of the different countries and agents composing that system will depend on the place they occupy in the system, on their interests, on whether alternative reactions are possible, etc.

The conclusion that the Chilean transformation process was viable from the viewpoint of external relations – although constrained within narrow boundaries – implies that the key to this process's ultimate successful development had to do with internal forces and with UP political leadership, rather than to external pressure. This conclusion does not contradict the fact that the UP initially underestimated the constraints imposed by the external sector. However, by 1973 the very important destabilizing impact of these constraints had already been substantially neutralized. By that time the Allende Government's foreign policy had in fact achieved its main objective of making the UP project viable insofar as this viability depended on the external situation.

Unfortunately, this development was not accompanied by the establishment of a coherent and effective economic planning system to guarantee an adequate response to the internal destabilizing forces.

The hostility of the Chilean dominant class towards the UP Government cannot be said to derive from the deterioration of the economic situation caused by external factors, and consequently could not be dealt with effectively. However when, later, hostility was generated in other social sectors by concrete economic problems, caused or magnified by the external sector, the internal response which was made did not deal adequately with such problems.

The *second* conclusion is that, despite all the obstacles and resistance which it encountered, the UP Government was able to carry out an important part of its programme: all things considered, the Government's achievements are remarkable and impressive, especially in the field of nationalizing the monopolized and foreign-controlled economic activities, and in the field of workers' participation. Yet the transformation process continued to be dominated by legal and political aspects and by the contradictions between immediate income distribution and structural reorganization of both production and consumption.

The *third* conclusion is, therefore, that the *coup d'état* was not actually instigated by the economic chaos in which the UP had plunged the country, but was the *only* alternative left to the opposition in Chile, because: (1) manifold signs indicated that the economy had started to recover; (2) the economic blockade was being broken; and (3) the UP was making continuous electoral gains.

Fourthly, the UP Government's policy of structural transformation was severely complicated by the economic and political necessity to simultaneously apply a short-term policy of economic reactivation. In theory the short-term policy was complementary to the UP Basic Programme of transformation, but in practice there were contradictions, and the UP Government proved unable to reconcile the two for various reasons.

First, the political struggle reached an unprecendented degree of violence: the opposition efficiently utilized the decomposition of the existing economic structure – which was both necessary to and largely planned by the UP Government – to create economic anarchy and chaos, and it simultaneously obstructed the creation of an alternative economic system.

Second, the way in which the transformation programme was executed created serious imbalances. For instance, the Area of Social Property (APS), which was under direct state control, did not fulfil its planned role as collector of surpluses; it did not achieve coordinated and coherent internal operation; and it did not guide or direct activities in the private sector. This was especially apparent in the industrial APS which, instead of collecting surpluses, directed them towards the private sector, thus significantly increasing the mass of speculative capital circulating in the economy and providing the opposition with the instruments to destabilize the economy.

Third, there was a political need to solve the immediate problems of the masses which supported the UP Government. Even a small increase in income meant that demand was rapidly expanded, necessitating a substantial and simultaneous readjustment in the production structure. However, the extent of the required restructuring had not been fully evaluated and the planned use of existing reserves of human, material and foreign exchange resources was inadequate to close the time gap between the two kinds changes. Consequently, the unprecedented increase in the level of economic activity created enormous internal and external disequilibria. Realization of the alternative production structure was seriously delayed and the consequent increase of consumption rapidly depleted foreign exchange reserves. Despite these difficulties the UP Government succeeded remarkably well in re-arranging Chile's foreign structure and in establishing alternative lines of credit by increasing credit from socialist countries, among others; this enabled the Government to rapidly extend its control over the external sector and thus introduce some degree of coherence and planning into its trade and commercial policies.

Less successful were the Government's attempts to control the domestic financial disequilibrium. Tremendous monetary expansion, which started in the public sector with the increasing deficit in the fiscal budget, became a permanent feature during the UP period. On the one hand, the Government's wage policy was nullified by the workers' long-neglected and justified demands; this caused a drastic increase in expenditure. On the other hand, the opposition in the National Congress systematically rejected all initiatives by the Executive to modify the tax system in order to properly finance increased expenditures through the income redistribution foreseen in the UP Programme. The difficulties in carrying out a coherent financial policy was further increased by the APS's growing deficit caused by, among other factors, the Government's deflationary policy which entailed only limited price increases for goods and services produced by this area. Analogously the exchange rate policy, aimed at maintaining a fixed type of exchange as a deflationary instrument, worsened the foreign exchange disequilibrium. Thus, in general, the initial expectations about the Government's ability to rapidly capture and use a significant proportion of the economic surplus and to control and increase foreign exchange reserves by nationalizing the basic sectors of production proved to be false.

The resulting economic crisis can be qualified as a crisis of transformation. Such a crisis should be distinguished from both the structural crisis that characterized Chile's economy during the 1960s and from a transition to socialism crisis, although the ultimate objective of the transformation initiated by the UP Government was indeed to construct a socialist and independent economy.

The UP Government's policies were determined by short-term economic problems which were worsened by the initial negative effects of the transformation process. To nullify these negative effects the UP Government would have needed, aside from theoretical insight into the implication of that process in a dependent economy, more political power than it had or more international support than many industrial countries were willing to give it. Management of an overall transformation process requires homogeneous and determined political direction. During the rapid transformation process in Chile, alternative solutions to many problems continuously emerged which could have given the UP Government more space to manoeuvre and more strength to resist, if it had been more united and if its leadership had been quicker to grasp such solutions.

The *fifth* conclusion is one that is now recognized by many: the UP Government implemented its programme without even minimally restricting individual liberties and always adhered strictly to the existing democratic framework. This made it even more difficult to realize the envisaged alternative structure and worsened the transformation crisis, which in turn supplied the material basis for the political destabilization process.

Although on several occasions it would not have been difficult for the UP to undermine the institutional order – an order shaped largely by the interests of those who were active in openly subverting the legitimate UP Government – it continued to defend the democratic system. Because of this approach the UP Government was able to enlarge its support and even to come close to sharing power with other important political forces; had the latter been realized, the UP programme would have enjoyed overwhelming majority support.

The *last* conclusion is that international cooperation should have been directed towards (1) closing the gap between production capability and the fulfilment of basic needs and provision of required inputs, while gradually readjusting income distribution; and (2) minimizing the possible negative reactions (of some countries and/or agents in the international system) to such a transformation process.

In general, the type of support from abroad which is given to dependent countries which are in the process of development is particularly important if democratic rule is to be maintained and radicalization is to be avoided. Such cooperation towards transition should enable wider political participation in the development process and should strengthen the developing country's capacity to absorb external as well as internal reactions to the process of structural change.

3. HOW THE RESEARCH FOR THE SEMINAR WAS SET UP

From the moment that a tangible proposal for research in preparation for the seminars started to take shape, it became obvious that an essential condition for successful analysis was the participation and cooperation of a considerable number of those Chileans who had been in charge of formulating and/or implementing the UP Government's policies. Indeed they were the persons who could best take on the responsibility of carrying out most of the research.

This phase of the project proved to be critical because it was extremely difficult to contact many of the contributors and participants and to explain the aims and organization of the research. In addition to being profoundly familiar with the general UP strategy and its policies, as well as being specialized in one of the areas to be analyzed in the seminars, the contributors had to be able to guarantee basic scientific standards in their work. Finally, agreement had to be reached among these contributors on a definitive research outline.

When the preparatory phase had been completed, it was decided that the project should be carried out in three stages.

During the first stage (May 1975 to April 1976) preliminary drafts on the various subjects were prepared and presented at the first seminar. Not only the contributors were invited, but also several other persons who for various reasons could be expected to contribute substantially to the discussions (see 'Participants in the Seminars' on p. xi).

The drafts were discussed, commented on, and criticized; various viewpoints and different interpretations were compared; alternative approaches were evaluated to eliminate unnecessary overlappings and indicate possible omissions: finally, issues which needed to be dealt with more specifically were pointed out.

Complications arose with regard to the divergences in the statistical data used in the preliminary drafts. As the various statistical sources used were not always consistent for the 1970-73 period, efforts were made to construct an agree-upon data base for at least the more general statistics (balance of payments, the external debt, etc.; see the Statistical Appendix following Chapter 2). However, the problem of consistent sources for more specific data remained, for the contributors have been denied access to original data and original publications of official institutions in Chile because they are forced to live in exile. Consequently, traditional academic standards with respect to source references could not always be maintained. On the other hand, it should not be forgotten that the contributors were high Government officials during the period examined and had final responsibility for collecting these data and/or formulating policies on the basis of them, whether they were officially published or not.

It was suggested during this first seminar that, given the relatively heavy urban-industrial bias of the chosen approach, an analysis should be included of the role played by agrarian reform in the system of interactions which was the general subject of the research. Apart from time limitations, the lack of specific data made it difficult to compile a separate contribution on the subject; instead, frequent references to agrarian problems are made in almost all the papers. (Some people, including David Baytelman, are working on this subject and it is hoped that such an analysis will be published shortly.)

It was also suggested that the volume should include a chapter that would briefly describe the Chilean economy's structural problems in the late 1960s. It was felt that such an introductory chapter would be useful for those readers who are not well acquainted with the Chilean situation.

During the second stage (April 1976 until July 1976), the contributors incorporated the observations, comments and criticisms made during the April seminar and they re-formulated their papers accordingly, so that their final drafts could be presented and discussed at a second seminar on 2-4 July 1976.

On the basis of suggestions that were almost unanimously voiced during the April seminar, and that confirmed both my and Ben Evers' ideas about the seminars, efforts were made to expand the political spectrum of the participants for the July seminar. The interest generated by the first seminar was exceptional and the principal constraint on honouring the positive response received from interested Chileans was limited financial resources. Furthermore, among the persons invited were many who were enthusiastic about the project and would have participated if personal or political circumstances had made it possible for them. In this regard, particular mention should be made of the interest expressed in the project by various leading figures in the Chilean Christian Democratic Party, both inside and outside Chile.

The April seminar had effectively proved that it had become possible to have a sincere, open and critical discussion on the UP experience among people of different political orientations. The July seminar reinforced this, despite the fact that the participants did not always agree, and could not have been expected to agree, with all the points presented in the papers. Some preferred other approaches and alternative interpretations of some facts were sometimes voiced. Nevertheless, the fact that the people who were ultimately responsible for the politics and policies of the UP Government could freely exchange opinions, without necessarily expressing their political parties' official view, was a significant step forward in the struggle to create a wider political alliance, and thus to reconstruct a better Chile.

During the third stage (July 1976 to July 1978) the papers were finalized, translated, and considerable editorial work was undertaken.

It is not necessary to summarize the discussions that took place during the April and July seminars because most of what was said has been introduced into the chapters in one way or another. In this sense this volume is genuinely a collective effort. Furthermore, because of the tone, content and political dimensions of these discussions, it would have been impossible for an outsider to adequately summarize them, at least in political terms. Also, the participants were promised complete confidentiality (which was why the discussions were not tape-recorded), for the success of these meetings has depended, to a significant degree, on the fact that the participants indeed felt sufficiently safe to be able to speak freely. Finally, because it was generally felt that it was necessary to place the seminar in a proper political context (a task which could only be performed by a Chilean), Clodomiro Almeyda was asked by all the participants in the seminar to write a separate chapter in which he comments on the major conclusions that can be derived from the seminars.

One of the conclusions reached is that dominant powers in the international system have played an active role in toppling the legitimate government of Salvador Allende and thus in destroying democracy in Chile. The international community therefore has a responsibility to help Chileans in their struggle to regain national dignity. This may take many forms. In the case of these seminars it took the shape of a forum in which UP economic policies could be reconsidered. Analyzing the past can be a starting-point for future coordinated, or possibly joint, action by the various Chilean political forces.

As organizers of this project, Ben Evers and I would like to express our personal gratitude to many people and institutions who have cooperated in working on the seminars and on this volume. We wish to thank the Dutch Minister of Development and Cooperation and many of his officials for their help. Furthermore, we are grateful to the Institute of Social Studies in The Hague and the Development and Research Institute of the University of Tilburg: both institutions have cooperated most effectively. Valeria de Baytelman has provided organizational support during the seminars, while Jean Sanders and Millie Blomhert have made possible the publication of this volume by solving extremely time-consuming and difficult translation and editorial problems. We would also like to thank Mrs A.Born-Doorschodt, Mrs G.W.Ackers-Jonker and Mr J.W.van Wieringen for their help in producing the book.

We do not consider it appropriate to individually thank the many Chileans who at various stages and in many ways have been helpful in the realization of the seminars and of this volume. However, we must make one exception for Orlando Letelier who, shortly after his participation in the July seminar, was assassinated in Washington, D.C. We dedicate this volume to him because his death once again affirms the urgency uniting all the democratic forces both in Chile and in the international community in the struggle to re-establish a democratic system in Chile which is based on respect for human dignity.

Sandro Sideri

ABBREVIATIONS

AID	Agency for International Development
AIFLD	American Institute for Free Labour Development
ALALC	*Asociación Latinoamericana de Libre Comercio* [Latin American Free Trade Association, LAFTA]
Andes	Andes Copper Mining Company
Andina	*Sociedad Minera Andina* [Andina Mining Corporation]
APM	*Area de Propiedad Mixta* [Area of Mixed Property]
APP	*Area de Propiedad Privada* [Area of Private Property]
APS	*Area de Propiedad Social* [Area of Social Property]
APSM	*Area de Propiedad Social y Mixta* [Area of Social and Mixed Property]
Basic Programme	*Programa básico de la Unidad Popular* (see Chapter 9, note 7 on the text of this program)
CAP	Pacific Steel Company
CAR	*Certificado de Ahorro Reajustable* [Readjustable Savings Certificate]
Central Bank	*Banco Central de Chile* [Central Bank of Chile]
CEPLAN	*Centro de Estudios de Planificación Nacional, Universidad Católica de Chile* [Centre for the Study of National Planning, Catholic University of Chile]
CEREN	*Centro de Estudios de la Realidad Nacional* [Centre for the Study of National Reality]
CESO	*Centro de Estudios Socioeconómicos* [Socio-Economic Studies Centre]
CHILEX	Chile Exploration Company
'Church Committee'	The United States Senate Select Committee to Study Government Operations with Respect to Intelligence Activities (chaired by Senator Church)
CIA	Central Intelligence Agency
CIAP	*Comisión Interamericana de la Alianza para el Progreso* [Inter-American Committee for the Alliance for Progress]
CIPEC	*Consejo Intergubernamental de Paises Exportadores de Cobre* [Intergovernmental Council of Copper-Exporting Countries]

CODELCO	*Corporación del Cobre* [Copper Corporation]
CORFO	*Corporación de Fomento de la Producción* [Corporation for Production Development]
CORVI	*Corporación de la Vivienda* [Housing Corporation]
CPI	Consumer Price Index
CUT	*Central Unica de Trabajadores* [Trade Unions' Confederation]
DAC	Development Assistance Committee of OECD
ECA	*Empresa de Comercio Agrícola* [Agricultural Trade Agency]
ECLA	Economic Commission for Latin America (*Comisión Económica para América Latína*, CEPAL)
Eximbank	Export-Import Bank
fob	free on board
GATT	General Agreement on Tariffs and Trade
GDP	Gross Domestic Product
GNP	Gross National Product
Gran Minería	*Gran Minería del Cobre* (the largest Chilean copper companies, including the Chuquicamata, Salvador, El Teniente and Exótica mines; formerly partly U.S.-owned, nationalized in 1971)
IDA	International Development Association of the World Bank
IDB	Inter-American Development Bank (*Banco Interamericano de Desarrollo*, BID)
IFC	International Finance Corporation of the World Bank
IMF	International Monetary Fund
ITT	International Telephone and Telegraph Company
JAP	*Junta de Abastecimento y Precios* [Council for Control of Supplies and Prices]
OAS	Organization of American States
ODA	Official Development Assistance
ODEPA	*Oficina de Planificación Agrícola* [Office of Agricultural Planning]
ODEPLAN	*Oficina de Planificación Nacional* [Office of National Planning]
OECD	Organization for Economic Cooperation and Development
PDC	*Partido Demócrata Cristiano* [Christian Democratic Party]
SB	*Superintendencia de Bancos* [Bank Superintendence]
SEREX	*Secretaría Ejecutiva de Relaciones Económicas Externas* [Foreign Trade Department of the Central Bank]
SNA	*Sociedad Nacional de Agricultura* [National Agricultural Society]
SOFOFA	*Sociedad de Fomento Fabril* [Industrial Development Society]
SOQUIMICH	Chilean Mining and Chemical Company
State Bank	*Banco del Estado de Chile* [State Bank of Chile]

TIAR	*Tratado Interamericano de Asistencia Recíproca* [Inter-American Treaty of Reciprocal Assistance]
UN	United Nations
UNCTAD	United Nations Conference on Trade and Development
UP	*Unidad Popular* [Popular Unity]
World Bank	International Bank for Reconstruction and Development
WPI	Wholesale Price Index
$	United States dollar
E°	Chilean escudo

Orlando Letelier
in memoriam

1

CLODOMIRO ALMEYDA

THE REASONS FOR SELF-CRITICISM OF THE UNIDAD POPULAR GOVERNMENT

We have before us a collective work of self-criticism written by close colleagues of President Allende on the economic policy of the *Unidad Popular* (UP) Government in Chile (1970-73), with special reference to its impact on international relations.

We define this work as self-criticism, meaning critique from within the reality that is criticized and assuming on the part of the practitioner an acceptance of the essential content of the process in which the criticized situation is set.

In this volume a basic supposition is shared by all contributors, namely that the UP Government's meaning and significance was its contribution to the revolutionary transformation of Chilean society towards socialism. This transformation was initiated with the idea of (1) breaking the ties that made Chile a politically and economically dependent nation, (2) reducing the preeminence in the national economy of national and foreign monopolies which distorted the economic structure in favour of their own interests, (3) deepening and broadening the scope of agrarian reform, and (4) setting up a system of social property which would eventually become the dominant sector of the economy, thus determining the socialist orientation of the revolutionary process.

To undertake such an examination of the economic experiences of the UP Government implies an evaluation in terms of these social transformation targets. The final balance has to be drawn up within this frame of reference.

We cannot judge these experiences in terms of the social and economic reproduction process that prevailed when the UP Government came to power, or according to its degree of success in the greater or lesser efficiency which it achieved in making the prevailing social and economic system work. On the contrary, it is necessary to judge whether the Government was capable of changing or altering this system and whether it could do so in such a way that the transformation could continue, self-managed and self-regulated, until Chilean society could be put on the road to socialism.

To measure the Chilean economy's efficiency in terms of conventional indicators such as increase of output, monetary stability, balance of payments, etc., is not an adequate standard for self-criticism. Greater or lesser efficiency in economic management defined according to conventional standards is useful only as a basis for or as a condition that favours or hinders the economic transformation process and the political assumptions that can give viability to that process. Efficiency in running the existing economic system is not an end in itself, but merely an element that begins to matter to the extent that it helps or hinders the continuation of the revolutionary process. In other words, efficiency in reproducing the system is important inasmuch as, from the political viewpoint, a minimal working efficiency is necessary to make its transformation feasible. It is the efficiency with which change is brought about which is of interest, the political efficacy in advancing the revolutionary process in which such noneconomic variables as the level of political leadership, political organization and political awareness play an important role. Conventional economic management efficiency criteria are conditioning factors in the process of developing these elements.

Propagandists of Chilean fascism present a frightening picture of the economy during the UP Government, but their criticism from outside the revolutionary process is of no value and means nothing at all to revolutionaries. Their criticism concerns the UP Government's inability to reproduce the existing system. Our self-criticism concerns the Government's ability to destroy the existing economic situation and at the same time rebuild the system on new political and value foundations, in such a way as to prevent the destructive aspect of revolutionary action from getting out of control and thus making impossible a socialist-oriented reorganization of the economy.

This collective volume does not claim to be a complete self-criticism in the sense just defined, partly because we are basically concerned with the economic aspects of the UP, particularly those aspects which have to do with international relations.

In the course of preparing the chapters in this volume and in the ensuing discussions, we became increasingly aware of the interdependence between the specifically economic aspects and the politico-institutional, politico-military and ideological aspects of the UP Government's management. These levels of social reality are not analyzed in their substantive right in this volume, despite the fact that the politico-military level is the most all-embracing and decisive, and that the political and institutional environment in which the political struggle took place was of prime importance in bringing together the social forces which determined the success of the fascist putsch in 1973. These levels are only considered to the extent that they impinge on economic factors. Obviously, the limited consideration given to noneconomic factors implies an inadequate coverage in that the deepest roots of the political process are not fully analyzed. But such an ambitious objective as complete coverage was not the inspiration for these studies.

In other words, this is a self-critical analysis dealing with the economic aspects of the UP Government's performance, an analysis which, for the reasons indicated, is incomplete and cannot be otherwise. Its conclusions provide working material which, if it is to be fully utilized, should be incorporated in an overall political evaluation of the UP Government. Such an attempt is not the aim of the present study which, albeit important, is not sufficiently comprehensive to allow a genuine self-examination of the whole reality. It is thus a support study of limited scope.

On the other hand, our study of the economic aspects also does not claim to be exhaustive. There are lacunae, points which are insufficiently clear, differences of opinion, aspects which are inadequately covered, etc., and we do not pretend to provide a detailed account of all the activities of the UP Government in order that it might be subjected to critical analysis. We have already noted the inadequacy of the conceptual framework in which ideological, politico-institutional and politico-military aspects are given only the relevance that stems from their necessary interdependence at different levels of the social structure. Furthermore, the UP Government's achievements in educational, cultural and social participation are also not discussed or evaluated. Although these achievements were limited, they constituted appreciable advances for Chilean society and also helped to clarify the sense and direction which the social change process was taking.

Far from reducing the value of this volume, these limitations are proof of its significance as a contributory work. Only by practising a basic modesty in presenting the partial results can we ensure that the self-critical approach which has been initiated will eventually lead to valuable conclusions.

These conclusions should be valuable to the extent that they are instructive. Self-criticism in the context of a revolutionary process is a necessary step if the process is to continue to develop and to overcome its limitations. For this reason, the Chilean revolutionary process will only succeed in developing for as far as it is capable of overcoming the mistakes and limitations revealed under the UP Government. This collective volume, although undertaken in an academic environment without party prejudice or political colour, is an integral part of the UP's political effort. It is a contribution to an unavoidable step in any revolutionary process. By offering constructive self-criticism from some of the people most concerned, it constitutes a yardstick of the Chilean people's revolutionary struggle against fascism, thus assuming an essentially political content.

It could not be otherwise. To marxists, social science in the contemporary world has no meaning except as an instrument of revolutionary action. 'Philosophers have so far attempted to explain the world', said Marx more than a hundred years ago; 'it is now their turn to transform it'. With these words he signalizes the essence of social knowledge in the present historical context, namely, that it is an indispensable and constituent element of revolutionary praxis which undermines capitalist society and at the same time builds socialism. When Lenin adds that 'without revolutionary theory there is no revolutionary action', he is referring to the role of self-criticism, an unavoidable element in the progressive task of social transformation.

It should be noted that all the contributors to this volume (with the exception of Dr. Sideri) have played dual roles, for besides writing the chapters they all were to a greater or lesser extent important actors in carrying out the UP's economic policy. Their reflections thus have a special value which is not customary in this type of work. They all were, and still are, active militant members of the popular parties, deeply committed to the political activities of the Chilean anti-fascist resistance. Because of this, the correct orientation of the contributors' self-criticism is reinforced and, I believe, the value of the contributions is enhanced.

Again, although this book appears to be a collection of studies by different writers, in fact the themes were actually decided upon after two fruitful meetings at which the contributors had the opportunity to exchange ideas, engage in mutual criticism, and adjust many of the opinions they initially held.

Furthermore, leaders of the parties in the UP were present at the meetings which preceded the final presentation of the working papers, and they actively participated in debates during which their ideas were taken up by the contributors. Even the views of anti-fascist Christian Democrats were represented in these debates. The perceptions and observations of the Christian Democrats, all of whom took a clear stance against the fascist junta, equally enriched the discussion.

We therefore have before us a work which in good measure is a collective effort, despite the fact that it is apparently an aggregation of independent studies. This characteristic is clearly shown in the considerable consensus between the contributors on the fundamental matters. Though there are admittedly differences in emphasis and style in the approach to some questions and even some significant discrepancies, ultimately there is a convergence of opinion on fundamental issues. Unity prevails over dissent. This is politically very significant because it relates to an important feature of the Chilean resistance movement, namely, that among the resistance groups which are the most stable and mature in terms of both quantity and quality, an extremely important, basic consensus is gaining ground not only on how to judge the past but also on how to plan for the future.

This phenomenon is found at all really important levels, whether inside the country or elsewhere, and allows the future course of the Chilean left to be viewed with some optimism. As in any progression this process of convergence is not without its cost, neither is it free from difficulties and pitfalls which, to the outside observer, might seem to indicate disunity and anarchy. Happily that is not the true situation. What is important is that in the broad mainstream of Chilean anti-fascism the various divergent trends are tending to come together, even though on the surface disagreements and disputes, protests and even violent altercations, are sometimes highlighted, which in truth are only the cost and consequences of the united advance in all its essentials. One should say with Don Quixote, 'the dogs are barking, a sign that we are walking'.

Nevertheless, one further point needs to be made. The opinions expressed in this collective volume are those of the contributors only. They are not as yet the final opinion of the political parties in which the contributors are activists, and far less the definitive judgment of the UP as a whole, on the experience which the Chilean nation underwent between 1970 and 1973.

The conclusions of the studies being undertaken under UP auspices, and also of this collective volume, will need to be carefully scrutinized by the political decision-makers of that political alliance before they are finally incorporated into the Chilean popular movement's ideological repertory.

As in any dialectical process, however, the work done in preparing this volume cannot fail to influence the criteria used by the political decision-markers. In the final result, therefore, these studies will constitute not merely a group of ideas which the UP will evaluate independently of the context in which they were conceived, for that very context will enrich the perspective from which these ideas will ultimately be judged.

The studies presented here have some important conclusions in common which might be said to represent basic consensus which emerges from their varied contents.

The first of these conclusions has to do with the viability of the so-called Chilean road to socialism. This term, which has been questioned many times, means nothing more or less than that the UP's political aims included an important strategy for capturing power which was based on Chilean reality. Its scope can only be measured in terms of the Chilean experience: conclusions cannot be extrapolated for use in other political contexts in other societies. This does not imply any disregard of the existence of fundamental laws that are valid for all revolutionary processes; it means that these laws have their individual expression in each society and that, in the case of Chile, the political project took national peculiarities into account.

Viewed from this angle the conclusions of all the chapters in this volume agree that the general, basic strategy for capturing power was viable, did not necessarily have to lead to failure, and that the negative results which ultimately frustrated the UP political experiment were due to errors and inadequacies in implementing the strategy and not to inherent weaknesses in its nature and structure. This statement, implicit in some contributions and explicit in others, is consistent with other conclusions which complement it and define its meaning more precisely.

Another conclusion that emerged, and which accords with the previous one, is that, in effect, the thwarting of the UP experiment can be attributed to internal factors in the implementation of the selected strategy and not to exogenous elements. Various decisive passages in the following chapters point out that external factors were important and might even have been decisive but only inasmuch as they were translated and converted into internal factors, which then combined to prevent the project's success. Possibly because these exogenous factors collided with internal reality, conditions were created which permitted the internal enemies of the Revolution to increase their strength and weakened that of its supporters.

A corollary of this important conclusion is that an analysis of events leads one to reallocate responsibility for what happened to the inadequacies of the internal organization rather than to the exogenous action of independent variables. Decisive as these variables may have been, they were only effective because of measures which were part of the domestic application of the strategy chosen.

This does not in any way diminish the weight of the external problems encountered by the revolutionary process. The Chilean economy, being dependent, is especially vulnerable to outside aggression. Responding to such aggression therefore demanded an exceptionally efficient handling of all factors to successfully counter the conjunction of internal and external oppositional elements which, in their totality, increased the reserves of strength of the internal counterrevolutionary forces. In other words, although the Chilean revolutionary process was viable, it had little room for manoeuvre and only very skillful leadership could have avoided the obstacles which it necessarily encountered as it developed.

The logical conclusion to this reasoning is that, during the UP Government experiment, no directive force was available which, in moments of acute political crisis, would have been capable of responding appropriately to the situation that was not foreseen during the early days.

One consideration might help to clarify the dimensions of this conclusion: although during even the most difficult period of the crisis, no adequate response or effective agent arose from within the process, nonetheless the very course of events generated reactive elements which typified both the shape that this response should take and the agent that should be created to deliver it. It cannot be said, therefore, that in Chile the centre of the revolutionary political and social forces showed no signs of restructuring its constituent elements in such a way that the situation could have been brought under control and the advance of the revolutionary process would have been ensured. The areas of foreign trade, monetary policy, distribution of goods, agriculture, and the general economic organization showed unequivocal signs of a new orientation that was likely to solve the problems raised by the crisis. But in politics the time factor is decisive. These positive trends did not coalesce into a new coherent economic policy which could have altered the overall situation. In any case, by mid-1973 the counterrevolution had gained its own momentum, consequently determining the overall situation to such an extent that it would have been very difficult for the mere emergence of an ideal economic programme to change the direction in which political events were leading. This assertion was to some degree proven beforehand, for early in July 1973 a coherent economic policy saw the light which clearly outlined a new approach to tackling the crisis. But the political whirlpool into which the country had been thrown made such projects inoperative; by this time they could no longer alter the course of events which were increasingly determined by the almost physical confrontation between struggling social forces and in which the military factor gradually acquired a more decisive role.

Nevertheless, the great improvement in the economic policy area which was laboriously surmounting the obstacles which the counterrevolution put in its way is shown by the fact that by July 1973 the economic blockade, sponsored by the imperialist nations in order to strangle the Chilean economy, had failed. Chile had managed to overcome the perilous situation in which it had found itself at the end of 1972. It had succeeded, with the aid of socialist countries, in avoiding a suspension of payments early in 1973 and, in the course of that year, had managed despite all difficulties to reconstruct credit lines in the West, thus allowing the Chilean economy to continue functioning without fear of imminent collapse.

To defeat the main thrust of the attempt to block the UP's political programme through external pressure, Chile effectively took advantage of the differences in the West between forces committed to the counterrevolution and those which remained more or less independent from this tendency and even openly sympathized with the Chilean experiment. The latter was basically the case of those Western European countries with a liberal democratic tradition, and particularly those states ruled by social democratic governments who did not hide their favourable predisposition towards the UP Government.

The fact that Chile came so close to victory over imperialism – an imperialism which made no secret of its intention to liquidate the Chilean revolutionary programme by any means available – cannot be explained without weighing the significance of the presence, importance and influence of the socialist countries, principally the Soviet Union, in the political arena of the world today. It was this which limited and still limits the options for imperialist action, and which decisively prevented the imperialist powers from fully utilizing all their enormous reserves of power to strangle the vulnerable and dependent Chilean economy.

The socialist world's contribution to Chile's revolutionary experiment should not be solely measured by effective assistance in carrying out economic development plans or in solving the grave crisis in the general balance of payments situation. An essential factor is the political effect that the presence of the socialist state system, with its policy of peace and *détente*, has in constraining counterrevolutionary activities on a world scale and in giving viability to the efforts of developing nations to secure their sovereignty, to build independent economies, and to progress towards advanced forms of social organization.

To the extent that the UP Government carried out its programme – thus adversely affecting the interests of imperialism, of the monopolies and the landowners – and particularly when it was realized that the Government's revolutionary course could not possibly be corrected through democratic means, the country's class struggle burst out of its institutional channels, thus involving all social sectors and becoming strongly articulated, so that all the international forces were working either for or against the Chilean revolution.

The conventional manifestations of political struggle at the congressional and electoral levels were soon overtaken by acute social conflict in all groups of national life. Later on this conflict reached the barracks, and ultimately it was the brutal and homogeneous intervention by the armed forces which determined the success of counterrevolutionary politics.

It is not the task of this study to pass judgment on the institutional and military policy of the UP Government, although a great deal could be said on the subject. It is, however, well worthwhile pausing to think about the factors which made it possible for the armed forces to successfully intervene in the political arena and to transform themselves into self-confessed and efficient agents of counterrevolution. There is no doubt that, among those factors, the country's worsened economic situation was of great influence. This predisposed significant middle sectors against the Government, and decisively shaped the alignment of social forces in the conflict which the armed forces could foresee when they decided to take power by force.

It is therefore necessary to delve more deeply into the nature of the economic strategy followed by the UP Government in order to determine whether it contained any fundamental flaws.

Study of the chapters in the volume shows a notable inconsistency between short-term economic policy, which the Government promoted from the beginning with the aim of obtaining political support from the electorate, and the long-term objectives of socialist transformation of Chile's economy and society.

During the first few months of UP Government the UP successfully carried out its policy of short-term economic reflation within the framework of the capitalist economic system. No significant alterations were made to the mechanism of regulating economic life according to the laws of the market. The nature of production was not changed, and no shift in the pattern of consumption was introduced in order to make economy's reflation compatible with a progressive socialist reorganization of the economy, not only as far as ownership of the means of production was concerned but in relation to the aims and objectives of the economic process.

The behaviour of economic agents continued to be ruled by motivations arising from the system's values and ideology. Under these circumstances it was impossible to pull down the main pillars on which the system rested, to control the economic process at every level, to convert the economy's dominant sector into socialized property and to promote socialist accumulation. The loss of control over the economic process, principally expressed in accelerating inflation, in shortages, hoarding and speculation, was the consequence of not having used socialist instruments in the short-term policy in order to ensure that the population's largest sector benefitted from the productive effort, and of not simultaneously eliminating conspicuous consumption and the waste of resources in the hands of the bourgeoisie.

Even if we suppose that such a daring and suggestive course were correct in the abstract, the question arises of whether it was politically feasible. Was there initially sufficient strength to combat tendencies which were strongly rooted in traditional patterns of behaviour? Without capturing total power, was it viable to try to lead economic actors along paths other than those which spontaneously arise from the system's process of reproduction? Or was the only possible course to first gain political support, thus aiding the total capture of power which, once in revolutionary hands, would have allowed those other socialist tasks to be carried out which initially had to be postponed?

It is impossible to give a definitive answer to such questions. From the general context of the chapters in this volume, we are given the impression that greater efficiency in the economic and political management of the process would have permitted more interrelationship and mutual support between the policy of reflation and that of economic change on the one hand, and the process of gathering power and politically strengthening the new regime on the other.

The query which this issue raises, and which is not clearly answered by the various chapters, reveals that much still needs to be explored in analyses of the Chilean political experiment. It is to be hoped that this volume will stimulate and accelerate the clarification of this and other key questions so that serious judgment can be passed on the UP Government.

This volume forms part of the collective effort by the Chilean Resistance, to find, through self-criticism of the route taken by the UP, the elements which will allow a deeper understanding of the Chilean reality and overcome the limitations and weaknesses of the revolutionary process which aided the success of the fascist *coup d'état*.

It has already been stressed that this *coup d'état* only temporarily interrupted the history of the Chilean people's advance towards socialism. The intensification of the class struggle to its greatest heights as a consequence of the UP Government's achievements, and the violent and brutal reaction which characterized and still characterizes the attempt of the propertied classes to maintain their preeminent role in society by destroying traditional democracy and setting up a fascist state – retrograde, cruel and bloody – has served the political education of the people. It has steeled and tempered their vanguard, made them realize who their enemies are, taught them how to combat those enemies and how to advance along the road towards democracy, progress and socialism.

Although public political activity in Chile is temporarily in abeyance and all means of expressing popular feeling are gagged, beneath the apparent 'order' and 'tranquility' – the peace of the grave – there is a new and powerful growth of anti-fascist awareness which is lucid and consistent, and which will be the motor of the people's actions when Chilean fascism reaches a crisis and the gates are once more opened, allowing the popular movement to advance.

In this new stage, sooner rather than later as President Allende would have said, the value of critical reflections on the Chilean process and on the whole of the UP Government's experience will be seen to be of fundamental importance. In these reflections the experience of the masses and their leaders is distilled, and theoretical and political capital is built up which will clarify the future road of the Chilean popular movement, in both the fight against fascism and in the subsequent stages when a new Chilean democracy will be built on the ruins.

The ideas contained in this volume, like so many ideas which have emerged from critical analysis of the Chilean experience after the military *coup d'état*, represent raw material for the progressive design of the historic programme which Chilean anti-fascists will have to draw up for rebuilding their country. They are ideas which do not belong to any particular party, elements for the great political undertaking which is being born in the fight against fascism; and they are destined to bring success to the activities of hundreds of thousands of Chileans, inside and outside their country, carried out under difficult circumstances to allow democracy to return to Chile and to open the way for socialism.

2

ALEXIS GUARDIA, ALBERTO MARTÍNEZ
AND
SERGIO RAMOS

GENERAL CONSIDERATIONS ON THE CHILEAN ECONOMIC STRUCTURE

Any effort at understanding a process so large and complex as that which was experienced in Chile under the *Unidad Popular* (UP) Government requires careful reflection to ensure the theoretical approach needed in gaining scientific knowledge. Nothing could be more alien to such an effort than an apology for, or an accusation against, such an experience.

In this social process the economic transformations had a significant effect at every level of Chilean society. In the pages that follow, some of the most relevant economic phenomena of this experience are highlighted: the successes and failures, the advances and limitations. It is certainly meaningless to attempt to isolate 'economic' and 'political' phenomena, the more so when we are dealing with very deep social change. But, with this in mind, it is not invalid to conduct an analysis stressing the economic aspects of a more general political struggle. This is even more worthwhile if, as in Chile, the struggle in the economic field played a role of primary importance in the political-social confrontation between those forces committed to change and those determined to maintain the *status quo*.

Almost without exception the chapters which follow adopt this 'economic viewpoint' not only as their subject but also as the basis for a more general understanding of the process as a whole.

The aim of this overview is to present to the reader the economic dimension of the historic context in which the process of transformation during the 1970-73 period took place and to set out some general considerations. The economic obstacles which arose on implementing structural changes during the period can be understood without difficulty only if one takes into account the results of many years of capitalist growth which was a legacy bequeathed to this process of change.

The economic aspect of the *via chilena*, the Chilean experience, is preceded

---

Footnotes and tables to this chapter may be found on pp. 30-33. The Statistical Appendix may be found on pp. 34-43.

by a type of development and growth which produced strains, imbalances and trends which, albeit the very nature of the process, were also symptoms of a malfunctioning which the structural changes were intended to correct. Their economic antecedents can be grouped into two large categories. The first is the relationship with the structural aspect of the economic context, that is to say, with the cumulative results of a capitalist development of a particular kind which constitute obstacles from the viewpoint the general interest. The second type of economic and political antecedent to consider is that of the economic climate in 1970, which both imposed restrictions upon and created breathing space for the short-term economic policy which began to be put into effect at the end of that year. Both antecedents, particularly the first one, were to be present explicitly or implicitly during the course of the structural transformation, and for that reason they warrant specific attention.

1. ANTECEDENTS IN THE STRUCTURE OF CHILE'S ECONOMY

There has always been a degree of relative underdevelopment and dependence in the Chilean economy; the concensus is, moreover, that this is a 'Third World' economy. Disagreement arises only when it is associated with the countries 'on the road to development', for it is argued that this would be wrong because one could, with propriety, also speak of a 'road to underdevelopment'. Nevertheless, whatever our interpretation of underdevelopment may be, it is important to emphasize that in a country such as Chile an economic project was embarked upon in which structural changes played a fundamental role in that these were aimed at the creation of a socialist society as a means of getting out of the existing state of underdevelopment.

Equally important is the consideration that such structural changes would be carried out in a society with a predominantly urban population (75%) and with a *per capita* income level of nearly \$600, higher than the average level in Latin America. At the same time the economy was diversified to a certain extent, with the industrial sector generating 25% of the national product in 1970 and employing 20% of the working population. On the other hand, the place of the economy in the world market was reflected by the fact that 85% of foreign exchange came from the export of mineral products, amongst which copper alone amounted to a little more than 75%. No less important was the level of the economy's external indebtedness at the end of the 1960s, reaching \$2.2 thousand million of net debts in 1970 (see Table XVII in the Statistical Appendix at the end of this chapter), requiring almost all of the reserves in order to service it (interest plus repayment of principal).

Certainly the effects of underdevelopment, which can be more or less dramatic, are not to be confused with its essential character. That is to say, the underdeveloped nature of the Chilean economy arises from its malfunctioning and the dependent nature arises from its place in an economic system with a given international division of labour. There is a very close relationship between the two. The structural changes were carried out precisely in order to change the nature of this phenomenon.

In order to evaluate the economic antecedents of greatest importance in terms of their influence on the transformation period, though running the risk of simplification implicit in all syntheses, we will cover the following aspects: distortion in the productive structure, the process of concentration and foreign control, and the external imbalance.

1.1. *Distortions in the Productive Structure*

The whole web of social relations involved in production generates, in the process of its reproduction, a determined productive structure. If we were to take a sample of the productive apparatus we would see this structure in terms of the composition of output and the employment of the labour force arranged by branch of activity. The structure would reflect the social productivity of labour attained at a particular point in time.

The Chilean economy in 1970 exhibited all the imbalances associated with underdeveloped capitalism, if these are considered from the point of view of social rationality, as from the standpoint of private rationality such a structure is internally consistent. All these imbalances were to be present during the process of structural change and formed an implicit restriction on the eventual fruition of such change. In Table 2.1 we can in effect identify the following significant facts:

(1) A high participation of the service sector in creating the total output (44%), with no relationship to overall productivity of *per capita* income, when compared to the same relationship in any industrialized economy.

(2) An excessive level of employment in the tertiary sector (49.5%) indicating to a certain extent the level of underemployment, as the high level of labour force absorption in this sector is related to the insufficient level of industrial capital formation and the dominance of capital-intensive technical progress.

On the other hand, the 60% of the working population involved in producing material goods and creating an economic surplus carried out its activities under varied circumstances. In fact, except for the large copper mining sector, the average productivity was very low. Yet, the low returns of this part of the labour force had nonetheless to support the remaining 40%, as much with consumer goods as with savings and investment capital, in addition to supporting the needs of the economically inactive population.

(3) A notably low productivity in the agricultural branch as compared to the rest of the economy, for 41% of global output came from that branch. Certainly, when we break down productivity differences by sector, we must note

that these not only have technological causes, but are also distorted by the pricing system used in valuing output: an example is the pricing of agricultural output at low levels to avoid inflationary pressures. Nevertheless if we consider the low growth rate, almost lower than that of the population as a whole, and the return on resources employed, Chilean agriculture will be seen to be patently backward, as innumerable studies have demonstrated.

It should also be noted that, mining excepted, productivity in commerce and financial activities is respectively 1.5 and 4.2 times greater than the overall average. Obviously this reflects the forms of appropriation of economic surplus generated in the productive sectors.

(4) If we consider the productivity increase by sector in the 1960-70 period,[1] we observe a fall in the service sector *pari passu* with labour force absorption by this sector, which was disguising underemployment. Again, productivity in agriculture and industry increased slightly more slowly than the population growth (2.5%), and showed signs of weak growth as previously indicated.

(5) Within the productive structure a certain degree of utilization of installed capacity and labour force existed. For the former it is difficult to estimate a utilization rate for the economy as a whole: it is known that in 1970 approximately one third of the industrial capacity was not used. From this viewpoint of use of the labour force an average of 6% unemployment of the active population was registered in 1971 and the Planning Office estimated unemployment equal to 9.7% of the economically active population (see Tables III and IV of the Statistical Appendix at the end of this chapter). That is to say, in absolute terms this meant that 325,000 people were apparently employed and 190,000 were openly unemployed, so that 515,000 people were pressing upon the labour market.

Finally, in this description of the productive structure it is necessary to add that by the end of 1970, the industrial sector had been significantly restructured. In fact, from 1960 to 1970 the growth rate in the dynamic industries was higher than the average growth of the industrial sector as a whole.[2] Such industries provide a large part of the consumer durables market – electrodomestic products, electronics and also automative production – which grew at 11% per year. On the other hand, the traditional consumer branches (food, footwear, clothing, textiles, furniture, etc.) showed little growth, less than the industrial average, so that their relative participation in industrial output diminished (see Table 2.2).

As shown in the discussion of Table 2.1 as well as in Table 2.2, a diversification process was taking place in the productive apparatus. This process corresponded to shifts in the demand pattern itself; it was not related to a sustained increase in overall levels of income (giving rise to the familiar Engels Law) but rather was linked to the model of income distribution which was used during this period – a model which did not show any symptoms of important changes. Thus at the end of the 1960s, 45% of Chileans received only

14% of income while, at the other extreme, around 9% received 35% of income. In between these two groups was a middle group which gave great impetus to this diversification: it represented 45% of the active population, receiving 50% of total incomes.[3]

On the other hand, the increased output of the dynamic industries did not represent an important relief for the unemployment problem because these industries were capital intensive. Moreover, such industries are large consumers of imported raw materials and thus introduced an inflexible element in the balance of payments, as any shortage of foreign exchange adversely affects the level of activity of an important part of industry.

1.2. *The Process of Industrial Concentration and Foreign Control*

A second important aspect of the Chilean economy is its tendency towards industrial concentration and foreign control. Concentration of property was manifest in all economic sectors but had acquired importance in the manufacturing and distributive industries. In industry, a small number of companies (3%) controlled a significant proportion of employment, value added, capital and gross surplus from production. Moreover, the management of the majority of these companies was also in the hands of an equally small group of persons which in turn extended its influence to finance, commerce, the construction sector and basic utilities.

The oligopolistic structure of the industrial goods market and of the distribution channels was the result of a type of capitalist development forced by the crisis in the foreign trade sector and not by any particular process of accumulation. The industrialization associated with import substitution developed through a protectionist policy of altering prices to favour national products, thus increasing industrial profits and hence capital formation. For this reason industry always took on an oligopolistic form from the start. The lack of competition from abroad and the almost exclusive orientation of the national output towards the national market gave rise to a high concentration of industry which was a constant feature of Chile from the 1940s onwards. In as much as the domestic market did not grow by extension and private capital formation was not all dynamic, the process of concentration became even more pronounced.

In this context we can say that the intervention of the state was of vital importance to maintaining not only capital accumulation but also effective demand, both necessary for the growth of the private sector. This is why in Chile from the 1940s onwards, the state began to play an important role in economic activity, creating basic utility companies and investing in the infrastructure in order to support the development of the private sectors.

Gross fixed asset formation in the Chilean economy always fluctuated between 14% and 17% of total output.[4] Nevertheless, to the extent that the growth of industry was being limited by the domestic market, the participation of the private sector in the efforts towards capital formation diminished and that of the state increased. This was the case during the 1960s as the state at the end of that decade was financing 50% of the direct and 25% of the indirect investments, having become the main investor. In addition the state had at that time direct control of the companies in electrical energy, extraction and refining of petroleum, the iron and steel industry, railways, air transport and other areas, which altogether thus constituted a nationalized sector within the economy.

During the 1960s the low rate of private capital formation forced the state to permanently sustain the level of overall demand, in an effort to avoid the tendency towards chronic stagnation resulting from the economic structure; in this sense state intervention was not directed at correcting such tendencies but rather at cushioning their effects. Therefore, we find in the Chilean economy of this period an investor state which was generating employment, fundamentally nonproductive and activating overall levels of demand; the limits of this type of intervention were fixed by the inflationary pressures which they unleashed.

On the other hand, the diversification of industry towards consumer durables achieved in this period was accomplished by reinforcing the tendency towards industrial concentration in these sectors, due to the technological demands made by capital-intensive processes. In the traditional industries where there already was a high degree of concentration, this was even further reinforced because of the stagnation of markets.

The regressive nature of income distribution was determined not only by the concentration of private ownership, but also by the negative effects of open and disguised unemployment: however, the state's distributive policies, which took place within given political situations, had a positive effect on income distribution.

Nevertheless, because an important part of capital accumulation was not being used in the domestic market, since 80% of the capital goods required were being imported, and the increase in overall demand was recurrent, the unequal growth of markets generally tended to lead to stagnation.

It was this inability of the system to promote a high rate of growth in domestic markets which induced a policy favourable to foreign capital, particularly during the 1960s. Foreign investment in industry and commerce, which until 1960 had only reached $40 million, grew by $200 million between 1960 and 1970. Of this figure $145 million entered the economy as direct investment and credits.[5] To this sum must be added more than $50 million used to acquire shares in already existent companies. This capital represented around 20% of the gross industrial fixed capital formation for the 1960-70 period. Nonetheless, the foreign share of ownership of industry attained a much more significant level. It is particularly noteworthy that this share was higher than that of the state, whose spending in industry was considerably greater (see Table 2.3).

This foreign capital was again concentrated in the largest companies: of the 261 largest industrial limited companies there were fifty-five in which more than 50% of the stock was foreign owned.[6] All this foreign control of industry did not imply that new markets abroad were opened, or even that technology was really transferred, for in the majority of cases the technology was managed and administered through the parent company. Moreover the subsidiaries established in Chile had satisfied the demand for both equipment and raw materials through their system of subsidiaries located in other countries, thus reducing the market prospects for the rest of Chilean industry.

It follows, therefore, that the process of increasing foreign control of industry represented neither a break in the trend towards stagnation nor an important increase in capital accumulation; on the contrary, it magnified all the problems of dependency in the economy, which previous to 1960-70 had been confined to mining.

We could not fail to point out as an important antecedent the fact that the agricultural sector, for long periods, had a growth rate which was lower than that of the population. To a certain extent, part of the industrial growth took place at the cost of a rapid increase in agricultural productivity, all of which resulted in a regressive distribution of agricultural incomes compared with what occurred in industry and the rest of the economy.

But the agrarian structure, which had a significant concentration of ownership known as the latifundia, was considerably modified from 1965 onwards by agrarian reform. In effect, from 1965 to 1970 1,408 latifundios were expropriated out of a total of five or six thousand; the criterion for these expropriations, as established by the agrarian reform law, was whether they had a surface area greater than 80 hectares of irrigated land. Albeit the process was slow and partial, it nevertheless represented a change in the landholding system which had existed for more than a century and under which 4.9% of the farms had controlled 79% of the agricultural land.[7]

The transfer of ownership to the *asentamiento*, an organization intended to be transitional and out of which the new private owners were to emerge, was achieved during the five-year period from 1965 to 1970 in some 19.4% of the irrigated land and by 1970 it had affected nearly 20,000 peasant families.[8] Even though the aim of the Government was to re-establish 100,000 families, the 20% of them which was affected represented a highly important change as it simultaneously stimulated the peasant movement and trade union organizations. Again, the fact that the minimum agricultural wage was raised at the beginning of this five-year period to the level prevailing in industry represented an increase in the size of the domestic market, which in part explains the growth of industry from 1965 to 1969.

It became more and more evident that economic growth implied breaking down the internal structural constraints resulting from the concentration of ownership and income; however, in solving this problem the constraints imposed by the external sector could not be ignored.

1.3. *The External Imbalance*

During the 1960s Chile's exports were not able to generate the necessary revenue to finance imports, remittance of profits and payment of interest on foreign capital invested in the country. This was true even at the end of the 1960s, when copper prices were exceptionally high (see Table 2.4).

The permanent deficit on current account was always financed by capital inflows in the form of either direct foreign investment or medium- and long-term credit, that is to say, by indebtedness.

On the other hand, the import rate was 14% of output throughout this period. This, however, does not indicate the Chilean economy's extreme sensitivity to variations in imports. In effect, the industrial diversification and import substitution which had taken place during the last thirty years caused an increase in the imports of non-food consumer goods, representing only 10% of all imports in 1970, and an increase in the relative weight of intermediate and capital goods, representing 83% of imports in that year. This meant that the level of domestic activity was strongly determined by the ability to import, as in general imports of raw materials and equipment for industry cannot easily be substituted on the short term.

The recurrent variations in copper prices meant that the purchasing power of Chilean exports became extremely unstable, so that capital imports and increased indebtedness were the only hope of keeping the economy functioning. Thus it was that the growth of the external debt in the 1960s was to create a feedback process which would decisively influence events in the 1970-73 period.

In effect, the process of external indebtedness became more noticeably pronounced between 1966 and 1970. Chile's external debt (public and private sector debts guaranteed by the state) for periods of longer than one year grew at an annual rate of 17% and, what was much more serious, the composition of the debt became even more unfavourable: while in 1960 60% of the debt was repayable over more than fifteen years, of the debts contracted between 1966 and 1970, only 34% were for more than fifteen years. The increase in the size of the debt and the changing composition of its time span meant that the burden of this debt, i.e. its servicing, increased from $125 million in 1967 to $280 million in 1971.

It is important to note that the presence of foreign capital or the existence of external indebtedness are not in themselves negative factors, if and when they are inserted into a particular global economic and industrial strategy, which converts them into a complementary and transitory factor. That is, a greater indebtedness should permit the material bases to be laid for reducing the vulnerability of the external sector and should create a certain dynamism in the internal sector.

The situation in Chile in the 1966-70 period was such that the growth in the external debt was based partially on investment projects with medium term pay-off periods and foreign capital participation, but it did not create any access to new markets, nor did it enlarge its control over the technological processes involved in the new industrial product lines.

The foreign trade sector was not able, at that time, to deal with modifying its structural limitations, either through indiscriminate entry of foreign capital, or through increase in foreign indebtedness. The undiversified nature of exports and the lack of control to prevent the departure of the economic surpluses continued to be the basis for a tendency towards chronic disequilibrium.

1.4. *The Crisis of Dependent Capitalist Growth*

The limitations on growth which we have indicated, and particularly the concentration of income, the foreign control of the economy and the external vulnerability, are all consequences of a more complex phenomenon known as dependence. The dependency relationships not only cover the strictly economic and financial fields but also permeate the whole of society, particularly the cultural, military and political aspects. Developed capitalism, and particularly its hegemonic centre, the United States' economy, through expansion via multinational corporations, has woven a network of relationships with economies such as that of Chile which sets a given framework for the development of these countries. That is not to say that these, and in particular the Chilean economy, act like mirrors and have no autonomy, but rather that this autonomy is fixed within the parameters of the dependent structure created by this expansion.

The 1960s served to only confirm the already evident exhaustion of the Chilean economic system, thus making its dependent character explicit; this was not only because during the 1960s the *per capita* income grew slowly, around 2% per year on the average, but also because at the same time the economic development was inadequate, something which affected the whole socio-political system, while the prospects for a take-off were remote – foreign indebtedness and the entry of foreign capital notwithstanding.

These antecedents create the impression that modernization of the system would not be able to generate any internal dynamism, because it would produce new contradictions – as agrarian reform had so clearly shown – whose solution is in a radical change in the basic operation and reproduction of the conditions inherent in a social formation such as that existent in Chile. Within this framework the programme of the UP Government proposed and carried out a process of structural change which in essence broke the bonds of the tendency towards concentration of economic activities, ruptured the dependency relationship and expanded the domestic market. This programme included a strategy for the medium term aimed at correcting the distortions in the productive structure and at adapting it to the new demand profile, which in fact meant an industrial reconversion and a relative diminuation of the importance of unearned income.

The economic programme of the UP, on postulating the democratization of the economy through planned management, created opportunities within this process of structural change for the non-monopolistic private sector, which was the greater part of the capitalist and entrepreneurial sector, in order to make it play an important role. Getting results from this policy was not easy, notwithstanding an economic policy which ultimately was favourable to the private sector, above all during the first year.[9]

2. THE ECONOMIC AND POLITICAL ANTECEDENTS OF THE ECONOMIC SITUATION

The economic and political circumstances under which UP came into power and their subsequent development established the framework of restrictions and possibilities to which implementing the basic programme had to be adapted. Despite the opposition of those affected by the implementation of this programme, the Government was able to bring about an important part of the structural changes planned. But the planning, consolidation and development of these changes was nevertheless limited and hampered by these circumstances.

The modernizing capitalist measures fostered by the Christian Democrats in 1965-70 were limited in conception and realization. Despite this – particularly in the beginning of the agrarian reform and the expansion of the peasant movement – they were sufficient to produce a deep split at the heart of the forces which traditionally managed the system of exploitation: on the one side were the most conservative groups defending the interests of the old alliance between the most powerful urban economic and financial groups and the latifundio; on the other side were the non-monopolistic sectors of the urban industrial bourgeoisie and, together with a strongly supportive petit bourgeoisie, a segment of the industrial, mining and agricultural workers.

The process of change begun by the Christian Democrats, despite its limited character, created great expectations amongst the mass organizations. The fact that these expectations were not satisfied added new strength to the popular movement, on the increase since the 1950s. Thus, in 1958, the candidate for the popular movement was narrowly defeated in the presidential elections. In

1964, a coalition between the conservative and reformist groups was necessary to prevent the electoral triumph of the left. The tensions produced from 1965 onwards made it practically impossible in 1970 to have an alliance similar to that of 1964. These circumstances considerably reinforced the position of the more committed reformist groups within the Christian Democrats who in effect ran the party from 1970 to 1972. This, and the simultaneous strengthening of the popular movement, allowed the UP to be formed; in this alliance the decisive influence was held by parties representing the majority of the working class and also a significant part, although a minority, of the petit and middle bourgeoisie.

The presidential candidate for the UP obtained his electoral victory over the conservative candidate by a narrow margin. From that moment the general rules of political struggle were changed throughout the country and this remained so throughout the 1970-73 period. The fact was that hostile social forces were directing different state institutions from the moment that the UP Government assumed power. On the one side were the working class and its allies; on the other, the monopolies, foreign capital and vast sectors of the urban and rural bourgeoisie. *The aim of this struggle was the control of political power*. In the centre were different social sectors with reformist tendencies, represented principally by the Christian Democratic Party. This political body was, in turn, divided into one group which was prepared to enter into certain limited agreements with the UP, while the other was an irreconcilable enemy. The influence of one or the other group would come to play a fundamental role in the later political situation. This relationship was decisive in forming the majority in the National Congress and in influencing an important part of the state bureaucracy, the armed forces, the administration of the justice and other state institutions.

The strength of the progressive wing of the Christian Democratic Party had at the end of 1970 made it possible for the UP candidate to be confirmed by the National Congress[10] through a formal agreement between the two parties. The agreement, in essence, implied that the strictly institutional character of the armed forces would be maintained and that the structural, judicial and political changes would be made within the framework of current legality or by legal modification of the same. In as much as the conservative forces continued to have great influence on the institutional system and could gather support from the reformist elements, these agreements implied serious limitations on implementing any measures requiring new legislation. However, the great development in state monopoly capital provided a wide field in which the Government could manoeuvre to apply its programme because it meant that the state had regulatory powers which were particularly important in the fields of market control, direct intervention in management and ownership of companies, conduct of foreign trade, and elsewhere. Completion of the UP's project nevertheless required considerably wider and stronger support. Only a movement of an overwhelming majority could carry out the contemplated transformations in the political, social and economic apparatus in an organized and complete manner.

The economic situation, for its part, had deteriorated increasingly during 1969 and 1970. The root cause of this was that the structure of the monopolistic system had remained in tact. All the efforts made in the first years of the 1965-70 period to raise the level of economic activity, reduce the rate of inflation and increase real income were dashed at this barrier. By 1967-68, the successes achieved in this field were completely reversed. In particular, it was not possible to raise the level of private capital accumulation and continue the recently begun process of income redistribution. The growth in output (expenditure of the gross national product) fell by an average of 2.8% annually and by 0.8% per person per year; unemployment once more returned to its previous growth rate and inflation accelerated. The phenomenon occurred despite a favourable external situation on the short term. In these years the international reserves increased partly because of improvements in the price of copper, more because of further acceleration of the foreign indebtedness on the medium and long term, and finally because of an increase in foreign investment.

The situation became frankly depressing at the end of 1970, when the conservative forces began economic sabotage. In that year the production of copper did not rise and the rest of the mining sector's output fell compared with 1969. Industrial output had an annual increase of only 0.8% and construction barely maintained its 1969 level, while the output in agriculture and fisheries was the only output which showed some improvement. As a consequence the unemployment percentage increased even above the high level of 1969. In the greater Santiago area, which includes almost a third of the economically active population, unemployment reached 6.1% and 7.1% in 1969 and 1970 respectively. In December of 1970 the unemployment figure rose to 8.1%. On the other hand, the rate of increase of prices, which had been 29.3% in 1969, reached 34.9% in 1970.[11] This made it necessary to complement the Basic Programme with a project made up of a series of economic measures which were applied immediately in order to take care of the most acute problems.[12]

The project presented, as its fundamental objective, the reactivation of the economy, reduction of unemployment, improvement of the living conditions in the most affected sectors through drastic redistribution of income, and starting to control inflation. It will be understood that this project was to be dovetailed into the Basic Programme. The nexus linking the two was, nevertheless, much stronger than a simple problem of coherence. There was no possibility of beginning to find permanent solutions to the problems of the economy as a whole without removing the structural obstacles. In effect, the framework of the political struggle in which the whole process took place and the UP's social nature obliged the UP to find the solution at the outset to a series of urgent problems affecting, above all, the populace in general. The conservative forces, on the other hand, had already begun to use all their power on the economic system in order to prevent any action by the future Government whatsoever, so that the need to increase the Government's capacity to direct and control was urgent. It is for these reasons that this project and the Basic Programme should not be conceived as juxtaposed: on the contrary, they were intimately related. Practice demonstrated that the objectives foreseen in one measure could not be carried out without bringing the other plans forward. This relationship was, nevertheless, not direct: that is it could be broken whenever one of the two levels got out of line.

A series of resources were available for implementing the Programme: underused industrial capacity, more than 30% in almost all sectors,[13] possibilities for considerably increasing the volume of building; labour force resources and finally around $400 million in foreign exchange reserves[14] which, despite being committed to a high foreign debt, ought to allow a certain increase in imports of raw materials and foodstuffs.[15] With these resources available it was possible to contemplate an increase in the different productive activities and of income at a significant rate within a certain period.

In order to ensure that this increase in income went mainly into the hands of the workers three fundamental methods were considered: increasing real wages, especially at the basic or minimum wage level; increasing consumption and social payments for education, health and welfare; and absorbing the unemployed by means of an increase in the general level of economic activity and a special housebuilding and public works programme. Improvement of real wages assumed that the price level would rise less than the wage increase set at 100% of the cost of living rise registered in the previous year. In other words, there would have to be a general squeeze on profit margins, particularly those of the more important companies. It was established that the increase was around 35% as a rule and an additional 5% would be considered to give a greater increase to the lower wage groups. Minimum agricultural and industrial wages would be raised 67%. On the other hand a top limit would be fixed of twenty times the minimum wage as the highest maximum for employees in the public sector.

Given the existing material and organizational infrastructure the increase in social expenditure did not present any difficulties, for there were state organizations experienced in social security, education and health throughout the country and a high degree of underuse of staff. The progressive increase in activity was principally related to the allocation of greater resources. From this viewpoint, the substantial increase in building similarly did not present significant problems. The activity of the state in this field had succeeded in creating a wide network of organizations for planning, execution and control over building projects.

These measures had at least three weak points. The first was the wage claims, which resulted in much larger adjustments than were foreseen, above all in 1972. The second was the problem of financing the public sector, that is the central Government, the decentralized agencies, the social security system and the state enterprises. This sector had to provide for the income increase in social expenditure and in the renumeration of its employees. It was estimated that to guarantee the necessary revenue it would be sufficient to be more exigent in collecting taxes and that the resources of the monopolistic sector now in the hands of the state could be relied upon. This point was to subsequently prove to be a source of serious economic, social and political problems. The third weak point was the difficulty in obtaining foreign exchange, a problem which became acute not so much because of the increase in imports during 1971 and 1972, but more because of the complete reversal in the movement of capital which had fed the balance of payments in the previous years, and the fall in the price of copper, the principal export.

It should be pointed out that the measures did not give proper attention to the need for improving and expanding the state apparatus for undertaking productive investment and for supporting possible private ventures. It was certainly foreseeable that the trend for such ventures would be downward, but despite the importance of preventing such a trend – which was tackled later – this problem was not given the same attention as those mentioned above. It was thought that the development of the public sector would suffice to ensure that the previous level of investment would be maintained. By 1970 investment was financed 75% by state resources and the state sector accounted directly for 50% of all investment.

Taken as a whole, the measures were adequate for the needs created by the situation which the country faced in 1970. Moreover, it does not seem feasible that a different direction for immediate action could have been chosen given the acuteness of the workers' situation and that of other strata in society, the politico-social character of the Government, and the programme of changes it planned to carry out. Adjusting the weak aspects would not have changed the essential nature of that programme, though it would have led to a more rigid handling both of the factors pressing on the internal and external weak spots and of the resources which would have permitted their control.

Contrarywise, neglect of these aspects allowed them to take on intolerable proportions, creating an increasingly unstable situation. The redistribution of income converted itself into inflationary pressures and external imbalances once it surpassed the state's capacity for controlling output and circulation of money. The neglect of measures which could reduce the tensions abroad reduced the margin for manoeuvre at home. These imbalances lead to a breakdown in the organization of economic activity, making it increasingly difficult to develop and derive any benefit from the basic economic and social transformations.

3. SOME GENERAL CONSIDERATIONS

Various issues and problems of great significance, such as the elements which determined the general course of the structural changes which occurred in Chile, constitute points of convergence among the different analysis presented in this volume. The observations made about them contain a degree of agreement which ought to be stressed, the more so when these opinions are the result of an increasingly more precise and well-researched study. Through such observations, purely emotional or intuitive opinions can progressively be replaced by the agreement which comes of a collective analytical effort. The correct evaluation of the lessons of the past, an indispensable basis for unity today, requires the farthest possible journey along the road of scientific analysis of the unique experience of the UP Government in Chile.

For this reason it is important to highlight a few points of agreement in the field of economics as well as of politics, if such a clear-cut distinction can be made, and in particular the following:

1. The transformation of Chilean society under the circumstances faced by the UP Government was an historic task capable of being accomplished successfully, although subject to restrictions and difficulties of great magnitude. The defeat of this attempt by the counterrevolutionary forces, both domestic and foreign, put an end to a process which took on specific forms in specific circumstances, which is not to say that the basic content of the process meant that it was condemned from the beginning to fail. On the contrary, at each phase of the process alternative courses of action were presented that were capable of modifying the balance of social forces in favour of the changes.

The *via chilena* was a viable process within the confines of a narrow path. At a certain moment possibilities existed, although limited, for gaining the support of the political majority which was indispensable for the change in the judicial and institutional framework demanded by the process of transformation. There were also precise circumstances under which it was possible to establish a broad alliance of social sectors in favour of changes. This is one of the conclusions of greatest importance which should be singled out and, no doubt, one with the greatest significance for the future.

Obviously, from the very moment that the UP Government was formed, given the character of its programme and its determined resolve to carry it out, the need for a new institutional order was inevitable to encompass the advances of a new legal and judicial order. All this, because of the specifics of the process, would be the collective majority consensus of all the social forces not bound up with those limited private interests affected directly by the structural changes. That is to say, an attempt was made to substitute the shattered hegemony of the existing domination system with a broad social block which would express that majority consensus through a broadening of the democratic system, and which would develop the conditions for control of political power by the popular movement. None of these factors were predetermined in any instance, nor did they constitute the crucial elements of the defeat.

2. The popular movement and its Government had to deal with the covert aggression of powerful enemies who did not hesitate before any step in defence of their privileges. In particular, the action of the principal power in the capitalist world has been justly singled out as a significant element in the defeat of the UP Government. Now abundantly documented, the actions of the United States' Central Intelligence Agency (CIA), the commercial and financial blockade, etc., in a word, the militantly aggressive policy against Chile arises as an explanatory factor of major importance for the ultimate outcome of the Chilean revolution. The evidence has been made available by the very Senate of the United States:

> Covert United States involvement in Chile in the decade between 1963 and 1973 was extensive and continuous. The Central Intelligence Agency spent three million dollars in an effort to influence the outcome of the 1964 Chilean presidential elections. Eight million dollars was spent, covertly, in the three years between 1970 and the military *coup d'état* in September 1973, with over three million dollars expended in fiscal year 1972 alone.[16]

Moreover, the bare figures are more likely to understate than to exaggerate the extent of U.S. covert action. In the years before the 1973 *coup d'état* especially, CIA dollars could be channelled through the Chilean black market where the unofficial exchange rate into Chilean escudos often reached five times the official rate.

> ...It financed activities covering a broad spectrum, from simple propaganda manipulation of the press to large-scale support for Chilean political parties, from public opinion polls to direct attempts to forment a military coup.[17]

Because of its nature, the imperialist aggression in its various guises appears as a whole range of 'external' elements, which were truly exogenous variables beyond all possible control by the elements inside Chile which were directing the process of change. Yet at the same time, given the gigantic political power which they represented, they tend to be considered as the most important explanation of what happened. Hence one frequently comes across attempts to evaluate the relative influence of 'external' and 'internal' factors on the final result of the process.

Let us consider the fact that, except for the case of military aggression in openly declared war, all acts of imperialism – whether carried out through imperialist agencies or jointly by local allies – produce their effects through and are functions of the prevailing internal conditions, while at the same time creating them. This was Chile's problem. The distinction between 'internal' and 'external' factors loses all significance as a pair of opposites and reveals its true nature as a phenomenon united in a single dialectical process. Imperialist aggression could attain its ends only by acting within the framework of characteristics which the socio-political conflict acquired in the country itself. Only in this sense can it be said that, in the interplay of external and internal factors, the latter played a decisive role. Certainly, as far as strictly economic phenomena are considered, it was also the internal situation, in the sense mentioned earlier, which multiplied or constrained the effects of external aggression intended to destabilize the economy.

3. As has previously been mentioned, during 1971 an imbalance was produced between the redistributive policy and the financing of such a policy in real terms. The short term reflationary policy exceeded the initially forecast targets and developed at a far greater speed than the general process of structural transformations, in the broadest sense of the term. Suffice it to say that the capacity of the state to appropriate and allocate surpluses, in line with the redistributive policy which was being implemented, fell short of the minimum requirements for attaining short-term equilibrium. Thus inflationary pressures and external imbalances developed which were to be felt and worsen in the next two years.

It is not difficult to realize that between the two policies, namely the redistribution policy and reflation on the one hand, and structural transformations on the other, there is a necessary relationship whose limits cannot be exceeded without causing serious problems in the general evolution of the economy. But, at the same time, it is no less clear that given the circumstances in Chile at the end of 1970 – and in view of the nature of the programme to be implemented by the UP – the simultaneous inception of both processes was essential, difficult as it may be. Moreover, from the point of view of the social interests at stake in such circumstances, the short-term reflationary policy and that of structural transformation represented, together and separately, the means for creating a new direction in the economy, this time in accordance with the interests of the workers and the majority of the population. While the degree and speed of application of one or other policy can be discussed on their merits, it would seem obvious that given their content it would have been out of the question to have opted for any direction which was essentially different. From this follows the fact that the necessity of carefully handling and strictly controlling economic policies, precisely to avoid problems, must be given top priority.

The immediate inception of the economic reflationary policy was an indispensable condition for carrying out one of the central policies of the Government, to wit, tackling the most urgent problems of the majority of the population. Not only the UP Programme but also other documents (e.g. 'the forty immediate measures') set out the needs for rapid action in this area. Again, the favourable political consequences for a Government that began to tackle these problems were clear to the UP leadership. Without falling into the tendency of seeking political support 'by satisfying the stomach' of certain social groups, it is certain that the political consequences of the economic reflation were a major element in judging the immediate situation.

If the above seems beyond doubt, the same cannot be said about the similarity between the basic content of both the policy of structural transformation and that of reflation. It has been maintained that while the former had as its objective the changing of the main characteristics of the economic system, economic reflation appeared to be based precisely on the traditional utilization of those market mechanisms which characterize of the system which was to be transformed. Hence a contradiction between the two processes arose – a contradiction which could have been avoided by using some other type of reflationary policy. Without ignoring the strength of arguments such as this, it is necessary to emphasize the urgency of tackling the immediate problems and the economic and legal instruments which existed at the time for doing so, which had extremely tight margins for operating. The basis for the effort was to be centred on raising aggregate demand which implied, under the circumstances, giving preference to the incomes policy and to the public expenditure increase. Certainly these were not the only measures, but they were without doubt the dominant and principal ones. One could imagine, for example, an increase in capital accumulation as a means of raising the level of activity (assuming, which is doubtful, a favourable reaction on the part of the private sector), or other mechanisms. Whatever they might have been, in the short run they would still have been measures in support of the reflation policy.

Thus the real discussion should be centred not on the direction and design of the reflationary policy, but rather on the degree of political control which was exercised over it. Exceeding the limits set in the reflationary policy and the consequent unbalanced rate of structural change was above all a problem of an insufficiently developed political awareness among the masses, more than of mistakes made in directing economic action.*

4. The development of the Chilean economic situation during the period is a good example of the existence of alternative courses of action which, although narrow and subject to conditions, allowed modification, while rigorously adhering to the Basic Programme's objectives, of the general direction of the process of transformation. These alternative courses had to do with either the manner in which the Area of Social Property (APS) was set up, or with the policy of satisfying the most urgent needs of the people, or with the anti-inflationary fight and the financial problems, or with external economic relationships, etc. In each and every case the forms that implementation of the Programme took on, and the contradictions they engendered, could have been presented differently and could have gained greater control over the anarchistic tendencies which they created. A large number of examples of the truth of this assertion will be found in the following chapters.

The ability to take advantage of the alternatives which presented themselves in order to ensure the growth of the economic system, thus stimulating the overall viability of the process of change, required a basic condition which was not fulfilled. This condition was the ensuring of steadfast united economic and, *a fortiori*, the political management of the economic transformations in progress. This unity of direction was an indispensable requirement for imposing a new rationality, this time of a social nature, on both the direct management of enterprises and on the allocation of resources in the economy as a whole. The absence of solid economic control became a factor of the greatest importance and explains the weak response to the natural tendency to economic disarticulation which structural changes invite.

This lack of control expressed itself, for example, in the failure to set up – within a meaningful time span – a national planning system capable of encompassing, in a coherent framework of economic policy, the different programmes and the multiplicity of measures being carried out. This lack of central planning and coordination alone created problems and led to waste which could completely and easily have been avoided. Furthermore, largely due to this lack of control, the powerful mass movement which developed in Chile during the period did not bring forth, at least not through the economic tasks it was assigned, the organizational environment indispensable for its own growth and maximum effectiveness. The participation of workers in managing and controlling the Chilean economy was limited primarily by the lack of planning and coordination by a single body.

5. Finally, it should be stressed that despite the economic and political aggression and the institutional siege of which the Government was a victim, this UP Government, with its successes and mistakes, always strictly respected the rights of individuals and their freedom of expression: never before in her history had Chile been such a free and democratic country. Furthermore the Government also kept its promise to carry out the Basic Programme, despite a background of the most pitiless opposition from the conservative factions in Chilean society. The transformations achieved represented a turning point in the historical development of Chile, a radical break with the tendencies prevailing until then. The immediate interests of the workers came to be, for the first time in the history of the country, the central motivations for Government actions.

The task accomplished in implementing an important part of the Programme was enormous. Listing only the economic transformations, which realized the dreams of generations of patriotic Chileans and whose symbolic example was the nationalization of copper, would suffice as a demonstration. But the period was characterized not only by economic transformations: to those must be added the multi-faceted expansion of cultural awareness and the various popular and artistic movements, the extraordinary growth in mass education, and the advances in the field of health, among others. The UP Government was the instrument for the free development of the individual and collective personality of the Chileans, and of the organization, in a great variety of forms, of the vast majority of the population and its prospects for uninhibited self-expression of the presence of Chile in the world as an independent, sovereign country guided only by the supreme interests of its people, and all this with the strictest regard for personal liberty and the conditions necessary for its expression.

The experience of nearly three years of UP Government in Chile is one of enormous theoretical and practical richness, not only for the principal actor – the Chilean people – but also for those throughout the world who are searching for a more just society through far-reaching changes.

NOTES

1. ODEPLAN, *Cuentas nacionales de Chile 1960-71* [National Accounts of Chile 1960-71] (Santiago de Chile, 1971), 22-23.
2. CORFO, *Datos básicos sector industrial manufacturero, período 1960-70* [Basic Data on the Industrial Manufacturing Sector for the 1960-70 Period] (Santiago de Chile, 1971), 9-10.
3. ODEPLAN, *Antecedentes sobre el desarrollo chileno 1960-70* [Antecedents of Chilean Development from 1960 to 1970] (ODEPLAN, Series I, no. 1, *Planes semestrales, Plan de la economía nacional 1971-76* [Half-Yearly Plans, Plan of the National Economy for 1971-76]) (Santiago de Chile, 1971).
4. ODEPLAN, *Antecedentes sobre el desarrollo*..., 155-157.
5. S. Bitar, 'La presencia de la empresa extranjera en la industria chilena' [The Presence of Foreign Enterprise in the Chilean Economy], *Desarrollo económico* [Economic Development], 150 (1973), 259 (Buenos Aires).
6. E. Acevado and H. Vergara, 'Concentración y capital extranjero en la industria chilena' [Concentration and Foreign Capital in the Chilean Economy], *Economía y administración* [Economy and Administration], 15 (1970) (Concepción, Chile).
7. ODEPA, *Plan de desarrollo agropecuario 1965-80* [Plan for Agricultural and Livestock Development from 1965 to 1980] (Santiago de Chile, Ministerio de Agricultura, 1970, Second Edition).
8. S. Barraclough, *Diagnóstico de la reforma agraria chilena* [Prognosis of Chilean Agrarian Reform] (Mexico City, Siglo XXI, 1974), 75.
9. Nevertheless, the problem of the middle classes involves much more than the economic behaviour of small and medium-sized producers. In this sense, the programme did not go far enough, but this will be discussed further from the political and economic viewpoint.
10. Because the candidate did not obtain an absolute majority, he had to be appointed by the National Congress.
11. These figures are taken from ODEPLAN, *Antecedentes sobre el desarrollo*...
12. 'Orientaciones básicas del programa económico de corto plazo' [Basic Orientations of the Short-term Economic Program], a typed, confidential document that was presented by the UP team of experts to presidential candidate Salvador Allende in October 1970.
13. ODEPLAN, *Plan anual 1971* [Annual Plan for 1971] (Santiago de Chile, 1971).
14. The World Bank, *Special Report on the Chilean Economic Outlook* (Washington D.C., October 1974), Vol. III.
15. An increase of 10% in industrial output required approximately \$50 million from imports. See *Comentarios sobre la situación económica (primer semestre 1973)* [Statement on the Economic Situation (First Half of 1973)], Departamento de Economía, Universidad de Chile [Department of Economics, University of Chile] (Santiago de Chile, November 1973, Second Edition).

16. *Covert Action in Chile, 1963-73. Staff Report of the Select Committee to Study Governmental Operations with Respect to Intelligence Activities* (Washington D.C., United States Senate, The U.S. Government Printing Office, 1975), 1.
17. *Covert Action in Chile...*, 1.
* It could be argued that this was also due to the limited theoretical insight into this contradiction, which at that time existed among those responsible for the UP economic policy. [The Editor]

Table 2.1. *The Production Structure of the Chilean Economy in 1970*

	Production			*Employment*			*Productivity 1960-70*	*Production ÷ employment*
	%		%	%		%		%
Primary and secondary sectors		56			59.5			94
Agriculture	9.6		17.1	23.1		38.8	1.8	41
Mining	10.4		18.5	3.5		5.8	4.4	297
Industry	25.0		44.8	20.0		33.0	2.1	125
Construction	4.8		8.5	6.2		10.4	1.0	77
Infrastructure	6.2		11.1	6.6		11.0	4.6	93
			100			100		
Tertiary sector		44			49.6			108
Commerce	21.5		48.9	13.7		27.6	–0.6	157
Banking, insurance	4.2		9.5	10.0		20.1		420
Public administration and defence	4.8		10.9	12.2		24.5	–0.4	39
Other services	13.5		30.7	13.7		27.6		98
		100	100		100	100		

Source: Production and employment figures are from ODEPLAN, *Cuentas Nacionales de Chile 1960-71* [Chile's National Accounts 1960-71] (Santiago de Chile, 1973), 18-20. Expenditure of GNP in market prices are in 1965 escudos. Productivity figures are from UN, CEPAL, *América Latina y la estrategia de desarrollo internacional: Primera evaluación regional* [Latin America and the International Development Strategy: First Regional Appraisal], 2 vols. (E/CN, 12/947, February 1973).

Table 2.2. *Comparative Growth Rates within Industry (percentage)*

	Composition of industrial output		*Growth rate (average)*
	1960	*1970*	
Traditional industries	55	45.5	3.6
Intermediate industries	30	32.0	6.1
Dynamic industries	15	22.5	10.0
	100	100	5.6

Source: ODEPLAN, *Antecedentes sobre el desarrollo chileno 1960-70* [Antecedents of Chilean Development from 1960 to 1970], (ODEPLAN, Series I, no. 1, *Planes semestrales, Plan de la economía nacional 1971-76* [Half-Yearly Plans, Plan of the National Economy for 1971-76]) (Santiago de Chile, 1971), Chapter 3, Part 2, 157.

Table 2.3. *Distribution of Paid Up Capital in Industrial Limited Companies (percentage)*

	1967	*1968*	*1970*
Foreign stockholders	16.5	16.8	20.3
Private stockholders of Chilean nationality	76.1	70.2	63.0
State-owned stocks	7.4	13.0	16.7

Source: División de Planificación Industrial [Division of Industrial Planning]. Cited in S. Bitar, 'La presencia de la empresa extranjera en la industria chilena' [The Presence of Foreign Enterprise in the Chilean Economy], *Desarrollo económico* [Economic Development], 150 (1973), 259 (Buenos Aires).

Table 2.4. *Internal and External Debt (in millions of dollars)*

	Balance on current account	*Balance of payments*
1960	–146.1	–44.0
1961	–253.7	–134.9
1962	–190.0	–70.9
1963	–167.7	–29.5
1964	–131.6	27.7
1965	–56.6	59.5
1966	–82.2	121.8
1967	–127.4	–25.0
1968	–135.3	127.0
1969	–15.4	222.8
1970	–64.4	108.2

Source: ODEPLAN, *Antecedentes sobre el desarrollo . . .*

STATISTICAL APPENDIX

Table I. *Gross National Product at Market Prices, 1970-73 (in millions of 1965 escudos)* [a]

	1970	*1971*	*1972*	*1973*
GDP	23,616	24,855	24,644	24,652
Rate of Growth		5.2%	−0.1%	–
Consumer expenditure	19,459	21,394	22,390	22,055
Gross capital formation	3,874	3,746	3,008	3,282
fixed capital	3,407	3,446	2,837	2,946
increase in stocks	467	300	171	336
Balance of payments	−638	−700	−979	−1,802
Adjusted for variations in the terms of trade	921	415	225	1,112
Net factor income from abroad	−615	−315	−164	−212
GNP	23,001	24,540	24,480	24,440
Rate of growth		6.7%	0.1%	−0.2%
GNP expenditure *per capita*	2,422	2,562	2,414	2,380
GNP *per capita*	2,521	2,605	2,537	2,493

[a] 1965: E°1 = \$0.3195

Source: ODEPLAN. Published in the Central Bank's *Boletín mensual* [Monthly Bulletin] (September 1975).

Table II. *Sectoral Indicators*

	1970	*1971*	*1972*	*1973*
Agricultural and livestock production				
Areas under 14 selected crops (1,000 hectares)[a]	1,251.0	1,262.0	1,295.0	1,028.0
Mining output (1968=100)[b]	103.1	106.7	104.7	108.1
Copper production (1,000 T)	691.6	708.3	716.9	742.7
Industrial output (1968=100)[c]	104.0	119.3	122.6	117.3
Construction industry				
Intermediate goods for construction (1969=100)[d]	104.1	113.2	123.5	117.8

Sources: [a] Instituto Nacional de Estadísticas [National Institute of Statistics] and Oficina de Planificación Agropecuaria [Office of Agricultural and Livestock Planning] (Santiago de Chile).
[b] Central Bank, Departamento de Estudios [Research Department].
[c] Instituto Nacional de Estadísticas.
[d] Sociedad de Fomento Fabril [National Society of Manufacturers]. Published in the Central Bank's *Boletín mensual* (September 1975).

Table III. *Employment in Greater Santiago (in thousands of persons, annual average)*

	1970	*1971*	*1972*	*1973*
Total population	2,927	3,041	3,160	3,318
Labour force	1,033	1,075	1,099	1,163
employed	959	1,016	1,058	1,109
unemployed	74	59	41	54
Unemployment rate (December)	7.1 (8.3)	5.5 (3.8)	3.7 (3.7)	4.7 (3.1)[a]
Sector of employment				
Agriculture	5.0	5.4	6.8	9.2
Mining	2.9	3.4	3.3	3.2
Industry	256.4	215.9	288.7	313.5
Construction industry	49.5	53.9	51.3	54.8
Commerce	150.6	152.6	164.8	161.4
Transport, storage, etc.	70.1	77.2	77.7	84.3
Government and banking	90.3	102.3	107.8	107.3
Personnel service	150.7	151.4	149.1	147.4
Other services	182.9	194.3	207.9	227.1
Unspecified	1.2	0.8	0.7	0.9
Total	959.3	1,016.5	1,057.7	1,108.8

[a] Month of June.

Source: Instituto de Economía, Universidad de Chile [Institute of Economics, University of Chile]. Published by the Central Bank's *Boletín mensual* (September 1975).

Table IV. *Employment in Urban Areas of Concepción-Talcahuano and Lota-Coronel, 1970-73 (in thousands of persons, annual average)*

	1970	*1971*	*1972*	*1973 (April)*
Total population	523	538	556	569
Labour force	149	152	154	158
employed	132	137	144	151
unemployed	17	15	10	7
Unemployment rate (October)	11.4 (11.4)	9.9 (9.3)	6.5 (7.3)	4.4 (–)
Distribution of employment				
Agriculture	1.5	1.8	2.5	2.5
Mining	11.0	12.1	12.4	12.5
Industry	33.7	36.2	37.3	39.7
Construction industry	9.8	10.8	10.7	10.2
Commerce	20.7	18.8	19.6	21.8
Transport, storage, etc.	10.0	10.2	10.5	11.2
Government and banking	6.1	7.2	8.7	8.2
Personnel service	17.9	16.3	14.2	14.7
Other services	21.4	23.1	26.3	29.1
Unspecified	0.1	0.2	0.7	1.2
Total	132.2	136.7	143.8	151.1

Source: *Encuesta semestral* [Half-yearly Survey]. Instituto de Economía y Planificación, Universidad de Chile [Institute of Economics and Planning, University of Chile]. Published in the Central Bank's *Boletín mensual* (June 1971 and July 1973).

Table V. *Wages and Salaries Index, 1970-73 (1970 average = 100)*

		Wages	*Salaries*	*Wages and salaries*
1970	October	108.8	115.3	112.0
1971	January	123.3	125.3	124.3
	April	152.6	144.5	148.7
	July	162.2	160.2	161.3
	October	168.9	171.3	170.1
1972	January	184.4	194.8	189.5
	April	200.0	217.4	208.5
	July	228.4	239.3	233.7
	October	367.5	385.6	376.3
1973	January	486.5	549.0	516.9
	April	524.8	629.6	575.8
	July	753.3	909.6	829.4
	October	871.2	1,164.2	1,013.8
1971	average	151.8	150.3	151.1
1972	average	245.1	259.3	252.0
1973	average	658.9	813.1	734.0

Source: Instituto Nacional de Estadísticas.

Table VI. *Annual Average Variation of Consumer Price Index, 1971-73 (percentage)*

	Total	*Food*	*Housing*	*Clothing*	*Miscellaneous*
1971	20.1	23.8	16.4	26.0	12.5
1972	77.8	115.2	27.6	59.0	60.8
1973	352.8	376.5	217.0	436.4	334.1
January-August 1972-73	241.7	295.3	128.0	390.0	179.4

Source: Instituto Nacional de Estadísticas.

Annual Average Wholesale Price Index Variation (percentage)

	Overall index	*Domestic products*			*Total domestic products*	*Imported products*
		Agriculture and livestock	*Mining*	*Industry*		
1971	17.9	25.5	32.8	13.9	16.7	22.2
1972	70.0	108.8	71.8	66.2	74.3	56.2
1973	511.4	428.3	473.0	476.6	465.8	552.0
January 1972- August 1973	190.8	330.0	156.1	185.2	209.6	127.8

Source: Instituto Nacional de Estadísticas.

Table VII. *Consumer Price Index, 1970-73 (1969 = 100)*

	1970	*1971*	*1972*	*1973*
January	106.80	136.85	170.82	478.84
February	112.21	137.84	181.90	498.66
March	116.18	139.50	186.87	529.49
April	118.97	142.97	197.45	583.51
May	121.50	146.99	205.85	696.72
June	123.88	149.96	210.15	805.75
July	126.28	150.40	219.50	929.02
August	129.49	152.02	269.43	1087.50
September	132.97	153.63	329.27	1271.07
October	134.07	156.20	379.40	2384.21
November	134.94	160.37	400.70	2520.11
December	134.94	164.80	434.12	2639.68

Source: Instituto Nacional de Estadísticas.

Table VIII. *Interbank Exchange Rates, 1970-73*[a] *(in escudos per dollar)*

Imports	*July 1970*	*December 1971* [b]	*August 1972*	*May 1973*
Food and fuel	12.21	12.21	20.00	20.00
Raw materials	12.21	15.80	25.00	25.00
Machines, tools and spare parts	12.21	19.00	40.00	65.00
Free port	12.21	25.00	80.00	120.00
Luxuries and nonbasic goods	12.21	25.00	80.00	240.00
Exports				
Copper and iron	12.21	15.80	20.00	45.00
Saltpetre, iodine and agro-industrial products	12.21	15.80	25.00	65.00
Industrial products	12.21	15.80	30.00	100.00

[a] Rate of exchange for dealing in goods. The date indicates the month in which it became effective.

[b] Until December 1971 there was a single exchange rate.

Source: Central Bank. Published in *Chile hoy* [Chile Today] 53 (June 1973) (Santiago de Chile).

Table IX. *Private Sector Monetary Holdings, 1970-73 (in millions of escudos) (December 1970 = 100)*

		E^om	*Index*
1970	September	8,812	87.7
	December	10,048	100.0
1971	March	13,263	132.0
	June	15,244	151.7
	September	17,851	177.7
	December	21,487	213.8
1972	March	24,961	248.4
	June	28,197	280.6
	September	32,352	322.0
	December	54,111	538.5
1973	March	73,198	728.5
	June	97,348	968.8
	September	134,968	1,343.2
	December	228,267	2,271.8

Source: The Central Bank's *Boletín mensual*, various issues.

Table X. *Government Incomes and Expenditure, 1970-73 (in thousand millions of 1970 escudos)*

	1970	*1971*	*1972*	*1973*
Current income	18.9	20.3	17.3	14.7
Direct taxes	7.1	6.4	4.7	5.0
persons and companies	3.8	5.1	3.9	4.2
copper	2.7	0.4	0.2	0.5
property	0.6	0.7	0.6	0.3
Indirect taxes	10.8	12.0	12.0	8.9
Current expenditure	15.3	22.0	24.4	17.8
Transfer payments to the rest of the public sector	5.7	9.8	10.8	8.9
Balance of current account	3.6	–1.7	–7.0	–3.0
Capital expenditure	6.1	7.4	6.4	5.9
Deficit (–) or surplus (+)	–2.5	–9.1	–13.4	–8.9
Deficit financing	2.5	9.1	13.4	8.9
Net foreign loans	–	0.2	2.2	–0.1
Domestic loans	2.5	8.9	11.1	9.0

$ value 1970: $1 = E°11.57
1971: $1 = E°12.21
1972: $1 = E°15.80
1973: $1 = E°25 (January-September)
$1 = E°340 (October-December)

Deflator: Variation on Consumer Price Index Annual Average
1971/1970 = 1.206
1972/1970 = 2.135
1973/1970 = 12.935

Source: International Monetary Fund, SM/75/47, and Ministerio de Hacienda [Ministry of the Treasury].

Table XI. *Consolidate Public Sector Income and Expenditure, 1970-72 (in millions of 1970 escudos)*

	1970	*1971*	*1972* [a]
Current income	30.4	34.8	43.2
Current expenditure	24.4	34.5	52.7
Balance of current account	6.0	0.3	–9.5
Other income	2.5	1.7	1.6
Capital expenditures	11.4	13.2	16.3
Total deficit	–2.9	–11.2	–24.2
Net foreign loans	1.3	–	1.1
Domestic loans	1.6	11.2	23.1

$ value 1970: $1 = E°11.57
1971: $1 = E°12.21
1972: $1 = E°15.80
1973: $1 = E°25 (January-September)
$1 = E°340 (October-December)

Deflator: Retail Price Index Annual Average Variation
1971/1970 = 1.206
1972/1970 = 2.135
1973/1970 = 12.935

[a] Provisional estimate.

Source: International Monetary Fund, SM/75/47, and Ministerio de Hacienda.

Table XII. *Government Income and Expenditure, 1970-73 (percentage of GNP expenditure at current prices)*

	1970	*1971*	*1972*	*1973* [a]
Current income	19.5	18.9	15.5	15.3
Current expenditure	15.8	20.5	21.8	18.5
(transfer payment to the rest of public sector)	(5.9)	(9.1)	(9.7)	(9.3)
Balance of current account	3.7	–1.5	–6.3	–3.1
Capital expenditure	6.3	6.9	5.7	6.1
Deficit	–2.6	–8.4	–12.0	–9.3
Net foreign loans	–	0.2	2.0	–
Net domestic loans	2.6	8.3	10.0	9.3

[a] Provisional data.

Source: Fiscal data: International Monetary Fund, SM/75/47, with sources from Ministerio de Hacienda.
GNP expenditure: Central Bank's *Boletín mensual* (September 1975).

Table XIII. *Consolidated Public Sector Income and Expenditure Account (percentage of GNP expenditure)*

	1970	*1971*	*1972*
Current income	31.4	32.4	38.6
Current expenditure	25.2	32.1	47.0
Balance on current account	6.2	0.3	–8.4
Other income	2.5	1.6	1.4
Capital expenditure	11.7	12.3	14.6
Total deficit	–3.0	–10.4	–21.6
Net foreign loans	1.3	–	1.0
Domestic loans	1.7	10.4	20.6

Source: International Monetary Fund, SM/73/153.

Table XIV. *Balance of Payments, 1970-73 (in millions of dollars)*

	1970	*1971*	*1972*	*1973* [a]
Trade account	+155.7	–18.1	–255.2	–260.8
Exports	1,111.7	996.8	847.4	1,346.9
copper	839.8	701.2	618.2	1,102.6
other	279.1	295.6	229.2	244.3
Imports	956.0	1,014.9	1,102.6	1,607.7
food	125.5	192.2	338.4	594.9
consumer goods	99.3	89.5	138.9	64.0
intermediate goods	445.0	485.0	460.2	663.8
capital goods	276.2	248.0	165.1	285.0
Services (net)	–260.6	–192.7	–156.8	–
Transport, insurances, etc.	16.2	11.2	1.9	–
Profit, interest, etc.	–199.4	–118.5	–59.3	–89.0
Other [b]	–77.4	–85.4	–100.4	–
Other current transactions [c]	2.0	5.3	7.2	6.0
Transactions on current account	–102.9	–205.5	–404.8	–379.8
Capital	+252.5	–49.9	+228.8	+150.5
Private	–2.6	–117.1	–5.6	–
Official	255.1	67.2	234.4	–
Errors and omissions	–72.9	–84.5	–169.8	–19.5
IMF special drawing rights	21.8	16.7	18.2	–
Balance of payments	+98.5	–323.2	–327.6	–248.8
(Net) Movements on reserves	–98.5	+323.2	+327.6	+248.8
Central Bank	–121.3	+243.7	+198.4	+145.3
Commercial banks	–1.9	+65.2	+125.1	+103.5
Others	+24.7	+14.3	+4.1	–

[a] Provisional estimates.
[b] Tourism, Government expense accounts, services, travelling expenses, etc.
[c] Gifts and nonmonetary gold.

Source: The Central Bank's *Boletín mensual* (September 1975) and 'Exposición de la Hacienda Pública de 1975' [Details from the Treasury], *El Mercurio* (25 October 1975).

Remarks on Table XIV

1. The presentation is slightly different from that made by the Central Bank. The two important changes are: (a) the 'Special drawing rights' allocations are presented without current transactions which are shown separately following International Monetary Fund's practice; and (b) the 'Compensatory capital flows account' has been called 'Movements in reserves' and has been moved to the end of the balance sheet, equally in accordance with the International Monetary Fund's formula.
2. The figures for the September 1975 *Boletín mensual* are different from those published in the first half of 1974 in that, for the years 1971, 1972 and 1973 the figures are still provisional. These differences are particularly important in the accounts for 'Imported goods', 'Capital movements' and 'Errors and omissions'.
3. The balance of payments presented by the International Monetary Fund in the document 'Chile Request for Stand-by Arrangement' (January 1974) is based upon provisional figures drawn up by the Central Bank. These figures are repeated, without any change, for the imports of good as given in the 'Chile-Request' document of March 1975 and in International Monetary Fund, SM/75/47.

Table XV. *Terms of Trade (1970 = 100)*

	1971	*1972*	*1973*
Unit value of exports	80	78	109
Unit value of imports	104	108	130
Terms of trade	77	72	84
Purchasing power of exports	74	64	76

Source: N. U., CEPAL, *Estudio económico de América Latina* [UN, ECLA, Economic Study of Latin America] (New York, 1973). Published in *Trimestre económico* 42 (1), No. 165 (Mexico City), 225-226, Table 5.

Table XVI. *Net Foreign Debt: Medium- and Long-term (in millions of dollars)*

	1970	*1971*	*1972*	*1973*
Total	2,067.4	2,187.3	2,419.9	2,703.1
Club of Paris	1,809.5	1,907.5	2,044.3	2,183.6
(to the United States)	(1,247.9)	(1,233.7)	(1,240.2)	(1,268.7)
Western Europe	0.2	5.6	50.5	112.7
Latin America	6.6	15.1	62.2	124.7
Other countries (People's Republic of China, Austria, Australia)	1.1	4.7	11.2	22.5
Other creditors	13.6	8.2	10.5	13.9
International institutions	175.9	193.4	193.9	204.1
Bond emissions	60.5	52.8	47.3	41.6

Source: International Monetary Fund, SM/75/47, with data from CORFO and the World Bank.

Table XVII. *Structure of the External Debt, 1970 and 1971 (in millions of dollars)*

	1970		*1971*	
	Net	*Gross*	*Net*	*Gross*
Total	2,067.5	...	2,187.4	2,793.2
Central Government	732.6	...	794.6	855.9
Decentralized institutions and public corporations	734.8	...	835.8	1,245.5
Largest mines (Gran Minería)	490.4	...	463.4	465.9
Banks [a]	74.9	...	56.7	177.8
Total public sector	2,032.7	...	2,150.5	2,745.1
Private sector subject to official guarantees	34.7	...	36.9	48.1

[a] Not including repurchase agreements with the International Monetary Fund.

Source: International Monetary Fund, SM/75/47, based on CORFO and World Bank data.

3

ALEXIS GUARDIA

STRUCTURAL TRANSFORMATIONS IN CHILE'S ECONOMY AND IN ITS SYSTEM OF EXTERNAL ECONOMIC RELATIONS

INTRODUCTION

In Latin America various international organizations, amongst them the Inter-American Development Bank (IDB) and the Economic Commission for Latin America (ECLA), proclaimed during the 1960s the need for the economy of the region to effect structural transformations aimed at breaking the classical constraints on economic growth, which were: the foreign trade stranglehold, the backwardness of agriculture, the inflexibility of the tax system, etc. During these years, the challenge presented by the Cuban experience persuaded the governments of Latin America to commit themselves, at least formally, to begin such structural transformations within the Alliance for Progress. In 1961 the United States Government, through President John F. Kennedy, undertook at Punta del Este to finance a type of Marshall Plan for Latin America, on the understanding that the transformations or reforms would be made within a democratic framework and without major breaks in the external economic relations of the region.

Within this context the structural transformations were limited mainly to agrarian and fiscal reform. The foreign loan agencies, through which the programmes of aid and technical assistance were channeled to those Latin American countries which introduced such reforms in their economies, demanded, in addition, that medium- and long-term economic plans be drawn up as a means of presenting in a coherent form the resource needs which would derive from the intended reforms.

In the course of the 1960s, the hopes of realizing a minimal programme of economic reform measures began to fade for at least two reasons: first, the total amount of economic aid promised by the United States to the Alliance for Progress, of the order of $1 thousand million per year, was gradually being lessened. Second, a large number of the Latin American governments did not

---

Footnotes and tables to this chapter may be found on pp. 91-101.

satisfy the political conditions necessary for carrying out these minimal structural changes. Thus it was that during this period attempts at reform were disintegrating and assumed secondary importance, while at the same time the number of development plans and planning boards proliferated. Slowly the foreign aid intended for financing the reform process began to be used for financing the permanent balance of payments deficits. Finally, in October 1969 President Richard M. Nixon, at a meeting with the Inter-American Press Association, admitted the failure of the Alliance for Progress.

Nevertheless, during this period, the situation in Chile could well be considered an exception in the region: in fact, the six-year period from 1964 to 1970 represented an epoch during which a process of reform began, the most important reform being that of the agrarian structure. Certainly, the agrarian reform process, despite its slow pace, had at the end of 1970 affected the expropriation of 1,408 latifundios of an estimated total of 5,040, which benefitted 20,970 peasant families occupying 19.4% of the irrigated land.[1] For the first time in the economic history of the country the vested interests of the landowning oligarchy were wounded. No less important was the fact that during this six-year period, Chile got the better part of the foreign aid that went to Latin America; the Alliance of Progress, by then in its death throes, especially was a source of this aid.[2]

It was in this way that the Chilean economy came to develop at the end of the 1960s. Thus the deep process of structural transformation which took place during the UP period cannot be interpreted as a mere continuation of the partial reforms of the previous six-year period, because this process was to affect the whole of the economic structure as well as its place in the system of international relations. Moreover, in this process the changes effected within the democratic system were to be set out from a socialist viewpoint.

The programme of economic transformations implemented under the UP Government was the result of a prognosis of the funtioning of the Chilean economy which was made at the end of the 1960s. All the economic analyses of the time confirmed not only weak and limited growth, but also the strengthening of the dependency links in the economic, financial and technical fields. There is an abundant literature on this topic, but it is nevertheless important to remember that much of the inspiration, at least in general outline, for the remedies proposed by two presidential candidates – one of which was the UP candidate – came from this source.[3]

1. FROM THE STRUCTURAL CRISIS TO THE TRANSFORMATION CRISIS

The structural changes, which took the form of a considerable series of nationalizations during 1970-73, were never considered to be an end in themselves, but rather a means of removing the obstacles to long-term economic growth; they would put in the hands of the state new instruments of economic policy which would permit the economy to be freed from its tendency towards economic stagnation and to take a different direction towards growth.

On the other hand, to push growth in the direction of including previously excluded social groups, either in terms of employment or consumption or participation, was another one of the objectives pursued in the changes, and equally important was the objective of attaining growth in conditions of reduced economic dependence, diversifying foreign trade relations and recovering some strategic decision-making centres. The basis of all structural change was the replacement of the traditional model for the operation and growth of the economy.

Nevertheless, in the process of implementing the changes in the economic structure there appeared new contradictions and obstacles to growth and development. During this period, which need not be identified with the classical stages of the transition to socialism, an economic crisis slowly began to emerge which was different from that in the Chilean economy before 1970. This crisis, which we could well call one of 'transformation', provided the material bases for the political destabilization to such a point that, once beyond a critical threshold, the solution was outside the strictly economic scope.

In order to identify the nature of the economic crisis which developed during the period of basic changes which we are discussing, we ought to point out a substantial difference in its origin as compared with the crisis of economic stagnation prior to 1970. Before 1970, in fact, the workings of a dependent capitalist economy such as the Chilean one produced an impression of modernization or false development once growth was induced in some productive sectors which, although lacking any priority in terms of social necessity, could be justified only on the basis of private profitability. That is, through the market mechanism a given demand structure directed the allocation of resources and encouraged unstable growth which quickly burnt itself out. Such a demand structure was naturally in harmony with the social relations in which production was undertaken, and it was in turn supported both by the heavy concentration of private property ownership and by the bargaining power which each social group succeeded in building up.

Thus it was that the productive apparatus began to slowly diversify, at a pace that was insufficient for absorbing all of the labour supply and for distributing the gains in productivity. In the industrial sector in particular, where growth had from the beginning been induced due to the problems in the external sector, there were sufficient profits for generating an import substitution industry. The industrial sector also diversified slowly until it reached the consumer durables range of products, particularly the electronics and automative industries. It is evident that income distribution is not alien to this process of industrial diversification: at the end of the 1960s, though 35% of income was concentrated in the hands of 7% of the population, there was also a middle sector of 48% of this population which absorbed approximately 46% of income.[4] Hence the domestic market for industrial products affected not only the highest income group but also the middle income segment in this economic system, which had an $600 average *per capita* income. Nevertheless this situation was compatible with the exclusion from the diversification process of the 45% of Chileans, who absorbed only 18% of income.

Therefore, the imbalance between productive capacity and the size of the domestic market partly set the limits for growth. The demand profile determined by the standard of income distribution established the degree of deformation of the industrial apparatus compared with the social needs of the majority of the population. Moreover, two structural limitations resulted and prevented self-sustained growth in Chilean capitalism. The first was Chile's presence in the world market as a copper exporter without access to the economic surpluses which were created in the mining sector and were largely transferred abroad as they were foreign property. The second limiting factor was that national and foreign industry in the traditional or dynamic branches had from the start been oligopolistic and for this reason the process of capital accumulation remained restricted by the domestic market and by the non-competitive character of the industry.

In this way the slow growth in some years, and at most rapid growth when favourable conditions for foreign trade existed – that is, when the copper price increased – combined with complete stagnation or even economic regression and ensured a tendency towards economic crisis not only because of a lack of growth but also because of an inability to generate capitalist growth.

In an underdeveloped capitalist economy, a crisis due to economic stagnation becomes more critical and explosive because there is a cumulative backlog of unsatisfied social needs and because only a part of the labour force is integrated into the economy; within this part only a minimum number are in the productive sector. In fact, during the 1960s an average 7% unemployment was registered and departures from this average were slight and transitory; moreover, underemployment was estimated at 9.7% of the economically active population.[5] It is certain that the intervention of the state as a source of employment in the nonproductive sector and as a redistributor of income partially alleviated the situation. Nonetheless, it was on the unemployed and underemployed labour force, as well as on the peasants and poorly organized workers, that the weight of the capitalist growth crisis rested.

In synthesis, the latent economic crisis in Chile before 1970, which was known to be structural, expressed the classical conflict between the conservative character of social relations in which production takes place – concentration of private property ownership, of economic surplus and of income – and the inability to develop a social exploitation of resources.

The acquisition by the popular movement of considerable political power allowed an economic programme to be put into practice which proposed to eradicate the fundamental causes of the structural crisis, and thus it aimed at two objectives which were to be embarked upon simultaneously. The first was the partial transformation of the capitalist economic structure to make way for state capitalism which would turn into socialism as it developed. (State capitalism is to be understood here as that stage – short or long – which precedes the period of transition to socialism.) The second aim was that such an economy should direct resources to satisfy the essential needs of the population; that is, it should try to gradually modify, in accordance with the new demand profile that was to be created, the supply structure which had been inherited from the period before 1970.

To achieve these objectives, the changes in the economic structure became associated with the series of nationalizations of the monopolistic centres which could be found in almost all sectors of the economy: agriculture, industry, mining, distribution, and the banks. It was out of this process in the economy that the Area of Social Property (APS) arose and, because of its wide and deep impact, it fundamentally modified the physiogomy of the Chilean economy. No less important was the fact that the concept of structural change, which previously had been ambiguous, became quite clear. The cause of the ambiguity is the fact that the notion of structure, when understood simply as a set of linked relationships at the level of economic analysis, can have two meanings: (1) when it refers to the social relations of production and amongst these, those of property, appropriation and use of the economic surplus, it means economic structure; (2) when it refers to relations of a technological and productive nature, as between different sectors of the economy or between different agents, it means of the productive structure. There is a dialectical relationship between these structures which needs no explanation here. For a long time the structural changes have been confused with changes in the productive structure, which generally are long-term, while the changes in the economic structure were considered as exogenous variables. In the Chilean case the difference between these areas became quite clear.

Simultaneously, on the other hand, a short-term economic policy was proposed whose aim was the expansion of the domestic market through an increase in real income and employment. Certainly modification of the prevailing distribution of income was not independent from the process of nationalization and therefore also can be considered as part of the structural transformations initiated. It is, moreover, important to remember that the series of nationalizations were carried out under two conditions which remained unchanged until the *coup d'état*: the first was that they were carried out within the existing legal framework and through the existing institutions, and the second was that they were carried out by a state apparatus which had not been substantially modified.

As is known, the nationalizations covered a wide field, and the APS incorporated the major mining companies, coal, saltpetre, iron ore and the banking system. Through intense application of the agrarian reform law nearly 4,000 latifundia were expropriated by the end of 1973; these, together with the 1,400 landholdings expropriated in the previous six-year period, accounted for nearly all the latifundia. Out of a total of 36,000 industrial enterprises, nearly 400 industrial enterprises were bought, or their management was taken over (*intervenidas*). Within less than three years the capitalist structure of production was subjected to one of the most profound alterations, and the state came to assume, besides its regulatory and supporting role for production, the function of producer and active participant in the generation of global demand and economic surplus. Nevertheless, notwithstanding the great influence gained by the state, the market mechanism continued to be the principal means by which the different social forces could express their desire to allocate resources in the directions which they preferred.

At the same time, this process also signified the partial dismemberment of the production system (the notion of system being understood here to include all structures) – that is, the capitalist system – without providing an alternative. This fact unleashed much tension in the management and organization of production, both in the state and in the private sector.

The economic crisis manifested itself first in a scarcity of some products and later became more acute because of accelerated inflation which occurred simultaneously with a domestic recession but had no similarity to the habitual stagnation described above. The substantial difference between the one and the other lay in the atypical behaviour of the traditional economic agents displayed during this period of transformation: that is, consumers, enterprises, the state and the foreign trade sectors altered their customary standards of behaviour on the market. In this way the process of accumulation was interrupted by the flight of capital or by the re-direction of profits into speculation; consumption was distorted by speculative tendencies or by exaggerated expectations of inflation; the foreign credit system crumbled for extra-economic reasons; normal financing of state activity proved to be impossible because of the political opposition to the Government in the National Congress; the economic estimates became distorted to such an extent that the prognoses used for making economic policy became increasingly meaningless, etc.

Moreover, the imbalances which effected economic activities differed from those which had been inherited from the previous period; the difference lay more in their origins and development than in the manner in which they manifested themselves, namely in price increases, fiscal deficits, balance of payments deficits, etc. The chronic crisis of capitalist growth described above was altering the very foundations of the system and thus became a crisis of structural transformation, as in this case the changes affected the dependent and oligopolistic nature of the Chilean economy. Consequently, the resultant economic crisis was not caused by the process of reproducing the 'dependent capitalism' structure, but by dissolving it. Thus undersupply, accelerating inflation, expansion of the money supply, and distortion in the pricing system were all factors which indicated the profound change which originated in the economic structure's transformation in the allocation of resources.

Obviously the magnitude of a transformation crisis is amplified when it occurs in a capitalist economy which is underdeveloped and dependent because, apart from the technological lag, one starts off with important structural imbalances. In this way the crisis of change cannot be attributed to structural change *per se*, but rather to the inability of underdeveloped capitalism, and the external economic relations which surround it, to accept fragmentary but significant changes in its structure. The natural rejection of the changes made in a part of the system, and of the social dynamics entailed in such changes, is translated into a deepening of the traditional imbalances. Only coherent, homogenous political action can really break through such an impasse.

In economic management one must know how to diagnose and anticipate such dynamics in the economic sphere. In selecting remedies for the inevitable difficulties raised by any truly structural changes, it is essential that one evaluates, foresees and offers viable alternatives. In the other chapters in this volume we will see whether in the Chilean case the ability to anticipate and act upon obstacles was or was not present in the economic policy.

2. THE LEGACY OF THE CAPITALIST ECONOMIC STRUCTURE

The legacy which was passed on to the period of transformation was in some cases a restrictive one but in other cases it played a more favourable role. While the aspects of this legacy which derived from the productive structure and the deformation of the industrial sector were restrictive, spare capacity, amounting to almost a third of industry, and unemployment amongst the labour force gave some degree of freedom to the policy of economic revival during the first year. Nevertheless there are two elements of this legacy which directly burdened the general economic situation and which need to be considered: structural heterogeneity and the external debt.

2.1. *Structural Heterogeneity*

Capitalist development in Chile gave rise to an imbalanced productive structure, although such development was consistent with the dynamics of the process of capital accumulation. The relative weakness in this structure caused a deformation in the productive apparatus in terms of absorption of the labour force, leading to the development of the service and commerce sectors independently from the average level of productivity. Again the favoured growth of consumer durables accentuated the unemployment problem because it was capital intensive; it also accentuated the weakness of the industrial sector in the face of fluctuations in import capacity, as a good part of industry's raw materials was imported. These tendencies became stronger when the industrial sector set out to satisfy an artificially diversified demand structure which had resulted from the absence of a sustained distribution of productivity gains extending over the whole population.

But we are not only dealing with 'national distortion'. The productive structure and the economic structure are not homogenously matched as far as the use of technology and the spread of property rights are concerned. In practice part of domestic product comes from small-scale enterprises which employ little or no salaried labour.

If we examine the data from the last industrial census (1967) we see that the handicraft and smaller industries, that is establishments employing between one and nine persons and ten and forty-nine persons respectively, constituted 80% of the industrial establishments in the country and represented 42% of industrial employment, creating 25% of industrial output (see Table 3.1).

From the technological point of view, the handicraft sector and small-scale industry utilized a capital intensity, with respect to employed labour, which was four times smaller than that in medium-sized and large firms, together with machinery and equipment which was, on the average, ten years old. That meant that the cost structure of industry was strongly influenced by its technologically backward sector, namely the small ownership and small commodity production sector.

A similar heterogeneity is also found in agriculture and commerce: in 1970, of the 120,000 existing commercial establishments, some 92% could be classified as small businesses, in terms of their capital, 6% as medium-sized and only 2% as large. On the other hand 9% of the agricultural labour force were small proprietors who neither sold their labour nor paid wage labour; another 35% were *minifundistas* with less than five hectares of irrigated land and who generally had to sell some of their labour in order to exist.[6]

Such heterogeneity can, however, lead to misinterpretation: small-scale industry can also be found in a developed capitalist economy or in a socialist economy; in both, small-scale and handicraft industries are important from the employment viewpoint. Complete uniformity in the use of technology and productivity differences has never existed. But these aspects have a completely different significance in an underdeveloped capitalist economy, because small output is not associated with increasing specialization of the labour force, without which large-scale production is unthinkable; it derives instead from insufficient growth and technological limitations. Hence heterogeneity is to be viewed as a product of both social relationships and productive structure.

Within each one of these sectors and especially in the manufacturing sector there is a link and a specific mode of interaction between the large and the small enterprises, in the same way as there is a particular functional relationship between the latifundio and the minifundio in agriculture. Oligopolistic profits in industry did not result exclusively from the noncompetitive prices or from prices determined by the marginal firm, but also from exploitative relationships between small and large enterprises, either through subcontracting of through supplying raw materials.

In the economic prognosis which served as the basis for formulating the Government's economic policy this aspect of structural heterogeneity was underestimated and the importance of the oligopolistic or monopolistic segment's influence was overestimated; thus the fact that this phenomenon is one of mutual interplay was forgotten. Without doubt the policy, through expansion of the domestic market, access to credit and use of an undervalued currency, favoured the small firm. Nevertheless, theoretical understanding of the *modus operandi* of oligopolistic industry operating amongst a large number of small producers was inadequate. This structural heterogeneity should be understood as having resulted from a high concentration, together with extreme diffusion, of size and property: this is because the dynamics of reproduction encompass both forms under very different guises as far as profitability, salaries, employment and technology are concerned.

It is important to highlight the two aspects of the monopolization of the Chilean economy because when the major industries were nationalized these, as enterprises, continued to operate just as they had previously. With the creation of the APS in all sectors of the economy, the nationalized enterprises and the part of agriculture which was affected by land reform began to coexist with small and medium-sized firms – without this involving any intention either of exploiting the smaller firms or of modernizing or abolishing leadership in the large enterprises. As there was no automatic growth of the cooperative relationship with small firms, the heterogeneity remained – though it was redefined organizationally through more advanced forms, such as cooperatives, and extended over a longer period known as a process of socialization.

2.2. *The External Debt*

The high level of the external debt in foreign currencies was another onerous legacy which the transformation process had to deal with under particularly unfavourable circumstances, for it coincided with the fall in the copper price and the closure of the traditional sources of foreign credit.

The net indebtedness (credits for more than one year) in foreign currencies recorded by the International Monetary Fund (IMF) amounted at the end of 1970 to $2,067.4 million, excluding interest (see the Statistical Appendix at the end of Chapter 2). Of this debt 60.4% was to the United States, which means that 69% of it was to the Club of Paris. This in itself indicates the character of Chile's external financial relations.

However, according to the Central Bank of Chile the net indebtedness in foreign currency was $2,581 million. This amount differs from the amount recorded by the IMF because the latter took into account only those debts incurred with governmental institutions or multinational organizations which gave credit according to the strict criteria which were applicable to all member countries. The Central Bank records all creditors because it has to service the debt through the years. Hence the difference results from considering as external debt the inflow of capital which took place at the end of the 1960s under Article 14 of DFL 258, which amounted to $111 million. This inflow had the peculiarity of being immediately payable on demand and basically was credits from multinational enterprises or foreign banks for loans in escudos to their subsidiaries or to other companies. Moreover, they included other debts which the IMF did not take into account and which, because they concerned real payments, the Central Bank had to register. In any case the proportions did not change fundamentally, as can be seen in Table 3.2.

The significance of these financial liabilities acquires its true dimension when the following is considered:

(1) The increase in external indebtedness took place from 1966 to 1970, and grew at a rate of 17% *per annum*, while during the same period exports grew at an average of almost 7% *per annum*. The most important point to stress about this period is, however, the change in the composition of the external debt, for it meant that servicing most of the debt was to take place in the period after 1970.

As shown in Table 3.3, one can discern a significant change in the composition of the debt by comparing the maturity dates and noting the increase in shorter-term obligations.

(2) The yearly expenses for servicing debts related to exports were much higher than had been traditionally acceptable, especially during 1970 and 1972. The traditional rates for six Latin American countries which held 80% of the region's debts in the period from 1964 to 1969 fluctuated between 18.6% and 22.2%.[7] The same calculation for Chile, before the renegotiation, indicated a rate of no less than 35% of estimated exports in 1971. Table 3.4 shows a calculation based on the real level of exports which makes the rate even higher for 1971 and 1972.

Debt servicing needs grew in comparison to previous periods: in 1967 only $125 million was needed, while during 1971-73 Chile had to write off $1,252 million for debt servicing, which is 37% of the total liabilities (including interest payments) of the debts incurred over the previous seventeen years.

(3) A final consideration about the influence of the legacy of the external debt is that up to 1970, while the Chilean economy was indeed deeply in debt, mechanisms of financial adjustment existed which specifically allowed for such a situation, to wit the net inflow of capital during the 1960s, which was a positive flow throughout that decade. After 1970 this mechanism stopped

functioning in the way it had previously, that is, it stopped at precisely the time when the highest payments for debt servicing were concentrated.

In the economic prognosis made in the middle of 1970 by the UP economists, the external debt legacy was not given the importance or significance warranted by the magnitude and complexity of the problem. This was due in part to a lack of information, for the figures were extremely inaccessible, especially to those who at that time were members of the opposition. Moreover, the level of the reserves, which was estimated at $340 million at the end of 1970, created illusions as far as the external imbalance was concerned, as this amount did not reflect sound foreign trade conditions because all reserves were committed to debt servicing once the price of copper fell.

3. THE NATURE AND EXTENT OF THE STRUCTURAL CHANGES

As was stated above, once the transformation process took place in Chile, the significance of the structural changes was no longer surrounded by ambiguity. But until then, in fact, structural reforms in Latin America had dealt with disparate aims, ranging from agrarian reform – which could be interpreted and put into practice simply as an extension of technical and credit assistance to small farmers – to a planned increase in the public budget for education and health, at best backed by *ad hoc* tax reform.

With the implementation of the UP programme it became clear that the changes were directed at the economic structure, that is the complex of social relationships in which production takes place. However, these changes were always considered a necessary but insufficient condition for bringing about a substantial modification in the way the economy worked: in addition to planned economic management at home, financial and technological support from the international community was also needed in order to discourage the tendencies which increased underdeveloped and economic dependency. For political reasons which will not be analyzed here, neither of these were forthcoming.

Only two important aspects of the process of change will be isolated for further examination. The first is the nature and degree of the transformations during the 1970-73 period, and the second is the hypotheses or assumptions made previous to the change about the possible economic effects of these transformations.

3.1. *The Nature and Degree of the Structural Changes*

The shift in the composition of the political and social forces in favour of change, which became a concrete reality in September 1970, permitted, for the first time in Chile's history, substantive transformations to be introduced in property relations which simultaneously affected the agrarian structure as well as the industry and mining sectors once the dominant centres in each were nationalized. The concept of nationalization which we shall use is simply the transfer of ownership of the most important means of production – whether foreign or national – to the state. Therefore nationalization is simply a legal change produced by political will.

From an economic viewpoint, however, this nationalization process opened the way for a period of socialization which was much more complex than the transfer in property ownership. Two distinct stages are combined within the phrase 'structural changes': one has to do with property relations and is associated with the judicial-political aspect of the process; the other has to do with the socialization process, that is the ability to effectively make provision for the means of production which is inherent in the social heritage.[8]

The process of socialization involves the basic and effective possession and control by society of the nationalized resources, of the output they produce, and of the distribution of the products from the APS. It indicates the efficiency with which state and societal resources are utilized in the broad sense; it ultimately indicates the real degree of economic management of social production. New organization and relationships in the nationalized enterprises must not only enable rises in productivity and efficiency, but also must set up the framework for growth in the existing capitalist sector. With a view towards a growing and sustained level of capital accumulation in the nationalized sector – as the only guarantee that economic growth be guided by the 'social interest' – the allocation of resources acquires a different significance. It is only in the socialization process that transformation of state property into social property can take place through the growth of democratic planning and participation by all the workers.

Having said this, we can state that in the case of Chile, the stage of socialization had hardly been embarked upon and had progressed with difficulty. Legal and political problems came to the fore in dealing with changes in the ownership of property; economic problems having to do with output, caused by the absence of central economic management, were predominant. These facts, together with the reversible nature of the change, allow us to affirm that the Chilean economy never, despite the wide-ranging nature of the transformations, became an economy in the process of transition to socialism, and certainly never became a socialist economy.

In summarizing the process of change in 1971 and 1972 we find the following characteristics:

(1) All of the transformations were carried out, although not simultaneously, in all sectors where the concentration of economic power played a dominant role in the allocation of resources and in capital accumulation.

(2) Despite the magnitude of the changes, oligopolies continued to exist in

the industrial sector. These oligopolies had strategic power within their respective market segments and were not nationalized.

(3) Nationalizations were carried out within the existing legal framework, that is to say by applying of the Agrarian Reform Law in 1967 and the Constitutional amendment permitting nationalization of the copper industry, which was passed in July 1971. Existing legal regulations were applied, such as Decree 520 of 1933, which allowed requisition of or intervention in firms abandoned or used for speculative purposes by their owners. When these regulations did not provide for the right to change ownership of property they at least allowed direct state control. In addition to legal instruments and direct negotiations with the owners, the market mechanism was used for purchasing shares, for instance in nationalizing the private banks. This mechanism had been used previously to the opposite effect, that is when the state sold its companies to the private sector.

(4) The magnitude of the structural transformations was demonstrated by state's share in output and employment: in 1970 the state's activities generated 19.4% of the Gross Domestic Product (GDP) and employed 14.1% of the working population. In March 1973 it was estimated that the state generated 50.4% of the GDP and employed 25% of the working population. This increased state intervention in the economy was distinct from previous interventions in that the entrepreneurial role of the state was accentuated because it came to administer and manage those large copper companies whose turnover was not less than $500 million, as well as some manufacturing industries. It was estimated that 30% of industrial output originated in state enterprises. On the other hand, by 1973 57% of irrigated land and 67% of the total agricultural land had been affected by agrarian reform. From the foreign trade viewpoint the state administered and controlled 85% of exports and made 65% of imports.[9]

(5) Nevertheless, though the degree of state participation in economic activity was greater than ever before, it was not dominant or hegomonic in terms of the general functioning of the economy. When ownership of the strategic means of production is changed, the predominance of social interests over private interests is not generated spontaneously, even when this is a necessary condition for making way for the new rationality. In part for extra-economic reasons (which will not be discussed here), the state played a dominant but not controlling role in economic activity. This phenomenon can, from the economic standpoint, be partially explained by both the lack of internal coherence in state production and the fragmentation of decision-making at the core of the economy's operation, as well as by the absence of real planning for these enterprises as a group and for the economy as a whole. But ultimately the problem was an intertwined mixture of economic and political factors, which lead to two questions: (1) why was there no real attempt at planning the economy; and (2) can a planning process exist when there is a tendency towards political destabilization?

If we place ourselves strictly within the bounds of economic analysis, and at the risk of losing sight of the richness which the process has when viewed as whole, it could be said that the major obstacle was the failure to link up the enterprises in the state sector through economic planning, which would have incorporated social objectives (including those determined by the business cycle) with a system of production targets and incentives, thus enabling the state to become the true driving force behind economic activity.

In the absence of such a plan the market mechanism inside and outside the state sector played a negative role not only by distorting the measurement of value but also by making it impossible to have any control over the state's output in relation to the private sector.

All these elements are indications of the inadequate degree of progress made by the socialization process: they place the Chilean economy of the 1970-73 period (regardless of the unstable aspects of the process) in a 'transitory situation' and certainly not in the stage of a 'transition to socialism'.

3.2. *A Theoretical Assumption on the Effects of the Changes*

The economic model which, it was hoped, could be attained once the structural changes had been carried out was based on the assumption of a certain set of economic effects. Amongst these it is important to highlight at least two: the mobilization and capture of the economic surplus, and the external sources of finance.

3.2.1. *The Mobilization and Capture of the Economic Surplus*

The Chilean economy generated a real economic surplus which was appropriated basically by the dominant centres of the economy, and an important part was transferred abroad through profit remittance, repayment of loan principal, unjustified royalty payments, services, and the flight of capital through under-invoicing exports and other speculative variants. In the Government's economic programme it was implicitly assumed that this surplus could be quite easily captured, but the facts demonstrated the reverse. Hence, it was assumed that control of the dominant economic centres by the state through nationalizations would put a stop to the leakage overseas of part of the surplus (through the nationalization of the copper industry and the foreign trade sector) and, with the state financial system reinforced by the nationalization of the banks, this would enable the surplus to be centralized both in origin and use.

The funds accumulated from the economic surplus would be used to increase the material bases for producing essential goods and thus gradually correct the deformation in the industrial sector which had been inherited from the period before 1970. At the same time, economic policy was directed towards realizing the potential economic surplus, once full use was made of installed capacity and the unemployed labour force. In this way the increased surpluses captured by the state through setting up the nationalized sector of the economy would reinforce the capital accumulation process in the direction previously indicated: in theory not only the generation but the utilization of the economic surplus by the state in a planned manner would be the guarantee of harmonious growth, that is growth with minimal inflationary pressures, and of a sustained increase in the real income of the workers.

It is not difficult to realize that this supposition fits with the way socialist economies work, but in no way suits a transitory situation such as that in the Chilean economy. On the contrary, the nationalization created a breakdown of the traditional forms in which production had taken place, which would have occurred under any system of change, but the fact was that the economic surplus was buried. That part of the surplus generated in the state sector was transferred partly to consumption by real increases in salaries and partly to the private sector through price controls affecting long-term inputs; the rest, which previously went abroad, was also used to support the increase in foodstuff consumption, as well as to finance the foreign trade deficit.

That part of the economic surplus which the capitalist sector still captured, primarily in the period when the domestic market was growing, increasingly lost its role of capital accumulation in the productive sector and was transformed into capitalist consumption or capital reproduction in the sphere of circulation, through speculation in goods and foreign currency.

In this way the growth of the state sector, which was often unplanned in the industrial sector, did not entail direct control over increased surpluses, except in the copper mining industry. Because of this situation a question arose at the end of 1972: *where* was the economic surplus? Without doubt an important part was generated in the private sector, mainly in the circulation of goods (commerce and transport), but a no less important part was potential in the productive state sector. The magnitude of the surplus captured in one sector or the other is indicative of the ability to direct and displace the real resources of each of the two; the exchange relationships between the nationalized and the state sector determined this ability precisely. In a situation of transition such as that in Chile, the problem has an extra-economic dimension which cannot be underestimated and therefore the problems of appropriation and use of economic surplus cannot be explained solely by the effective use of the market mechanism.

Consequently, the generation and appreciation of surpluses in the nationalized sector is not only the result of a change in property ownership but also of the development of the socialization process. The legal and political acts of changing property relationships also predict a partial dismantling of the traditional mechanisms for the appropriation of such economic surpluses. The case of Chile clearly indicated that structural transformations are compatible with increased output over a period, but if such transformations take place in a context where there is no planned direction for resource allocation, the long-term result is a production decrease which imperils the whole process of change. Moreover, one cannot forget that in part this process of change was excessively motivated by economicist tendencies which had roots in a distant past and affected not only the social base of support for the UP Government but also important sectors in the opposition. This fact alone was an important obstacle in the way of capturing the economic surplus.

3.2.2. *The External Sources of Finance*

Another important supposition, and one which inspired the first steps of the policy of structural transformations, is the assumption about external finance which essentially states that nationalization of the major copper mines and state control of foreign trade (and eventually its planning) would allow the retention within the country of a major part of the surplus in foreign exchange. These resources, plus the economic solidarity of the socialist camp and the continuation of the traditional relationship with capitalist Europe, would finance the increased need for imports arising from the expected increased levels of output, as well as the need for capital accumulation.

Despite the fact that the state managed to get hold of significant foreign exchange resources through nationalization and credits from socialist countries, these were inadequate for coping with the balance of payments gap. This imbalance was caused in part by factors which were only vaguely understood before the Government took office, as for example the legacy of financial obligations. Other unforeseeable factors also existed, such as the trend in the international business cycle which implied a change in Chilean import prices and a fall in the price of copper; also, no precise prognosis was made of the economic cost, especially in qualitative terms, of breaking away from political and economic dependence on the U.S. hegemonic centre. Furthermore, nothing was understood about invisible blockades or about the difficulties involved in speeding up aid coming from the socialist camp. Hence the model for the process of change had, through experience, to be adjusted the real situation.

In practice the two assumptions described above were transformed, once the change in property relationships within the strategic means of production had taken place, into the central objectives of a new economic policy which began in the middle of 1972. For political reasons, however, they never became operational.

4. THE INTERNAL ECONOMIC EFFECTS OF THE CHANGES

It is difficult to distinguish the direct internal effects generated by a change in the economic structure of the economy as a whole. Global output and capital formation are subject both to factors which are exogenous to the process, that is import prices, and to consequences which appear indirectly or after a certain time lag, for example the economic blockade. Moreover, any analysis of the macro-economic variables in the Chilean experience, in this case output and capital accumulation, ought to take into account that in the two years and ten months that the experiment lasted, there were social and political upheavals which have no parallel in the history of Chile. One can say that at least the last eight months of 1973 were totally abnormal: a military putsch in June, pre-insurrectional strikes in July and August, sabotage of production and overt political destabilization.

Nevertheless during 1971 and 1972, which were considered to be the 'normal' years, there was significant economic growth in the first year and a fall in the second year, accompanied by a reduction in the capital investment rate compared to the previous level. By analyzing the behaviour of these two variables some hypotheses can be inferred on the elements which influenced them, among which were the effects of nationalization.

4.1. *The Effects on Output*

The Chilean economy grew by 7.6% in 1971, stagnated in the following year, and radically decreased in 1973 by -3.7%. Nonetheless there was, during these three years, a rather important change in income distribution since at the end of 1972 the wage earners received 59% of the national income as opposed to only 51% in 1970.[10]

What was the extent of the influence these changes had in property ownership, the international business cycle and political destabilization? It is difficult to give a single answer, for it is necessary to analyze each sector in which changes occurred – agriculture, mining (especially of copper) and industry. In agriculture and industry the economic cycles mentioned above were also present: the increase in agricultural and livestock output was 5.1% in 1971 and only 1.1% in 1972 (with a 1% fall in agricultural output); industrial output grew by 14.6% in 1971 and by 2.8% in 1972. Output from the major copper mines grew regularly at about 21,000 tons per year but was below full capacity utilization due to the expansionary plans in 1967-70.[11]

Each sector has its own peculiar characteristics which explain the tendencies in it; for the economy as a whole, however, the hypotheses which explained the variations in the business cycle, and also provide an overview of each sector, are as follows:

1. The first element to be considered is the economic policy's use of the existent margin of inherited spare capacity. Here we cannot forget that when the UP Government took over, the economy was semi-paralyzed and had underused capacity caused by the recessionary drop in the business cycle – above all in industry and construction; spare capacity also existed in agricultural and ologopolistic industry where its causes were structural.

The use of this capacity was initially undertaken through the market mechanism in the form of a major increase in overall demand. Domestic supply reacted to this very vigorously, growing by 7.6% in 1971 and reducing unemployment to only 3.8% by December of that same year after having reached 8.3% in 1970 (see Table 3.5). Despite the revival of the economy and the substantial increase in production, the margins of spare capacity in each sector or branch were not uniform and consequently supply in the economy generally grew with partial bottlenecks, producing at the end of 1971 localized specific shortages parallel with increases in output.

Naturally when factories work two or three shifts, independent of any intermediate goods bottlenecks, increases in output can only arise from an improvement in labour productivity and an increase in installed capacity. The latter becomes even more important when bottlenecks appear. For this reason, in Chile the increases in output based on a spontaneous absorption of spare capacity were short lived, as was observed in the manufacturing industry from the end of 1971 onwards.

2. A second factor, which in this case had a negative effect on output, was the restrictions, caused by a shortage of foreign exchange, on importing raw materials and spare parts for industry, as well as on reducing the supply of raw materials coming from the agricultural sector.

In the second quarter of 1972 the fall in the purchasing power of exports began to be very noticeable, above all in industry, on account of the drop in the copper price in 1971-72 as compared with the previous five years and the rise in the cost of imports. Some of the difficulties in foreign trade were independent of the process of transformation, for example the variation in international prices, but these difficulties were magnified internally because of the effects of structural change. A typical example of when the two variables meet is the increasing demand for imported foodstuffs at a time when the introduction of new forms for organizing agricultural output had not yet led to increases in agricultural productivity.

Both of the two factors considered – the use of the margin of spare capacity and the shortage of foreign exchange – rendered prolonged economic growth impossible: for this reason the fundamental problem at the end of 1971 was to support economic growth by productivity increases and to improve the use of potential reserves by more planning of the productive process.

3. A third factor which had an important influence on production, and most

particularly on productivity, was the nationalization process and the time lag in setting up new social relationships in production.

We have suggested in the previous pages that the nationalization process is distinct from that of socialization: the degree of economic transformation attained clearly indicated this difference. The legal change of property ownership was never identified with a developed societal capability for directing the global process of production. The lack of a planning system as a means of directing and managing the economy typified the situation. Nevertheless one should not forget that the changes were carried out against the background of a political conflict of unprecedented intensity, and during a domestic and foreign blockade by those economic and political interests affected by changes, so that it became even more difficult to administer the effects of this situation.

Consequently, the increased output achieved and the need for even greater productivity existed within a very singular set of circumstances: an important breakdown in capitalist production relationships had occurred, but these relationships had not been replaced by socialist production relationships. This is the definition of a transitory situation and not of an economy in the transitional phase of socialism.

How did this situation affect the productive process?

In the first place one could detect a partial breakdown in the customary interaction of the nationalized industries, either because the supply of manufacturing inputs had to adopt itself to the restricted foreign trade situation, or because the distribution of the output of nationalized industries had to adapt to black markets. The APS enterprises which were faced with this disarticulation, lacking a normative plan which would have arrested these tendencies, realized that their production organization was affected both at the enterprise level and at the level of the economy as a whole.

Second, in general, when an enterprise is transferred from the private to the social sector the coercive element inherent in the system of production disappears. It is precisely this element that keeps productivity at a certain level; it is based on the fear of unemployment and on the internal management structure of the enterprise; when it disappears a new social discipline, congruent with the new property relationships, does not spontaneously arise. Consequently, during this transformation period the tendencies towards absenteeism, lack of discipline and demands from the workers increase. (In Chiquicamata, the major copper mine, there were 102 partial stoppages in 1972 amongst different groups of workers.)

These two trends – breakdown in the previous relationships in enterprises and in capitalist discipline – were considered to be direct effects of change in property ownership, and were not as dominant in agriculture as in industry. The problem of organizing agricultural production is much more complex and affected the productive system for a much longer period. In a major part of this sector it was a case of changing from pre-capitalist relationships, in paternalist forms, to those relationships which presuppose a more efficient management from a social point of view. It has been said repeatedly that when the role of the *'patrón'* is eliminated, the organization is also eliminated; though this may seem backward and traditional, the paternalist organization assigned tasks and functions and put into operation its own methods of labour force control. In agriculture the organizational aspect is not a short-term problem: it has no overall economic management and development of a new and superior organization of labour cannot be achieved solely through more investment in technical assistance or more credit.

In the industry and mining sectors the situation is again different. Here the changes are started within fully developed capitalist relationships at the production unit level, where the necessary elements exist for linking the labour force to the productive apparatus in such a way that there is a minimum flow of output guaranteed by technology. For this reason industry is different from agriculture: the structural changes in industry affect production only in the short run, with negative effects primarily on productivity. The material and organizational basis of the industry remains within the enterprise and is independent from the disappearance of the capitalist (shareholder) as owner and ultimately as organizer so long as the technical capability of management, found amongst the engineers and technicians, is not fundamentally altered. But it is necessary, starting on this basis, to attain a higher level of organization of production and labour; as we have said, this does not spontaneously occur upon merely changing the ownership of property, and it cannot be confused with merely increasing production.

In general, when the problems of organizing production are being resolved at a higher level, the economy is creating a new rationality. This involves an increasingly more homogeneous and planned behaviour by the nationalized sector, and with this comes the safeguarding of the social interest. However, organizational problems are not always solved at the economic level but rather at the political and legal levels. It is from these levels that the new institutional body should have arisen in Chile to legitimize the new economic structure, thus opening the way to a new economic rationality which would guarantee self-sustained growth in output within a process of economic development. It was precisely these features which never reached a satisfactory realization in the case of Chile: the negative aspects predominated in the process of change, notwithstanding the first year's increase in output, as in the second year there was a decrease in overall productivity.

4.2. *The Effects on Capital Accumulation*

The increase in output during 1971 and its stagnation in 1972 occurred when there was a drop of nearly 20% in the copper price as compared to the average for the previous five years at the same time a fall in the level of investment was observed, particularly during 1972, with a trend towards recovery in 1973 (see Table 3.5). The fact that production grew in 1971 while at the same time copper prices and investment were declining was totally unprecedented in the traditional standards of short-term growth in Latin American economies.

From the supply viewpoint the explanation for the economic expansion hinges upon the fact that there was an improvement in the capital output ratio, that is, there was an increase in output per unit of capital invested due to more intensive utilization of installed capacity. However, the decline in the purchasing power of Chilean exports caused by the fall in the copper price and the rise in international prices affected the level of imports; the result for industry was that an additional constraint was put on its initial growth and impetus, as the shortage of foreign exchange at the end of 1971 profoundly affected the import of raw materials and spare parts.

It is also important to note in this context that the decline in the rate of investment which occurred during the 1971-73 period, when it averaged 13.8%, compared with the 1966-70 period, when it reached an average of 17.4%, is much less if we consider that the latter average was very strongly influenced by the unusually high investment in the major copper mines. In fact, during the 1967-70 period investments in copper mining reached nearly $730 million, and were all financed by foreign exchange; this fact changed the long-term level of investment in mining, increasing its share in overall domestic investment from 1.7% in 1966 to 17.1% in 1969. If we now exclude the three years of mining investment from 1967 to 1970 from the long-term rate (fixed capital investment divided by output) this rate drops to only 14% during 1965-70, which is lower than the rate reached in 1960-64, which was 16.3%.[12]

Nevertheless, the reduction in the investment rate, either as fixed capital formation or gross domestic asset formation, expressed as a percentage of output, is significant for the period we are analyzing because, apart from the fact that it occurred when terms of trade were deteriorating, the output increases, and the subsequent stagnation in the second year, clearly reveal the efforts put into the productive process because these increases took place during the course of important economic transformations.

Although the redistribution of income, and the resultant wage increase, is usually given as the explanation for the reduction of investment, the true cause is the process of changes in its entirety. Because the Chilean economy in 1970 had a state sector which accounted for 50% of the gross capital formation, an estimated 57% fall in private investment was balanced out by a 60% increase in state investment, particularly in the construction industry, so that the overall investment rate was less affected.[13]

Although the state controlled 50% of investment and some 25% additional indirect investment (development credit for the private sector), there was during 1972 a serious decline of 20% in overall investment compared with 1971, and this pushed the investment rate to its lowest level, that is 12.3%. This decline, the result of a continued decrease in private investment, compelled the state sector to increase its share in investment, resulting in a slight recovery in 1973 of 9.1% compared to 1972.

But the problem was not one of linear substitution of private investment by state investment, because the former is very important for employment; furthermore, the simple reproduction of investments by expansion created bottlenecks in production which were very significant for the overall level of economic activity.

Hence the progressing quasi-paralysis of private investment, mainly due to postponement of all expansion of enterprise, which took place despite the increase in the domestic market, and the subsequent failure to renew equipment and replace parts, created serious problems of input shortages, particularly as the economy was growing rapidly. Furthermore, private investment in small and medium-sized establishments is different from state investment in industry because smaller establishments are labour intensive. Thus the fact that private investment was seen to decrease increased the demand for the state sector to create employment.

In a major nationalization process such as that in the Chilean economy it was foreseeable that investments by the large, oligopolistic enterprises would decline, which would result in a decline throughout the private sector, including those small and medium-sized establishments which, according to the Government's programme, were not to be expropriated. However, we should not forget that half of the investments in the Chilean economy was in the construction industry, where the private sector is practically irreplaceable on the short term.

The negative influence on private investment originated neither in the economic policy nor in the nationalization process *per se*, but rather in the political impossibility of defining exactly what was to be expropriated and guaranteeing the inviolability of the rest. The economist Oscar Lange, in a work which has become a classic, pointed out that:

> If a socialist government socializes the coal mines today and declares that the textile industry will be socialized after five years, we can be certain that the textile industry will be ruined before it will be socialized.

Later he says:

> On the other hand, as a complement to its resolute policy of speedy socialization, the socialist government has to declare an unmistakable way that all property and enterprise not explicitly included in the socialization measures is going to remain in private hands and to *guarantee its absolute security*.[14]

Although in the case of Chile the Government was not strictly socialist, the suggestion made by Lange is absolutely valid for the Chilean experience. The President of the Republic explored every opportunity for arriving at a political agreement on this matter, that is, for establishing the limits of especially the state sector in industry, but this was not possible for reasons which lie outside the scope of this chapter and which go beyond the strictly economic field.

During 1970-73, on the other hand, the criteria for allocating state investment changed diametrically as compared with previous criteria, for the new criteria gave priority to projects which had a short maturity period, which would absorb the labour force and which were designed to change the supply structure. Nevertheless, the fact that the private sector did not share in this effort meant a decrease in overall productivity in industry, as at the intersectoral level the supply shortfalls affected the economy as a whole. Still, during this period the private sector realized that the domestic market was expanding rapidly, and although there may well have been a fall in profit margins, with cheap credit and an undervalued currency the total volume of profits grew. This profit flow was withdrawn from productive accumulation and was partly directed towards unproductive stock formation and foreign exchange holdings, thus seriously affecting the market outlets for goods and creating black markets. This was the principal consequence of the freeze on private investment.

5. THE REACTION OF OTHER COUNTRIES TO THE CHILEAN STRUCTURAL CHANGES

In the previous sections we have tried to measure and conceptualize the process of transformation in the Chilean economic structure; thereafter we have attempted to study some of the internal effects produced by these changes. In this section we will account for the reciprocal effects of the changes and the external economic relationships. It is very difficult to separate internal from external effects, as they are closely interrelated and, in general, social and economic phenomena are governed by endogenous variables.

The first symptoms of difficulties in foreign trade and finance appeared at the end of 1971 and became more widespread in 1972; the months of 1973 were distinctly abnormal as far as foreign trade was concerned even though the foreign exchange crisis showed the first signs of recovery.

There were at least two factors at the core of the foreign trade problems experienced by Chile: first, the desire to break away from political and economic dependence; and second, the vulnerability of the Chilean economy in coping with partial change in external economic relationships.

Nationalization of the major copper companies, which affected two large U.S. multinational corporations, Kennecott and Anaconda, created the most important conflict, especially as the U.S. Government identified itself totally with these companies and stated their case before all the international organizations and multinational banks. When nationalization occurred in other sectors the treatment of foreign capital, be it in industry or commerce, was the result of negotiations between the Chilean Government and the foreign private interests, and generally they ended in agreements which were scrupulously adhered to by both parties. In the case of copper there was the additional issue of the previous excess profits because of the non-renewability of this resource. This of course set a legal precedent for the treatment of such investments in the Third World.

The economic changes cannot of themselves explain the shift in Chile's position on the international scene; the expansion of Chilean ties with the socialist camp and the Third World is linked to the independent, nationalist stance in foreign policy. When seen in this light the initiation of diplomatic and economic relations with the socialist countries, as well as the important work done by Chile to stress the independence and economic defence of the underdeveloped countries, are also meaningful for understanding the attitude of the United States and the rest of the developed capitalist countries.

From the economic point of view the Chilean experiment represented for foreign capital not only the eventual loss of markets or the impossibility of gaining access to natural resources, but it also meant a questioning of the traditional norms which regulated such capital in Latin America. These norms were set out in the investor's statute of the Andean Pact and Chile had promoted and practised them faithfully. Yet the economic policy made it quite clear from the beginning that the economic development which was to be promoted required acquisition of foreign capital, preferably in cooperation with the state, with the aim of bringing technical progress to areas where it was deemed necessary. The automotive industry policy was implemented on the basis of this criteria, and foreign capital was accepted according to a framework of rules which guaranteed the return on capital and the social priorities set out in the policy. But those providing foreign capital also perceived that, at the heart of the Chilean economy, the capitalist system was being seriously questioned and the changes were leading towards creating a mixed economy with socialist leanings. Very revealing indeed is the hesitation of a U.S. financier who, during the negotiations on debt rescheduling, asked: 'Why should capitalism have to finance the building of socialism in Chile?'

Another key to understanding the problems of external finance is the degree of vulnerability of the foreign trade sector, which was 80% dependent on a single product for its foreign exchange earnings. The structure of exports and imports is also important because of the strong predominance of U.S. and European markets: 14.1% of Chilean exports went to the United States and 60% to Europe (including Great Britain) during 1970; in that same year imports coming from the U.S. represented 36.9% of the total, while 28% came from Europe (see Table 3.6). A considerable proportion of Chilean the imports purchased on the U.S. market were strategically important because to a large extent no substitutes could be found for them in other markets on the short term. Lastly, copper is a raw material whose price fluctuates constantly with the business cycle of the developed capitalist countries, and this fact creates great instability in the Chilean capacity to import.

But more important than all these facts is a proper understanding of the traditional mechanism of financing foreign trade, which until 1970 had been the accepted mode of doing business in Chile. Through the years, and certainly during the 1960s, the balance of payments had had a net positive inflow of capital – that is, foreign investment, movement of short-term private capital and credit from governments and international organizations. This inflow allowed the balance of payments on current account to be partially or totally financed, as in general there was a deficit even when the price of copper improved. Such a mechanism for debt financing certainly maintains a diversified level of consumption but, rather than solving the problem of external finance, it simply delays making payments abroad. The important thing to note is that this capital inflow financed part of the imports or raw materials, spare parts and foodstuffs. During 1965-70 conditions were very favourable for foreign capital and in these years the net inflow of capital amounted to $1,167 million.[15] This inflow, despite having the effect of taking industry out of national hands and increasing indebtedness on the short-term foreign exchange account, played a valuable balancing role which, after 1970, was no longer the case.

Apart from cyclical movements in international trade, fluctuations in this compensatory capital inflow depend generally on guarantees and facilities for distributing profits and on the foreign capital 'business climate', as well as on the economic and political system's stability. With the initiation of the economic transformation all these traditional variables were affected; in other words, the dependency relationship was shattered and this capital inflow stopped. This could have been relatively easily foreseen during the time which it would have taken to re-establish a new *modus operandi* and a guarantee for foreign capital; what could not be foreseen was that long-term credit administered by such international agencies as the World Bank and the IDB would also be frozen.

At the end of 1971 it was quite evident that the foreign sector was vulnerable, and also that the domestic productive apparatus was equally sensitive. Thus, although the import rate (imports divided by national output) was 11%, 52% of all imports in 1970 were raw materials and spare parts, and some 35% of the gross fixed asset formation needed imported components; furthermore 80% of machinery and equipment purchases originated abroad.[16] Hence, any foreign exchange limitation had an immediate effect first on the level of industrial activity and subsequently on capital accumulation.

Most of the foreign trade and finance problems of the 1971-73 period (up to the *coup d'état*) were the results of extra-economic factors. That is, there was covert economic aggression which was aimed at creating the basis for political destabilization. This covert aggression, known as the 'invisible blockade', took various forms, the most evident being the denial of long-term credit to the Chilean Government by the World Bank and the IDB through the stealthy veto by the U.S. representatives in the technical and bureaucratic departments of these organizations. The embargo on Chilean goods in New York, which was requested by Anaconda in February and March 1972 and menaced all state purchases made on the U.S. market, was another form of legal covert action. This measure meant that purchases, especially for the copper industry, had to be shifted to other markets with all the technological problems entailed. Later further embargoes, this time on copper shipments once they had arrived at European ports, were attempted by Kennecott. The date on which these embargoes were put into effect, September 1972, coincided with the campaign launched by the Chilean copper companies which, with an eye towards 1973, aimed to reopen and increase copper sales in Europe. The two key motives behind this blatant aggression were to introduce an element of doubt amongst the purchasers of Chilean copper and to prevent supply contracts from serving as collateral for new credits. Furthermore, besides this aggression, other measures were taken: one was that Chilean purchasers of capital goods were confronted with demands for cash down payments; these down payments were higher than accepted international practice, for Chile was asked for 30% while the going rate was fluctuating between 15% and 20% of the purchase price.

All these measures, along with the 'invisible blockade', seemed to be operations designed to weaken Chile and to create an image of an 'insolvent' country. The insolvency image was built up into a vicious circle, so that without specifically forbidding trade the same effect was achieved: the movements of goods and credit to the Chilean economy were halted. However, these measures only marginally affected the economy: they created technical problems and resulted in wasting administrative time, but they were not the fundamental causes of the foreign trade crisis; for that reason they are not directly reflected in the balance of payments.

The economic difficulties which stemmed from the transformation process could have been alleviated if the import capacity of the Chilean economy had looked promising for the future. Such difficulties arise not only because of the changes *per se* but also from the direct and indirect affects which are generated when economic and political interests are affected; these interests will not necessarily give way, even in a sharpening conflict which makes itself economically apparent in a thousand different forms.

The nationalization of copper affected two multinationals, thus producing a dynamic situation in external economic relations which found partial expression in the unfavourable situation for foreign trade financing. Apart from the 'invisible blockade' – one of the most studied aspects of the Chilean experience but not necessarily the most important – the external obstacles which the process of structural change encountered, or at least two of them, are of an endogenous nature: the renegotiation of the external debt and the collapse of short-term finance for foreign trade. These two factors were negatively related to the process of change: to them we can add those which are unrelated to structural change, for example the increase in international prices and the fall in the copper price. The first two factors reflected the reaction abroad to the transformation process, while the latter two are elements of the business cycle which merely served to widen the foreign trade deficit.

5.1. *Renegotiating the External Debt*

The legacy of high indebtedness in foreign currency was one of the most complex economic and political problems the UP Government had to face. During the first eleven months of 1971, that is until the 9 November, the country faithfully fulfilled its obligations, paying nearly $300 million in capital and interest on debts. During this period, debt servicing absorbed nearly all the net reserves, which equalled $343.2 million in 1970.[17] These reserves, built up earlier when favourable copper prices and exceptionally high net capital inflows were recorded, revealed their weakness as they did not stem from sound foreign trade, and were in effect needed for debt repayment whenever the slightest decrease in the copper price occurred.

Looking back on the balance of payments and external debt problems, it seems that the UP Government made a grave error when, at the beginning of 1971, it failed to ask the Club of Paris for renegotiation of the debt, in anticipation of the economic and political consequences of breaking the dependency relationship. The debt servicing programme indicated that 30% of repayments would be concentrated in 1971-74 and that the burden of paying interest would amount to not less than 35% of the value of annual exports. At the beginning of 1971 Chile's bargaining position *vis-à-vis* foreign capital was much stronger than thereafter, when the foreign exchange financing capacity had been reduced by a 20% fall in the copper price as compared to the 1970 quotations.

The basis of this error of evaluation could well have been produced by the illusionary international reserves situation, which was in effect little more than a medium-term liability, and by the hope that there would be a recovery in the copper price. At the end of 1971 the traditional debt mechanism ceased to function, that is the net positive inflow of capital, part of which was new debts to repay old, did not take place, so that there was a negative balance in capital movements of $50 million (see Table XIV in the Statistical Appendix at the end of Chapter 2). The inflow of credit and investments was less than the outflow of capital at exactly the time when the copper price dropped from $0.64 per pound in 1970 to $0.49 per pound in 1971.[18] Under these circumstances the Government had no alternative but to ask for a renegotiation of the debt, but they did not begin discussing this in the Council of Ministers until October.

During the discussions in the Government on how to proceed with negotiation, two possible options were found. The first consisted of saying that an underdeveloped country which is in the middle of a period of transformation, as Chile was, could not commit more than a certain percentage (15 to 20%) of its exports for debt servicing payments. Chile would present this principle as a general one which affected all the underdeveloped countries with debt problems. The second option was to simply enter into traditional negotiations and try to get maximum financial relief. The first option was rejected because it represented a diplomatic effort which was beyond the available means and involved a high risk of failure as the creditor countries were not prepared to accept such a precedent.

The Government asked specifically for the renegotiation of debt servicing for the period extending from November 1971 to December 1974. Excluded from this renegotiation were credits for periods of less than a year, credits from international organizations (the World Bank and the IDB), credits from Latin American and socialist countries, and also credits already renegotiated in 1965. Hence, the renegotiable credits were those from suppliers of goods guaranteed by official export insurance agencies, and Government credits. Moreover, the request for renegotiation implied the immediate suspension of scheduled payments of all renegotiable items until such time as an agreement could be reached with the Club of Paris. All other debts were conscientiously repaid.

The creditors in the Club of Paris, which includes fourteen advanced capitalist countries, negotiated with the Chilean Government during February and April of 1972. An agreement with this group of creditors had two meanings: the first was financial, for new credit was in fact received; the second, and perhaps the most important one, was that an agreement with the Club of Paris opens all the doors to the international financial system.

The strategy for dealing with the creditors was drawn up in the full knowledge that, while half the debts to be renegotiated were with the United States, litigation was taking place concerning the financial terms for nationalization of two U.S. multinationals which, through constitutional decrees approved unanimously by the National Congress, were nationalized in June 1971. For this reason two series of renegotiations were attempted: one with the U.S. Government and another with the rest of the creditors (Europe, Japan and Canada). The aim was to localize the conflict and prevent the United States from taking the problem with the multinational copper corporations, which was being litigated in court, to the Club of Paris, thus transforming the Club of Paris into a forum for political pressure. This attempt failed in practice because of opposition from European governments: these governments thought that two series negotiations would involve the risk of additional advantages for one or the other camp, although Chile had promised not to give more favourable treatment to the United States than to the Europeans, Japanese and Canadians.

In the discussions with the creditors two important political problems arose. The first was that, as a prelude to renegotiation with the U.S. Government, the problem of compensation for the U.S. copper multinationals had to be discussed. The second, which was a general source of concern amongst all the creditors, was the need to sign a stand-by agreement with the IMF as a prerequisite for arriving at an agreement over renegotiation.

The Chilean Government had already indicated that it was present at the Club of Paris meetings to renegotiate the external debt and not to debate on Chilean policy. If the two political problems mentioned above were to gain general approval this would represent a setback of the process of change which was going on in Chile at that time. The nationalization of copper had not yet been completed because, given the legal provisions approved in the constitutional amendment, there were still various institutions to which the companies could appeal. Should the copper companies not recognize the Chilean law, international law based on United Nations Resolution 1803 of 1962 also recognized the rights of sovereign states to their natural resources.

Nevertheless the hazards presented by these two problems were partially avoided and in effect postponed to the next renegotiation. The problem of compensating the copper multinationals was reduced to a court case between Chile and the United States. During the closing sessions of the Club of Paris meeting (19 April 1972) the policy for the treatment of foreign capital was established, as far as nationalization was concerned, in the following terms:

> The Chilean representatives confirmed their policy of recognizing and discharging all foreign debts and of the acceptance of the principle of paying just compensation for all nationalizations in accordance with Chilean and international law.[19]

Chile did not sign a stand-by agreement as its creditors asked; instead a declaration on the objectives of monetary policy was signed, as was an agreement on certain minimal rules for the conduct of foreign trade, to wit: limits on indebtedness, maintenance of a given average in reserves, etc.

During the five months that negotiations lasted, external economic and political affairs were severely tested. There is evidence that, amongst the major creditors and governments belonging to the Club of Paris, there was no marked common approach for dealing with the case of Chile in an understanding and strictly technical manner. Only governments such as Sweden, Italy and, paradoxically, Spain had a more open attitude to the Chilean economic problems and tried to prevent the Club of Paris from making judgments which went beyond strictly technical points of the structural reform programme. On the other hand, during this time the pressures on Chile from creditors were increasing. The comments by the Director of SEREX (the Foreign Trade Department of the Central Bank) were very revealing:

> A difficult period for the Chilean monetary authorities. Quite a few countries, quite a few multinational corporations either directly or indirectly tried to take advantage of the situation, promising their vote or influence on the decision of this or that Club of Paris delegate on the condition that certain problems they had in Chile 'solved' or that they should be given certain special tax concessions denied to the majority or which were outside the foreign exchange, monetary or commercial policy which Chile was following at the time.[20]

From the economic viewpoint, the results of the renegotiation were inadequate. Only the debt servicing for 1972 was renegotiated: that for 1973 and 1974 was not renegotiated although Chile had requested it. Moreover, 30% of the services in question, and not 5% as requested by Chile, were to be paid. The postponement of 70% of the 1972 interest payments represented a financial relief of $165 million but at the same time Chile paid $230 million during that year for the servicing of that part of the debt which was not renegotiated.[21] For this reason one can only speak of a partial respite in the balance of payments problem; unfortunately the UP Government presented the renegotiations with the Club of Paris as a success without clarifying its true significance.

Once general agreement had been reached with the creditors, bilateral negotiations took place which lasted throughout 1972. In January 1973 almost all the debt negotiations had been completed, except those concerning the United States. Negotiations with the United States were actually never concluded, as the bilateral level of negotiation raised once more the question of compensation for the copper companies. The Chilean Government foreseeing that this situation would slow down the Club of Paris renegotiations for 1973 (renegotiations which were also not concluded as the creditors delayed up to the moment of the *coup d'état*) suggested to the U.S. Government that the legal dispute should be resolved according to treaties existing between the two countries.

> The Government of the United States has insisted on linking the renegotiation of a foreign debt with this nation, with the nationalization of the major copper companies and especially with the compensation for two private U.S. companies. Chile has rejected these proposals and we have suggested that our differences which cannot be resolved directly by both parties should be settled through the channels set out in the treaty on resolving disputes signed in 1914 by both Governments, as it is considered to be the appropriate legal instrument existing for the resolution of difficulties such as those we have today.[22]

The U.S. Government at the beginning of 1973 repudiated the treaty which Chile wanted to invoke in the dispute. In the Presidential Message of 1973 it was stated:

Until now the United States Government has not accepted any agreement to use the said treaty and so the existence of diverse points of conflict is prolonged, with negative consequences for our economic circumstances and prejudicing a normal development of our relationships.[23]

This impasse between Chile and the United States ended with renegotiation of the 1973 debt being blocked and the prospects of trade between the two countries being frozen.

As was noted previously, in general renegotiation of a foreign debt entails something more than the granting of credit by means of the postponement of debt servicing. The Club of Paris, and the agreements which come from it signify an endorsement of the creditor country's monetary policies in the public and private sector. Consequently, because Chile did not pay interest on the debt with the United States, as the United States stood in the way of a bilateral agreement, and because later, during 1973, Chile did not pay the debt with the rest of the Club of Paris in the futile hope of reaching an agreement, Chile entered into conflict with companies, suppliers and banks which demanded the Club of Paris endorsement, and in this way got into a vicious circle in which the image of an 'insolvent' country grew stronger.

5.2. *Short-term External Finance*

The most consequential economic effect on the breakdown of external economic relations in the face of the transformations was the reduction in short-term finance and the difficulties this implied in obtaining ordinary import requirements. The main difficulty with foreign trade finance was in fact the narrow operational and financial limits for importing raw materials, spare parts and foodstuffs.

Until the end of 1970 an important part of Chilean imports were financed with credit from foreign suppliers. At the end of 1971 the first indications of a change in attitude with regard to exports made to Chile began to be noticeable: the Export-Import Bank (Eximbank), which had traditionally insured and guaranteed these exports, stopped doing so. (It is known, through the United States Senate investigations, that this was a political decision of the U.S. Government to put an end to the Chilean experiment.)

Nevertheless the most serious aspect was the reduction in the short-term credit previously provided by the U.S. banking system. This banking system in fact exercised a central role in financing Chilean foreign trade. Credits were authorized for imports from any part of the world and were automatically renewable every 180 days. The Chilean banks had links with U.S. banks for carrying out these operations: that is, the Chilean banks were clients of the U.S. banking system for importing not only from the United States but also from the rest of the world. It was estimated that at the end of 1970 some 80% of imports was financed by the U.S. banking network.

The short-term credit lines which were recorded as authorized by the U.S. banks for Chile amounted to $220 million in August 1970. This is, however, an underestimate of the short-term finance available, as the U.S. banks permitted many credit lines to Chile which had no fixed limit and which are not included in this figure. One can estimate that for an import turnover of $884 million (the 1970 figure), short-term credit lines renewable every 180 days would be needed to the amount of at least half that figure, that is $442 million.

The U.S. banks were cancelling credit lines throughout 1971 and 1972, and by January 1972 these lines had been decreased to $20 million of fixed amount credit; they rose to $32 million in June 1972 and remained frozen at that level until the *coup d'état*. The credit lines without a fixed amount were also decreased, but there is no information on which lines disappeared entirely because they are difficult to quantify.[24]

With the initiation of the transformations and their assimilation, short-term finance plummeted alarmingly: the closure of credit lines was gradual but irregular, so that the effect was lagged. This meant that trade had to be redirected to other areas in a very short period of time; most of the shortages which began to appear in 1971 were due to this situation, that is the impossibility of finding finance for raw materials, medicines, etc., which had previously been financed automatically by telex.

The reasons adduced by the U.S. bankers for closure of their credit lines were that there was no agreement with the Club of Paris on how to deal with Chile's external debt, and that the country was ceasing to be 'solvent' and for that reason there was no 'confidence' in dealing with Chile. However, once an agreement was made with the Club of Paris for dealing with the Chilean external debt, the U.S. banks did not modify their policy. The argument that there was a deterioration in the Chilean economy has little value in this context because the credit closures were made long before 1973, when deterioration set in. This deterioration was not unrelated to the virtual monetary strangulation of Chile, which was engineered by the U.S. banking system.

In sum, the breaking of the dependency links and the transformation involved an economic expense which stemmed from the nature of the external financing which was inherited from the previous period. When this financing was stopped, a change had to be made in the traditional framework of foreign trade relationships. The advantage which the hegemonic centre had was that they had erected an economic barrier around Chile at minimal political cost: it appeared as if the interested parties in the financial world were simply taking the measures which are normal when a debtor becomes insolvent. Certainly the criteria used for describing solvency went further than a strictly financial judgment.

5.3. *Exogenous Factors*

The international economic context in which the Chilean experiment took place played a negative role and made the problem of external finance even more acute. During 1971-72 two international economic events affected Chile: the copper price quoted in the London Metal Exchange fell substantially, and the parity of the dollar was changed through devaluation against other currencies, creating a wave of international price increases which particularly affected the foodstuff and raw material import prices paid by Chile. In 1973 there was a recovery in the copper price, but meanwhile world inflation grew, and this was reflected in the unit value of world exports expressed in dollars (see Table 3.7). The fall of the copper price was such that the 1971-72 average was 19.1% less than that of 1965-70; this alone caused a loss of some $280 million. Furthermore, the devaluation of the dollar meant an increase by industrial countries in international export prices and therefore an increase in Chilean import prices, particularly in foodstuffs, which represented a third of the total import bill. The index of international prices for foodstuffs increased from December 1972 to December 1973 by 44%. All international price increases implied a reduction of purchasing power, which was estimated at 11.5% in 1972 compared to 1970.

The fall in copper prices, combined with the reduction of purchasing power, meant a decrease in the earning capacity of Chilean copper exports in 1971-72. This partly eliminated the immediate economic effects of copper nationalization, that is the capturing of the net surplus.

The index of the dollar purchasing power for Chilean imports takes into account the increase in prices of the goods and services exported to the countries from which Chilean imports originated and the changes in dollar parity of the currencies of these countries.

According to Table 3.8 there was 25% less purchasing power for each physical unit of copper exported between 1970 and 1971, and a 33.1% decrease occurred by 1972 compared to 1970. The net effect of the variations of the terms of trade for copper represented a cumulative loss of $413 million in the 1971-72 period compared with 1970 revenues, assuming constant exports of $700 million.

The deterioration of the terms of trade for copper by a third compared with the base year of 1970 determined the extent of the influence of the international business cycle on the Chilean economy at the moment when this economy was embarking upon its policy of structural changes. The calculation of the terms of trade for Chilean exports as a whole show a similar trend (see Table XV in the Statistical Appendix at the end of Chapter 2), with a fall of 23% and 28% for 1971 and 1972 respectively.

6. THE EXTERNAL STRANGLEHOLD

So far we have considered the influence of structural changes on the conduct of traditional intermediaries in foreign trade. These intermediaries created problems which made it more difficult to consolidate the structural changes; this meant reorganizing production in order to improve the economy's production level. The foreign trade obstacles played a destabilizing role in the normal functioning of the economy and the deterioration of the terms of trade similarly did not help to counterbalance these tendencies. Intensive gowth in the economy could not take place because of the foreign exchange crisis, among other things.

If it is certain that the drop in overall productivity in 1972 and 1973 was due to various different factors, it is equally true that a dominant and constant element was the bottleneck in import capacity.

The balance of payments deficit reached during the 1971-72 period, an annual average of $325 million, reflects the reactions of the traditional intermediaries in foreign trade, the delay and mediocre results obtained in renegotiating the external debt, the closure of credit lines, the weakening of the terms of trade, and the short-term economic policy – particularly the prices and incomes policy.

In the context of the foreign trade relationships, which were restrictive and the source of much conflict, there were two significant events: the changes in the composition of imports and the centralization of foreign trade.

6.1. *Changes in the Composition of Imports and Their Real Evolution*

During the transformation period excessive stress was put on the argument that imports, having increased substantially, were causing the crisis in foreign trade. Nevertheless, new data reveal a different situation: the definitive figures on the 1971 and 1972 balance of payments (the 1973 figures give imports licenced but do not indicate the imports actually made) which appeared in October 1975, indicate an increase in the value of imports of 6.2% for 1971 and 8.5% for 1972; however, correcting these figures to take price increases into account shows a smaller growth. Unfortunately the Central Bank of Chile stopped compiling an index of import prices after 1966. A calculation was made for 1971 by the general economic workshop of the University of Chile's Faculty of Economics, which obtained a figure of 5%. Only two calculations were made thereafter: ECLA gave a figure for the unit value of Chilean imports, and the *Corporación del Cobre* (CODELCO) [the Copper Corporation] calculated a figure, shown in Table 3.9, which is a weighted average of consumer prices estimated by the Organization for Economic Cooperation and Development (OECD), adjusted for parity changes against the dollar. This average indicated an 8.4% increase, thus differing from the ECLA estimate of a 3.8% price increase in 1972. Taking the workshop's figure for 1971 and that of the ECLA for 1972, the increase in real imports was 1.1% in 1971 and 4.5% in 1972.

Therefore, it follows that in the period of full expansion there was only a small increase in real imports; subsequently, when production ceased to grow (1972) there was a significant increase in real imports caused by imported foodstuffs, but the overall average increase of 2.8% in real imports was lower than the average 3.8% growth rate for the economy as a whole.

The important points to note are that the increase in real imports took place when the terms of trade were deteriorating, and that such an imbalance could not be maintained for very long. This problem stemmed not from the changes themselves, but rather from the magnitude of the income redistribution policy, which did not take the adverse international economic conditions sufficiently into account.

On the other hand, there is an important change in the composition of imports during the 1971-72 period. The proportion of total imports which consisted of foodstuffs rose from 14% to 30% in two years. The increase in value (42.3% in 1971 and 76% in 1972) and also in real terms (estimated at 37% and 55% respectively) of this line of imports reflects the importance and magnitude of income redistribution, and especially the introduction into the economy and social security system of some 200,000 persons with high income elasticity of demand for foodstuffs. But at the same time imports of capital goods declined considerably, that is from 29% of the total in 1970, when extraordinary investments in the major copper companies took place, to 15% in 1972, a figure which in any case is abnormally low. Finally, the imports of intermediate goods closely followed the level of economic activity, increasing initially and subsequently falling in 1972 (see Table 3.10).

6.2. *Centralization of Foreign Trade*

The foreign exchange crisis described above developed simultaneously with a tendency on the part of the state to increase centralization in foreign currency transactions. Certainly one cannot infer any correlation between these two phenomena, because the first was influenced by much more relevant factors than the second.

This more centralized control of the use and allocation of foreign exchange was a consequence of the nationalization process, as this put into the hands of the state the whole of the returns from copper mining; from the demand side, the transfer to the state of the banking system as well as many industrial enterprises made the state the principle user of foreign exchange. The control of foreign trade by the state constituted at the end of 1972 the beginning of planning in this sector, and for the first time mandatory budgeting of foreign exchange was introduced in state enterprises. In 1973 the state sector became the main user of foreign exchange, accounting for 70% of the total (see Table 3.11).

Centralization of the market of imports also coincided with increasingly centralized control by the state over external finance, which meant that the geographical and financial allocation of resources could be carried out by one planning operation. This was of great importance in facing the external finance difficulties, although these measures could not be implemented until the end of 1972. The structure and evolution of the balance of payments deficits during the first two years indicate that the policy intended to fill the gap in foreign trade was overwhelmed by the force of the external imbalance. For that reason measures to finance rather than reduce the deficit predominated because new parameters of foreign trade had not yet been established, so that the emphasis was on short-term finance (see Table 3.12).

7. THE EXTERNAL FINANCING POLICY AND THE DEFICIT

If an exhaustive overview were made of external economic problems, it would become clear that answers had to be found for two basic questions. The first is whether it was possible to foresee the negative effects arising from resistance to the transformation process, as expressed in the balance of payments. The second question is whether false forecasts were made.

The answer to the first question is that some of the reactions were foreseen, for example the reduction in the inflow of capital and especially foreign investment, and the increase in the demand for imported foodstuffs and raw materials, although this was underestimated for 1972. Of course other variables could not be foreseen, for example the fall in the copper price during 1971 and world inflation in 1972-73. Furthermore, it was not foreseen that the international organizations from which Chile requested credit for projects evaluated and approved before 1970 would set up an economic blockade.

The answer to the second question is that a false impression was created by the supposition that the conflict with U.S. copper companies could be localized without adversely affecting external financing.

In the course of 1971 and at the beginning of 1972 the effects of the economic policy, and of the process of change in the economic structure, on foreign trade became evident. There are always, in a process of economic change, risks and uncertainties which can only be spelt out in detail through experiment: in this case the foreign trade crisis, which could even have jeopardized the very changes, became the centre of attention in economic policy-making, because this policy included measures to reduce the deficit (which are not analyzed in this chapter) as well as measures aimed at reconstructing a system of external economic relationships.

Therefore renegotiation of the external debt was considered to have top priority, as we have observed; the same priority was given to intensifying relationships with socialist countries and rebuilding the short-term financing system to provide the finance which the U.S. banking system had suspended.

7.1. *The Economic Relationship with the Socialist Countries*

The crisis in the traditional system of external financing could be dealt with by finding alternative sources, obviously sources which had no direct or indirect economic involvement with the nationalization process, for instance the socialist countries. However there was, above and beyond the prospects for credit offered by these countries, an enormous potential for developing trade, as in 1970 Chilean imports from socialist countries represented less than 1% of the total.

Thus it is important to bear in mind some of the essential characteristics of foreign trade involving socialist countries, the most important of which is the exchange of technology. In fact, the problems of technological backwardness in some sectors in the socialist economies, and the spreading among the masses of the new consumption standards resulting from a more diversified demand structure, form the guidelines for the foreign trade of these economies. The singular feature generally distinguishing trade in socialist countries from trade in developed capitalist countries is that on the one hand, the socialist countries import machinery and equipment with up-to-date technology from, and export raw materials to, developed countries; on the other hand, their trade with the underdeveloped countries is based upon exporting machinery and complete plants and importing raw materials and, in some cases, goods manufactured by the same plants.

The distinguishing characteristic of Chilean foreign trade was that it was cyclical, that is the need for short-term financing for importing foodstuffs, raw materials, and spare parts predominated. In addition not only the suspension of multilateral credits, but also the embargoes in the United States, which the former owners of the copper mines imposed on the two state institutions – CODELCO and the *Corparacion del Fomento de la Producción* (CORFO) [Corporation for Production Development], blocked a good part of the spare parts and raw materials purchases made in the United States. Furthermore, one has to bear in mind that the Chilean economy's production facilities were built up on the basis of the technology of advanced capitalist countries; this created a certain inflexibility in the supply sources for spare parts and some inputs, which in circumstances such as those in the Chilean economy meant either looking for alternative markets or substituting such imports at very high cost.

Because of the situation in both the socialist economies and the Chilean economy, the development of trade with the socialist countries could not fully satisfy the Chilean economy's needs.

7.1.1. *The Relative Growth of Trade*

Foreign trade with socialist countries involves the rigidities inherent in a centrally planned economy and this fact affected Chilean purchases in such economies, as is shown by the great difference which existed between applications for import licences and imports actually realized (see Table 3.13).

Unless the real import figures are false, the difference noted in Table 3.13 can only be explained by the rigidity of the socialist economies when it came to including Chile's purchases in their foreign trade plans. The first negotiations began in 1971; in that year it was difficult to increase trade between the countries for reasons already given. What is surprising is that imports remained stationary in 1972 and did not reach a significant figure until 1973. That is, according to these figures, the Chilean economy was not considered as a special case, but followed the normal trade patterns of the socialist countries. For this reason imports coming from socialist countries only represented 2.5% of total imports in 1971, and 2.7% in 1972, and rose to 7.7% in 1973. On the other hand Chilean exports to socialist countries represented 7% and 6.3% of the total Chilean exports in 1972 and 1973 respectively. As to Chile's imports from socialist countries, the largest share was that of Cuba (40%), and the second largest was the Soviet Union (20%). Chilean purchases from socialist countries during 1972-73 amounted to 60% capital goods, which is a perfectly normal standard for foreign trade with these countries and is in accordance with the finance facilities offered for such purchases.

7.1.2. *External Financing from Socialist Countries*

The Chilean Government's efforts in the socialist countries between mid-1971 and mid-1972 centred fundamentally on obtaining grants of long-term credit for the purchase of machinery and industrial plant. The credits reached a figure of nearly $380 million at the end of 1972. The Soviet Union had agreed to grant $102 million for industrial plants and technical assistance programmes, plus increasing the credit given to the previous Government for acquiring separate pieces of machinery and equipment, so that altogether $115 million was made available by the Soviet Union.

In general the monetary conditions attached to these credits were better than these of the non-socialist markets, at least as far as the interest rate was concerned, for it varied between 2% and 5%, while no interest was charged for Chinese grants, for which the first payment varied between 0% and 15%. The credit obtained by mid-1972 amounted to $302 million (not including the Chinese grants which are computed in yuans in Table 3.14) but by the 15 August 1972 some $232 million, that is 77%, had been used up, as well as 21% of the Chinese credit. By 'used up' we mean the actual spending of the credit by Chile, so that the socialist countries could start filling the orders which had been placed. If $115 million – the amount which corresponds to the increase in a previously authorized Soviet credit, of which $40 million had been used up in 1971-72 – is added to the list of authorized credits, the total level of credit available for capital goods purchases in socialist countries at the end of 1972 was $417 million, of which only $272 million had actually been spent. The Chinese credits are excluded as they are not convertible, but the most important credit, that of $67 million, awarded by China for purchasing machinery, gives an approximate idea of the importance of credit received from the socialist camp.

While it is certain that the credits granted by socialist countries for purchasing machinery, complete industrial plants and technical assistance were more than adequate, short-term credits for financing current imports were insufficient in the face of the concrete needs of the Chilean economy generally.

There were four basic procedures for obtaining for short-term external finance from the socialist countries: short-term credit lines, payment agreements, suppliers' credit, and freely convertible currency credit.

Bankers' short-term credit lines in socialist countries were limited as compared with those authorized by non-socialist countries. They reached $20 million on 30 June 1973, that is 3.5% of the sum of all credit granted Chile on that date (see Table 3.15). Although the estimated level of imports originating from these countries in 1973 was 16%, of which only 7.7% was ultimately imported, a high proportion were capital goods, which do not require this type of credit. In general the short-term credit lines granted by the socialist countries were bilateral, so that they could not be used for transactions outside the markets of these countries (Table 3.15).

Nevertheless the socialist countries supplemented the inadequate short-term credit lines by other means of financing. Amongst these were two agreements on payments: one with Poland for $1 million, and the other with China, which had no fixed limit and was renewable annually; it was estimated that its value would have been $15 million had it been used throughout 1973. Agreements on payments are accounting methods for clearing the net balances after goods have entered or left the country; payment is made at the end of an agreed period either by cash or further credit.

Chile was also awarded two short-term credits: the consortium of banks in the socialist countries granted $50 million to finance purchases of goods other than capital goods in capitalist and socialist markets; another $50 million was authorized by the People's Republic of China as an interest-free advance payment for Chilean copper exports. These two credits gave considerable relief to the cash flow situation during 1973.

A third type of credit was suppliers' credit. This type, consisting of medium- or long-term payment for current imports (which would normally be paid directly in cash) was requested by the Chilean Government as it was the preferred way to develop trade with the socialist countries. It was thought that, although this trade would not be balanced in the beginning, the imbalance would tend to narrow towards 1976. The request for such credit, which was drawn up in the early part of 1972 and presented by the President Allende himself during his visit to the Soviet Union at the end of 1972, did not receive the welcome expected by the Chilean Government. In 1972 these credits amounted to very little, less than $20 million. By 1973 they had reached a higher level as some $5 million were offered by various European socialist countries (see Table 3.16). It should be mentioned that at the end of 1972, Cuba gave a gift of sugar which was equivalent to $8 million; the significance of this gesture of solidarity can only be understood in terms of the economic problems which both countries were going through at the time.

Lastly, credits in foreign currencies were granted to Chile by the Soviet Union: in 1972 $100 million was granted which was renewable in 1973 at the commercial rate prevailing in international capital markets. This credit, as well as suppliers' credit, were the quickest means of overcoming the Chilean economy's foreign currency crisis.

When one speaks of a lack of short-term credits from the socialist countries, one does not mean that the short-term credits were of little importance but simply that they were not meeting the external financing needs for current imports which the general level of economic activity in 1972 and 1973 was creating. The forecast made at the end of 1972 of import needs for 1973 estimated that $500 million of agricultural goods and raw materials for industry would have to be financed from the socialist camp in order to maintain the level of employment in industry, and sustain the consumption levels per inhabitant for basic goods, which had been reached in 1971. The figures already given show what in fact happened.

Only a third of the current import finance requested from the socialist countries to cover 1973 was granted. On the other hand, capital goods finance, assuming a normal import level for capital goods in the Chilean economy, reached almost $300 million and, *ceteris paribus* as far as technological problems were concerned, were entirely financed by the socialist countries. This situation could be considered as an asymmetrical process of economically integrating Chile into the socialist system. To this should be added the fact that the problem of rigidity in the foreign trade of socialist countries produced a lag between the financing of imports and their actual importation, for the difference between the number of import licences granted and the amount of real imports was far greater than normal.

7.2. *Re-establishing Short-term Credit Lines with the Rest of the World*

In the previous sections we have indicated that until 1970 the flow of imports on current account was basically financed by the U.S. banking system, both private and governmental; all imports from any part of the world passed, directly or indirectly, through this network. Once the process of structural change had begun, this method of financing went through a crisis which took the form of a rapid and sustained decline in lines of credit. This reaction, albeit foreseen, was not measured accurately, nor was its extent realized. It was not until later than the dependence of the Chilean economy was fully understood. Understanding of this dependence was not gained through its ramifications or through its mechanisms of operation: only the experience of a process of structural change such as that which was occurring in Chile could reveal the profundity of economic dependence in an underdeveloped country.

The credit finance crisis in Chile's imports affected the normal operation of the productive apparatus through difficulties in obtaining imports of raw materials and spare parts, particularly those of U.S. origin. In this way the administrative, financial and technological difficulties in moving trade from one market to another and looking for *ad hoc* finance were extremely complex.

At the beginning of 1972 the economic leadership decided to launch a campaign to reconstruct and change the short-term finance system, giving the Central Bank all the necessary powers for directing the operation; the operation lasted throughout 1972 and part of 1973. The objectives were to diversify external sources of finance and replace the almost total monopoly which the U.S. banks had previously enjoyed with both the European banking system and that of Latin America and the socialist countries.

Chile set out to look for finance, offering to the market her import turnover of nearly $1 thousand million in 1972. Finance was sought directly with the supplying countries as the customary system of U.S. bank credit lines no longer existed; it was emphasized that Chile's real demand for imports was backed by the real capacity to import. Thus Chile was willing to buy, but it would be necessary for the banking system of the selling country to fill the role of the U.S. financier; should this not be possible, Chile would have to move its purchases to other markets.

It was not long before the European banks reacted positively, in fact the European banking system began to replace the U.S. system, granting credit lines which by 1972 had reached the sum of $252 million, including special short-term credits. By the 30 June 1973 – two months and some days before the *coup d'état* – Chile had rebuilt and diversified a substantial part of its system of external finance (see Table 3.17).

Despite the considerable increase in this type of credit some limitations should be indicated, the most important being that 67.6% of the total credit was bilateral. Of the credit from European banks, 54% was bilateral, while all the credit from Latin American banks was bilateral. Thus a substantial part of the credit could not be used for financing purchases from third countries; this created a certain rigidity in Chilean foreign trade which indicated the abnormal situation the country was passing through.

Nonetheless in Europe, as in Latin America, Chile was gradually opening up normal trade channels. The Central Bank became the guarantor through endorsement of all these operations; this was another indication of the abnormal situation although understandable given the circumstances.

Short-term credit took other forms which differed from the classical credit lines; some of these were already indicated in describing the financing provided by the socialist countries (section 7.1.1). The key issue was the cash flow difficulties of the Central Bank: in order to re-establish and consolidate new finance, the Bank sought new ways of obtaining greater flexibility in acquiring foreign currency; one important result of this was the credit obtained from the European banks on the basis of copper exports, amounting to $20 million by June 1973. Resource was also made to special operations credits, which were basically imports by foreign companies of Chilean raw materials and spares. In practice these credits provided some $67 million in additional funds. Finally, there were the transactions called confirming credits, which consisted of endorsements by European banks on certain Chilean imports; these were not very significant and amounted to only $4 million.

Table 3.14 shows the total of short-term finance (including the loans in currency obtained from socialist countries in Europe, known as finance credit) which in June 1973 amounted to $574 million; thus a considerable volume of resources meant that the economic blockade which had been woven round Chile could be partially broken.

Despite all the efforts made, short-term finance was insufficient for the turnover of $1.5 thousand million in 1973; moreover, international prices increased during that year. For these reasons the finance problems dragged on throughout the months of 1973 previous to the *coup d'état*.

The direct effects of building up a new system of external finance were principally the changes in the composition of foreign trade. Among these changes the modification in the regional structure of imports was important, especially because Chile increased its imports from Latin America and from European multinationals based in Latin America; meanwhile, imports from the United States decreased significantly.

8. CONCLUSIONS

It is difficult to arrive at definitive conclusions about such a complex process as that undertaken in Chile under the UP Government. Nevertheless, we can make some tentative conclusions which may also be used as working hypotheses:

1. The Chilean economy went through a profound process of transformation of its economic structure; during this process the institutional, legal and political framework was not fundamentally modified. This imbalance created

tensions in the whole fabric of society and particularly in the operation of the economy. In this way the increasing political destabilization was furthered.

2. Nationalizations embody on the one hand the political will to, and on the other the legal act of, the transfer of ownership of the strategic means of production; in any case the process takes place amidst sharp strife. Nationalization does not mean *per se* the effective participation of society in the resources common to all through the national patrimony, for this requires a mediating process of socialization in which higher forms of organization of production are developed. The APS was created for this reason and laid the material foundations for precisely such a process of socialization in the economy. When the *coup d'état* occurred the transition to this stage of socialization had barely begun; planning was emerging as the main aspect of the new economy and was thus contributing to a process of economic development within a democratic system.

Nevertheless the socialization process, which generally takes a long time – especially when it occurs in an underdeveloped and dependent economy such as the Chilean one – was only beginning. This process, intended as the optimal utilization of resources in the context of new social relations, was paralyzed because of the danger of the changes being reversed (as reflected in the tendency towards political destabilization) and also because the mechanisms for planning in the nationalized sector of the economy remained inadequate, given the magnitude of the change.

These two facts define a 'transitory situation' rather than an economy in 'transition to socialism'. For this reason, despite the profundity of the changes which occurred in the Chilean economy during the UP period, this period cannot be labelled and judged as an example of a 'transition to socialism'. The term 'transitory situation' indicates that precisely the instability of the change was a dominant characteristic: this term is, therefore, more suited to the Chilean case.

3. It is important to note that the traditional indicators of economic growth and of the business cycle are inadequate and unsatisfactory for measuring and evaluating a process of structural change. Changes, when they affect the economic structure, also affect the fundamental parameters which measure precisely the type of growth and development which is to be changed.

When one deals with the reproduction of a given economic structure, analyzing the economic trends can indicate the greater or lesser efficiency of the system in reproducing itself; however, when one deals with a structural change, efficiency is related to the viability and irreversibility of the process of change as a whole. Therefore such a process of change is not inefficient because production or productivity decreases, or because the rate of accumulation falls below the previously recorded average, but because of the political inability to confront the decline of each one of these variables which are inherent for a brief period in all transitional processes. Hence the indicators for measuring and assessing the process of structural change can only be those which arise from the dialectical link between political and economic variables. Unfortunately this chapter has a technocratic basis which specifically prevents a scientific understanding of the process as a whole.

4. Nationalization of the dominant centres of the Chilean economy in agriculture, industry, mining and the banks produced not only what we have called a transformation crisis, but also direct and indirect effects in external economic relations. Nevertheless, the external economic problems were not exclusive to the period of change, nor were they caused exclusively by these changes.

There was in fact always a chronic tendency towards disequilibrium in the Chilean balance of payments; except for short periods when the copper price rose, the economy always had problems in external finance. At the same time it is also clear that this economy created its own adjustment mechanisms through the expansion of external indebtedness (in 1965 the debt was renegotiated) and through unrestricted short-term credit. During the structural changes a breakdown occurred in precisely this traditional adjustment mechanism, and within the short period of two years it led to a crisis in foreign exchange reserves.

On the other hand, if we say that the changes are not exclusively responsible for the external finance problems, then we must add that before the implementation of the Government's Basic Programme, and consequently before the nationalization of copper, the United States had decided to intervene in the political system of Chile and to harm her economy. Within the week during which the results of the presidential elections became known, the traditional authorized lines of credit from the United States banks began to be suspended. On 15 November 1970 President Richard M. Nixon, Secretary of State Henry Kissinger and Secretary of the Treasury John Mitchell agreed to 'make the economy scream'.[25] A few weeks later the Chilean Ministry of the Treasury made a public declaration which paralyzed all economic activity. Thus the process of change was carried out in the presence of permanent external aggression which, though it certainly was not the cause the balance of payments disequilibrium, had its effect on the finance mechanism and on the financial image of the country.

5. The collapse of short-term finance made it difficult to maintain a flow of imports for current consumption; this was the most concrete indication of the crisis in the traditional sources of finance. Moreover, the refusal of the international loan agencies to grant long-term credit, and the refusal of the Eximbank to ensure exports to Chile, are expressions of the same phenomenon: all these measures considered in isolation have no decisive influence on the foreign reserves crisis if one considers the amounts of external finance directly involved. But if one considers these measures together, the prospects of stability

in Chilean foreign trade are seen to be greatly reduced. Thus, for example, the delay in the renegotiation of the external debt, the embargoes on Chilean goods abroad, the pressures put on the European banks by U.S. multinationals, etc. were actions with a cumulative effect; these actions are also the vehicles for spreading the crisis of external economic relations, a crisis which had been motivated by the will for economic independence which the programme of transformations represented. Thus, an economy which is going through a period of dissolving its dependency relationships in order to transform them into interdependency relationships and thus lessen external vulnerability needs short-term financial support from the international community in order to counteract the tendencies towards destabilization and cope with the effects of the transformation crisis.

6. Those outside Chile reacted to the changes in Chile in diverse ways. The aggressive attitude of the multinational enterprises and the solidarity of some governments, in particular that of the United States, with these enterprises did not openly appear to be a complete break. Nonetheless all the traditional mechanisms of external finance were used to express the rejection of the Chilean transformations: an investment freeze, a slow but systematic closure of credit lines, etc. Possibly the most overt reactions were those of the copper multinationals through their embargoes, and of International Telephone and Telegraph (ITT) which even went so far as to consider directly implementing a *coup d'état*, as the hearings in the U.S. Congress have revealed.[26]

It is, however, also clear that European companies were interested in a share of the Chilean market and hoped that the new rules of the game would become clear. The automobile industry tenders are further proof that foreign capital other than U.S. capital was not inclined to abandon the prospects offered by the Chilean economy.

7. Chile succeeded during the period of transformation in partially reconstructing a system of short- and long-term finance. The creation of relations with the socialist countries, as well as with some Western European and Latin American countries – particularly Mexico and Argentina – allowed a substantial diversification of external finance and, hence, of trade, thus achieving less vulnerability, as compared to the situation when the UP Government took office, as long as these new relationships consolidated themselves and grew.

But the efforts to reconstruct external finance, albeit positive, were inadequate, particularly in terms of short-term credit. There are at least two factors which gave rise to this inadequacy. The first was the fall in copper prices and the deteriorating terms of trade, which generated a decline in the purchasing power of Chilean exports at the very moment when the traditional financing mechanisms were breaking down because the transformations in Chile were unacceptable. The second factor was that the short-term economic policy had an important influence on the external disequilibrium. Thus the maintenance of an imbalance between overall supply and demand not only produced a distortion in relative prices – including the rate of exchange – but also sustained a level of demand which, with declining export purchasing power, prevented a correction of the external debt, while at the same time jeopardizing the long-term process of state capital accumulation. That is, the increase in foodstuff and raw material imports, which was brought about by the redistribution of income at a time when international prices were rising, meant that persistent pressure was being put on the capacity to import which, for its part, ran up against the constraints imposed by the crisis in traditional financing.

8. There is a clear relationship between short-term policy and structural changes. Short-term policy basically involves control of prices, wages, public expenditure and the money supply. In Chile this policy was begun in the context of a semi-paralyzed economy and for that reason the aim of stimulating the level of economic activity was of prime importance, at least in the initial stages. The policy of structural changes involves new forms for organizing production and extends over a longer time span than the short-term policy. The relations which are established between the two policies are not necessarily complementary; they can even be contradictory and conflicting, as was shown in the case of Chile. The fundamental contradiction stems from the fact that short-term policy tends to reproduce the system through an increase in consumption, including consumption by the higher income groups. This was the populist side of the process, in its Keynesian version. Agrarian reform, nationalization of copper, of the banking system and of some industrial monopolies comprise the revolutionary and transforming aspect of the process. Recognizing that there is an interaction between the two policies (which cannot be analyzed here), the short-term policy should have been subordinated to the transformation process, enabling this process to become viable and irreversible and not endangering it. Certainly this is a theoretical problem of great practical significance, and for this reason it is stated more as working hypothesis than as a definite conclusion.

9. To summarize, the struggle to open a road towards a new type of economic development, and therefore a change in resource allocation, encountered obstacles which stemmed from the economic system which had existed previously; however, it also had to deal with difficulties induced by the process of change itself. There is a feedback relationship between the two aspects which in this chapter was called 'the transformation crisis'. Analysis of the evolution of external economic relations *pari passu* with structural change provides a good example of a transformation crisis, and in this sense the lesson taught by the 'Chilean case' is a rich one.

NOTES

1. S. Barraclough, *Diagnóstico de la reforma agraria chilena* [Prognosis of Chilean Agrarian Reform] (Mexico City, Siglo XXI, 1974), 75.
2. 'Between 1961 and 1970 the United States Government and U.S. controlled international agencies lent Chile some $1,536 million (Committee on Foreign Affairs 1971). According to Simon Hanson, Chile with 3.5% of Latin America's population received some 13.4% of net *per capita* aid (Hanson Latin American Letter, 1970). In the 1960s Chile ranked second to Vietnam in *per capita* economic aid.' See Albert L. Michael, 'The Alliance for Progress and Chile's Revolution in Liberty 1964-70', *Journal of Inter-American Studies and World Affairs*, 18 (1976), No. 18.
3. Pedro Vuskovic, 'Distribución del ingreso y opciones de desarrollo' [Income Distribution and Development Options], *Cuadernos de la realidad nacional. Revista del Centro de Estudios de la Realidad Nacional (Universidad Católica de Chile) (CEREN)* [Notebooks on the National Reality. Review of the Centre for Studies of National Reality (Catholic University of Chile)], 5 (1970), 41-60.
4. ODEPLAN, *Antecedentes sobre el desarrollo chileno 1960-70* [Antecedents of Chilean Development from 1960 to 1970] (ODEPLAN, Series I, No. 1, *Planes semestrales, Plan de la económia nacional 1971-76* [Half Yearly Plans, Plan of the National Economy for 1971-76]) (Santiago de Chile, 1971).
5. ODEPLAN, *Balance de recursos humanos 1971* [Human Resources Audit 1971] (Santiago de Chile, 1971), Tables I and II.
6. Instituto Nacional de Estadísticas [National Institute of Statistics], *Censo de comercio 1967, Censo de la agricultura 1965* [Commercial Census 1967, Agricultural Census 1965] (Santiago de Chile).
7. Luis Landau, 'Endeudamiento externo de los países en desarrollo, con especial referencia en Latinoamérica' [Foreign Indebtedness of Developing Countries with Special Reference to Latin America]. Lecture presented at the Tenth Meeting of Central Bank Experts from the American Continent Caracas, November 1971.
8. Charles Bettelheim, *Economic Calculations and Forms of Property* (London, Routledge and Kegan Paul, 1976), Chapter III.
9. *Mensaje presidencial* [Presidential Message], 1972 and 1973 (Santiago de Chile), especially the chapters on Agriculture and Industry; see also ODEPLAN, *Plan de la economía nacional 1971-76* [National Economic Plan, 1971-76] (Santiago de Chile, 1971).
10. Report of the Chilean Government to the ECLA meeting in Quito, April 1973.
11. Report of the Chilean Government to the ECLA meeting.
12. Alban Lataste, 'El proceso de inversiones bajo el Gobierno Popular' [Investment under the Unidad Popular Government], *Revista de la Universidad Técnica del Estado* [Review of the State Technical University] (May-June 1973).
13. *Mensaje presidencial* [Presidential Message], 1972, Chapter VI.
14. Oscar Lange and Fred. N. Taylor, *On the Economic Theory of Socialism*, (ed) B. Lippincott (New York, McGraw Hill, 1964), 123, 124.
15. ODEPLAN, *Antecedentes sobre el desarrollo....*
16. ODEPLAN, *Antecedentes sobre el desarrollo...*, 180-182.
17. The World Bank, *Special Report on the Chilean Economic Outlook* (Washington D.C., October 1974), Vol. III, Tables 3 and 4.
18. CODELCO, Departamento de Estudios [Research Department] (Santiago de Chile) and the General Agreement on Tariffs and Trade (GATT).
19. *Mensaje presidencial*, 1972, Chapter on Foreign Affairs.
20. *Mensaje presidencial*, 1972, 122.
21. *Mensaje presidencial*, 1972, 120 and *Mensaje presidencial*, 1973, 110.
22. Eduardo Trabucco, *Chile and the Principal Problems of Short Term Finance During the Period 1970/73* (Bonn, Friedrich Ebert Foundation, 1974).
23. *Mensaja presidencial*, 1973, 113.
24. Report of the Chilean Government to the Meeting of the Inter-American Committee for the Alliance for Progress, 1971 and 1972.

25. *Hearings before the Select Committee to Study Governmental Operations with Respect to Intelligence Activities of the United States Senate*, 94th Congress, 1st Session, Volume 7, *Covert Action*, 4-5 December 1975 (Washington D.C., U.S. Government Printing Office, 1975), 96.
26. See *Hearings before the Select Committee to Study Governmental Operations....*

Table 3.1. *Distribution of Handicraft and Small-Scale Industry*

	Handicraft industry(1)	*Small-scale industry(2)*	*All industry(3)*	*(1) + (2) ÷ (3)*
Number of establishments	26,701	5,356	36,220	80
Number of persons employed	76,116	106,287	425,292	42

Source: Dirección de Estadísticas y Censos [Office of Statistics and Census], *Censo industrial 1967* [Industrial Census 1967] (Santiago de Chile).

Table 3.2. *Estimated Foreign Debt according to the Central Bank, Payable in Foreign Currencies as of 31 December 1970*

Institution or country		*Net Debt ($m)*		*%*
1. Multinational institutions		248.0		9.6
2. Countries		1994.0		77.3
United States	1334.0		51.7	
Federal Republic Germany	147.0		5.7	
Great Britain	157.0		6.1	
France	48.0		1.9	
Italy	90.0		3.5	
Spain	43.0		1.7	
Japan	65.0		1.5	
Others	110.0		4.2	
3. Other creditors [a]		339.0		13.1
Total foreign debt		2581.0		100.0

[a] This figure includes loans immediately repayable on demand.

Source: Central Bank and CORFO, Departamento de Crédito Externo [Foreign Credit Department], *Revista finanzas públicas* [Public Finance Review], 15 (April 1972).

Table 3.3. *The Composition of Indebtedness in Terms of Repayment Periods (percentage)*

	1966	*1966-70*
1–5 years	0.4	11.1
6–8 years	6.2	12.7
9–10 years	14.5	11.0
11–15 years	17.5	30.9
Subtotal	38.6	65.7
More than 15 years	61.4	34.3
Total	100.0	100.0

Source: International Monetary Fund, SM/72/47, 28.

Table 3.4. *Debt Servicing (Repayments plus Interest) (in millions of dollars)*

	1971	*1972*	*1973*
Repayments plus interest [a]	433.0	409.0	410.0
Value of exports of goods and services[b]	1,132.8	978.2	1,466.9
Debt servicing ÷ value of exports (%)	38	42	28

Sources: [a] Central Bank and CORFO, Departamento de Crédito Externo, *Revista finanzas públicas*, 15 (April 1972), 120.
[b] Central Bank, *Boletín mensual* [Monthly Bulletin], (October 1975).

Table 3.5. *Growth and General Economic Indicators (percentage)*

	1965-70	*1971*	*1972*	*1973*
Annual growth				
National product [a]	3.9	7.6	−0.1	−3.7
Agriculture and livestock [b]	1.8	5.1	−3.6	. . .
Mining [b]	5.0	1.7	−6.6	. . .
Industry [b]	3.8	12.9	3.1	. . .
Average unemployment	5.1 (1970)	5.5	3.7	4.7
Productivity growth	2.3	2.7	−1.8	. . .
Copper price ($ cents per pound) [a]	61.0	49.3	48.3	80.0
Rate of investment [a]	17.0 (1970)	15.3	12.3	13.9

Source: [a] ODEPLAN (1975), particularly its Statistical Appendix, and also CODELCO.
[b] The World Bank, *Special Report on the Chilean Economic Outlook* (Washington D.C., October 1974), Vol. III., Table 2.2.

Table 3.6. *Change in the Structure of Imports According to the Region of Origin (percentage)*

	1970	*1971*	*1972*	*1973*
United States	36.9	27.3	17.0	16.3
Latin America	21.6	23.9	28.0	26.8
European Economic Community	28.0	24.8	27.7	27.1
Socialist countries	0.5	2.5	2.7	7.7
The rest of the world	13.0	21.5	24.6	22.1
	100.0	100.0	100.0	100.0

Source: Central Bank, *Boletín mensual* (1971 and October 1975).

Table 3.7. *Prices of Copper and of World Exports*

	Copper prices		*Unit value of $ world exports*
	Average ($ cents per lb.)	*Index number*	
1965-70	61.1	100.0	...
1971-72	49.4	80.9	...
1970	64.2	100.0	100.0
1971	49.3	76.8	106.0
1972	48.5	75.5	115.7
1973	80.0	124.6	140.3

Source: CODELCO, Departamento de Estudíos [Research Department] (Santiago de Chile) and the General Agreement of Tariffs and Trade (GATT).

Table 3.8. *The Terms of Trade for Copper (base: 1970 = 100)*

	1971	*% of change*	*1972*	*% of change*
Purchasing power for Chilean imports	96.6	−3.4	88.5	−11.5
Terms of trade for copper (annual average)	74.2	−25.8	66.9	−33.1

Source: CODELCO, Departamento de Estudíos, Oficina de Ventas [Sales Office] (Santiago de Chile, 1973).

Table 3.9. *Trends in Real Imports*

	1970	*1971*	*1972*
Import of goods ($m) [a]	956	1015.0	1102.0
Index of import values	100	106.2	115.2
Index of import prices [b]	100	105.0	109.0
Index of real value of imports	100	101.1	105.7
Terms of trade	100	77.0	72.0

Sources: [a] Central Bank, *Boletín mensual* (October 1975).
[b] Index calculated by the Taller de Coyunctura, Facultad de Economía, Universidad de Chile [Economic Workshop, Faculty of Economics, University of Chile] (1972) for 1971. The price variations for 1972 were calculated by the Economic Commission for Latin America (ECLA).

Table 3.10. *Composition of Imports (percentage)*

	1970	*1971*	*1972*	*1973* [a]
Foodstuffs and food industry imports	14.1	19.0	30.7	37.0
Intermediate goods	46.5	48.0	42.7	41.3
Capital goods	29.0	24.4	15.0	17.0
Consumer goods	10.4	8.6	12.6	4.0

[a] Calculated from import licences granted in 1973.

Source: Central Bank, *Boletín mensual* (October 1975).

Table 3.11. *Distribution of Imports (percentage)*

	1970	*1971*	*1972*	*1973* [a]
State sector	34	44	62	70
Private sector	66	56	38	30

[a] For 1973 the foreign exchange budget figure is used.

Source: *Mensaje presidencial* [Presidential Message], (Santiago de Chile, 1973). The figures are based on import licences.

Table 3.12. *The Balance of Payments (in millions of dollars)*

	1970	*1971*	*1972*
Balance of trade	155.0	−18.1	−255.2
Balance on current account	−102.9	−205.5	−404.8
Net capital movements	252.5	−49.9	228.0
Balance of payments	98.5	−323.2	−327.6

Source: Central Bank, 1975. The sum of the balances on various accounts does not equal the balance of payments deficit due to the lack of the 'errors and omissions category' and the allocation of special drawing rights (SDRs).

Table 3.13. *Trade with Socialist Countries (in millions of dollars)*

	1970	*1971*		*1972*		*1973*	
		L[a]	R[b]	L	R	L	R
Exports	28.8	38.6		38.6	60.0	110.0	158.0
Imports	5.8	46.0	24.0	165.0	25.6	232.0	83.0
Balance	23.0	−7.3		−90.0	34.4	−122.0	75.0

[a] L = Import licences.
[b] R = Real imports.

Source: Central Bank and SEREX [Foreign Trade Department of the Central Bank]. The figures for 1973 were estimated in March of that year. The figures for real imports were taken from the Superintendencia de Aduanas [Customs Office] and published by the Central Bank in the *Boletín mensual* (1975).

Table 3.14. *Loans from Socialist Countries*

Country	*Amount*	*Purpose*	*Terms*	*Interest*	*Taken up by 14 August 1973*
Bulgaria	$20,000,000	Industrial equipment and technical aid	15% down, balance over 12 years	2.5%	$16,056,100
Bulgaria	$20,000,000	Industrial equipment, preinvestment and project studies	5% down, balance over 12 years	2.5%	$17,651,800
Bulgaria	$5,000,000	Assorted equipment	15% down, balance over 8 years	5.0%	$2,238,617
Bulgaria	$10,000,000	Purchase goods	100% over 3 years	6%	$4,526,284
Czechoslovakia	$5,000,000	Industrial equipment	10% down, balance over 8½ years; minimum order $ 5,000	4.5%	$28,211
Czechoslovakia	$15,000,000	Assorted equipment	5% down, balance over 3 years according to amount: $50-200,000 8½ years; $200-500,000 10 years; $500,000+ 12 years	3%	$2,630,687
China	Yuan 118,160,000	Complete plants, technical aid, machinery and equipment	100% over 20 years with 10-year grace period	0%	–
China	Yuan 30,721,600	Purchase goods	100% over 20 years with 10-year grace period	0%	Yuan 31,026,000
Hungary	$10,000,000	Purchase goods	3% down, balance over 2 years	5%	$768,727
Hungary	$15,000,000	Complete plant purchase and technical assistance	15% down, balance over 12 years with 1-year grace period; minimum order $800,000	2.5%	$1,219,850

Table 3.14, continued

Country	*Amount*	*Purpose*	*Terms*	*Interest*	*Taken up by 14 August 1973*
Hungary	$5,000,000	Assorted equipment	10% down, balance over 12 years, etc. as above	6%	–
Poland	$25,000,000	Complete plants	5% down, balance over 13 years; minimum order $500,000	3%	$1,607,313
German Democratic Republic	$20,000,000	Complete plants, assorted equipment and technical aid	5% down, balance according to amount. Less than $200,000 4 years; $200-500,000 4-6 years; $500-600,000 6-8 years; $600,000 + 8-10 years	3%	
German Democratic Republic	$5,000,000	Purchase goods	5% down, balance 1 year	5%	–
Korean Democratic Republic	$25,000,000	Assorted equipment and technical aid	100% over 10 years	0%	–
Romania	$20,000,000	Complete plants and assorted equipment	5% down, balance according to amount: $1-5 million, 8 years; $5+ million, 10 years	5%	$169,081
Union of Soviet Socialist Republics	$102,000,000	Complete plants and technical aid	100% over 12 years with 1-year grace period	2.5%	–
Union of Soviet Socialist Republics	$115,000,000	Machinery and equipment	–		$40,000,000

Source: Central Bank, ‘Créditos de suministro de los paises socialistas para 1973’ [Supply Credits from the Socialist Countries during 1973] *Boletín mensual*, 545 (July 1973), 761-763.

Table 3.15. *Lines of Credit as of 30 June 1973 (in millions of dollars)*

Country/Area	*Total*	*Bilateral*	*Multilateral*	*Committed*	*Specific*	*Financial*	*Copper*
Total	574.1822	274.5192	131.8117	4.2814	67.8024	75.209	20.6045
Western Europe	303.1140	94.1192	79.5617	1.4814	34.2382	75.109	18.6045
Federal Republic of Germany	57.0989	38.8366	9.6000	.5677	.946	10.0	–
Spain	6.3342	6.3342	–	–	–	–	–
France	74.6219	10.2829	18.3987	.4635	6.1588	32.0	7.318
Portugal	.050	.05	–	–	–	–	–
Switzerland	19.3073	1.6218	9.5765	–	–	8.109	–
Belgium	15.367	5.367	–	–	10.0	–	–
Denmark	1.3559	1.3559	–	–	–	–	–
Finland	4.2	4.2	–	–	–	–	–
The Netherlands	2.7359	2.7359	–	–	–	–	–
Great Britain	59.3317	11.2085	20.8865	.4502	5	25.0	1.2865
Italy	57.513	9.163	21.1	–	17.25	–	10.0
Norway	.15	.15	–	–	–	–	–
Sweden	5.0482	4.8134	–	–	.2348	–	–
North America	46.7	8.95	34.75	–	1.0	–	2.0
Canada	10.75	6.0	2.75	–	–	–	2.0
United States	35.95	2.95	32.0	–	1.0	–	–
Asia, Africa and Oceania	41.0642	3.45	2.5	2.55	32.5642	–	–
Australia	14.156	–	–	–	14.1560	–	–
Hong Kong	.5	–	–	.05	–	–	–
Japan	4.2082	2.9	.5	.5	.4082	–	–
Libya	4.0	–	2.0	2.0	–	–	–
New Zealand	18.25	.25	–	–	18.0	–	–
South Africa	.3	.3	–	–	–	–	–

Table 3.15, continued

Country/Area	*Total*	*Bilateral*	*Multilateral*	*Committed*	*Specific*	*Financial*	*Copper*
Socialist Countries	20.05	20.05	–	–	–	–	–
Bulgaria	2.0	2.0	–	–	–	–	–
Czechoslovakia	6.0	6.0	–	–	–	–	–
Hungary	2.05	2.05	–	–	–	–	–
Romania	1.0	1.0	–	–	–	–	–
Union of Soviet Socialist Republics	4.0	4.0	–	–	–	–	–
Yugoslavia	5.0	5.0	–	–	–	–	–
Latin America	163.2	147.95	15.0	.25	–	–	–
Argentina	62.25	62.25	–	–	–	–	–
Bolivia	7.5	7.5	–	–	–	–	–
Brazil	22.4	22.4	–	–	–	–	–
Colombia	1.1	1.1	–	–	–	–	–
Mexico	60.75	45.75	15.0	–	–	–	–
Panama	.25	–	–	.25	–	–	–
Paraguay	.5	.5	–	–	–	–	–
Peru	8.45	8.45	–	–	–	–	–

Source: Central Bank, Gerencia de Operaciones Internacionales [International Operations Management]. Published in the Central Bank's *Boletín mensual* (1973).

Table 3.16. *Suppliers' Credits from Socialist Countries for 1973*[a] *(in millions of dollars)*

Bulgaria	10
Czechoslovakia	5
Hungary	10
Romania	1
German Democratic Republic	5
Union of Soviet Socialist Republics	27
Total	58

[a] Granted at the end of 1972.

Source: Central Bank, 'Créditos de suministro . . .'.

Table 3.17. *Bank Credit Lines for Short-term Loans as of 30 June 1973 (in millions of dollars)*

		%
Western Europe	173.6	42.8
Canada and The United States	43.7	10.8
Asia, Africa, Oceania	5.9	1.4
Socialist Countries	20.0	4.9
Latin America	163.0	40.1
Total	406.2	100.0

Source: Central Bank, Gerencia de Operaciones Internacionales. Published in the Central Bank's *Boletín mensual* (1973).

4

CLODOMIRO ALMEYDA

THE FOREIGN POLICY OF THE UNIDAD POPULAR GOVERNMENT

1. The foreign policy proposals contained in the Programme of the *Unidad Popular* (UP) showed clearly that its political objectives had an international dimension. This was inevitable because a socialist transformation of Chilean society affected substantial foreign interests. It also disturbed the political *status quo* in Latin America and introduced an element of strife and disruption into the inter-American system (basically the Organization of American States (OAS) and the Inter-American Treaty of Reciprocal Assistance (TIAR)). It therefore had an influence on the world political scene of which the main feature is the struggle between the capitalist world, led by the United States, and the socialist states led by the Soviet Union.[1]

The Chilean political experiment took place at a particular moment in world history and in a particular context. While it remains true that the essential characteristic of our age is the transition from capitalism to socialism – and the UP shares this idea – the UP leadership believed that such a transition takes different forms in distinct circumstances. The specific forms are determined by the concrete circumstances under which the process of transition occurs, and it is these which give it its specific character. In other words, the way in which the transition takes place is dependent upon the circumstances.

The so-called 'cold war' represented one such set of circumstances, while the climate of *détente* constitutes another. Within the Western hemisphere, whether an event took place before or after the Cuban Revolution is of fundamental relevance. The same applies for the October 1962 crisis at the end of which the United States accepted the presence of a socialist state in Western hemisphere, while at the same time resolving to stop the spread of communism and similar systems on the American continent by any means. This decision led to the formulation of the so-called Johnson Doctrine after the United States intervened in Santo Domingo. In Latin America – more specifically in South America – nationalist regimes and political forces that are

---

Footnotes to this chapter may be found on pp. 132-134.

more or less anti-imperialist predominate at certain times; at other times, however, a quite different situation may emerge as openly pro-U.S. regimes and political forces that cooperate with the United States in achieving its political objectives come to dominate the politics of the subcontinent. The situation for Chile, when the governments in charge in its neighbouring states are friendly and understanding, is quite different from when the country is surrounded by hostile and distrustful neighbours.

All of these factors interrelate at various geo-political levels, from the broad but decisive context of world politics to the situation prevailing in the southern cone of South America. Together these interrelations make up the external context of the UP experiment.

This external context, as well as the international situation prevailing in 1970, was such that the UP's political objectives, though difficult to achieve, were not unrealistic. They might even have been achieved if there had not been, at the same time, many potential obstacles that were capable of postponing, distorting or totally frustrating them.

In saying that the UP's political objectives were not unrealistic, we must remember that there was a link between the external context on the one hand, and internal factors that favoured or opposed the proposed changes on the other.

Let us now examine the links that can exist between the external context of a political system which is undergoing profound change and the internal factors that can be either supportive or destructive to that change. To do this we must distinguish between what might be called a war situation and a peace situation. In the latter, relations between two states are conducted in various ways and through various channels which do not involve armed conflict. In a war situation, on the other hand, the final outcome of a conflict between two states or political systems is determined by military factors.

The part played by internal factors in countries that are party to a conflict will differ according to whether there is a situation of war or peace. When there is peace, the influence of external factors on the internal processes of a system must be channelled through groups and individuals that can be seen to operate within the system. External factors can help to either strengthen or to weaken certain political forces that are already operating in the system and, if the need arises, can contribute to new internal factors becoming involved in the political struggle. In other words, external factors operate through internal ones and thus their impact can only be discerned in relation to these internal forces which they either create or destroy or merely influence in one direction or another.

In a war situation, on the other hand, external factors operate directly on the political system through the application of military force. Here, the balance of internal power is determined by military factors and it is at this level that the conflict is finally resolved.

When we say that the UP's political objectives were viable, though at the same time difficult to achieve, we are assuming two things: first, that the experiment would be carried out in a peaceful context; and second, that armed confrontation was both possible and undesirable.

In the following pages we shall examine the external viability of the UP's political objectives, given a peace situation. Thereafter we shall analyse the external threats which made these objectives more difficult to achieve. In order to do this, we shall first discuss the international situation in 1970 in relation to the Chilean experiment; subsequently we shall see how the objectives which the UP was trying to achieve influenced the external context, as this context was perceived by the political leadership which formulated and carried out Chile's foreign policy.

2. Examination of the overall international situation prevailing in 1970 led to the idea that the UP experiment was viable. Assuming that the Chilean Government's behaviour was reasonable, it should have been possible to avoid armed intervention by the United States. The invasion of Santo Domingo could not be repeated in Chile: since the UP Government had been democratically elected in accordance with the Constitution, opposition within the United States to any threat of invasion, and the international repercussions which would have resulted from such a course of action, made armed intervention almost impossible. In any case the United States did not, in the end, need to resort to such extreme measures. Other means which were equally as effective and less politically damaging could be used to achieve the same ends.

Again, because the UP had come to power through democratic elections, the Chilean experiment attracted a great deal of sympathy in Western Europe, and this was a source of support for Chile in its confrontation with the U.S. Government. The fact that the socialist countries had pledged their friendship to the UP meant that high risks were associated with any aggressive policy *vis-à-vis* Chile. Moreover, the deep involvement of the United States in the Southeast Asian conflict had brought its popularity to an all-time low throughout the world. It did not seem prudent, under such circumstances, for the United States to embark upon another warlike adventure, particularly one that was much more difficult to justify.

Generally speaking, despite the Vietnam war and the Middle East conflict, there was a climate of *détente* in relations between the Eastern and Western blocks; this facilitated the development of the Chilean experiment and made things more difficult for hardliners in the United States who harboured aggressive intentions.

Military intervention in Chile, if it was to take place at all, was far more likely to come from the countries neighbouring on Chile, with whom relations were complicated by unresolved problems that could flare up at any time. The United States could encourage such countries to raise such problems in a manner that might require a military solution and that could create difficulties – perhaps insoluble difficulties – for the UP Government.

In fact, the governments of the neighbouring countries were all, to a greater or lesser extent, potentially hostile to Chile. The military government in Argentina, which was openly pursuing right-wing policies, was unhappy about the fact that a left-wing regime in which the marxist and communist influence was strong had taken over in neighbouring Chile. Chile and Argentina were also involved in a long-standing dispute – which remained unresolved – on the question of sovereignty over some islands situated to the south of the Beagle Canal. In the past, relations between the two countries had deteriorated considerably as a result of incidents connected with this dispute. Even when border questions were not at issue, such disagreeable problems as the Laguna del Desierto incident in the 1960s, when border patrols from both countries almost became involved in a major armed confrontation, could easily be repeated. It was quite feasible that incidents might be staged in the southern border area with the intention of disrupting Chile's internal political processes and providing a pretext for a *coup* by Chilean armed forces for so-called reasons of national security.

Relations between Chile and Bolivia had not been good since the War of the Pacific in the 1880s. Bolivia became a landlocked country as a result of that war, and its repeated demands for a port on the Pacific had soured relations between the two countries. Diplomatic relations were broken off during the Alessandri Government (1958-64) as a result of a conflict about the use of water from the Lauca River; they had not been re-established at the time the UP acceded to power. In 1970, left-wing tendencies were dominant in the government in Bolivia; while this reduced the probability of conflict it did not eliminate it. Moreover, in view of Bolivia's chronic political instability, a military *coup* could at any moment bring a chauvinistic and reactionary government to power in La Paz, and such a government would have been doubly anti-Chilean. This is indeed what happened later, when President Torres' left-wing government was deposed and the General Bánzer's ultra-reactionary regime took over. While Bolivia in itself did not pose a real military threat to Chile, there was always the danger that the disputes in which Chile was involved with Bolivia and Argentina would flare up simultaneously, facing the Allende Government with a serious international situation.

In addition, the Brazilian military regime was openly opposed to what was happening in Chile and, given its influence on the Bolivian Government, was capable of stimulating Bolivian hostility towards Chile.

Although there was perhaps some affinity between the UP and the progressive military government in Peru, this was neutralized by the anti-communist attitudes of certain groups within the Peruvian armed forces and by memories of the War of the Pacific, which sustained feelings of mistrust and hostility in certain political and military circles *vis-à-vis* Chile as a nation.

Neither Ecuador, nor Colombia, nor Venezuela – and certainly not Paraguay – showed signs of genuine friendship with Chile. Under these circumstances the new UP Government had to face the danger that Chile might become isolated, both politically and economically, and that this isolation might have military implications. The possibility that the United States might want to encourage Latin American countries to isolate Chile, perhaps even to provoke violent conflicts, could not be discarded, since such a course of action might very well put an end to the Chilean experiment by force, without the United States becoming directly involved.

3. While the possibility of U.S. armed intervention with the intention of eliminating the new Chilean Government was very remote, the risk that the United States might try to destroy that Government in some other way was real: we have already mentioned the possibility of the United States exploiting the problems existing between Chile and its neighbours, thus provoking a serious conflict in the area.

To better understand this question, it may be useful to examine the ways in which the UP Government represented a threat to the United States.

It is often thought that the main reason why the United States from the very beginning expressed its total opposition to the Chilean experiment (to the point where President of the United States Richard M. Nixon ordered the Central Intelligence Agency (CIA) to use any means to prevent Allende from taking power after the 1970 elections[2]) was the threat which a UP Government might represent to the economic interests of U.S. investors. Given the significance of the U.S. copper interests in Chile, the projected nationalization of the Gran Minería (the largest copper mines) posed a serious threat to the largest copper companies, particularly as it was thought that a fairly strictly regulated compensation procedure would be adopted. Moreover, other nationalization measures were expected in the mining sector (iron) and in public services (telephone) as well as in those areas of industrial production which were wholly or partly U.S. owned.

There is no denying that U.S. investments in these sectors were in jeopardy; moreover, for many reasons, not the least of which was the precedent which these nationalizations (and the compensation procedures associated with them) might set for the future, these expected measures would affect the interests of the United States as a nation. But despite this, I do not believe that the open hostility which the United States from the very beginning showed towards the UP Government can be explained primarily in terms of such considerations. In my view, the reasons behind that hostility were essentially political and went far beyond the threat of nationalization that hung over the U.S. companies operating in Chile.

The U.S. Government is not, and has not been in the past, merely the representative of the *general* interests of the capitalist economy which sustains its political and ideological structure. It is not, and was not in the past, merely an agency charged with the task of regulating, defending and sustaining the rules of the game which enable the reproduction and development of the capitalist economy, whether that capital be invested at home or abroad. The Government, or better, the state of course performed those functions which were designed to sustain capitalism in the United States, but it also acquired an additional role within the existent world economic system.

Gradually, especially since the beginning of the cold war, the U.S. Government has become the main support of a structure designed to put down revolutions throughout the world. This role forces the United States to act on the basis of political and geographic factors which subsume and integrate U.S. private interests with those of the rest of the capitalist world. In other words, the United States' dominant position in the Western world since the beginning of World War II has given rise to a 'para-political' structure designed to defend the common and general interests of the entire capitalist world against the threat of revolution and socialism; this structure is also designed to defend those interests in the dependent and underdeveloped countries that constitute an organic part of the worldwide economic and political system.

Let us examine this idea in greater detail. The October Revolution and the consequent breakdown of the world capitalist system, followed by the emergence of a socialist state which took a decisive part in the direction of future revolutionary movements throughout the world, marked the beginning of a new chapter in the development of imperialism. In the classical stage of imperialism, so well defined by Lenin, one of the main features is the inter-capitalist rivalry which emerges as a result of increased competition among monopoly interests at the international level. These interests constantly struggle to control supplies of energy, raw materials and cheap labour, to find markets for their manufactured goods as well as profitable areas for investing their economic surplus.

After the October Revolution, and particularly after World War II and the beginning of the cold war, a new tendency emerged, a trend towards unity among rival imperialist countries, based on the idea that all have a common interest in sustaining the world capitalist order against the threat of revolution. This was not seen so much as a threat to specific monopolies or to particular capitalist countries, but as a danger to the world capitalist system as such. Therefore the response had to be at that level, and a global policy, designed to defend the system against the assaults of the revolution, had to be developed.

The need for a counterrevolutionary policy, as a response of the capitalist-imperialist system to the threat of revolution, did not imply the disappearance of inter-capitalist rivalries; it merely implied that, in view of the threat to the common interests of the capitalist countries, these contradictions within the imperialist system had to be muted. An essential element of capitalism is that private interests should compete against each other, whether in a system of more or less free competition, as in the early years, or through monopolies or oligopolies closely linked with individual states. Nevertheless, at a time when the struggle between revolution and counterrevolution overshadowed every other struggle, a joint counterrevolutionary policy was bound to emerge in defence of capitalism as a system.

The first indication that a worldwide counterrevolutionary policy had emerged came at the time of the undeclared war which the imperialist powers waged against the fledgling Russian revolution after these powers had won the 1914-18 war. U.S., British, French, Japanese and Czech soldiers joined the White Russian armies in the anti-revolutionary struggle. They did not succeed in crushing the revolution, but their joint attempt was a clear indication that the capitalist countries had common interests and pursued common policies when faced with what they regarded as a global menace.

A similar path was followed during the cold war, although under different circumstances. There was an attempt to stop by any means the expansion of the system of socialist states which had emerged as a consequence of World War II. The readiness of U.S. imperialism to use every means at its disposal to influence the internal decision-making processes in the countries that were likely to move toward socialism was demonstrated by the events surrounding the Italian elections through the years after World War II. But the fundamental objective was to set up a network of military pacts with countries bordering on, or geographically close to, the Soviet Union in order to isolate it politically and militarily, and to place it in a difficult defence position. It was in this context that the North Atlantic and the South East Asian Treaty Organizations (NATO and SEATO) were set up, and that the inter-American system was reorganized to make room for the OAS and the TIAR, as well as for the network of inter-American military pacts that complement these alliances. Later, the United Kingdom signed a treaty with pro-Western countries in the Middle East as part of this strategy of containment. Lastly, we cannot omit the so-called Marshall Plan which made the extension of socialism to Western Europe more difficult by committing U.S. capital to the economic reconstruction of that area.

The United States formed the mainstay of this network of political and military commitments and alliances for many reasons: its economic, technological and military strength, and finally its prevailing ideology of counterrevolution and anti-communism – all circumstances which were not present to the same extent in the other countries belonging to the network.

It was only natural, therefore, that the United States should assume a position of hegemony among capitalist countries, and that a world counterrevolutionary political structure was established with the United States as its dominant force. Think, for a moment, of the role that the United States has recently played in Angola.

This supra-national counterrevolutionary system can be qualified as 'para-political' because, while its role is to sustain both the prevailing structure of international relations and the capitalist mode of production, it has not generated a supra-national political authority which can fulfil a role comparable to that of the national state in relation to the various capitalist interests within a given country. In the absence of such an authority, the void has been filled by the United States! However, this does not prevent the different parts of its system as a whole from being run according to a specific rationale which has as its fundamental objective the permanence and continuance of the existing international relations and the established socio-economic substrate.

The UP's accession to power represented a threat to the U.S.-led world counterrevolutionary structure that was far more serious than the economic difficulties of the multinationals which were faced with the prospects of nationalization; it was that threat which was the reason for U.S. hostility towards the Allende Government.

Chile's success in moving towards socialism within a context of liberty set a highly attractive and provocative example to other countries in South America which were undergoing a period of severe discontent. The Argentinian 'military revolution' had been a failure and elections would sooner or later have to be held. The example of a democratic Chile progressing steadily toward socialism and overcoming all its political and economic difficulties would have important implications for such an election because people would naturally want to follow Chile's lead. In Uruguay, the *Frente Amplio* ('Large Front') was about to be created and, *mutatis mutandi*, was likely to follow the same lines as the UP in Chile. The left-wing populist government which was in power in Bolivia would also be strengthened if the Chilean experiment proved successful. All this would enable the socialist world to form a bridgehead in the southern part of the continent and would deprive the United States of its control over the situation. If we add to this the fact that the military government in Peru was taking an independent nationalist line and also developing closer relations with socialist Cuba, it becomes clear that a successful socialist experiment in Chile would have negative consequences for the United States and the counterrevolutionary forces, and also that the consequences would be worldwide.

The threat posed by the UP's triumph was aggravated by the fact that it had been democratically elected. Under the circumstances these democratic credentials attracted a great deal of sympathy, which made it very difficult to use the same arguments against Chile that had been used against Cuba and other countries moving towards socialism, whose political systems did not correspond to the liberal democratic orthodoxy prevailing in the West. It also meant, as was mentioned earlier, that armed intervention in support of counterrevolution was politically infeasible.

It goes without saying that the Communist Party's influence on the Chilean people and Government, and its close cooperation with the socialist and other parties in the coalition, were sufficient to persuade those in control of the counterrevolutionary world system that the Chilean experiment was indeed a dangerous one. A division within the Chilean left, which would separate the Communists and their allies or the marxist and non-marxist parties in the UP, seemed impossible. Only the growth of ultra-leftism seemed to favour counterrevolution, for it corroded the unity in the left and the provocative nature of its actions caused reactions which strengthened domestic counterrevolution. Unhappily, the consequences of ultra-leftism later played a major part in the process that led to the restoration of fascism in Chile.

It follows, therefore, that U.S. hostility towards the UP Government was mainly caused by the UP's challenge to the counterrevolutionary structure; this challenge also motivated the various forms of intervention which were carried out in Chile. This does not mean, of course, that the importance of the U.S. economic interests which were directly affected by the Chilean Government's nationalist policies did not contribute significantly to the acceleration and intensification of the counterrevolutionary thrust, but this factor was not the decisive one.

It is interesting that Chile's sovereign decision to follow a particular road did not prevent the United States from performing an 'international police' function. The way in which President of the United States Gerald Ford expressed his attempt to explain U.S. intervention in Chile through the CIA clearly proved that the United States has assigned itself a tutelage role which apparently qualifies it to violate other countries' sovereignty whenever it considers that 'world security' in some other part of the world is threatened by antithetical political interests (see note 2 of this chapter). And if that principle is valid in general, how much more it must apply in the American hemisphere, where the United States has traditionally exercised an almost undisputed hegemony! In other words, the notorious 'Johnson Doctrine' – which was formulated on the occasion of the armed invasion in the Dominican Republic and states that the United States appropriates the right to intervene by force anywhere on the American continent to prevent the rise of Communist or similar regimes – is fully operational. This was clearly shown by the behaviour of President Nixon and of Henry Kissinger – by the latter in his role as Chairman of the National Security Council, which authorized the disbursement of millions of dollars to 'destabilize' the UP Government. This was also shown by President Ford's attempt to justify these actions.

4. At no point during the period of UP Government did the U.S. Government, either through its embassy in Santiago or through statements by official spokesmen, clarify its real policy or the motives on which that policy was based.

In official communications between the two Governments, transmitted through their embassies, the United States persistently objected to the compensations procedure adopted with regard to the nationalized copper companies. Most of all they disliked the fact that according to this procedure, the financial obligations between the Chilean Government and the enterprises just about cancelled each other out, so that the companies were ultimately to receive no monetary compensation whatsoever. The United States' objections were based on a supposed violation by Chile of a principle of international law which, in cases of nationalization, states that a 'just, prompt and effective' compensation should be paid. The Chilean Government rejected this principle and considered that the doctrine of international law which was the correct one to apply in this case was that arising from United Nations Resolution 1803.

In order to solve this critical difference of opinion, the Chilean Government turned to the only judicial instrument in existence designed to deal with such situations, i.e. the Chile-United States Treaty of 1916, under which conflicts were to be submitted to an Arbitration Committee whose members were to be appointed by the affected parties. In cases of disagreement between the two parties, the Arbitration Committee would issue an opinion on how the conflict should be resolved. The parties were under no obligation to accept that opinion.

This matter was discussed by officials of the two countries on four occasions but the U.S. representatives would not agree to this legal solution which Chile had suggested, arguing that it provided no assurance that a prompt and satisfactory solution to the problem of compensation could be reached. The United States insisted on direct negotiations on the substantive question – the procedure and amount of compensation – without considering that this would require an amendment of the Chilean Constitution which, given the prevailing political climate, the Government was unwilling to propose and the Chilean National Congress would not have countenanced. This impasse continued until the military *coup d'état* in September 1973.

In addition to the problem of compensating the copper companies, Chile wanted the Arbitration Committee to deal with other conflicts between the two countries such as the position taken by the United States in the international financing agencies. The U.S. position was based on the well-known Gonzalez Amendment, which was designed to block credits to countries that had expropriated U.S. property, as Chile had done. Other conflicts which Chile wanted the Committee to deal with included the United States' initiatives in setting up an economic blockade against Chile which, according to the UP Government, represented an affront to Chile's national sovereignty; undue pressure to force a change of policy; and even open economic aggression. All of these measures are condemned by the Charter of the United Nations and in particular by that of the OAS. During one of the meetings between Chilean and U.S. officials, the U.S. officials were told that Chile would possibly ask the Arbitration Committee to consider those violations of the nonintervention principle which had resulted from CIA activities in Chile. Some of these activities have since become public knowledge as a result of the publication of the ITT documents in both U.S. and Chilean newspapers in April 1972.

5. In statements made by U.S. officials, and in Senate investigations into U.S. involvement in Chilean affairs, it has been clearly shown that the objective of the U.S. Government was to 'destabilize' the Allende Government.[3] For reasons which have been discussed above, this could not be achieved by means of a military invasion such as the United States had mounted against the Dominican Republic. What was possible, however, was to disrupt the Chilean Government's policies by means of measures designed to weaken its economy. This would create not only problems for the UP Government but also a great deal of popular discontent. The economic difficulties that these measures would cause would move the population to oppose the UP and to support the opposition parties in any future election; or they might create conditions favourable to intervention by the armed forces.

The investigation into CIA activities, which was conducted in the U.S. Senate by the Church Committee, shows that during the period between President Allende's election and the day on which he was to assume office, the CIA not only tried to stop the Chilean National Congress from ratifying the choice of the electorate and encouraged military intervention against the winning candidate (a manoeuvre which led to the assassination of General Schneider), but also attempted to stimulate a climate of financial panic in the business world so that the way would be open for any operation designed to prevent President-elect Allende from taking power.[4] Plans prepared by the ITT, with the complicity of the CIA, which are now widely known, were designed to achieve the same objective.

None of these manoeuvres succeeded, although a climate of panic was indeed created in the private sector as a result of the activities of the CIA and the multinationals. Consequently, as soon as the UP Government took office, it was faced with a very difficult situation, a main element of which was a crisis of confidence augmented by foreign intervention.

Attempts to prevent Allende from taking office were wide-ranging, though they stopped short of direct military intervention: they included bribes offered to members of the Chilean Congress and encouragement of military insurrection. When these proved ineffective and the UP Government was inaugurated, the anti-Allende forces revised their objectives and launched a systematic campaign designed to politically destabilize the UP Government. The basis for this was the political and strategic judgment that the Chilean Government represented a grave hazard and would consequently have to be coerced into abandoning its programme and/or altering its political support base (this judgment included the possibility that this might come about as a result either of an election or of combined action by the subversive civilian opposition and the armed forces). On the whole the U.S. State Department, the Pentagon and those enterprises directly affected by Chilean politics gave their support to this approach. While their tactics might have differed, there is nothing to support the belief that they disagreed with this approach in any significant way. Any eventual opposition there may have been within the State Department to these policies was rendered futile by the personal attitude of President Nixon, who ordered that whatever means necessary should be taken to prevent Allende's rise to power, as well as by the attitude of Secretary of State William Rogers, but above all by Kissinger who, using his position as Chairman of the 40 Committee, funded the destabilization operations. All this was confirmed in statements made by the White House, the armed forces and the intelligence agencies to the 40 Committee.

The relationship between the U.S. Government's policy *vis-à-vis* Chile and the private interests involved became clear when joint meetings were held between U.S. Government officials and representatives of companies with capital invested in Chile; the purpose of these joint meetings was to coordinate the anti-Chilean operations.[5] It is in the nature of the U.S. political system that there should be close relationship between government policies and those of monopolies and transnational companies, although the two are not always in complete agreement. This is because of the higher and more general responsibilities which the U.S. Government has assumed in the context of the counter-revolutionary 'para-political' structure which transcends the more limited views of private interests. In the case of Chile, however, substantial differences do not seem to have existed between government policies and those of the business world.

A summary of the various economic measures that were planned and carried out in order to destabilize the Chilean Government presents the following picture:

1. *Government action through public lending agencies*. In June 1971, the Export-Import Bank (Eximbank) suspended credits and guarantees to Chile; official sources said this was due to the disagreement on the question of compensating the nationalized copper companies.

In 1970, the Agency for International Development (AID) stopped granting loans to Chile, restricting the extension of 'technical assistance' to 'selected Chilean nationals'.

2. *Government action through international lending agencies*. The World Bank stopped granting loans to Chile; such loans had previously amounted to almost $80 million per year.

The Inter-American Development Bank (IDB) restricted its credit operations. While the UP Government was in power only two loans were granted, to the *Universidad Católica* [Catholic University] and the *Universidad Austral* [Southern University], totalling $11.6 million. (These loans had been approved by the Board of the IDB a few days before the September 4 elections.) Through the Gonzalez Amendment, the President of the United States is empowered to order U.S. representatives on the boards of international lending agencies to oppose loans to countries which nationalize or expropriate U.S. property.

3. *Government action designed to obstruct renegotiation of the Chilean external debt.* At a meeting of the Club of Paris in early 1972, U.S. representatives tried without success to link renegotiation of the Chilean external debt to a favourable solution to the problem of compensation for the copper companies.

4. *Action by private U.S. banks.* Short-term credits made available to Chile were reduced from $220 million in November 1970 to $35 million at the end of 1970; these credits were not renewed. Before the Allende Government came to power, over 78% of the credits made available to Chile came from the United States; by 1972 U.S. credits had declined to 6%. Moreover, the percentage of total Chilean imports coming from the United States declined from 40% before the UP Government to 20% in 1972.

5. *Action by the nationalized copper companies.* In the United States and elsewhere, the copper companies took legal action against Chile, with the result that the European banks suspended short-term credits which previously had been guaranteed by receipts from copper sales.

The attempt to destabilize the Chilean Government involved far more than purely economic measures. In the political sphere, the CIA was both persistent and effective in its attempts to undermine the UP. Having failed to prevent Allende's accession to the presidency, during the transmission of power following the elections, the CIA began to work toward medium-term objectives with the authorization of the 40 Committee and of its chairman, Henry Kissinger. This is not the place to go into the well-known results of the investigation carried out by the U.S. Senate Committee chaired by Senator Church, but it is worth mentioning that the CIA activities were directed toward the following objectives:

(1) Helping those political forces that were opposed to the UP Government by subsidizing their election expenses, giving financial support for the purchase of radio stations and to the opposition press, particularly *El Mercurio*, which had enormous influence on Chilean public opinion.

(2) Providing financial assistance to trade unions and professional associations that organized strikes for the purpose of destabilizing the UP Government during its final months in power (the truck drivers strike, for example).

(3) Providing advice to the opposition forces on matters of propaganda. This continued after the *coup d'état*, as is shown by the CIA's involvement in preparing the *Libro blanco*, published by the junta to discredit the UP Government. That this advice was more than purely political is demonstrated by the so-called Plan Z, designed to provide an aura of legitimacy for the *coup d'état* in order to satisfy public opinion. There is evidence to suggest that this Plan was produced on the advice of the CIA.[6]

Even more important than the CIA's clandestine political operations was the infiltration of the Chilean armed forces by the intelligence services of the three branches of the U.S. armed forces, especially by the Naval Intelligence Service,[7] to the point that these military agencies participated in the technical preparation of the *coup d'état*. The presence around the time of the *coup d'état* of U.S. warships off the Chilean coast under the pretext of Operation Unitas IV, and of fighter aircraft in Paraguay, make it reasonable to believe that the U.S. armed forces were involved in the *coup d'état*. The visit to Chile at the same time of 150 U.S. specialists in aerial acrobatics also seems to indicate that direct armed intervention was contemplated and might even have taken place. Many other factors, which the limited scope of this chapter do not allow us to discuss, also point to the same conclusions. It is public knowledge that the systematic infiltration of Latin American armed forces in various ways is a key element of U.S. policy.

It is worth mentioning that the U.S. economic blockade of Chile, defended on the grounds that the conflict concerning compensation for the copper companies had not been resolved, did not affect credit lines for purchases by the Chilean armed forces. The U.S. representatives at the compensation negotiations were asked the reason for this but were unable to provide a plausible explanation.

Given the scope of this chapter, it is not necessary here to examine the other ways in which the destabilization of the UP Government was pursued. However, a significant role was played in this respect by certain U.S. (or U.S.-controlled) organizations, most particularly the American Institute for Free Labour Development (AIFLD).

This brief summary of U.S. attempts to destabilize the UP Government, devised by people at the top of the U.S. decision-making structure, can help us understand the Chilean Government's behaviour *vis-à-vis* the United States, which will be examined below.

6. Those responsible for formulating and carrying out Chile's foreign policy under the UP Government were well aware that U.S. hostility toward Chile was based on political considerations and that these, in turn, had to do with the United States' role as leader of the counterrevolutionary forces throughout the world and as the hegemonic power in the Western hemisphere. At the same time they realized that a reasonable policy on the part of Chile, designed to avoid provocation, would ensure that neither armed intervention on the part of the United States, nor an official financial and commercial blockade such as was applied to Cuba, could be viable courses of action. The international situation did not allow it. It was known that the CIA and the military intelligence services were engaged in clandestine action to undermine the Chilean Government, strengthen the opposition and influence the armed forces. It was known that companies affected by the nationalizations were pressing for a hard-line policy *vis-à-vis* Chile. But it was also known that concessions to the United States on the question of compensation for the copper companies

would not change that country's hostile attitude, which would soon be expressed in other ways. Despite all of this the United States claimed, as we have mentioned earlier, that the question of compensation was the only significant obstacle to improving relations between the two countries.

Within this general framework, the objective which the Chilean Government pursued in its relations with the United States was to ensure that no pretext could be used to facilitate or legitimize either a strict economic blockade of Chile or other measures that could be harmful to the UP Government. In the same spirit, the idea was to reduce the number of conflict situations to a minimum and to ensure that those that could not be eliminated should not become more serious, while always keeping within the limits set down in the UP Programme.

It was felt that, to achieve these objectives, the Chilean Government needed to demonstrate its strong commitment to the principle of nonintervention. This would make it more difficult for the United States to adopt a tough and openly interventionist policy and, moreover, would make it easier for Chile to ensure that West European and Latin American countries, as well as the rest of the capitalist world, would not cooperate with U.S. attempts to wreck the Chilean economy. This emphasis in word and deed on the principle of non-intervention was of special relevance in Latin America because there was a tendency to regard the Chilean experience as being similar to that of Cuba; the Chilean Government was compelled to discredit this distorted view, which was being propagated in order to legitimize a policy of hemispheric isolation against Chile.

As long as the Chilean Government upheld the principle of nonintervention and the related idea of self-determination, it was difficult for other countries to justify hostile measures designed to isolate Chile. But this could not stop the hypocritical indirect or clandestine activities against Chile, as was clearly evidenced by subsequent events.

Efforts were made to reduce possible areas of conflict with the United States and to avoid situations that might increase tension between the two countries. Thus when, at the beginning of the UP's term of office, the United States unilaterally decided to withdraw its paramilitary installations from Easter Island, disregarding Chilean sovereignty, the Chilean Government did not make an issue out of it, nor did it publicize the matter.

Both the UP Government in its official statements, and the newspapers which supported the UP, were always very careful not to stir up difficulties with the United States by using immoderate language. Only in December 1972, when President Allende spoke before the General Assembly of the United Nations, did Chile formally denounce the economic blockade which had been imposed on the country. Even then Allende did not make a direct attack on the U.S. Government in spite of the widespread belief in Chilean Government circles that the U.S. authorities were directly participating in the pressure placed on Chile.

This policy of caution and non-provocation, which adhered faithfully to the anti-imperialist content of the Government's programme, was maintained until the end. There is little doubt that it helped to undermine the U.S. destabilization policy insofar as certain measures which were being contemplated, and which would have seriously damaged the Chilean economy, were not in fact taken for fear of political repercussions. It must not be forgotten that Chile's economic dependence on the United States allowed Washington a wide margin for action, but the cautious manner in which Chile managed its relations with the United States prevented the latter from making full use of that possibility.

7. We have already seen that the possibility of Chile becoming politically and economically isolated within Latin America had to be avoided by all means possible within the limits of the UP Programme. Chile's foreign policy in Latin America was mainly directed towards the achievement of that objective.

From the beginning, the Chilean Government was interested in the initiation and promotion of 'ideological pluralism' as a way to ensure peaceful and constructive coexistence in Latin America. Allusions to ideological pluralism are contained in all joint statements issued by Chilean authorities and their Latin American counterparts: for instance, the statements to which Chile subscribed jointly with Colombia, Argentina, Ecuador, Mexico, Cuba and Venezuela. The fact that several of these countries were governed by conservative administrations gave special relevance to such agreements which constituted yet another version of the principle of nonintervention, which Chile scrupulously observed in its relations with its fellow Latin American nations. The UP thus effectively blocked attempts to isolate Chile within Latin America on the pretext of the Government's political orientation.

Relations with Argentina were given special attention. The dispute on the question of the Beagle Canal was given priority, and the two Governments agreed to submit their difference to arbitration, thus eliminating the risk that any other interested party might exploit the situation in order to awaken Argentinian chauvinism against Chile.

President Allende's visit to Salta and President Lanusse's to Antofagasta clearly showed that friendly relations prevailed between the Chilean and Argentinian Governments despite their different ideologies and political orientation. Trade between the two countries also increased considerably during the 1970-73 period, and Argentinian credits for financing Chilean purchases of equipment and short-term operations amounted to approximately $350 million.

Argentina's goodwill was thus extremely important to the Chilean economy, and the Chilean Ministry of Foreign Affairs did everything possible to maintain friendly relations between the two countries. The danger of political and economic isolation was consequently eliminated on one of Chile's most vulnerable external fronts.

The Chilean Government also gave consideration to Bolivia's traditional problem, that of access to the sea. Promising attempts had been made under the Torres Government to solve this problem in the spirit of friendship among Latin American nations, which was one of the bases for the UP Programme. However, the fall of President Torres and the inauguration in Bolivia of a reactionary and anti-Chilean military regime brought these consultations to an end: mutual trust between the parties, an essential precondition for a favourable outcome, disappeared and negotiations on this delicate matter could not continue.

The UP Government attributed a great deal of importance to Andean economic integration as provided for in the Andean Pact, which resulted from Cartagena Agreement. At first, the initiative was regarded with misgiving by Chile's left-wing parties, who felt that nothing in the Agreement could prevent the U.S. monopolies from becoming the main beneficiaries of the expanded market which integration was designed to create. These reservations disappeared when, during the first few months of the UP's term of office, Decision 24 on the common treatment of foreign capital by the Andean countries was approved with Chile's wholehearted support. In effect, the decision ensured that the advantages of this market expansion would accrue mainly to the Andean Pact member countries, and that the main economic activities under foreign control would gradually be taken over by nationals of the host countries.

Owing to the difficult situation in which the UP Government found itself, the political dimension of Andean integration was perhaps of even greater importance than the economic advantages. Reciprocal ties multiplied among the Andean Pact members, thus increasing their interdependence while they at the same time were being asked to accept the principle of ideological pluralism as the political basis for that Pact. It was felt in certain business circles of some member countries that integration could not proceed satisfactorily if one of the members chose to pursue a socialist-type economic policy. Happily, however, this attitude won little support. In fact not only Chile, but all the member countries, particularly Peru, had policies that were state-oriented to some degree. As a result it was difficult to argue that only Chile's economic policy was incompatible with the Pact.

The Chilean Government was a strong supporter of Andean integration, and this support proved to be decisive when the first agreement on sectoral economic programming in the metal engineering industry was approved. The country's balance of payments problems caused some Chilean resistance to those regulations that involved payment in foreign exchange for imports coming from within the subregion. In the end, the position advocated by the Chilean Ministry of Foreign Affairs prevailed and it was agreed that the economic costs involved in the observance of Andean commitments were at that moment more than offset by the political significance of Chile's commitment to the process of Andean integration. In spite of this, however, during the last months of the UP Government, Chile had to take recourse to the special escape clauses provided in the Pact, seeking temporary exemption from the common regulations on interregional trade because the country was in the grips of an economic crisis at that time.

President Allende's tour of all the Andean countries – except Bolivia, which was undergoing a political crisis – provided an excellent opportunity for him to assure Columbia, Ecuador and Peru of the Chilean Government's Latin American orientation, its commitment to the principles of nonintervention and of Andean integration, its resolute defence of the sovereign right of all countries to deal with their natural resources as they see fit, and its condemnation of unlawful attempts by foreign elements to impede the full exercise of that sovereign right.

Mexico's decision to re-orient its foreign policy toward Latin America and the Third World, which became apparent during the second year of President Echeverria's Government, opened the way for closer economic and political ties between Mexico and Chile. This was confirmed by the very successful visit which President Allende made to Mexico City at the end of 1972.

A few days after the UP Government took office Chile re-established diplomatic, economic and cultural relations with Cuba. The immediate consequence, on Chile's part, was to dispute the legitimacy of the OAS agreement which obliged its members to sever relations with Cuba, and to affirm its willingness to intensify Chilean-Cuban relations. This willingness was immediately manifested by several agreements of various types between the two countries and by an exchange of visits between President Allende and Prime Minister Fidel Castro.

As could be foreseen, the UP's accession to power was not warmly received in Brazil. At first, Brazil was thoroughly hostile to the new UP Government and it seems reasonable to assume that it was prepared to support any attempt to isolate Chile within the hemisphere. However, the care with which Chile managed its relations with Brazil, and the success of the Chilean Ministry of Foreign Affairs in neutralizing potentially hostile attitudes of other Latin American countries towards Chile, led the Brazilian Government to change its attitude. Thus, the principle of 'ideological frontiers' that had been sustained by Brazil gave way to that of 'ideological pluralism'.

To be sure, political relations between the two countries remained cool; on the other hand, economic relations did not deteriorate. In fact, when things became very difficult for Chile as a result of a shortage of foreign exchange and of short-term credits for current operations, Brazil extended short-term credits to Chile amounting to $30 million to facilitate the payment of a similar sum for the purchase of urgently needed equipment.

To summarize, Chile's resolute policy of sustaining and improving relations with other Latin American countries frustrated attempts to politically isolate the country. It also softened the impact of both the balance of payments difficulties and the U.S. economic blockade because it encouraged short-term credits from and expanded trade with other Latin American countries.

8. U.S. hostility, which had been foreseen, caused the Chilean authorities to attach great significance to maintaining relations with Western countries; this was firstly because economic relations with the West could become very significant in the event of a U.S.-sponsored blockade; secondly it was because these countries held an influential position in the international community and could block any possible attempt to isolate Chile internationally.

These friendly overtures towards Western Europe appeared to be viable because of Chile's traditional ties with these countries, and because many of these countries had left-oriented or social democratic governments, so that they were predisposed to look kindly on the UP Government. European public opinion was particularly attracted to the Chilean experiment because of the democratic electoral process by which President Allende had come to power, and because of the UP's objective to create a socialist society in the context of democracy, pluralism and freedom.

Relations between Chile and the Western European countries did not deteriorate: a favourable, cooperative and friendly attitude towards Chile was maintained despite pressure from U.S. financial circles and the U.S. Government. Economic relations – commercial as well as financial – continued to develop in a normal manner. This close relationship was illustrated by the joint communiqué and the economic, technological and cultural cooperation agreements which resulted from the Chilean Minister of Foreign Affairs' visit to Europe in 1972.

The UP's emphasis on maintaining friendly relations with this important group of countries caused most of the governments in Western Europe to give the military junta a very cool reception after the *coup d'état* of September 1973.

Some mention should also be made of the fact that Chile's relations with Japan, Canada and Australia developed within a similar context during this period. In the case of Japan, for instance, private economic interests did not discontinue their plans for investing in Chile. While it is true that some projects did not materialize, and that an ambitious plan for commercial and industrial cooperation between the two countries had to be abandoned, these setbacks were due much more to U.S. pressure on the Japanese Government than to attitudes prevailing in Japanese business circles.

It is also interesting to note that the Spanish Government encouraged the development of closer economic ties with Chile. Import credits increased considerably and, in the field of industrial cooperation, very substantial agreements were signed regarding the automobile industry.

These facts are emphasized here because they show that Chilean foreign policy succeeded in reducing ideological conflicts even with such countries as Spain, where the prevailing ideology was profoundly antithetical to that of Chile. Again, the result was to reduce the effectiveness of policies whose purpose was to isolate Chile economically.

Another clear example of this is provided by the failure of U.S. attempts to block the renegotiation of the Chilean external debt during discussions in the Club of Paris early in 1972. Chile got its way despite the United States' insistence that an agreement should be conditional upon a Chilean commitment to compensate the owners of expropriated foreign capital, in accordance with U.S. interpretation of international law. Although other creditor countries had interests similar to those of the United States in that they also had capital invested in Chile, they did not support the U.S. position; in fact, they offered Chile reasonable conditions for repaying debts which helped the Chilean authorities to manage the economy in a difficult period.

Governments in many of these creditor countries complained to the Chilean Government on behalf of firms owned by their nationals which had been nationalized or in which management had been taken over by the workers. Although genuine efforts were made by the Chilean Government, it was not always possible to find a solution that was acceptable to both sides. However, unlike the United States – which threatened to take reprisals against Chile – these governments tried in good faith to find a solution that would not lead to a break in economic relations. Thus, despite the serious harm done to Chile as a result of the embargo placed by U.S. companies on Chilean copper sold to Europe, by mid-1973 Chile had succeeded in obtaining normal credit for the purchase of many items which could no longer be purchased in the United States.

9. Another factor of interest is the broad and far-reaching political consensus which provided the backdrop against which relations between Chile and the socialist countries were defined while the UP was in office. There is evidence of this not only in the statements and speeches of high level Chilean Government spokesmen, but also in the joint communiqués issued by Chile and the socialist countries. Such statements served to define the political basis for relations in many areas, including trade, industrial cooperation, technical assistance, finance and cultural exchange.

The visit of Chile's Minister of Foreign Affairs to Eastern Europe in the summer of 1971 inaugurated a series of important agreements regarding joint projects in industry, mining, agriculture-related industries and transportation, for which financial and technical assistance was provided by the socialist countries. These projects had previously been contemplated in Chile's economic planning; it should be stressed that many of them were carried out with financial and technological aid from the West and from Japan. The fact that negotiations were held with socialist countries about some of these projects did not imply that Western proposals were rejected by Chile, but merely that Chile had a wider range from which to choose and was able to select those that were most favourable to her own interests. In the case of the Soviet Union in particular, some of the projects to be carried out had been under study since the Frei Government and had been negotiated by that Government.

Credits for long-term projects which the socialist countries had granted totalled approximately $500 million, of which some $70 million were actually spend before the military *coup d'état*. These amounts do not include credits for projects which had been agreed on only in principle. The plan to modernize the transportation system and energy installations, which was being discussed with the Soviet Union, would have added a considerable amount to these figures. The socialist countries which provided credit also included the Chinese People's Republic, with which important trade and industrial cooperation agreements were reached as a result of a visit by the Chilean Foreign Minister to China early in 1973 (see Chapter 3, Table 3.14).

Although the volume of trade between Chile and the socialist countries increased considerably during the UP period, that is from 2% to 12%, it was still quite a small share of total Chilean trade (see Chapter 3, Tables 3.6 and 3.13). Far more important, given Chile's short-term requirements for foreign currency at the end of 1972 and early in 1973, was the financial aid given by the Soviet Union and other socialist countries. The former twice provided untied financial aid, totalling $106 million; the Chinese People's Republic granted $65 million in the form of prepayment for future copper deliveries and credits for the purchase of Chinese products, which constituted savings in foreign currency. The other socialist countries awarded slightly more than $10 million, also in the form of import credits (see Chapter 3, Table 3.15). In view of Chile's pressing need for foreign currency at that time, this financial help from the socialist countries enabled her to avoid defaulting on her debts, with all the implications that this would have had. The financial aid given by the socialist countries was decisive not so much because of its volume but because it came at the right moment. During 1973 the relative improvement in the balance of payments, due in part to the rise in copper prices, the reopening of credit lines to Western Europe, and the important new Argentinian credit, all without any reduction in Brazilian credits, enabled the country to do without the kind of emergency financial aid which it had been forced to ask from socialist countries towards the end of 1972.

10. An essential characteristic of our age is the emergence of national liberation movements in those areas of the world which, until recently, were colonial possessions of the capitalist powers, and in those countries whose political independence has not prevented them from falling prey to imperialism and neo-colonialism.

In keeping with its Programme, the UP Government demonstrated its solidarity with these movements. Through bilateral relations and participation in international gatherings and organizations, the Chilean movement gave its support to the peoples of the Third World in their struggle for political independence, in their search for autonomous economic development and in their efforts to carry out plans for social reform.

It is in this context that we must, in the first place, view Chile's denunciation of the OAS as an instrument of U.S. domination in Latin America, and that we must appreciate the Chilean proposals for a fundamental reform of the inter-American system. These proposals were aimed at challenging the idea that North and South America have similar objectives and interests, for this idea, apart from being untrue, was and is an anachronism left over from the cold war. The fact is that there is more that separates than unites North and South America: thus an institutionalized inter-American system could only make sense if it were intended to give form to a dialogue between the United States and Latin America as a whole in the hope of solving the conflict through negotiation. This was the position taken by Chile in the OAS: this denunciation was intended as an initiative towards promoting better understanding among Latin American countries so as to bring about a more accurate assessment of the inter-American system; it was seen as an aspect of the Latin American orientation of the UP's overall foreign policy. This orientation was also expressed in support for the idea of economic integration and in the effort to revitalize the Economic Commission for Latin America (ECLA) as an agency designed to work out a common position among Latin American governments *vis-à-vis* the world community.

Secondly, in keeping with its policy of solidarity with the developing world, the UP Government joined with the nonaligned countries and cooperated actively with those who promoted the independence of Third World countries, helping to break their ties of dependence on imperialism and working for greater cooperation between them and other progressive forces; particularly the socialist countries.

The UP Government accordingly supported the Vietnamese people's struggle for independence; it established diplomatic relations with the Democratic Republic of Vietnam, with the Revolutionary Government of South Vietnam, with the Royal Government of Cambodia and with the Popular and Democratic Republic of Korea. It severed relations with the puppet government of Taiwan and recognized the Chinese People's Republic as the only legitimate government of that country; it also supported the latter's claim for membership of the United Nations.

As to the Middle East question, Chile supported both the just demands of the Arab peoples for the return of territories occupied by Israel during the 1967 war, and the Palestinians' legitimate right to national expression.

Furthermore, Chile supported the liberation movements in the Portuguese colonies, condemned apartheid and all those who support racism and segregation, and generally identified itself with the struggle for the liberation of oppressed peoples.

Chile supported all countries in their claims to sovereignty over their natural resources, which includes sovereignty over those resources within the 200-mile offshore limit. At the same time, Chile condemned interventionist and neocolonialist manoeuvres designed to maintain dependence relationships and campaigned for a reform of international economic relations in the light of principles of justice and equity as a way of correcting serious disequilibria which do great harm to the developing countries. Through both the Group of 77, and the various specialized agencies of the United Nations – particularly UNCTAD, whose third session was held in Santiago de Chile in 1972 – and through the nonaligned countries, Chile strongly supported the demands of developing countries for basic changes not only in the commercial, financial and monetary structures but also in the regulations governing the transfer of technology, all of which demonstrate the predominance of Western capitalism in the world economic system.

Finally, Chile gave full support to the United Nations, considering it to be the best instrument for achieving peace, *détente*, disarmament and world security, and for promoting international cooperation.

11. The objective of the UP Government's foreign policy was to ensure that the external relations that would facilitate implementing the internal social transformation envisaged in its Programme. The discussion above shows that this objective was achieved. We shall now evaluate the policy that was followed and then look into whether a different foreign policy might perhaps have led to better results.

The UP Government's foreign policy prevented Chile from becoming isolated in Latin America and enabled it to develop friendly relations with the other nations on the South American continent, particularly with its more important neighbours. In keeping with the UP Programme, Chile pressed for Andean integration and put forward policies that were Latin American in orientation and also critical of the inter-American system. Problems that could be anticipated with the United States were reduced to a minimum so that U.S. policy-makers would have no pretext for openly obstructing the Chilean Government's revolutionary policy. Successful efforts were made to ensure that satisfactory economic and political relations could be maintained with the United States' West European allies and with Japan. Relations with socialist countries were developed in every field, and Chile made common cause with the countries of the Third World, particularly the nonaligned nations, thus ensuring that for the first time in its history Chile's voice would be heard in the international community.

These achievements were the result of the general strategy adopted by the

Chilean Ministry of Foreign Affairs to cope with the difficult international situation which confronted the new Government when it took office. In the end the emphasis on the principle of nonintervention, the ability to avoid direct confrontation with the imperialism of the United States and its allies (thus depriving these countries of motives for a policy of open intervention in Chilean affairs) and the attempt to divide and neutralize its potential opponents through appropriate and reasonable concessions, all ensured that external factors would not cause insuperable problems for the Government, while a simultaneous attempt was made to maximize economic and political support from abroad for the Chilean revolutionary experiment.

What conclusions can be drawn? First, it is obvious that the UP Government's strategy in foreign policy was very different from that followed in domestic problems. In my opinion, there was a marked tendency in dealing with domestic issues to overestimate the strength of pro-Government forces while underestimating that of the opposition. As a result, an incorrect strategy was drawn up which favoured the opponents of the UP, permitting them to gain support among the uncommitted at the expense of the Government. Unwillingness to contemplate tactical agreements with those opposition forces which were likely to be most susceptible to neutralization, and the tendency – which was never overcome – to believe that a final confrontation of a social or even military character would resolve the conflict in favour of the left, prevented the adoption of a single, reasonable and consistent domestic policy based on objective conditions rather than on wishful thinking, which might have progressively opened the way for the uninterrupted advance of revolutionism.

While this inaccurate perception of reality and of the balance of political power had a negative impact on domestic affairs, in the international field there was, from the outset, a much more objective appreciation of the external circumstances which made it possible to apply strategies and tactics that were adequate, consistent and effective.

This political orientation in foreign policy enjoyed overwhelming support within the UP. Those who did not agree refrained from public criticism, thus decisively facilitating its application. Moreover, President Allende had the full and constant support of the Ministry of Foreign Affairs, and decision-making in foreign policy matters was free of partisan and other disruptive influences. As a result, the Government's foreign policy was conducted in a spirit of unity, consistency and decisiveness.

The important question that must now be examined is: what role did external factors play in the developing political crisis which culminated in the fascist military *coup d'état* of 11 September 1973?

There are people who believe that external factors were primarily responsible for the failure of the revolutionary experiment in Chile: they emphasize in particular the effect of the U.S. financial blockade, the economic and technical aid which the CIA channelled to the UP's opponents, and the ways in which the United States influenced and infiltrated the Chilean armed forces. All these factors are said to have tipped the balance of power in favour of the counterrevolutionary movement.

To judge how true this is, it is necessary to first find the correct analytical criteria for judging the situation and the reciprocal influence of internal and external factors which contributed to the Government's downfall.

There are two ways in which external agents can undermine and even destroy a revolutionary project in a given country.

The first is by launching an economic, political and/or military attack against that country, directly inciting a situation of internal 'destabilization' that is so serious that the revolutionary project is paralyzed and eventually destroyed.

The second way is to exercise external influence on those internal factors which are already undermining the Government's authority, thus increasing their destabilizing effect and eventually causing an irreversible political crisis that will lead to the Government's fall. This is what happened in Chile, as indeed in the majority of cases. External factors that aimed to encourage the UP Government's overthrow operated through existent internal factors of destability, thus strengthening their impact and opening the way for a successful military *coup d'état*.

The U.S. economic blockade and the obstacles to Chilean-U.S. trade contributed both to the balance of payments crisis and to certain problems in supply of consumer goods, but it cannot be said that they were the primary cause of these difficulties. If we are to make some attempt to identify causal factors we must examine the internal dialectic of the Chilean process, whose determining elements were the Government's economic policy and the reactions of the dominant classes to that policy.

It is now obvious that the worsening balance of payments situation and the shortage of certain commodities played a significant part in creating a climate of scarcity and in aggravating inflation which, in turn, generated and increased the dissatisfaction felt in important sectors of society – particularly the middle class – thus increasing the likelihood of a successful military rebellion.

Having said this, however, we cannot assume that the behaviour of the middle classes would have been radically different had the economic situation not deteriorated as much as it did. Certain sectors in the middle classes favoured a military *coup d'état* and the hostility shown towards the UP Government did not derive from any externally caused deterioration of the economic situation. It was rather the result of counterrevolutionary attitudes that emerged in response to the implementation of the Government's revolutionary programme and to the dawning realization that the process might be irreversible. What was indeed a direct result of the worsening economic situation and of external factors was the way in which this hostility towards the

Government spread to other social sectors, which thus became more vulnerable to manipulation by the advocates of military intervention.

The financial support which the CIA and the opposition parties gave to the right-wing press and to the leaders of the *gremios*, who organized the lockouts in October 1972 and August 1973, had a similar effect. It helped to increase the efficiency of their political activities and of those of the press, as well as of those whose subversive manoeuvres led to the lockout, but it cannot be said that these were caused by outside help. Due to this support more people voted for the right, mass communication media controlled by the right gained more influence, and the lockout organizers found it easier to achieve their purpose.

Of even greater relevance than the foreign intervention described above was U.S. interference in the affairs of the Chilean armed forces, mainly through the activities of the military intelligence services. U.S. influence in inducing the Chilean military to set up a *coup d'état* was significant because the technical and professional assistance which was provided helped to retain unity while subversion was being planned. Once again, however, external action was fruitful because it was directed towards those members of the military who were already amenable to the idea of military subversion. In fact, the great majority of officers in the Chilean armed forces, given the basically reactionary character of their subculture, were impervious to, and thus could not be incorporated in, the Government's revolutionary policy, a policy which they naturally questioned and tended to resist. Only the tradition of professionalism – a tradition established at a time when the base of the social order was never seriously threatened – and their long-standing habit of obedience to legally constituted governments, temporarily neutralized their tendency to oppose a government which, as they saw it, threatened the very basis of nationhood and the social order. If the armed forces had not been predisposed to oppose the UP Government, the Pentagon's call for a military uprising would have gone unheeded.

Although the Chilean armed forces' political orientation did predate the U.S. incitement to counterinsurgency, the importance of the systematic anti-communist indoctrination to which hundreds of officers were subjected in Panama and in the United States must not be minimized: this indoctrination enforced and modernized the reactionary political subculture in the Chilean military.

Moreover, the UP never really attempted to make any changes in the Chilean officer corps' leadership and composition. This policy, recognized *a posteriori* by all concerned as suicidal, was without doubt the main reason why it was so easy for the military leadership to side with the *coup d'état*.

In other words, U.S. interference in Chilean military affairs, besides being undeniably significant, related well to an internal situation whose most important dimension – the composition of the officer corps and the political attitude – had unfortunately not been given Government attention, notwithstanding the considerable opportunities for doing so.

It is now apparent that a well planned military policy would have been of greater significance than either the UP's economic programme or its foreign policy. Such a military policy should have dealt with the entire question of violence in the revolutionary process, putting special emphasis on the need to ensure military support for the Government and to neutralize and combat U.S. anti-revolutionary influence in the Chilean armed forces.

To sum up, U.S. activities designed to destabilize the UP Government – activities which the U.S. authorities have cynically acknowledged – did not create the factors which caused the UP Government to fall but rather increased and intensified the impact of those factors.

Whether or not foreign intervention was necessary or sufficient to tip the scales in favour of the pro-*coup* forces is a question which is impossible to answer. However, it is obvious that foreign intervention in the country's political, economic and military affairs directly prior to the *coup d'état* was significant and that its impact was strongest in matters affecting the armed forces' behaviour.

In my opinion, military subversion would have occurred in any case, even without the influence of external forces, but it is impossible to say whether it would then have had the same result.

The next question is whether Chilean foreign policy could have halted or at least significantly reduced U.S. intervention aimed at destabilizing the UP Government. I maintain that it could not have done so. To substantiate this opinion I shall examine two possibilities: the first is that the Government's foreign policy could have eliminated or reduced the causes and pretexts for U.S. intervention.

Working from the principle that the UP Programme could not be renounced and that the Government was not prepared to surrender its sovereignty, the Chilean Ministry of Foreign Affairs did everything in its power to avoid provoking U.S. intervention.

If a more conciliatory position on the question of compensating the copper companies had been taken, it would have meant surrendering the very sovereignty which had been upheld when the Chilean National Congress unanimously adopted its procedure for resolving problems of compensation: and this procedure was ultimately carried out.

It is also highly probable – I would go so far as to say certain – that even if the Chilean Government had reached an agreement with the copper companies on the question of compensation, despite the political cost and surrender of sovereignty that this would have implied, the U.S. Government would have continued with its clandestine 'destabilizing' activities through the CIA and the intelligence services of the armed forces, with the aim of provoking disorder throughout Chile, of strengthening opposition, and of inciting the armed forces to rebel. It was the impact of foreign intervention on these elements which most influenced the relative strength of the forces involved in determining the final outcome. It might have been possible to obtain a relaxation of the economic blockade by accepting an unworthy solution to the compensation problem, but this would not have increased the ability of the UP Government to suppress a military *coup d'état*.

I am convinced that U.S. interference in Chilean affairs was motivated primarily by the political liability which a successful Chilean revolution would have represented for the United States. Although the U.S. Government publicly proclaimed that the question of compensating the copper companies was the most important outstanding issue between the two countries, in reality it was a question of secondary importance. In adopting this attitude, U.S. diplomacy sought a way to give its anti-Chilean policy an aura of legitimacy while continuing its destabilizing activities. There was no likelihood that these activities would cease since they were determined in the context of the general counter-revolutionary strategy that was at the core of U.S. foreign policy.

To sum up, it is my contention that a more conciliatory policy *vis-à-vis* the United States would have had no significant effect on the level of the latter's interference in Chilean affairs, or its contribution to the success of the military *coup d'état*.

The second possibility to be examined is that a tougher foreign policy could have eliminated or reduced U.S. intervention in Chile, or could have altered the balance of power in the Government's favour.

A more uncompromising policy *vis-à-vis* the United States would of necessity have involved the following measures: (1) earlier and/or more violent denunciation, before the international community and Chilean public opinion, of the anti-Chilean manoeuvres of the United States; (2) refusal to negotiate with the United States on a legal basis for a solution to the problem of compensating the copper companies; (3) breaking diplomatic relations, which would have resulted from Chilean denunciations of U.S. intervention.

It is my belief that such measures, whether adopted singly or jointly, would neither have eliminated nor reduced intervention and the threat that it represented.

It would indeed have been possible to denounce U.S. interference at an earlier time than President Allende's speech at the United Nations, and to have done so more violently, but this would not have altered the course of events in Chile's favour. Similarly, although Chile could have refused to participate in negotiations on the compensation problem, while still remaining faithful to constitutional principles, this would not have changed things for the better. On the contrary, the only possible consequence of such a course of action would have been a weakening of Chile's case. Chile maintained that it was trying to find a legal solution to the problem on the basis of an existing treaty which laid down a procedure for resolving disputes between the two countries. If Chile had refused to negotiate, the position she was maintaining would have lost all its validity in the eyes of the international community, particularly in the Western European countries where the situation was being closely followed.

The conflict could also have been handled in such a way that a break in diplomatic relations by one of the parties could have been justified, but such a course of action would have been disadvantageous to Chile. Given the prevailing political climate in Chile in 1973 and the attitude of the middle classes, a diplomatic break would have narrowed the Government's political base. This would hardly have been compensated by increased militancy among the UP's active supporters who, given their stronger anti-imperialist feelings, were the only people likely to be motivated by such a measure.

Moreover, a tougher policy would have been neither understood nor supported by most Latin American governments; it thus would have created a situation in which attempts to isolate Chile could be successful, and the Chilean Ministry of Foreign Affairs was trying to avoid such a situation at all costs.

Even more serious, however, was the fact that a break in diplomatic relations with the United States would have both hastened and strengthened the military insurrection. Support for counterrevolutionary plans would have grown more rapidly, and the *coup d'état* would have taken place sooner. The reasons for this included Chile's dependence on the United States for the supply of arms. Breaking relations would have provided an excellent pretext for legitimizing the seditious feelings prevalent among the officer corps, as it could have been argued that a break with the United States would seriously weaken the armed forces and thus compromise the national security for which they felt responsible. The irresolution and conflict of loyalty felt by some members of the armed forces would have disappeared immediately if Chile had broken relations with the United States.

It seems clear, therefore, that a more cautious or tougher policy would have had no significant effect on U.S. resolution to destabilize the UP Government.

Yet another question is whether the balance of internal power, which in the end resulted in the *coup d'état*, could have been changed if more help had been received from the socialist countries.

The answer has to be negative. An increased contribution by the socialist countries towards Chilean economic development would have had little effect on the balance of internal power. The favourable economic effects of this cooperation for the Government were of a long-term nature and could not have altered the political situation which gave rise to the military *coup d'état*. The same would have applied to any increase in trade relations.

With respect to financial aid, which was of great significance during the foreign exchange crisis in late 1972 and early 1973, it is obvious that the help given by the socialist countries saved Chile from defaulting on its debts. We have already seen that the relative improvement in the balance of payments situation in mid-1973 made it possible for Chile to meet its financial commitments without requesting further hard currency from the socialist countries. Conceivably the Government could have obtained credits for the import of large quantities of food and other goods which started becoming scarce when the political crisis began in the second quarter of 1973. But by then it was already clear that the majority of social and political forces that opposed the Government and harboured subversive ideas would not have been mollified by any improvement in the supply of consumer goods. The appeal from the counterrevolutionary groups might perhaps not have been heard by quite so many people if the shortages had been eased, but this would not have essentially altered the domestic political situation, which was determined by the gradual development of a counterrevolutionary awareness based on experiences and expectations which were far more important in determining political behaviour than the shortage of consumer goods. These shortages were mainly caused by the Government's domestic economic policy and were worsened by the U.S. economic blockade.

12. In conclusion, it is my opinion that the UP Government's international policy, within the limits which were necessarily imposed upon it, was able to achieve its principal objective, that is the viability of the Chilean revolutionary project insofar as this depended upon the external context. Moreover, taking into account the strategic priority that had to be given to achieving the internal revolution, the international policy also succeeded in giving support to those progressive forces throughout the world that struggle for peace, democracy and socialism and for political and economic emancipation of dependent peoples.

NOTES

1. See *Covert Action in Chile, 1963-73. Staff Report of the Select Committee to Study Governmental Operations with Respect to Intelligence Activities* (Washington, D.C., United States Senate, the U.S. Government Printing Office, 1975). This report (known as the 'Church Report' as Senator Frank Church chaired the Committee) claims that in an off-the-record conversation with a journalist a few days after the Chilean elections (on 16 September 1970), 'Henry Kissinger warns that Allende's election was irreversible, might affect neighboring nations and would pose "massive problems" for the U.S. and Latin America' (58).

2. According to *Covert Action in Chile...*, 58, on 15 September 1970 President Nixon 'instructs CIA Director Richard Helms with the task to prevent Allende's accession to office. The CIA is to play a direct role in organizing a military *coup d'état*. This involvement becomes known as Track II [Pista Dos].'

3. See *Covert Action in Chile...* and *Hearings before the Select Committee to Study Governmental Operations with Respect to Intelligence Activities of the United States Senate*, 94th Congress, 1st Session, volume 7, *Covert Action* (Washington, D.C., The U.S. Government Printing Office, 1975).

4. See *Covert Action in Chile...*, 58. On 8 and 14 September 1970, '40 Committee dis-

cusses the Chilean situation. The Committee approves $250,000 for the use of Ambassador Korry to influence the 24 October Chilean Congressional vote'.

5. In October 1971, Secretary of State Rogers met with representatives of Anaconda, Ford Motor Company, First National City Bank, Bank of America, Ralston Purina and International Telephone and Telegraph (ITT). A possible embargo on spare parts and materials for Chile was discussed, as were the U.S. Government's plans to stop all aid to Chile under the Hickenlooper Amendment. ITT presented a detailed memorandum requesting that pressure be put on Chile and suggesting the formation of a special unit within the National Security Council to take charge of these types of measures.

6. There is, in *Covert Action in Chile...*, 59-61, evidence that the following measures were supported in order to influence Chilean political developments and 'destabilize' the UP Government:

1970

14 October: '40 Committee approves $60,000 for Ambassador Korry's proposal to purchase a radio station....'

13 November: '40 Committee approves $25,000 to support Christian Democratic candidates.'

19 November: '40 Committee approves $750,000 for clandestine operations in Chile.'

1971

28 January: '40 Committee approves $1,240,000 for the purchase of radio stations and newspapers and to support candidates in municipal and other activities of anti-Allende parties.'

22 March: '40 Committee approves $185,000 additional support to the Christian Democratic Party (PDC).'

10 May: '40 Committee approves $77,000 for purchase of a press for the Christian Democratic Party newspaper. The press is not obtained and the funds are used to support the paper.'

20 May: '40 Committee approves $100,000 in emergency aid to the Christian Democratic Party to meet short term debts.'

26 May: '40 Committee approves $150,000 for additional aid to the Christian Democratic Party to meet debts.'

6 July: '40 Committee approves $150,000 for support of opposition candidates in a Chilean by-election.'

9 September: '40 Committee approves $700,000 for support to the major Santiago newspaper, *El Mercurio*.'

5 November: '40 Committee approves $815,000 support to opposition parties and to induce a split in the Popular Unity coalition.'

15 December: '40 Committee approves $160,000 to support two opposition candidates in January 1972 by-elections.'

1972

11 April: '40 Committee approves $965,000 for additional support to *El Mercurio*.'

24 April: '40 Committee approves $50,000 for an effort to splinter the Popular Unity coalition.'

16 June: '40 Committee approves $46,500 to support a candidate in a Chilean by-election.'

21 September: '40 Committee approves $24,000 to support an anti-Allende businessmen's organization *Sociedad de Fomento Fabril*.'

26 October: '40 Committee approves $1,427,666 to support opposition political parties and private sector organizations in anticipation of March 1973 Congressional elections.'

1973

12 February: '40 Committee approves $200,000 to support opposition political parties in the Congressional elections.'

20 August: '40 Committee approves $1 million to support opposition political parties and private sector organizations money is not spent.'

15 October (after the *coup d'état*): '40 Committee approves $34,000 for an anti-Allende radio station and travel costs of pro-junta spokesmen.'

7. 'In the case of aggression against Chile, the CIA was designed as the responsible coordinator for clandestine operations, while the Naval Intelligence Service was the responsible

coordinator for military problems.' Pedro Vuskovic, *Acusación al imperialismo* [Accusation Against Imperialism] (Mexico City, Fondo de Cultura Económica, 1975), 24.

5

FERNANDO FAJNZYLBER

THE EXTERNAL SECTOR AND THE POLICIES OF THE UNIDAD POPULAR GOVERNMENT

INTRODUCTION

The object of this study is to examine the way in which Chile's external economic relations affected the transformation of its economy while the *Unidad Popular* (UP) Government was in power. To do this, we must pay special attention to the following points: (1) the level and 'style of development' that prevailed before this transformation process was initiated; (2) the policies contained in the programme of economic transformation and the way in which they were carried out; (3) the behaviour and relative strength of the social groups, inside and outside Chile, which supported or were affected by this transformation process.

The discussion that follows has been organized within this frame of reference. It should be kept in mind that this chapter is merely part of a larger study dealing with the international system and the internal situations in the developing countries as interdependent phenomena; that the role of foreign trade is only one dimension of the problem; and that Chile represents a specific experience from which it is possible to derive lessons that may be useful for other countries.

In the first section we shall discuss the main features of the Chilean economy during the 1960s, with particular emphasis on the external sector. Here we shall focus on trade relations with the United States and we shall try to measure their impact on the Chilean economy.

In the second part we shall examine the way in which implementation of the UP Government's Programme affected the external sector. This will be followed by an analysis of the Government's policies and achievements in relation to the external sector. We shall conclude with some general comments on the economic blockade.

The basic argument of this chapter is that the transformation process in Chile between 1970 and 1973 was shaped and determined by internal factors.

Footnotes and tables to this chapter may be found on pp. 168-181.

We must not, of course, minimize the significance of external constraints for there are indeed lessons to be learned from them that might be useful to other countries. However, we are drawn to the conclusion that these external constraints were unavoidable and that in fact they were not applied to Chile with as much rigour as they might have been. Thus the problem should be seen as one of managing the process of change in such a way as to be able to cope with the kinds of external constraints that are certain to emerge whenever genuine social transformations are attempted.

1. THE CHILEAN ECONOMY DURING THE 1960s

1.1. *Introduction*

We shall begin discussing the main features of the Chilean economy during the 1960s by giving a general survey of the economy during that period; this will be followed by a more detailed discussion of Chile's trade relations with the United States. (The evolution of the external sector in general is discussed in Alexis Guardia's 'Structural Transformations in Chile's Economy and in its System of External Economic Relations' (Chapter 3 of this volume) and will therefore not be examined here.)

Because of the fact that Chile's major external conflicts involved U.S. companies and the U.S. Government, it seems useful to probe the relationships with them in order to establish whether they really had a 'strategic' character and to obtain a general picture of the ways in which the United States was able to affect the Chilean economy.

The fact that a country has attained a certain level of industrial development makes it more vulnerable to external constraints. In semi-industrialized countries, import restrictions affect mass domestic consumption through the effect on the level of economic activity and the creation of new jobs. Obviously the political consequences of import restrictions in this kind of situation are quite different from what they might be in a situation where only high income groups are affected.

This is one of the issues which makes us feel that a close examination of the 'style of development' in which the transformation process was launched is necessary.

1.2. *Problems in the Chilean Economy during the 1960s*

During the 1960s it was becoming obvious that Chile's capitalist economic system was in difficulty. *Per capita* income was growing slowly at an average rate of about 2% *per annum* during this period, but by the end of the decade the rate had dropped to about 0.8%, partly as the result of a lack of investment. In spite of a continuing flow of foreign capital into Chile, the rate of investment remained at about 15% to 17% in relation to output, and was decreasing at the end of the decade.

At the same time, income distribution continued to be highly regressive. At the end of the decade 45% of Chileans received only 14% of national income, while at the other extreme about 9% of the population received 35% of the national income. Between those two groups was a large middle sector which accounted for 45% of the economically active population and received approximately 50% of income.[1] These figures help to explain why an increasing number of people came to question the economic system's capacity to meet the people's rising expectations. Given the slow growth rate, the struggle for a better and more equitably distributed income gained intensity. The trade union organizations, which had historically been closely linked to the large left-wing parties, were the means for expressing these expectations, which emerged as a result of the obvious ineffectiveness and inequity of the existing economic structure and power configuration.

These features of the Chilean economy reflected two basic structural characteristics: a significant concentration in ownership of the means of production and a high level of foreign control of the economy through ownership of strategic firms and through the external debt. Until 1965 the agricultural sector was dominated by the latifundio system and a high proportion of agricultural land was in the hands of a few landowners. Agricultural production was stagnating and the peasants were practically outside the money economy; they had neither social nor trade union organizations and were culturally as well as politically under the landowners' control. After 1965 there was an agrarian reform which, by 1970, had led to expropriation of some of the latifundios and organization of part of the peasantry into trade unions. Concentration of property and of the means of production was particularly high in the industrial and banking sectors. The groups which controlled these activities absorbed a high proportion of credit and financial resources. This economic power was the basis of their political power.

Nevertheless, while industrial property and financial resources remained concentrated in a few hands, the private sector's share in financing national investment was decreasing. Both public sector investment and foreign investment were increasing at the expense of the Chilean private sector.[2]

During 1965-70 attempts were made to introduce partial reforms designed to breathe some life into the capitalist economic structure and to eliminate the main obstacles. In the mining sector, Chile reached an agreement with the copper companies which made it possible for the state to acquire part of the foreign companies' shares without prejudicing their interests. In the industrial sector, a number of joint ventures were set up with private and public participation and a substantial amount of foreign credit and capital flowed into Chile.

The idea was not to bring about a fundamental transformation but rather to modernize the existing structures. As a result, the reformist policies merely accentuated the historical tendencies toward increasing indebtedness and greater foreign penetration of the economy.

The main expressions of Chile's dependent status were: (1) a large external debt; (2) a large proportion of exports being controlled from the outside; (3) a rapid denationalization of the industrial sector and (4) inadequate technology.

The persistent tendency towards high indebtedness, regardless of the economic policies pursued by various governments, demonstrated that the economic structure was incapable of achieving self-sustaining growth. In 1960 the external debt was $598 million; by the mid-1960s it had reached $1,846 million and in 1970 it was $1,975 million.[3] The result was that Chile had the highest *per capita* external debt in the world and foreign interests were able to use their power as creditors to keep Chile in a subordinate position.

Exports generated by foreign firms added to the vulnerability of the Chilean economy. Copper accounted for the lion's share of exports, reaching 77% of the value of total exports in 1970. During that year the two largest mines, which were basically controlled by U.S. companies, were producing 80% of Chile's copper and therefore controlled 60% of total exports. Other important export industries, such as the nitrate and iron industries, were also controlled by foreign firms. In 1965 the Frei Government initiated a programme of joint ventures with the U.S. copper companies called the 'Chileanization' of copper. The state purchased 51% of the shares in one of the largest mines (Kennecott) and 25% of the shares in the other (Anaconda). Both transactions were negotiated with the companies and there was no element of coercion. The agreements were advantageous to the companies and brought them higher profits. As a result there was a great deal of pressure – some of it from the Government's own ranks – for a policy change. In 1969 new negotiations took place between Anaconda and the Chilean Government, and nationalization was discussed. However, the end result was again a compromise and the state's share merely increased from 25% to 51%, with an option to purchase after 1973; but the companies' management remained in foreign hands.[4]

1.3. *Trade Relations with the United States*

The role of the United States in Chile's foreign trade will be examined in order to establish the degree to which these bilateral trade relations were 'strategic' in 1970. This will enable us to assess both the intensity of external pressure on Chile and the logic of the U.S. decision to set up an invisible blockade around the Chilean economy.

1.3.1. *The Diversification of Foreign Trade*

Table 5.1 shows that in 1970, the value of imports from the United States was about twice that of Chilean exports to that country. Those imports accounted for approximately 36.9% of Chile's total imports, while exports to the United States represented 14.1% of total exports.

The volume of imports from the United States was comparable to that of imports from Europe, the United Kingdom and Canada combined, or to that of imports from all Latin American, Asian, African and European socialist countries taken together.

A significant diversification of Chilean trade took place between 1950 and 1970, particularly in exports. In 1950 trade between the United States and Chile accounted for more than half the latter's exports and half its imports. By 1970, as we have seen, these figures had dropped to approximately 14.1% and 36.9% respectively.

1.3.2. *The Structure and Strategic Character of Imports from the United States*

Let us examine how the $343 million of imports that came from the United States in 1970 was composed.

To assess the 'strategic' character of imports, we must first of all say what we mean by 'strategic' goods. For the purposes of this discussion we will define 'strategic' goods as those goods (1) whose unavailability would seriously harm the economy; and (2) for which finding alternative sources of supply would be a slow and difficult process.

Concerning (1) we will further assume that the economy would suffer seriously if the unavailability of certain goods were to lead to a paralysis of: the marketing of exports, which is the source of foreign exchange needed to purchase the blockaded goods from other suppliers; the manufacturing of essential and widely needed consumer goods; the manufacturing of items that are essential for production in a large number of areas; and provision of basic services – transportation, energy and communications.

Concerning (2) we will assume that finding alternative supply sources would be a slow and difficult process in cases where the United States had a monopoly over the production and distribution of the goods in question.

In general terms it would appear that the following Chilean imports fulfil condition (2):

– Spare parts for equipment manufactured in the United States: this is especially true of equipment which has particular design features and is produced in small quantities. Whether or not the equipment is old constitutes a complicating factor.

– Raw materials and finished products in the chemical, petrochemical and pharmaceutical sectors: while few of these products are manufactured exclusively in the United States, many are produced outside that country either by subsidiaries of U.S. companies or under patent, licencing or other types of agreements with U.S. firms.

– Crude oil: while this was not imported directly from the United States, 63% of crude oil supplies came from U.S. distributing companies.

These examples demonstrate that the concept of 'strategic' goods is a fairly broad one. However, for the purposes of this discussion we must focus on a certain limited number of products.

Other ways of defining groups of 'strategic' goods might be as follows: (1) products which come mainly from the United States; (2) products for which finding alternative supply sources would be a slow and difficult process; (3) products mentioned in (2) which are essential to the country.

For the sake of analysis, imported goods have been categorized in a way which perhaps brings out Chile's dependence on U.S. supplies; the results are presented in Tables 5.2 to 5.5. We find that, of the $340 million of imports from the United States in 1970, $114 million were spent on products supplied mainly (75% or more) by the United States. (It should be noted that imports with a value of less than $100,000 a year are not included.) Those products for which there was a heavy reliance on the United States, at least on the short term, represented 13.5% of total imports. If we add the products for which 50% of the total supplies came from the United States, this figure rises to 26.6% of total imports.

As for imported intermediate goods, 67.8% came mainly (75% or more) from the United States, as did 29.2% of imported capital goods and 3% of imported consumer goods. $3.4 million was spent on the latter category (that is consumer goods that came mainly from the United States) while $33.2 million was spent on capital goods and $37 million on intermediate goods. As for products of which more than 50% was imported from the United States, consumer goods amounted to $8.8 million, intermediate goods to $150 million, and capital goods to $65 million.

It seems clear that our analysis must concentrate on intermediate and capital goods because of the large volume of trade in these types of goods, because of the problems of substitution which would emerge if a sudden shortage occurred, and because of their importance for the national economy.

1.3.3. *Intermediate Goods*

In 1970, $490 million of intermediate goods were imported into Chile, of which about $190 million, thus some 39%, came from the United States. These intermediate goods could be grouped in the following categories: spare parts (about $121 million), chemical products (about $97 million), agricultural raw materials ($60 million), fuels ($60 million) and raw materials originating from the textile, mechanical engineering, leather, construction and other industries (altogether $150 million).

Among the various types of intermediate goods, spare parts, chemical products and fuels appear to have a 'strategic' character. We shall therefore concentrate on them.

If we classify imports of intermediate goods in terms of the economic sectors which make use of them (Table 5.6), we see that the most crucial sector is mining. Over half of the imports of intermediate goods for this sector were made up of goods which came mainly (75% or more) from the United States. This accounted for $15.7 million of imports, which is what it would have cost in 1970 to build up a stock of these products for the mining sector in order to have a year's breathing space to find alternative suppliers.

If we examine other sectors in the same way, it would seem that the value of the 'overstock' necessary to cover requirements for intermediate goods which came mainly (75% or more) from the United States would be $77 million. However, alternative suppliers could have been found fairly rapidly for many of these goods so that it was not necessary to build up a stock for them. Moreover, there are other products which do not need alternative suppliers simply because they do not play a decisive role in the productive process. Thus the figure of $77 million should be used only as a point of reference.

1.3.4. *Spare Parts*

If we examine imports of specific types of spare parts with an annual value of $500,000 or more, we find that over 50% of them came from the United States. The specific percentages are: 61.2% in 1967, 67.6% in 1968, 65.2% in 1969 and then a drop to 55.6% in 1970. Obviously the supply of spare parts was closely associated with the nature of the existing industrial infrastructure – as we shall discuss further on. The decrease in U.S.-supplied spare parts in 1970 was due to the diversification of equipment imports during the late 1960s.

As for imports of spare parts with an annual value of under $500,000, those from the United States accounted for 45.7% in 1968 and 44.7% in 1970.

Taking all imports of spare parts with an annual value of $100,000 or more together, we find that the total value of such imports in 1970 was about $121 million, of which $63 million (53%) came from the United States.

Looking at types of spare parts which came mainly (75% or more) from the United States, we find that in 1970, the value of imports amounted to $22 million, or 18.3% of the value of all imports of spare parts (see Table 5.6). This $22 million rises to $54 million if we consider the types of spare parts of which 50% came from the United States. This is the level of investment that would have been necessary to build up a one-year stock of the parts which would normally be imported from the United States.

The automobile industry accounted for $33 million of the $120 million spent on importing spare parts into Chile in 1970. Some $19.1 million (59%) came from the United States. Thus we see that dependence on the United States for spare parts was greater in the automobile industry than in other industries. It would have been extremely difficult to find alternative supplies of parts for older vehicles. Approximately 30% of vehicles were more than twenty years old and for these, practically no suppliers existed outside the country where they had been manufactured.

Diversification of the automobile stock in Chile during the 1960s is reflected in the drop in imports from the United States. In fact in 1967 and 1968 only 70% of parts were U.S. imports.

There was, for the automobile industry, a possibility of finding supplies outside the United States because the models available in Chile were manufactured in several countries. But there was also the possibility that U.S. subsidiaries abroad would not be allowed to sell to Chile (as was the case for Cuba until 1974).

In industries where special equipment was used, the situation was more serious because of the relative importance of U.S. suppliers and the problem of finding alternative suppliers. For example, imports of spare parts by the *Corporación del Cobre* (CODELCO) [Copper Corporation] reached $8 million in 1970, of which 90% came from the United States. Most of the equipment was U.S.-made and much of it was manufactured only in the United States.

In 1970 the National Petroleum Company (ENAP) imported $7 million of spare parts, of which 87% came from the United States. Thus in these two key industries (copper and petroleum), dependence on U.S. suppliers for spare parts was almost absolute.

1.3.5. *Intermediate Goods of Chemical Origin*

In 1970, $97 million worth of this type product was imported into Chile, of which about 36% – worth nearly $35 million – came from the United States.

However, one group of these products was imported from the United States for 75% or more and had a value of $14 million. In this group we find simple, double and triple superphosphates, with a value of $5.5 million, 98% of which came from the United States; and urea, with a value of $2.1 million, all of which was imported from the United States. Other products which came mainly from the United States included silica gel, phosphopentasulphate, butyl alcohol, octanes, vinyl acetate, phosphorites and tetraethyl lead.

If we consider the products of which 50% or more came from the United States, we get a figure of $25 million, which is the level of investment that would have been necessary to build up a one-year stock of those products that come mainly from the United States. Of course there would have been a tendency to concentrate on products for which alternative suppliers could not easily be found. It appears that it would have been possible to find alternative suppliers for most of the intermediate goods for the chemical industry. However, for certain products, particularly certain chemical catalysts used in the mining industry, some time was needed to complete laboratory analyses required to establish whether the new suppliers' products fitted the technical specifications.

In the pharmaceutical industry, the value of imports was approximately $25 million, of which almost $7 million came from the United States. For the U.S. imports, the problem of finding alternative suppliers was closely tied up with the Government's policy *vis-à-vis* U.S. pharmaceutical laboratories in Chile. This is a concrete example of the interdependence of commercial and industrial policy.

1.3.6. *Petroleum*

Imports of crude oil in 1970 accounted for approximately 70% of the total amount of oil refined. Although this oil was not imported from the United States, it was marketed to a significant extent by U.S. companies. Almost 63% of imported petroleum was purchased from U.S. companies (Esso and Gulf); the rest came from European firms, mainly British Petroleum (United Kingdom).

The contracts which took effect in 1970 were valid until 1974. They ensured full supplies for 1972 and partial supplies for 1973 and 1974, which meant, in short, that this was a vulnerable sector.

1.3.7. *Capital Goods*

Analyzing the structure of capital goods is an essential task for two reasons: first, this structure is very closely associated with imports of spare parts, which constituted the most 'critical' link with the United States; second, expansion of productive capacity in certain U.S.-equipped plants and industries was dependent upon the prospects for maintaining supply links with the United States.

In the late 1960s there was a slight drop in the proportion of equipment purchased from the United States. For imports of equipment with an annual value of $500,000 or more, the annual average in 1967-68 and 1969 was about 50%, while in 1970 it dropped to 46%. In 1970, 37% of the equipment imports annually valued at between $100,000 and $500,000 came from the United States.

If we compare these figures with corresponding figures for spare parts, we find that Chile's dependence on U.S. supplies was greater for spare parts than for new equipment, which shows that a larger proportion of the older industrial plant came from the United States.

Another way of probing the industrial infrastructure in terms of its country of origin is to examine the sources of credits for the purchase of equipment over the course of the years. If all credits for which there were debit balances in 1970 are taken together, they amount to $1,428 million. This corresponds approximately to capital goods imports between 1964 and 1970. Of this sum, $692 million, or 49%, was provided by the United States for purchases benefitting the mining and manufacturing industry in approximately equal proportions.

If we analyze capital goods imports in terms of the economic sectors which make use of them, we find that, like intermediate goods, the mining industry exhibits the highest degree of dependence on U.S. suppliers (Table 5.7). Some 53.8% of imported mining equipment came mainly (75% or more) from the United States. Its value in 1970 was $9 million. Equipment for the construction of transportation material 75% or more of which came from the United States accounted for 25% of all imports. Valued at $12.4 million, this represented a higher volume in absolute terms than that for the mining industry.

As it is interesting to analyze, along the same lines, the absorption of capital goods by public sector enterprises, we have examined a group of enterprises in the *Area de Propiedad Social* (APS) [Area of Social Property] in strategic sectors of the economy. In 1972, capital goods imports by these enterprises amounted to $270 million, of which $89 million (33%) came from the United States. This amount is lower than the corresponding figure for the late 1960s but it is still significantly high, particularly as these enterprises were in strategic sectors of the economy. Industries which accounted for the largest amount of imports included fishing (48.5%), steel (69.1%), rubber (83.3%), petroleum (81.2%), electronics (100%) and transportation (43.7%).

Among the key industries which had plans for importing a substantial proportion of their inputs for 1972, the following are worth mentioning: INSA (tyres, 83.3%), ENAP (petroleum, 98.5%), ELECNA (electronics, 100%), CHILECTRA (electricity, 80.6%), National Television Channel (100%) and Channel 13 (90.1%). (These figures were collected in 1971 and indicate these industries' plans for 1972.)

It is possible that in certain cases, the imported goods were meant to complement existing installations of U.S. origin, and thus the importer's freedom of choice was limited. But the tendency to look to U.S. suppliers can also be attributed to technical and bureaucratic inertia on the part of civil servants, and perhaps even to their political orientation. In any case, it was necessary that the Government should make people realize that finding capital goods suppliers in other countries was an important task.

1.4. *The Strategic Character of Trade with the United States*

The preceding analysis demonstrates that the U.S. Government and the private U.S. companies were in a position to inflict serious damage on the Chilean economy. This was not so much due to the volume of trade with Chile as to the strategic character of that trade. The technology, equipment and spare parts used by key export industries, services and supplies all came from the United States. This, combined with the lack of alternative suppliers for the mining industry and the dominant role of U.S. firms in supplying petroleum, made Chile highly vulnerable to U.S. pressure. In fact, very little action on the part of the United States was needed to cause a good deal of damage. It could take any one of a number of specific measures, from tightening up long-term credits, which would have paralyzed expansion in key industries, to quietly instructing U.S. subsidiaries abroad not to sell to Chile.

The economic blockade became more effective as such obstacles as these were increased in number and intensity. At the same time, however, the political costs of the operation were becoming greater at the international level and there was always the danger of provoking an increasingly strong movement in support of the Chilean Government.

Had European or Latin American subsidiaries of U.S. companies indeed been prevented from selling to Chile, the situation would undoubtedly have been more difficult for the Chilean Government but relations between the U.S. Government and the Latin American and European governments would have also suffered. The situation for Chile would have been especially difficult if subsidiaries located in Argentina, Brazil and Mexico had been prevented from selling because, despite ideological differences, the UP Government had good economic and political relations in these countries.

As we shall see later on, the U.S. Government did indeed put pressure on Chile in various ways, but by no means did it pull out all the stops.

2. FOREIGN TRADE POLICY

In this section we shall analyze the impact of the Government's Programme on the external sector and the means that were used to deal with the disequilibria that were generated.

2.1. *The Impact of the Government's Programme on the External Sector*

Two areas will be examined: the first is the transfer of ownership of the means of production in strategic sectors to the 'social area' (APS) of the economy; the second concerns short-term economic policies designed to reactivate a sluggish economy and drastically redistribute income. The external sector felt the impact of the policies adopted in both of these areas.

The following fall into the first area: the nationalization of the copper companies,[5] state ownership of the banks,[6] the creation of a social area (APS) in the industrial sector,[7] and agrarian reforms.[8]

These transformations, and the prospects which they offered for a transition to socialism, alienated Chilean interests in industry, banking, distribution and agriculture; they also alienated foreign interests in the extractive and service industries, U.S. financial interests and the U.S. Government itself. Foreign industrial interests were not directly affected and their reaction was more moderate or, at any rate, more discrete.

The ensuing reactions of external agents had an impact on the Chilean balance of payments; the most obvious reactions were: (1) a flight of short-term capital to the amount of approximately $60 million in the first few months; (2) a complete lack of new direct investment; (3) pressure from the U.S. State Department on the members of the Club of Paris to avoid renegotiating Chile's external debt and to make that renegotiation conditional upon an agreement with the copper companies; (4) the refusal by the Export-Import Bank (Eximbank) in July 1971 to grant a loan for purchasing aircraft; (5) the State Department's instruction of U.S. representatives at the Inter-American Development Bank (IDB) and the World Bank to reject loan applications from countries that nationalize property without compensation; (6) statements by President Richard M. Nixon, Secretary of State William Rogers and other officials to the effect that expropriations without compensation would affect the level of aid to underdeveloped countries, constituting a threat which did not apply only to Chile; (7) legal action by the Braden Copper Company against CODELCO, which in 1972 resulted in the freezing of the deposits which the main Chilean state agencies had made in U.S. accounts; and later, throughout 1973, efforts by Braden to set up embargoes against Chile in various European countries; (8) legal action by Anaconda against CODELCO and the *Corporación de Fomento de la Producción* (CORFO) [Corporation for Production Development] affecting those spare parts and other goods which had been ordered by CODELCO but were still in the shippers' hands; (9) reduction of export loans from U.S. banks as follows:[9] November 1970, $220 million; November 1971, $88 million; January 1972, $36 million; and December 1972, $32 million. (10) Lastly, the refusal by the World Bank, during the entire period of UP Government, to award Chile a single loan, despite the fact that projects meeting the current criteria of profitability and efficiency were submitted.

Suspension of short-term credits led to a drop in current imports; this caused economic activity in certain specific areas to slow down. As a result there was some black market speculative activity, particularly in spare parts. There were also supply problems, and whenever these affected widely used inputs or spare parts they tended to disrupt the productive process.

It was possible to compensate for the lack of short-term credit as long as foreign reserves were sufficient, but that was the case for only eighteen months. Moreover, the drop in foreign reserves damaged Chile's financial reputation abroad and this was used to make Chile's search for new sources of financing even more complicated.

The unwillingness of the U.S. Government's financial agencies and of multilateral organizations such as the IDB and the World Bank to extend long-term credits had an effect on purchasing equipment for maintaining and expanding the productive apparatus. As mentioned earlier, large sections of the industrial machinery stock came from the United States. Certain types of equipment, particularly spare parts, had to be brought to Chile in one way or another; on many occasions they had to be paid for in cash from the reserves. This was the case particularly in the copper mining industry and in petroleum; it contributed to the drop in reserves and this drop was subsequently used by the international financing agencies to justify rejection of Chilean loan applications.

In addition to the difficulties caused by the problems with spare parts, there were also political problems associated with the climate of uncertainty surrounding prospects for expanding the economy's strategic sectors. This was especially true for key public enterprises and the affects it had were cleverly and systematically used by the opposition to paint a very pessimistic picture of the future (rationing of electricity and other fuels, etc.).

The flight of short-term capital, lack of new direct investment, and problems in renegotiating the external debt all contributed to the liquidity problem that developed when external financing was suspended.

So far we have only discussed the obstacles that emerged as a result of measures related to the structural transformation process described in the Government Programme. We must add to these obstacles those which emerged as a consequence of short-term economic policies. Measures designed to reactivate the economy and to redistribute income affected the external sector insofar as they led to increased imports – particularly food imports – and to a reduction in industrial and agricultural surpluses available for export. These problems, combined with the traditionally slow growth rate of the agricultural sector (which was simultaneously being disrupted by agrarian reform), contributed to a substantial increase in the trade deficit.

Besides the factors mentioned above, all of which are associated with implementing the Government's Programme, other difficulties must be kept in mind, such as the drop in copper prices and the rise in the prices of such imported goods as cereals, petroleum and its derivatives, meat and raw materials of chemical origin.

To summarize, in addition to the factors that have traditionally led to deficits in the Chilean economy, three types of problems contributed to a significant deterioration in Chile's balance of payments: reprisals on the part of interests affected by the structural transformation, repercussions of short-term economic policy decisions and (adverse) cyclical factors affecting the national economy (the drop in copper prices and the rise in import prices).

This situation led to shortages of certain goods. It also gave support to certain external forces that were trying to slow down or distort the Programme's application. At the same time the deterioration of the external situation was used as an argument to discourage other market economy countries, notably Japan and the Western European countries, from expanding their trade with Chile.

Notwithstanding the normal interdependence between internal and external factors and the complex behavioural interaction of the various agents, there is little doubt that it was the structural transformation process – and more specifically the reaction of powerful interests both inside and outside the country – which most fully accounts for the mutual reinforcement of internal and external obstacles. Cyclical factors, such as the drop in copper prices and the rise in the price of imports, were not new to Chile, but they had always been resolved through external financing. The consequences of redistributive and reflationary policies could also have been neutralized in the traditional manner since there were also precedents – more modest ones to be sure – in that area.

What set off that sequence of reactions was the Government's intention to transform a 'style of development' which had prevailed for many years and in which minorities within the country, in collusion with powerful outside interests, had been the main beneficiaries. What made the issue even more serious from the U.S. viewpoint was the fact that, had the Chilean Government became consolidated, it might have caused a shift in the correlation of forces at the international level.

So far, we have not touched on the Government's foreign trade policy, and it would be absurd to claim that it was unrelated to the events that have already been briefly described. Thus we shall analyze the principal measures taken by the Government in the area of foreign trade.

2.2. *Foreign Trade Policy*

Until 1970 foreign trade activities were essentially private and decentralized. A large proportion of exports were generated by foreign firms, while imports were brought in largely by private or public enterprises on the basis of microeconomic criteria. Short-term financing came largely from private banks while long-term financing was negotiated by public and private enterprises with the state acting as guarantor. Adequate external financing was always available to resolve deficit problems because the model which Chile adhered to at that time was regarded as 'respectable' by international financing agencies.

With the nationalization of the large, foreign-owned copper mines, and of the iron and saltpetre industries, most of Chile's exports came under state control. A similar process took place on the import side as leading industrial enterprises which were major importers were transferred over to the social area (APS). These two developments, coupled with the external constraints that have already been described, led the Government to reconsider its entire commercial policy. This meant, in the first place, a centralization of foreign trade policy both in terms of its formulation and its operation. It was hoped that foreign trade policy would thus become an instrument of general economic policy, that it would support and strengthen Chile's overall foreign policy and help the country face the challenges from outside. More specifically the idea was to: (1) guarantee supplies of inputs, equipment and food in keeping with the needs and priorities established by domestic economic policies; (2) increase the level of Chilean exports so as to bring in as much foreign exchange as possible, in addition to meeting domestic demand; (3) re-direct commercial ties on a regional basis so as to avoid predictable obstacles and ensure stable supplies and deliveries; (4) reconstruct the system of short- and long-term financing on the basis of a regional structure that would be congruent with foreseeable levels of commercial flows; (5) renegotiate the external debt; (6) encourage import substitution in certain strategic sectors; (7) ensure that constraints emanating from the external sector be taken into account in the formulation of general economic policy.

We now have a clearer appreciation of the importance of external constraints than we had in early 1971, when there was still an adequate amount of international reserves and forecasts for copper prices, and when production levels led to the belief that the external sector would not constitute a decisive constraint. Moreover at that time it was felt that, as was the case in the industrial sector where there was spare capacity to be used, the external sector constituted a reserve which would provide support for short-term economic policies that were designed to reactivate the economy and consolidate political support for the Government.

This unfounded optimism was based on several factors. The first was that the nationalization of copper was being carried out through a strictly constitutional procedure which had the unanimous support of all the political parties; second, the problems arising from a reorientation of external trade had been underestimated; and third, prospects for obtaining financial support and technological assistance from the socialist countries were viewed in what can now be seen as a too optimistic vein.

It is impossible to say which of these factors weighed most heavily, but the truth is that during the first year of UP Government, the external sector was not seen as a constraint. On the contrary, the general feeling was that it could provide some space for manoeuvring to compensate for the effects of domestic economic policies. There are clear indications of this feeling in the fact that the Government waited a full year before requesting renegotiation of the external debt and in that the task of centralizing the formulation and execution of foreign trade policy was given low priority.

At the end of 1971 it was becoming obvious that, far from providing a margin for manoeuvre, the external sector imposed an additional constraint. It was at that point that the Government began to take measures designed to neutralize this new type of constraint. The principal measures taken by the Government are described below.[10]

2.2.1. *The Creation of SEREX*

The Government set up the *Secretaría Ejecutiva de Relaciones Económicas Externas* [The Executive Secretariat for External Economic Relations] (in effect the Foreign Trade Department of the Central Bank), known as SEREX, to be responsible for formulating and carrying out the Government's foreign trade policy. The reasons for doing this should be understood in relation to three features of the UP Government.

First, because of legal and political difficulties, the Government was prevented from restructuring state institutions to fit the requirements of its Programme. Had the Government attempted to set up a Ministry of Foreign Trade, for example, it would have had to submit a bill to that effect to the National Congress and there was no chance that such legislation would have been passed. Thus the new foreign trade functions had to be assigned to an organization that could fit into the existing institutional framework; some functions of the Central Bank were transferred to SEREX and the Bank's infrastructure was used to carry them out. At the same time, SEREX was placed under the jurisdiction of the Ministry of Foreign Affairs. To all appearances a group of Central Bank employees were still carrying out duties that were in the Bank's area of jurisdiction but they were doing so under the authority of the Minister responsible for the country's external relations. It was hoped that in this way, coherency within the Government's foreign policy could be guaranteed, so as to ensure that the new organization would be able to operate effectively and, at the same time, to give it a substantial amount of independence *vis-à-vis* both the Central Bank and the Ministry of Foreign Affairs. The technical personnel and the authorities of these two fairly traditional institutions were not particularly committed to the objectives of the UP Government. As the political conflict sharpened throughout the country it became increasingly clear that this *sui generis* organization was meeting resistance from the institutions with which it maintained organizational links.

The second feature has to do with the UP's make-up and manner of operation. Each time a new institution was set up, levels of authority had to be defined and assigned to individual appointees. At this stage – and also later on when the organization was operating in a normal way – it was often difficult to arrive at a distribution of responsibilities which satisfied all of the political groups that made up the UP coalition. The formation of the coalition had clearly been an important factor in the electoral victory of September 1970, and it gave rise to the broad vision which is implicit in the Programme. But there is no doubt that it had a negative effect on decision-making and on the efficiency of Government operations.

The third feature, which is closely linked to the second one, has to do with the poor performance in managing the Government's economic policy. There is no doubt that this created numerous problems in the general area of economic management and it explains in part why global planning was weak and why, as a consequence, formulating a foreign trade policy was so difficult. In the absence of a national plan, and even of clearly defined sectoral development plans, programming the external sector was anything but smooth sailing. Nevertheless, as it became obvious that the external sector was becoming rigidly constrictive, the Government began to feel the need to approach the task of managing that sector in a systematic manner. This explains the Economic Committee of Ministers' decision to the effect that a disaggregated foreign exchange budget should be worked out and that SEREX should be given the responsibility for this task.

2.2.2. *Setting Up a Foreign Exchange Budget*

At the beginning of 1972 foreign exchange budgets and external trade programmes (which emphasized the need to allocate foreign exchange for import purposes) were worked out. The aim was to distribute available foreign exchange to various sectors and firms in accordance with stated priorities. Moreover, these budgets and programmes could be used in negotiations with other countries. The availability of centralized information on Chilean export products and import requirements greatly strengthened the country's position in international negotiations. This was particularly important because the Government was also trying to diversify its international trade and, among other things, expand its trade relations which the socialist countries.

It is interesting to note that in spite of its obvious technical deficiencies, this approach to external sector programming helped to initiate a process of partial planning which made reorganized participation by personnel and by administrators at all levels possible. Since the availability of foreign exchange was a well-defined constraint on imports, it came to be regarded as an objective indicator in formulating the various sectoral production and distribution programmes. When the time came to work out the 1973 foreign trade programme there was an attempt to elicit the participation – and thus the commitment – of the personnel, particularly those working in industrial plants in the APS. A tentative sectoral allocation plan, which discussed basic options for levels of food and industrial imports, was submitted to the Economic Committee of Ministers on the basis of global forecasts. This plan included a trade-off between food consumption, for which a significant proportion of the supply was imported, and industrial production, which relied heavily on imported inputs: more of one inevitably meant less of the other. Once this preliminary allocation was made, the sectoral institutions disaggregated their share in order to set tentative targets at the level of production units. These targets were then used as reference points to work out production programmes; thereafter discussions were held regarding additional sectoral allocations and, subsequently, global allocations. The latter were then submitted to the Economic Committee of Ministers and the resulting 'definitive programme' was used to control the allocation of foreign currency and the issue of import licences.

In spite of the obvious technical deficiencies of such a scheme, and of some questionable choices with respect to importation of certain consumer items (particularly meat), this method of working out foreign trade priorities demonstrates the enormous potential of worker participation and commitment at the plant level: it also provides a glimpse at the kinds of results that could have been achieved if participation had occurred in a continuous and systematic manner. To achieve this objective, there obviously has to be a sense of direction in both the economic and the political spheres so that popular participation in Government management can be stimulated and guided. Enthusiasm for and commitment to participation are no substitute for the lack of a sense of direction.

To give substance to these programmes and open the way for concrete foreign trade operations, it became necessary to set up operational units to take charge of imports and exports on a sectoral basis. The *Empresas de Comercio Exterior* [Foreign Trade Agencies] were set up for this purpose.

2.2.3. *The Foreign Trade Agencies*

The idea was to either create or reinforce sectoral agencies with the capacity to carry out foreign trade operations within a given sector. This would have several beneficial effects, including strengthening Chile's bargaining position *vis-à-vis* the rest of the world, encouraging the process of commercial and financial programming, facilitating the regional restructuring of external trade and at the same time ensuring that in each sector the technical personnel would cooperate closely with specialists in international commerce in solving the purely commercial aspects.

The approach was a flexible one in the sense that in certain sectors external trade was taken over by one or more leading producers (for instance, Pacific Steel Company (CAP) in the case of petroleum and its derivatives); in certain other sectors specialized agencies were created, such as ECETEX for textiles and leather and ENARA for automobile parts; in still other sectors, existing agencies that were already involved in national or international commercial operations were strengthened, as was the case with the *Empresa de Comercio Agricola* (ECA) [Agricultural Trade Agency].

All of these agencies maintained links with sectoral organizations which had final authority (CORFO) as well as with SEREX. CORFO emphasized the need to obtain the quantity of supplies which it considered was necessary, while on the other hand SEREX and the Central Bank stressed the need to keep within the 'maximum' levels of available foreign exchange. The more they consulted with each other, the more the level of activity in both groups of institutions tended to increase.

There was also an attempt to centralize export operations by transferring them to a small number of specialized agencies. Because of the structure of Chilean exports, this was a much easier task than centralizing import operations. CODELCO handled the exports of the large mining companies while the National Mining Company (ENAMI) dealt with those of the smaller ones. The Chilean Mining and Chemical Company (SOQUIMICH), which was set up when nitrate production was nationalized, took care of nitrate exports. When the iron mines were nationalized, responsibility for exporting iron was handed over to the Pacific Steel Company (CAP). Together these four enterprises were responsible for 90% of the country's exports. The Government set up a new foreign trade agency, SOCORA, for exporting agricultural products; this agency worked together with private firms to bring Chilean agricultural products to the world market.

On the whole, creating a small number of agencies which were specialized in foreign trade and linked together through a foreign trade programme indeed helped to achieve the initial objectives of strengthening Chile's bargaining power, reorienting commercial flows on a regional basis and increasing the prospects of obtaining external finance.

The last objective was an essential one from the viewpoint of carrying out the Government's foreign trade policy; for this reason it was decided that responsibility for obtaining and channelling external financing should be centralized by handing it over to the Central Bank.

2.2.4. *Centralizing External Financing in the Central Bank*

Short-term financing had previously been handled by commercial banks; thus it had been controlled by the various industrial, agricultural and commercial groups that were linked with these specific banks. The decision to centralize short-term financing in the Central Bank was taken for several reasons, including the need to: (1) re-direct productive activities; (2) cope with the effects of the discontinuation of credits lines available formerly; (3) reorganize the entire system of financing; and (4) ensure that the financing system should operate in accordance with national priorities.

Long-term credits designed to finance expansion in large public and private enterprises were usually negotiated and used by the individual firms with the state serving as guarantor. Here again, for reasons similar to those discussed above in relation to short-term financing, it was decided that all aspects of long-term financing activities should be centralized in the Central Bank, including such activities as the search for new credits, negotiations with creditors and allocation of funds.

Another reason for centralizing external financing in the Central Bank was the need to renegotiate the external debt, which required full information on and strict control of external financing agreements and of the way in which external credits were used.

When external financing from multilateral sources and from U.S. Government agencies (the Export-Import Bank (Eximbank) and the Agency for International Development (AID)), was cut off, Chile had to turn to suppliers of capital in other market economy countries, and to the governments of socialist countries, for new credits. In cases of the first type, approval by the insuring agencies of the governments concerned was always required. In the case of Europe and Japan, attempts to obtain external financing were tied up with problems of external debt renegotiation and with U.S. pressure on this question. Consequently, such attempts were really negotiations of a political character that had more to do with foreign policy than with economics. The same applied to relations with socialist countries, though of course for different reasons.

As financing was connected with buying equipment which had to be acquired in the country providing the credit, the problem was to ensure that the equipment available in that country had the specific technological features required by Chilean plants. Freedom to acquire other capital goods and technology from new suppliers was limited by a number of factors, including the level of diversification and industrial development, the predominance of equipment manufactured in the United States, the type of professional training the technical personnel had received and their widely differing degrees of commitment to the Government's policies. The commitment factor applied especially in the large public sector enterprises where middle-level technical personnel, most of whom had many years' experience with the enterprise, had a great deal of direct and indirect influence on how the plants were run. Whenever it became necessary to make a technical evaluation of the various options that were open to the management of a given plant, the task required such a high degree of specialized knowledge that it was necessary for technical personnel to play a key role in preparing decisions.

However, in the course of the three years of UP Government the technical personnel's attitude clearly changed. This seemed to confirm the point that initial attitudes had been based on prejudice which tended to disappear through direct contact with and the experience of the new Government.

Other Latin American countries – particularly Mexico, Argentina and Brazil, with whom the UP Government developed much closer commercial and financial relations than previous governments had done – played an important role in reorganizing short- and long-term financing. This situation, which would have been difficult to forecast in 1970, was achieved in large measure through foreign policy measures. Not only did the Government's foreign policy succeed in avoiding the international isolation which certain outside forces were trying to impose, but it also elicited the interest and support of Latin American governments and Latin American public opinion despite substantial differences in domestic policies.

In Europe, very useful links were established with private banks and with some governments. The European banks' interest was stirred by the prospects of taking the place of U.S. private banks in a country that could play an important role in the Andean Pact (Chile's relations with this subregional body had always been excellent). On the other hand, pressure from the United States and from the more conservative political groups was directed mainly toward the Finance Ministers of European countries who had jurisdiction over the insuring agencies whose approval was required to extend long-term credits.

The merits of Chile's foreign policy also became apparent with the development of excellent relations with Spain and the Scandinavian countries. Moreover, various European governments extended political support in various international forums and through statements supporting the Chilean position at meetings of the Club of Paris, for the persons responsible for the financial decisions taken at those meetings were mainly the Finance Ministers.

Thus, generally speaking, the Government's policy on short-term financing problems was successful. By early 1973 a financing scheme of the same order of magnitude as that which had existed in 1970 had been established. The absence of credits from U.S. sources had been compensated by new sources of finance coming from Latin America, Europe and the socialist countries. Some of the credits were obtained by linking them with Chilean copper sales; others were associated with the creditor countries' desire to develop new commercial links with Chile, as was particularly the case with some Latin American countries. With respect to current imports, short-term financing facilities were reasonably satisfactory in 1973, both in terms of the volume of credits and of the policies of creditor countries involved.

The situation regarding long-term credits for purchasing equipment was much less favourable. There was far less scope for finding alternative suppliers than there was in current imports (food and raw materials). Credits had to be obtained from countries where equipment with the right specifications, as worked out by the user plants' technical personnel, could be obtained. Normally this meant that there would be only a limited number of potential suppliers. What in fact happened was that credits from socialist countries were obtained for purchasing machinery and equipment in larger quantities than could be absorbed on the short term. As we said earlier, it takes a certain amount of time to make the switch from one source of technological supplies to another, and the process requires re-training technical personnel and even changes in political attitudes at various levels of bureaucracy. The problem may not be so serious for countries in a very early stage of industrialization, for in such cases it is not so much a question of switching from one source of technology to another as one of launching an industrialization programme on the basis of a technology acquired in countries other than those which have formerly supplied most of the imported consumer goods.

The long-term credits obtained from Latin American countries were used basically to purchase transport equipment since this was a relatively developed sector, mainly because of the activities of subsidiaries of transnational companies. A large proportion of the other capital goods which the economy required had to be acquired in Western European countries and in Japan, as access to U.S. suppliers was closed. Credits were made available by these countries but not in sufficient amounts. This applies particularly to Japan, for of all the developed capitalist countries other than the United States, Japan took the hardest line *vis-à-vis* the UP Government.[11]

Despite the fact that relations with socialist countries were extremely good, capital goods imported from those countries in 1973 still only accounted for a modest 15% of such imports.

Because of the importance of Chile's relations with Western Europe, the need to link copper sales with external financing, and the usefulness of having direct and permanent contracts with private European banks, it was decided in mid-1973 that a permanent mission of the Central Bank of Chile should be established in Western Europe with headquarters in London. The mission was expected to also take part in renegotiating the external debt and coordinating the work of the Chilean foreign trade agencies operating in Europe. The fact that such a mission was set up shows that the management of external financing had become well organized by then, that there was some coordination in dealing with commercial and financial questions, and that after two-and-a-half years the Government had made significant advances in its attempt to neutralize the invisible blockade. It must be re-emphasized that until 1970, the state's role in international and economic relations was very discrete and passive, and that most officials dealing in this area had been trained in that sort of work climate. Consequently the technical personnel working in this sector for the new Government had very little experience in taking a more active role.[12]

2.3. *Some Results of the Foreign Trade Policy*

The problems of Chilean foreign trade during the 1970-73 period was only partly the result of the policies discussed above. What it basically reflected was the Government's overall economic policy combined with a series of factors over which the Government had no control. In the following section we shall examine only those dimensions of the problem that are directly associated with the policies just discussed. More specifically, we shall examine the changes that have taken place in the following areas: participation of the social areas (APS) in foreign trade, centralization of operations into a few agencies and the regional structure of commercial flows.

2.3.1. *Participation of the APS in Organizing Foreign Trade*

The increasing share of the APS in foreign trade was due to a combination of the following factors: (1) the transfer of private firms to the APS; (2) the trend towards APS firms assuming responsibility for foreign trade operations previously carried out by private sector firms; (3) the fact that APS firms demonstrated greater dynamism than private firms in carrying out foreign trade operations. This situation also had to do with the difference between the types of products handled by the APS and those handled by private firms. Obviously these factors weighed more heavily in some sectors than in others, but nevertheless it may be useful to examine the situation for 1973, which was the last year of UP Government. If we classify imports according to the level of the share of the APS (Table 5.8) we find that 76% of current imports correspond to products for which the APS share was higher than two thirds, while 8% of imports went to the *Area de Propiedad Mixta* (APM) [Area of Mixed Property] and 16% to the private sector (also called the *Area de Propiedad Privada* (APP) [Area of Private Property].

We also find (Table 5.9) that practically 100% of imports for the agricultural and foodstuff sector were made by the APS. Imports which went to the private sector were concentrated in certain areas of the manufacturing industry (mainly paints, pharmaceuticals, cosmetics, plastics, construction materials, rubber, leather and footwear). Imports by firms in the APM were for the food and automobile industries. The APS was predominant in textiles, mechanical engineering, electricity and certain subsectors of the automobile industry.

As for exports, the level of the APS share was large because the major exporting firms had been transferred to the APS; the mining sector (copper, iron, nitrate), in which the APS share was very large, accounted for approximately 85% of exports (see Table 5.10).

According to the export programme planned for 1973, the APS was to account for 93% of all exports. Comparing the level the share of the social, mixed and private sectors, we find that 85% of the value of exports corresponded to products coming mainly (two thirds or more) from the APS, while 15% corresponded to products coming mainly from the APM. There were no export products came mainly (two thirds or more) from the private sector.

Breaking down the figures by economic sector, we find that in the 'agriculture, livestock and fisheries' sector, the APS exported mainly forestry products and fish, the APM mainly agricultural products, and the APP mainly livestock.

In the industrial sector, APS firms were heavily involved in the production of timber, transport equipment, metal products, machinery and electrical goods, with the rest of the sector remaining in the hands of the APM and APP.

In summary, therefore, a decisive part of Chilean imports and exports were channelled through APS firms. Because of this, it became possible to work out a more sophisticated foreign trade programme and, what is more important, Chile's bargaining power abroad was strengthened as far as two major issues were concerned: linking increases in imports to rising demands for Chilean products and using trade expansion as an incentive for obtaining financing.

2.3.2. *Foreign Trade Agencies*

The high level of the APS share in foreign trade operations did not necessarily indicate a greater capacity for international management, and a need was felt for agencies specialized in carrying out foreign trade. These agencies would have to develop a programming function, look for markets, and negotiate and administer financial transactions with some degree of autonomy, while at the same time keeping within the parameters established by the overall foreign trade programme.

It may be useful to examine the relative importance of these foreign trade agencies during 1973.

As Table 5.11 shows, the ten largest firms absorbed 68% of imports; all these firms were in the APS. Some of them were foreign trade agencies (ECA, ECETEX, the Fertilizer Department of the State Bank and ENARA); others were APS firms involved in production and occupying a dominant position in their own sector, and to which the Government had given the responsibility of centralizing imports and exports in their respective sectors. Such was the case for ENAP (petroleum and derivatives), CAP (mechanical engineering) and INSA (tyres). As to copper, CODELCO had almost achieved the centralization of all imports for that industry.

The main private sector importers are listed in Table 5.11; they are firms in the automobile, paper and cardboard, and detergent (Indus-Lever) sectors.

It is interesting to note that most imports, and mainly those of a 'strategic' nature, were administered by ten APS firms, including some specialized foreign trade agencies and a number of leading productive enterprises with special units to handle foreign trade.

For obvious reasons, the degree of concentration is higher on the export side. According to the plans for 1973, the ten largest export firms were to account for 91% of all exports. The highest degree of concentration was in the mining sector, where the three biggest exporters accounted for 83% of the total. This contrasts with the dispersed origin of industrial and agricultural exports: in the industrial sector, the three largest exporting firms accounted for only 4% of exported manufactured goods; in agriculture, livestock and fisheries sector the corresponding figure was 3.1%.

The high degree of concentration in export activities can be fully appreciated when we realize that the ten most important export products accounted for 92% of total exports (mining, 87%; industrial products, 5%).

Among all the attempts to develop an international marketing capacity for Chilean products, efforts in the area of copper marketing stand out. Having begun with a situation in which marketing copper was controlled entirely by foreign companies, it was found that it was possible to develop an international marketing capacity using only Chilean technicians and specialists. The international copper market's complexity, the obstacles raised by the copper companies and the positive results of Chilean Government efforts in this area, all lend little credence to the argument – often put forward by foreign companies – that less developed countries are in no position to handle the international marketing of their export products. From its headquarters in Santiago or through its main branch office in London, CODELCO achieved many positive results not only in marketing copper but also in negotiating both imports of basic supplies and external financing. Moreover, CODELCO helped develop plans for increasing the production and export of products manufactured from copper.

The activities of the foreign trade agencies were coordinated within the framework of the foreign trade programme. Participation in bilateral and regional international negotiations was not restricted to the commercial and financial organizations but involved the foreign trade agencies as well.

Taken as a whole, the substantial achievements in foreign trade can be seen to have contributed to greater efficiency in implementing policies and carrying out foreign trade operations.

2.3.3. *Changes in the Regional Structure of Foreign Trade*

Because of the external constraints that have already been discussed, and in the attempt to come to grips with problems originating outside Chile, one of the objectives of the foreign trade policy was to alter the regional structure of Chile's foreign trade. This objective was decided upon in order to cope with the problems that developed with traditional markets and suppliers. It was not a question of shifting commercial flows for reasons of principle but rather one of reacting to very real problems mainly arising *vis-à-vis* the United States.

The foreign trade programmes and a limited number of foreign trade agencies were set up to effect this policy. Let us now examine the regional structure of Chile's foreign trade and the changes that the policy had introduced by the end of the period of UP Government.

On the whole the changes were not very drastic. The United States share dropped and there was a rise in the shares of the Latin American and, to a lesser extent, European and socialist countries. The share of the latter group was still less than 15% after three years of UP Government.

In terms of the volume of imports, the three largest suppliers were Argentina, the United States and Australia. Argentina was by far the largest supplier, exporting agricultural products (meat, leather, wool, industrial fodder etc.) and transport equipment (automobiles, trucks and buses). The United States supplied basic industrial inputs (mainly chemical products and spare parts) and Australia exported cereals. Table 5.12 shows the relative share of Chilean imports provided by the three largest suppliers, according to type of product. It may be noted that the socialist countries are not usually among the three largest suppliers. The Soviet Union and Romania are listed in Table 5.12 under 2.2 'Transport Equipment' because large numbers of trucks and tractors were imported from these countries in 1972. As to the edibles listed in Table 5.12 under 3.2.1, Cuba was mainly an exporter of sugar, Poland provided mainly vegetable oils, and Argentina, as one of Chile's main trading partners, supplied a wide range of products.

The close economic ties with Argentina, Brazil and the rest of Latin America show clearly that Chilean foreign policy was successful not only in avoiding isolation from its Latin American neighbours, but also in actually strengthening ties within the region.

The regional structure of imports is clarified by looking at products that accounted for the largest volume. Table 5.13 gives figures for the ten most important imported products, which together accounted for 44% of total imports. Major suppliers are indicated for each product. We see that except for petroleum and cotton, all imports were in the foodstuff sector. This brings out the fact that the Government's income redistribution policy had a very strong impact on the external sector, and that an attempt was made to avoid shortages at all costs.

The situation regarding petroleum imports was uncertain because of the U.S. companies' and Government's ability to put pressure on Chile's two largest suppliers, Iran and Saudi Arabia.

Let us now examine the relations with the United States in as much detail as possible. Looking at the imported products of which the United States was an important supplier, and comparing the 1973 figures with those for 1971 and 1972, we get the following results, as shown in Table 5.14: the U.S. share in supplying consumer goods dropped from 21.4% in 1971 to 10.8% in 1972 and to 5% during the first half of 1973. The U.S. share in supplying intermediate goods remained steady at about 33%, though the figure for the first half of 1973 is less than 20%. The U.S. share in capital goods decreased from 27.1% in 1971 to 14.3% in 1972 and to 6% during the first half of 1973.

Mere quantitative analysis of this decreasing U.S. share in Chilean imports does not quite reflect the problems that emerged as a result of shortages of certain items, especially certain types of chemical catalysts for the mining industry which were indispensable even though the quantities required were not large.

What the figures do reflect is that the reduction in the flow of supplies from the United States was progressive, so that no one realized the magnitude of the problem. Obviously supplies could have been much more drastically reduced and the damage to Chile's economy could have been much greater, but such a course of action would have produced adverse political reactions which the U.S. Government wanted to avoid.

The regional structure of Chilean exports was determined fundamentally by the copper market. Even prior to 1970, the main consumers of Chilean copper were Europe (particularly the Federal Republic of Germany and the United Kingdom) and Japan. These three countries together absorbed approximately half of Chile's total copper exports. During the period of UP Government the U.S. share in Chilean exports dropped from 14% in 1970 to 11% in 1971, 8% in 1972 and around 5% during the first half of 1973.

Thus for imports Chile's major trading partners were the Latin American and Western European countries. This did not change during the three years of UP Government. For imports, on the other hand, there was a shift away from the United States and towards Latin America and Western Europe.

The percentage variations shown above do not reflect the full extent of the difficulties that emerged during the process of modifying the structure of external trade. This was especially the case for copper because of the problems involved in establishing the nationalized copper companies' trade system and in simultaneously finding new sources of imported goods and external financing. However, on the whole, we can say that the shift in the regional structure of external trade was carried out reasonably efficiently.

3. SOME CONSIDERATIONS ON THE ECONOMIC BLOCKADE DURING THE 1970-73 PERIOD

Several of the chapters in this volume refer to the mechanics and economic consequences of the economic blockade. In this section we shall try to provide a frame of reference as an aid in understanding the scope of U.S. economic pressures on Chile. These pressures must be seen in the context of the overall policy of the United States *vis-à-vis* the UP Government. Thus in this section our objective is to identify both the motives for this policy and the means that were used to carry it out.

In the light of information made public since the *coup d'état* in 1973 and of events in Latin America, Asia, Africa, Europe and the United States, it seems clear that the central objective which U.S. policy toward Chile was meant to achieve was in the area of 'national security'.[13] The idea was to prevent left-wing forces from coming to power, regardless of the means such forces might employ to try to gain power. If left-wing groups did manage to form a Government despite the pressures against them, an attempt would be made to provoke their downfall or, at the very least, to ensure that their progress towards their aims was either distorted or thwarted.

The 'logic' behind this policy is this: the presence of left-wing elements in a 'western' country's government can cause a shift in the international balance of power in favour of the socialist world which (according to the United States) must be avoided at all costs.

The Chilean experience shows quite clearly that the goal of preventing a left-wing victory was formulated as soon as it became clear that the Chilean left might be in a position to win an election.[14]

After the UP won the September 1970 election there were a series of manoeuvres designed to prevent the President-elect from being appointed by a joint sitting of the two houses of the National Congress. Shortly before the scheduled date of appointment, the Commander-in-Chief of the Army was assassinated. Attempts to prevent the UP from exercising the power it had gained in a democratic manner had thus begun even before the President-elect took office.

The fact that their manoeuvres had failed did not discourage the anti-UP forces; it simply led them to devise new ways of preventing a Government – whose legal claim to power was completely well-founded – from carrying out its Programme.

A number of features in the course of events in Chile – including the way power was distributed, the choice for the electoral method and the country's democratic tradition – all combined to elicit a great deal of international interest in what was happening in the country. If the UP Government were successful a precedent might be created that could have a powerful impact on other countries in Latin America and in Europe.

On the other hand, there was also the fact that the United States' natural allies in Chile clamoured for U.S. help to prevent the left from gaining power and consolidating itself. Although this factor was not as influential as the ones already discussed, it had some importance insofar as Chile was a test of U.S. willingness to stand behind its natural allies in Latin America and in the rest of the world.

While these political motives seem to have been paramount, they were reinforced by a number of economic considerations which applied specifically to Chile.

1. Chile's importance as a copper exporting country, coupled with U.S. involvement in that sector, meant that a strong left-wing presence in the Government would have important implications – first because nationalizing copper could hurt the companies financially and second because control of the Chilean copper industry by a government that would act independently from the United States threatened long-term U.S. economic interests.

Added to this was the fact that nationalization was to be achieved by means of a completely legitimate constitutional procedure and that the companies' 'excess profits' over the past years were to be taken into account in calculating compensation – a precedent that had international implications.

In this context, it seems clear that even an agreement on the amount of compensation would not, in itself, have solved the copper problem. There was far more to it than the question of the economic losses suffered by the companies. This is not to say that other approaches to the compensation question might not eventually have had some influence on the companies' attitudes. What we are saying is that in this case, the companies' local and particular interest was only one dimension of a situation that had far-reaching implications.

2. The transnational copper companies' interests coincided with those of other transnational companies that dominated the industrial sector and were heavily involved in commerce, banking and insurance. Yet on the whole, the behaviour of these other transnationals differed from that of the transnationals involved in the extractive sector. This is because, in the first place, the extractive companies' investments are concentrated in a small number of countries (those with the right kind of natural resources) and consequently nationalizing a single subsidiary tends to affect a high percentage of their assets and profits.[15] For the other types of transnationals, though the major market is the United States, the rest of the foreign market is usually spread over a large number of countries. Thus Ford, for example, regarded its Chilean operations as almost insignificant whereas Anaconda's investments in Chile accounted for a substantial proportion of its total investments. Another point which helps to explain the difference in the behaviour of the two types of transnationals is the fact that the extractive companies have become more fully aware of the widespread desire among Third World countries to re-appropriate and make use of their own natural resources; it becomes vitally important to these companies that governments likely to accelerate this process of regaining control of natural resources should not succeed. Lastly, transnational companies with industrial interests seem – formally, at least – to be contributing to the industrialization effort, which is a key objective for Third World countries.

To summarize, the conflict between the host countries and the transnationals active in the manufacturing sector is much less intense than that which pits the Third World against the extractive transnationals because the former have the advantages associated with greater diversification in investments and the fact that their activities do not appear to run counter to the host country's national interests.

None of this suggests that transnationals involved in manufacturing, commerce or finance might either support or be indifferent to the processes of social transformation, as was also demonstrated by International Telephone and Telegraph.[16] It simply means that they tend to react differently from the extractive transnationals whenever such processes take place.

It is important to study the behaviour of the transnationals in the manufacturing sector very carefully because the Chilean experience might seem to indicate that the Allende Government had successfully neutralized them by capitalizing on the conflicts of interest between U.S., European and Japanese firms and by replacing the first by the other two.

Since the lessons taught by the Chilean experience must be of benefit to other countries, it is essential to understand the structural tendencies which govern the behaviour of industrial transnationals. We shall now discuss the type of behaviour that can be expected whenever these transnationals are faced with prospects of social transformation. On the whole, it would seem that they oppose such transformation.

In the first place, their leadership role is certain to be affected by the 'national programme' which the left might try to carry out. Since it is this very leadership role which guarantees that the prevailing model will fit their interests, any attempt to question this role becomes a matter of deep concern.

Second, whatever the objectives which government might put forward for the initial period of transition, there will always be a well-founded fear that events will unfold in such a way as to jeopardize the transnational companies' interests within the host country.

Third, the way in which transnationals evaluate developments in a particular country will be influenced by the nature of their interests in other developing countries, either in the same region or in the rest of the Third World. In other words, the companies must not only take into account the threat to their interests within the given country, but they must also weigh the consequences of setting undesirable precedents.

Transnationals play a leading role in the international capitalist system and thus they have a large stake in expanding that system. At the same time, the idea that development should give priority to the basic needs of the people in the developing countries is gaining currency. This type of development model emphasizes the need for developing countries to overcome their dependency situation, to have control over the development of their natural resources and to promote cooperation among the Third World nations. All of these points can be seen as representing obstacles to the international capitalist system's continued expansion.

Finally – and this point will be developed below – the transition processes may affect the strategic interests of the transnationals' home country, and this may constitute an additional reason for opposing the process.

We can therefore expect that in general transnationals will oppose the transition process. The manner in which this opposition is likely to be expressed will depend on a variety of factors including the 'national programme's' specific political implications and the political forces on which it is based, the degree of cohesion in the programme's support, the magnitude of the interests that are affected and their interaction with local interests, the struggle's impact within the country and at the international level and, finally, the implications which a successful outcome of the transition process might have for East-West relations.

Both the pace at which the various politico-economic measures are applied and the technical efficiency of state initiatives during the transition period can have an influence on the behaviour of the transnationals. While these factors are unlikely to have the same influence as the ones discussed above, it seems obvious that the specific measures that are adopted and the technical efficiency in implementing can, to a moderate extent, make it easier or more difficult for various elements supporting one side of the issue or the other to act together.

Once transnationals are confronted with a set of restrictions during the transition period, they must either choose to accept them – which in no way prevents them from simultaneously trying to slow down or distort the process – or they must abandon the market. If they abandon the market and the transition towards a new style of development is carried out successfully, they will probably find it extremely difficult to regain that market. If, on the other hand, they officially agree to the changes the state demands, they will survive the transition and continue to operate within the new model.

The other possibility is that the transition process might be aborted. If the companies have abandoned the market before this occurs, there is no guarantee that they will be able to regain their previous positions if the situation should revert to what it was, unless of course their departure has been part of a plan designed to block the transition process, in which case they would then return in triumph.

If they appear to be adjusting to the measures taken by the state and the transition process fails, they can still continue to operate. It is unlikely that a new government would take reprisals against transnationals that had continued to operate during the transition period, particularly if they have contributed to the failure of the 'national programme'.

Transnational corporations involved in industrial activities do seem to be reacting in a somewhat more flexible manner to restrictive measures taken by the governments of their host countries. The Chilean experience has confirmed this trend, which could be attributed to an intensification of the process of oligopolistic competition at the international level, resulting from the rapid expansion of Japanese and European transnational companies during the last twelve years. Transnationals that decide to abandon certain markets for political reasons now fully realize that their place will be taken by other members of the international oligarchy.

Another factor which encourages greater flexibility on the part of transnationals is the experience which they are beginning to acquire in dealing with countries with centrally planned economies (that is, in selling technology, coproduction agreements, increases in trade, etc.).

Furthermore, the transnationals are certainly and increasingly aware that new forms of social organization, designed to cope with the disequilibria produced by the existing model, are being promoted in the Third World countries, and that they must come to terms with these developments. However, this does not prevent them, individually or collectively, from simultaneously attempting to combat these developments at the national and international levels.

Finally, it is becoming increasingly clear that the transnationals have had conflicts with various social groups – and at times even with the governments – in their home countries. This is a powerful factor which indirectly increases the host countries' ability to impose restrictions on the transnationals operating in their territory.

While we may seem to have strayed from our topic – the economic blockade against Chile – our purpose has been to gain an understanding of the nature and magnitude of the major obstacles to the social transformation process, including certain types of pressures which were not applied to Chile to the full extent possible because of certain national and international circumstances.

The main conclusion of this analysis of the motives behind the economic blockade is this: the United States attempted to prevent the UP's electoral victory, subsequent progress and consolidation in power; it did this for reasons of national security, reinforced by strategic political and economic interests. The goals of the U.S. policy were not affected and could not be altered by the nature or efficiency of this or that measure.

We must of course try to learn from the mistakes that were made in formulating and carrying out Chile's own policies, but we must also keep in mind that certain forces will continue to oppose the social transformation process, whatever the manner of effecting that process may be. Since the objectives pursued by these opposing forces compel them to fight to the very end, the methods which they are prepared to use are various and unpredictable. That, in any case, was one of the lessons of the events of Chile.

3.1. *The Nature of the Blockade*

The fact that the present volume deals primarily with economic questions might give the impression that it was economic pressure that had the greatest impact on the social transformation process initiated by the UP. This was not the case because, as was already pointed out, the key objective was to ensure that the UP's political programme would fail. The best way to achieve this objective was to encourage unity and cohesion among domestic social forces likely to oppose the social transformation process. The greater the cohesion in the domestic opposition to the UP, the more discrete and less apparent U.S. intervention would be.

In this context, the United States had to take action at various levels in order to stimulate and support domestic opposition to the UP Government. Action taken at the economic level represented only one type of measure, and the impact of such measures was dependent upon the kind of political context which could be created and upon changes in the attitudes and behaviour of various social groups and political parties.

This was not a new field of action for the United States. We have already established that the Chilean economy was highly dependent upon the U.S. economy, but there was more to it than strictly economic dependence. It was obvious that, in the armed forces, for example, the years of ideological and technical training received by generations of Chilean officers, plus the fact that the United States was Chile's main source of military equipment, had some influence on the behaviour of the military. The situation in the trade unions was similar: U.S. agencies had been doing systematic work in this area and they had been particularly successful with white collar workers and professionals. Information made available after the *coup d'état* showed unequivocally that U.S. penetration of Chilean trade unions had a great deal of influence on the most significant labour conflicts (with transport, with copper, and with the professional associations) which the UP Government had to solve.[17]

On the basis of evidence now available regarding aid given to the *El Mercurio* newspaper chain, it is clear that one of the highest priorities was communications.[18] Support of the opposition press within Chile was coordinated with an international campaign carried out by U.S. press agencies, designed to create the image of a chaotic and bankrupt country with which it was dangerous to maintain normal economic relations.

Cultural and ideological pressure, applied through a wide variety of means over a long period of time, provided a background for support for initiatives aimed at specific social sectors or groups. The impression that emerged was that, whatever the concrete results which the UP Government might achieve, the entire process was leading to a form of social organization that was 'ethically unacceptable'.

Thus the attack was on two fronts: first, there was an attempt to ensure that the outcome of Government policies would be as unfavourable as possible; and second, the idea was hammered home that, apart from what the Government was successful in doing, socialism itself had to be rejected. The economic pressures mentioned in this and in other chapters complemented, and were themselves reinforced by, what was being achieved on those two fronts.

The closure of long-term credits lines is a good example of this. On the short term, the absence of long-term credits had a very limited impact; it simply meant that certain types of urgently needed equipment had to be paid for out of reserves, which reduced the amount of liquidity available to import other goods. The most serious consequence of using these reserves was the creation of the impression that it was becoming increasingly difficult to ensure the expansion of the productive apparatus. Rationing of electricity was forecast for four or five years hence, steel production was to drop and the copper industry was to be unable to raise production. The technical and professional personnel displayed a remarkable lack of zeal – mostly for ideological reasons – in searching for ways to use new suppliers of equipment and technology. The result was that the impression was given that the UP Programme was unlikely to be viable either on the medium or the long term.

All of these difficulties were seen by the military as a threat to 'national sovereignty' and by the professional groups as a potential cause of further unemployment on the medium term.

Consequently, it was quite clear that the various methods of applying pressure on the Chilean Government – whether those pressures came from inside or from outside the country – were interdependent. However, it is worth pointing out that, despite the increasing economic difficulties during 1972, the Government enjoyed more political support in March 1973 than it had in September 1970.

There is no doubt that the economic blockade contributed to Chile's economic difficulties and that these difficulties in turn alienated certain social sectors of Chilean society which might otherwise have supported the Government. The most important result of the blockade, however, was that it stimulated, strengthened and brought together several social forces, including the military, and thus created an invincible alliance of adversaries to the UP Government's Programme.

NOTES

1. These figures are taken from *Antecedentes sobre el desarrollo chileno 1960-70* [Antecedents of Chilean Development from 1960 to 1970] (ODEPLAN, Series I, No. 1, *Planes semestrales, Plan de la economía nacional 1971-76* [Half-Yearly Plans, Plan of the National Economy for 1971-76]) (Santiago de Chile, 1971).
2. In 1961 direct public investment accounted for 39% of total investment. In 1970 this figure rose to 50%. In addition the state transferred resources to the private sector. This indirect public investment also increased rapidly during the 1960s, rising from 8% to 25% of total investment. Taking everything into account, the public sector was providing almost 75% of total investment in 1970; this situation can be explained in terms of the political power of private groups and of their influence on the state's management.
3. ODEPLAN, *Antecedentes sobre el desarrollo....*
4. See Eduardo Novoa, *La batalla del cobre* [The Copper Battle] (Santiago de Chile, Quimantú, 1972).
5. See works by Eduardo Novoa, including *La batalla..., Nacionalización y recuperación de recursos naturales ante la Ley Internacional* [Nationalization and the Regaining of Natural Resources in International Law] (Mexico City, Fondo de Cultura Económica, 1974), and *Defensa de las nacionalizaciones ante los tribunales extranjeros* [Defence of the Nationalization in the Foreign Tribunals] (Mexico City, Prensa Universidad Nacional de México, 1974). See also Carlos Fortin's 'Nationalization of Copper in Chile and its International Repercussions' (Chapter 6 of this volume).
6. In 1970, the state controlled approximately 50% of bank deposits through the State Bank. By the end of 1972 it controlled 95% through the thirteen private banks (there were fifteen altogether) in which the state had purchased shares. See Minister of the Treasury Americo Zorrilla's *Exposición sobre el estado de la hacienda pública y de la política económica del Gobierno* [Statement on Public Finance and the Economic Policy of the Government], presented to the *Comisión Mixta de Presupuestos* [Mixed Commission on Budgets], 15 November 1972 (Santiago de Chile, Ministerio de Hacienda, Dirección de Presupuestos [Ministry of the Treasury, Office of the Budget], 1972) and Alfonso Inostroza's 'Nationalization of the Banking System in Chile' (Chapter 8 of this volume).
7. According to the Government's Programme, the ninety firms that made up the APS, along with the firms that were already in the public sector in 1970, accounted for more than 40% of industrial production, 20% of employment and 70% of the assets of manufacturing industries. See *La economía chilena en 1972* [The Chilean Economy in 1972] (Santiago de Chile, Instituto de Economía y Planificación, Universidad de Chile [Institute of Economy and Planning, University of Chile], 1973) and Alberto Martínez's 'The industrial Sector: Areas of Social and Mixed Property in Chile' (Chapter 7 of this volume).
8. That is, expropriation of all farms with eighty basic hectares or more. In September 1970 35% of agricultural land and 45% of irrigated land had been reformed. See Zorrilla, *Exposición sobre el estado de la hacienda pública....*
9. See the Report of the Chilean Government to the Meeting of the Inter-American Committee of the Alliance for Progress, 1971 and 1972.

10. We refer only to measures directly affecting the external sector. Obviously other types of economic measures, such as prices and incomes policy, monetary policy and fiscal policy, also have an impact on the external sector.
11. Despite substantial Chilean exports of iron to Japan, and despite the possibility of expanding Chilean capital goods imports from that country, the credit granted by Japan was only $10 million.
12. These sectors had never been engaged in using more modern technology.
13. See *Covert Action in Chile, 1963-73. Staff Report of the Select Committee to Study Governmental Operations with Respect to Intelligence Activities.* (Washington, D.C., United States Senate, The U.S. Government Printing Office, 1975), 51-52 (known as the 'Church Report').
14. Documents published after the *coup d'état* show unequivocally that the United States had intervened in Chilean elections in 1958, 1964 and 1970. See *Covert Action in Chile...*, 9.
15. See Fortin's 'Nationalization of Copper...' for a discussion of the background of this question.
16. See Fortin's 'Nationalization of Copper...'.
17. See *Covert Action in Chile...*, 30-31.
18. See *Covert Action in Chile...*, 29.

Table 5.1. *Distribution of Chile's Balance of Trade (in millions of dollars, with percentages)*

	1950			*1955*			*1960*			*1965*			*1970*		
	Exports	*Imports*	*Balance*	*Exports*	*Imports*	*Balance*	*Exports*	*Imports*	*Balance*	*Exports*	*Imports*	*Balance*	*Exports*	*Imports*	*Balance*
United States	159.0	126.6	32.4	200.9	169.4	31.5	93.1	260.7	–167.6	157.9	230.3	–72.4	177.2	343.6	–166.4
%	55.2	49.5		40.8	42.9		10.2	23.9		23.3	36.7		14.1	36.9	
Canada	0.3	2.3	–2.0	0.2	3.6	–3.4	0.4	5.4	–5.0	0.0	10.0	–10.0	0.5	11.6	–11.1
%		0.9			0.9		0.2	0.5			1.6			1.2	
Latin America	41.1	52.8	–11.7	77.3	82.1	–4.7	38.9	94.9	56.0	57.1	150.3	–93.2	161.1	201.2	–40.1
%	14.5	20.0		15.7	20.8		4.2	8.7		8.4	24.0		12.9	21.6	
United Kingdom	15.5	31.6	–16.1	83.8	25.2	58.6	88.1	38.3	49.8	84.8	39.4	45.4	154.2	58.1	96.1
%	5.4	12.4		17.0	6.4		9.6	3.5		12.5	6.3		12.3	6.2	
Continental Europe				126.5	98.7	27.8	230.0	138.0	92.0	286.2	153.5	132.7	600.5	249.1	351.4
%				25.7	25.0		25.1	12.7		42.1	24.5		47.9	26.8	
Rest of the World	72.2	42.4	29.8	4.0	15.7	–11.8	464.2	553.0	–88.8	92.9	43.4	49.5	159.9	67.2	92.7
%	25.1	16.6		0.8	4.0		50.7	50.7		13.7	6.9		12.8	7.2	
Total	228.1	255.7	32.4	492.6	394.7	97.9	914.7	1,090.3	–175.6	678.9	629.9	32.0	1,253.4	930.8	322.6
%	100	100		100	100		100	100		100	100		100	100	

Source: Balance of payments, Central Bank.

Table 5.2. *1970 Imports* [a] *(in millions of dollars)*

	Total Imports	*Imports from the U.S.*	*U.S. imports in percentage of total*
Consumer goods	143.4	24.5	17.1
Intermediate goods	490.2	189.5	38.7
Capital goods	208.6	89.4	43.5
Subtotal	842.3	303.4	36.0
Total	930.8	343.6	36.9

[a] Only products with an import value of over $100,000 have been included.

Source: Superintendencia de Aduanas [Superintendence of Customs] (Santiago de Chile).

Table 5.3. *Distribution of Imports in 1970 with a value of over $100,000, by Sector and According to the Percentage Imported from the United States (in thousands of dollars)*

% of imports from the U.S.	*Consumer goods*	*Intermediate goods*	*Capital goods*	*Total*
75 or more	3,395.2	77,061.5	33,171.2	113,627.9
74.9 to 50	5,403.4	72,802.7	32,105.8	110,307.9
49.9 to 0.1	15,741.1	39,663.9	24,090.5	79,495.5
Less than 0.1	118,942.2	300,676.8	119,249.8	538,868.8
Total from the U.S.	24,539.7	189,528.1	89,363.5	303,431.3
Total	143,481.9	490,204.9	208,613.3	842,300.1

Source: Superintendencia de Aduanas.

Table 5.4. *Percentages from Table 5.3, by Sector*

% of imports from the U.S.	*Consumer goods*	*Intermediate goods*	*Capital goods*	*Total*
75 or more	2.3	15.7	15.9	13.5
74.9 to 50	3.8	14.9	15.4	13.1
49.9 to 0.1	11.0	8.1	11.5	9.4
Less than 0.1	82.9	61.3	57.2	64.0
Total from the U.S.	17.1	38.7	42.8	36.0
Total	100.0	100.0	100.0	100.0

Source: Table 5.3.

Table 5.5. *Percentages from Table 5.3, According to the Import Level*

% of imports from the U.S.	*Consumer goods*	*Intermediate goods*	*Capital goods*	*Total*
75 or more	3.0	67.8	29.2	100.0
74.9 to 50	4.9	66.0	29.1	100.0
49.9 to 0.1	19.8	49.9	30.3	100.0
Less than 0.1	22.1	55.8	22.1	100.0
Total from the U.S.	17.0	58.2	24.8	100.0
Total	8.1	62.5	29.5	100.0

Source: Table 5.3.

Table 5.6. *Distribution of Total and U.S.-Imported Intermediate Goods in 1970, by Economic Sector (annual imports of over $100,000, in thousands of dollars)*

Sectors	*Total imported*	*Imports from the U.S.*					
		75% or more	*% of total*	*74.9 to 50%*	*% of total*	*49.9 to 0.1%*	*% of total*
1 Unclassified intermediate goods	33,947.7	9,107.4	26.8	4,008.7	11.8	4,385.2	12.9
2 Agriculture, livestock, forestry and hunting	36,905.0	5,862.7	15.9	6,367.1	17.3	2,583.4	7.0
3 Fishing	314.7					17.9	5.7
4 Mining	29,927.1	15,652.5	52.3	5,127.5	17.1	744.0	2.5
5 Foodstuffs, beverages and tobacco	42,471.5	10,131.0	23.9	62.5	0.1	527.2	1.2
6 Textiles, footwear and clothing	36,899.0	144.5	0.4	747.9	2.0	1,399.9	3.8
7 Paper, printing and related industries	7,581.5	1,034.8	13.6	1,382.1	18.2	694.0	9.2
8 Rubber and leather goods	13,609.9	...	0.0	1,097.0	8.1	1,518.8	11.2
9 Chemical products	60,597.5	6,077.3	10.0	8,081.9	13.3	5,896.7	9.7
10 Petroleum and coal products	39,781.2	...	0.0	85.4	0.2	1,092.8	2.7
11 Manufacture of nonmetalic mineral products and basic metal industries	20,975.0	4,221.6	20.1	2,103.4	10.0	2,050.6	9.8
12 Manufacture of metal products and machinery	69,585.5	12,914.0	18.6	16,860.2	24.2	8,669.5	12.5
13 Manufacture of electrical products and machinery	31,342.5	850.5	2.7	10,130.7	32.3	3,948.5	12.6
14 Manufacture of transport material	57,993.8	10,940.6	18.9	13,372.5	23.1	6,062.1	10.5
15 Construction	8,273.0	124.6	1.5	3,375.8	40.8	73.3	0.9
Total	490,204.9	77,061.5	15.7	72,802.7	14.9	39,663.9	8.1

Source: Superintendencia de Aduanas.

Table 5.7. *Distribution of Total and U.S.-Imported Capital Goods in 1970, by Economic Sector (annual imports of over $100,000, in thousands of dollars)*

Sectors	*Total imported*	*Imports from the U.S.*					
		75% or more	*% of total*	*74.9 to 50%*	*% of total*	*49.9 to 0.1%*	*% of total*
1 Unclassified intermediate goods	19,699.2	491.7	2.5	1,699.9	8.6	5,057.9	25.7
2 Agriculture, livestock, forestry and hunting	15,537.6	1,214.8	7.8	3,737.3	24.1	1,297.7	8.2
3 Fishing	14,073.7	. . .	0.0	382.4	2.7	45.5	0.3
4 Mining	16,773.5	9,024.4	53.8	2,664.6	15.9	1,132.7	6.8
5 Foodstuffs, beverages and tobacco	2,204.8	. . .	0.0	58.8	2.7	241.3	10.9
6 Textiles, footwear and clothing	6,243.2	. . .	0.0	. . .	0.0	338.3	5.4
7 Paper, printing and related industries	13,357.6	1,057.8	7.9	716.8	5.4	2,396.5	17.9
8 Rubber and leather goods	929.4	. . .	0.0	. . .	0.0	99.0	10.7
9 Chemical products	2,359.5	121.0	5.1	268.6	11.4	443.6	18.8
10 Manufacture of nonmetalic mineral products and basic metal industries	511.1	. . .	0.0	190.3	37.2	5.3	1.0
11 Manufacture of metal products and machinery	16,058.8	. . .	0.0	2,669.6	16.6	2,862.8	17.8
12 Manufacture of electrical products and machinery	33,260.4	5,356.0	16.1	6,594.4	19.8	4,157.6	12.5
13 Manufacture of transport material	50,569.0	12,435.7	24.6	7,540.5	14.9	3,550.4	7.0
14 Construction	17,035.5	3,013.4	17.7	5,578.6	32.7	2,479.9	14.6
Total	208,613.3	32,714.8	15.7	32,101.8	15.4	24,090.5	11.5

Source: Superintendencia de Aduanas.

Table 5.8. *Share of the APS in the Value of Imports in 1973 (in thousands of dollars)*

Share of APS	*Imports*	%
More than 2/3	840,933.3	75.7
Between 1/3 and 2/3	91,828.7	8.3
Less than 1/3	177,643.1	16.0
Total	1,110,455.1	100.0

Source: Central Bank, SEREX [Foreign Trade Department of the Central Bank].

Table 5.9. *Structure of the Programme for Imports in 1973 (in thousands of dollars)*

	Total	%	*APS*	%	*APP*
1 Agriculture and foodstuffs	483,107.8	94.9	458,286.2	5.1	24,821.6
2 Fishing	5,466.0	70.2	3,838.0	29.8	1,628.0
3 Mining	73,377.0	93.6	68,663.1	6.4	4,714.8
4 Industry	512,583.7	57.0	292,226.6	43.0	220,357.1
5 Services	22,338.7	55.0	12,392.1	44.5	9,944.6
6 Government	13,583.0	100.0	13,583.0	0.0	0.0
Total of planned imports	1,110,455.1	76.4	848,989.0	23.5	261,466.1

Source: Central Bank, SEREX.

Table 5.10. *Share of the APS in the Value of Exports in 1973 (in thousands of dollars)*

Share of APS	*Exports*	%
More than 2/3	932,144.6	85.3
Between 1/3 and 2/3	160,751.4	14.7
Less than 1/3	...	...
Total	1,092,896.0	100.0

Source: Central Bank, SEREX.

Table 5.11. *Main Imports According to the 1973 Programme (in thousands of dollars)*

Name of enterprise	*APS*	*APP*	*Total*	*%*
1 ECA (food)	365,228.4	–		
2 ENAP (petroleum)	106,224.0	–		
3 ECETEX (leather and textiles)	73,315.6	–		
4 IANSA (sugar)	52,783.9	–		
5 CAP (steel and iron)	47,000.0	–		
6 CODELCO (copper)	43,000.0	–		
7 State Bank (banking)	24,000.0	–		
8 INSA (rubber)	13,740.0	–		
9 SOQUIMICH (nitrate)	13,000.0	–		
10 ENARA (automobile spare parts)	11,279.1	–		
Subtotal	749,571.0	–	749,571.0	
Cumulative total	749,571.0		749,571.0	67.5
11 Indus-Lever	–	8,000.0		
12 Automotora Franco-Chilena	–	7,265.3		
13 F.F.C.C.	6,589.0	–		
14 S.N.S.	6,000.0	–		
15 ENAMI	6,000.0	–		
16 Citroën	–	5,556.0		
17 Laboratorio Chile	5,400.0	–		
18 Fiat	–	5,020.1		
19 Cia. Manuf. Papeles	–	4,800.0		
20 Shell Industrial	–	4,600.0		
Subtotal	23,989.0	35,241.4	59,230.4	
Cumulative total	773,560.0	35,241.4	808,801.4	72.9
21 CORMECANICA	–	4,261.0		
22 Esso Industrial	–	3,850.0		
23 Quimica Bayer	–	3,983.1		
24 IRT-ILESCO	3,728.0	–		
25 BASF Anilquimica	–	3,600.0		
26 COSAF	–	3,430.5		
27 Cia. Chilena de Tabacos	3,208.6	3,208.6		
28 Pizarreño	–	3,254.8		
29 Mantos Blancos	–	3,200.0		
30 MADECO	3,200.0	–		
Subtotal	10,136.6	25,579.4	35,716.0	
Cumulative total	783,696.6	60,820.8	844,517.4	76.1

Name of enterprise	*APS*	*APP*	*Total*	*%*
31 Shell Distributor	–	3,150.0		
32 Química Hoechst	–	3,060.0		
33 LAN CHILE	3,047.0	–		
34 Mobil Oil Chile	–	2,750.0		
35 Ind. Química Ciba Geygy	–	2,685.0		
36 Minera Santa Fe	2,670.0	–		
37 D.A.E.	2,481.0	–		
38 Philips	–	2,320.0		
39 C.C.U.	2,000.0	–		
40 Disputada de las Condes	1,953.4	–		
Subtotal	12,151.4	13,965.0	26,116.4	
Cumulative total	795,848.0	74,785.8	870,633.8	78.5
41 FEMSACO	1,802.1	–		
42 SOINCA	–	1,766.4		
43 ENACAR	1,738.0	–		
44 CHIPRODAL	–	1,730.0		
45 Dirección de Vialidad	1,701.0	–		
46 Ind. Nac. de Explosivos	1,700.0	–		
47 British Leyland	–	1,665.6		
48 Fca. Nac. de Máquinas de Coser	–	1,650.0		
49 RECSA	–	1,638.8		
50 MANESA	1,600.0	–		
Subtotal	8,541.1	8,450.8	16,991.9	
Cumulative total	804,389.1	83,236.6	887,625.7	80.0
Total planned imports	848,989.0	261,466.1	1,110,455.1	

Source: Central Bank, SEREX.

Table 5.12. *Structure of Imports in 1972 by Country of Origin (in thousands of dollars and percentages)*

	Total imports	*Proportion represented by sample*	*Main countries of origin*	*%*	*Imported from the U.S.*
1. Consumer goods	276,584.8	85.0	Argent./N.Zeal./Brazil	41.6	
1.1. Foodstuffs	202,417.4	97.1	Argent./N.Zeal./Brazil	47.8	
1.1.1. agricultural origin	11,589.9	83.6	Ecuador/Poland/Spain	97.1	
1.1.2. industrial origin	190,827.5	97.9	Argent./Brazil/N.Zeal.	50.3	
1.2. Non-food products	76,167.4	51.9	U.S./Spain/Brazil	32.9	11.4
1.2.1. pharmaceuticals and medicine	36,375.6	54.5	U.S./GDR/Switzerland	47.9	21.3
1.2.2. tools and instruments	5,683.2	27.9	GDR/Spain/U.S.	63.1	9.8
1.2.3. others	32,108.6	53.2	Brazil/Spain/Argentina	60.4	
2. Capital goods	341,828.5	86.6	Romania/U.K./U.S.S.R.	28.0	
2.1. Machinery and equipment	158,493.5	77.3	U.S./France/U.K.	43.1	10.2
2.2. Transport equipment	173,312.7	95.8	U.S.S.R./Romania/Argent.	45.1	
2.3. Animals for breeding	10,022.4	75.5	Argent./Urug./Netherlands	100.0	
3. Intermediate goods	843,274.1	80.8	Argent./U.S./Australia	40.6	16.7
3.1. Raw materials of agricultural origin	237,432.9	98.1	Argent./Australia/U.S.	75.4	19.1
3.1.1. edibles	167,453.1	99.0	Argent./Australia/U.S.	83.8	20.4
3.1.2. non-edibles	69,979.8	95.7	Argent./Mexico/U.S.	78.8	15.9
3.2. Raw materials of industrial origin	267,455.4	70.1	Cuba/U.S./Argentina	35.2	11.5
3.2.1. edibles	98,357.8	92.4	Cuba/Argent./Netherlands	59.4	
3.2.2. non-edibles	169,097.6	57.2	U.S./GDR/Mexico	41.2	22.3
3.3. Industrial intermediate products	90,051.7	55.0	GDR/U.S./U.K.	48.3	15.2
3.4. Spare parts	123,797.2	82.2	U.S./Argent./GDR	52.7	26.9
3.4.1. machinery and equipment	48,611.3	80.8	U.S./GDR/U.K.	67.1	33.8
3.4.2. transport equipment	75,185.9	83.2	Argent./U.S./Italy	55.9	22.6
3.5. Fuels and lubricants	101,428.9	96.4	Saudi Arabia/U.S./Iran	52.8	13.0
3.6. Parts for assembly line production	23,108.0	49.7	Japan/Spain/Brazil	66.3	
Total	1,461,687.5	82.9	Argentina/U.S./Australia	38.8	

Source: Central Bank, SEREX.

Table 5.13. *Main Imports for 1972 (in millions of dollars and percentages)*

	APS	*APP*	*Total*	*Main countries of origin*	%
Meat	92,277.0	20,783.1	113,060.1	Argent./Brazil/N.Zealand	69.4
Wheat for consumption	91,391.8	9.6	91,401.4	Australia/Argent./Romania	96.6
Crude oil	68,831.1	–	68,831.1	Saudi Arabia/Iran/Venezuela	72.3
Milk	43,939.9	1,472.9	45,412.8	N.Zealand/France/Ireland	87.3
Sugar	42,022.4	2,049.4	44,071.8	Cuba/Brazil/Australia	98.3
Corn for consumption	41,879.4	35.0	41,914.4	U.S./Argentina/Bolivia	100.0
Leather	629.6	27,331.1	27,960.7	Argentina/U.S./Paraguay	90.0
Raw cotton	1,013.7	21,869.0	22,882.7	Mexico/Brazil/Peru	96.7
Vegetable oil for human consumption	1,826.3	15,853.0	17,679.3	Netherlands/France/Poland	57.8
Rice for consumption	15,788.6	1,128.6	16,917.2	Peoples' Rep. China/Spain/ Pakistan	76.2
Total	399,599.8	90,531.7	490,131.5		

Source: Central Bank, SEREX.

Table 5.14. *Distribution of Imports of Over $1,000,000 of which the United States is Among the Three Main Exporters to Chile (in thousands of dollars, and percentages)*

	1971					1972				
	Total imports	*Imports in the sample* [a]	*Imports in the sub-sample* [b]	*Imports from the U.S.* [c]	*(4)÷(3) %*	*Total imports*	*Imports in the sample* [a]	*Imports in the sub-sample* [b]	*Imports from the U.S.* [c]	*(9)÷(8) %*
	(1)	*(2)*	*(3)*	*(4)*	*(5)*	*(6)*	*(7)*	*(8)*	*(9)*	*(10)*
1. Consumer goods	234,800.0	177,942.1	44,170.1	9,440.4	21.4	276,584.8	236,358.1	52,789.6	5,693.4	10.8
Foodstuffs	144,842.0	101,367.7	7,009.4	1,454.6	20.8	202,417.4	196,512.2	21,329.0	...	0.0
1.1. Foodstuffs of agricultural origin		11,015.3	...	...	...	11,589.9	9,686.4	–	...	...
1.2. Foodstuffs of industrial origin		120,352.1	7,009.4	1,454.6	20.8	190,827.5	186,855.8	21,329.0	...	0.0
1.3. Foodstuffs of non-edible industrial origin	69,637.4	46,574.4	37,160.7	7,985.8	21.5	74,167.4	39,815.9	31,460.6	5,683.4	18.1
1.3.1. medicines and pharmaceuticals	27,699.0	14,337.2	14,337.2	3,741.6	26.1	36,375.6	19,838.2	19,838.2	4,218.5	21.3
1.3.2. tools and instruments for the foodstuff industry	10,720.5	3,973.3	3,973.3	465.2	11.7	5,683.2	1,587.1	1,587.1	155.0	9.8
1.3.3. others	51,237.9	28,263.9	18,850.2	3,779.0	20.0	32,108.6	18,390.6	10,035.3	1,319.9	13.2
2. Capital goods	204,400.0	156,778.1	113,373.6	30,752.0	27.1	311,828.6	306,130.0	164,896.7	23,499.0	14.3
2.1. Machinery and equipment	189,000.0	88,977.4	61,983.5	21,049.1	34.0	158,493.5	127,959.5	74,018.3	13,876.0	18.7
2.2. Transport equipment	62,000.0	60,911.8	51,330.1	9,702.9	18.9	173,312.7	189,619.4	90,876.4	9,623.0	10.6
2.3. Animals for breeding	8,100.0	6,888.9	...	...	...	10,022.4	8,520.6	–	–	

	(1)	(2)	(3)	(4)	(5)	(6)	(7)	(8)	(9)	(10)
3. Intermediate goods	728,987.7	613,914.6	266,210.3	89,120.3	33.5	843,274.1	708,910.4	352,080.0	118,522.4	33.7
3.1. Raw materials of agricultural origin		163,764.5	62,023.1	13,594.7	21.9	237,432.9	234,334.6	116,537.1	45,812.6	39.3
3.1.1. edibles		100,784.3	56,636.1	9,854.8	17.4	167,453.1	167,331.3	101,542.0	35,213.7	34.7
3.1.2. non-edibles		62,980.2	5,387.0	3,739.8	69.4	69,979.8	67,003.3	14,995.1	10,628.9	70.9
3.2. Raw materials of industrial origin		185,416.7	73,308.7	28,499.5	38.9	267,455.4	204,215.9	83,405.7	23,078.2	27.7
3.2.1. edibles		69,902.3	15,242.6	4,114.6	27.0	98,357.8	92,737.0	14,541.5	279.1	1.9
3.2.2. non-edibles		115,514.4	58,066.1	24,384.9	42.0	169,097.6	111,508.9	68,864.2	22,799.1	33.1
3.3. Industrial intermediate products		35,187.9	25,399.8	6,564.4	25.8	90,051.7	51,529.4	39,297.2	7,900.3	20.1
3.4. Spare parts		103,950.6	78,655.8	26,741.4	34.0	123,797.2	103,562.3	85,731.8	28,092.9	37.8
3.4.1. for machinery and equipment		41,906.0	41,906.0	16,097.2	38.4	48,611.3	41,028.8	41,028.8	13,753.3	33.5
3.4.2. for transport equipment		62,044.6	36,749.8	10,644.2	29.0	75,185.9	62,533.5	44,703.0	14,339.6	32.1
3.5. Fuels and lubricants		112,913.5	22,591.7	12,554.7	55.6	101,428.9	99,902.7	22,547.1	12,815.5	56.8
3.6. Parts for assembly line production		12,681.4	4,228.2	1,165.6	27.6	23,108.0	12,365.6	4,561.1	792.9	87.4
Total	1,165,587.7	948,634.8	423,754.0	129,312.7	30.5	1,461,687.5	1,251,428.5	569,766.3	147,714.8	25.9

[a] The sample includes all imported products with a value of $1,000,000 or more in 1971 and/or 1972.
[b] The subsample includes those of the products above for which the United States is one of the three largest exporters to Chile.
[c] Imports from the United States which are included in the subsample.

Source: Central Bank, SEREX.

6

CARLOS FORTIN

NATIONALIZATION OF COPPER IN CHILE AND ITS INTERNATIONAL REPERCUSSIONS

Nationalization of the large, partly U.S.-owned copper companies, jointly known as *Gran Minería del Cobre*,[1] was a major promise in the Programme with which Salvador Allende was elected President of Chile in 1970. Within eight months of his inauguration the promise had been fully carried out and in a manner, moreover, that can be described as uncompromising: the Government refused to engage in any negotiations with the companies regarding compensation and instead proceeded to deduct from the amount owed to the companies all excess profits made during the preceding fifteen years. This effectively ruled out payment of direct compensation above what had already been paid out by the previous Government for the purchase of 51% of the companies' assets.

As was to be expected, nationalization gave rise to a bitter legal and commercial international confrontation between the Chilean Government and the U.S. companies; it is also generally regarded as one of the reasons for the intervention by the U.S. Government in order to isolate Chile economically and to 'destabilize' the Allende Government, which, in turn, appears as an important factor in the ultimate demise of the UP experience.

The first question that arises is, naturally, was the conflict necessary? In other words, were the decisions to nationalize copper and not to pay compensation essential to the achievement of the domestic socio-economic transformations proposed in the UP programme? To answer this question we need to analyze the presence of foreign interests in Chilean copper in terms of its impact on the economy generally and on the Government's project of basic social change; we must also examine the possible alternatives and compare their probable costs with the Allende Government's evaluation of the probability and costs of the nationalization conflict.

Next, we must assess the effects of the conflict on the viability of the Allende Government. This calls for an examination of the impact of the state take-over in terms of productivity of the mining operations, technological

Footnotes and tables to this chapter may be found on pp. 216-220.

requirements and marketing, including an evaluation of the policies followed by the new management in these areas. We shall then have to enquire into the effects of the U.S. companies' response to nationalization of the copper industry and to the Chilean economy as a whole.

Finally, we must examine the relationship between, on the one hand, the copper nationalization conflict and, on the other, the economic blockade and direct intervention by the U.S. Government in Chile during the 1970-73 period; this will be considered in the light of the UP Government's ultimate fate. More specifically, two questions will be asked: what was the real significance of the question of compensating the copper companies in determining the U.S. Government's policies *vis-à-vis* Allende? How did the conflict influence the attitude of other industrialized countries?

In this chapter we shall propose some answers to these questions. It seems useful to begin by situating the problem of copper nationalization in its historical context, and thus the first section of this chapter will briefly review the development of the copper industry in Chile from the turn of the century up to 1970. We shall pay particular attention to the role of international capital, its impact on the economy and its interaction with the power structures in Chilean society. In section 2 the process of nationalization will be described, with emphasis on the objectives pursued by the Chilean decision-makers and the options that were open to them at various times: this will allow a clarification of the rationale of the chosen courses of action. In the third section we shall evaluate the effects of copper nationalization and of the subsequent conflict on the Chilean economy, on the international position of the Allende Government and, ultimately, on the UP's viability as an experiment in radical change. Finally, we shall try to arrive at some general conclusions about the way in which internal and external factors interacted, and about the ability of Chilean leaders, as well as those of the other countries involved, to control both sets of factors.

1. CHILE AND THE U.S. COPPER COMPANIES, 1920-70

1.1. *Politics, Economics and the Copper Industry up to 1960*

U.S. investment in Chilean copper mining goes back to the 1810s. Copper had of course, been exploited in Chile long before that, and by the nineteenth century the industry had acquired world importance; in fact, between 1830 and 1880 Chile was the world's leading copper producer and had an industry made up of small independent operations owned by Chileans.

The subsequent development of richer copper deposits in the western United States meant a rapid decline of the Chilean copper industry, that by the 1900s had dropped to sixth place in the world, after the United States, Mexico, the Iberian Peninsula, Japan and Australia.[2]

However, a new situation arose between 1899 and 1903. The discovery and development of new technologies for extracting and processing made the exploitation of low-grade ore profitable. Suddenly the Chilean deposits began to look attractive, and U.S. capital started to show interest in investing in the Chilean copper industry.

In 1904 a U.S. engineer named William Braden bought the rights to exploit the deposits at El Teniente, south of Santiago, and set up a company in the United States, the Braden Copper Company, with a capital of $625,000. In 1909, Braden Copper was bought by the Guggenheim Exploration Company, another U.S. firm, which invested $2,500,000 to start exploiting copper on a large scale. Braden Copper was transferred in 1919 to the Kennecott Copper Corporation, another company controlled by the Guggenheims; by the 1950s El Teniente had become the largest underground mine in the world.

In 1912 the Guggenheims bought the rights to the other major Chilean copper deposit, an open-pit mine in the north of the country called Chuquicamata, and invested about $12,000,000 to begin mining operations. During the 1922-29 period the Guggenheims sold the rights to exploit Chuquicamata to the Anaconda Copper Company; in 1927 Anaconda started a new mining operation at another northern site called Potrerillos.

Thus by 1930 the Chilean copper industry, which had already replaced the nitrate industry as the country's main exporter, was dominated by two large U.S. companies, Anaconda and Kennecott.

One of the main reasons why Chilean copper was so attractive to U.S. capital was the exceptionally privileged treatment offered to investors. Until 1925, the Anaconda and Kennecott operations were typical mining enclaves with few linkages with the national company and with a tax regime which, according to one estimate, 'was well below 5% of the value of sales' and represented 'the least important link between the industry and the rest of the economy'.[3]

The first significant departure from this situation occurred at the time of the Great Depression when the Chilean Government had to try to increase its share of the income from copper exports. This was done in two ways: first, from 1934 onwards the U.S. companies were forced to convert dollars into Chilean currency at a special net rate to cover part of their expenditures in escudos. This rate did not change until 1955. Second, the tax on profits began to rise until it reached 39% in 1941.

The first of these measures touched on a problem that was much debated in Chile until 1970: the question of the 'returned value' (*retornos*) from the copper industry. What is meant by 'returned value' is that part of the income from the sale of copper to the rest of the world is re-injected in the Chilean economy in the form of hard currency. Obviously, the companies had to bring in enough dollars to cover taxes and costs in Chilean currency. But beyond that they had no further obligations, so that they could keep in their foreign current accounts all their profits, whether distributed as dividends or not, and funds to cover their costs in foreign currency, including depreciation and repayment of loans and interest.

With respect to the tax regime, in 1942, when copper prices were rising because of the wartime demand, Chile introduced a new tax of 50% on windfall profits. This tax was applied to profits generated by increases in the copper prices above $0.10 per pound of electrolytic copper fob New York. The rate was raised to 60% in 1947. However, Chile derived little benefit from this tax as, throughout the war, the United States and its allies set the price of copper at $0.115 per pound (only marginally higher than the price during the Depression years). The *Corporación del Cobre* (CODELCO) [the Copper Corporation] later calculated that this decision cost Chile $500 million during this period. At the same time, the U.S. companies were receiving loans and subsidies from the U.S. Government and were selling copper from their mines in the United States at considerably higher prices. Because of this, for the first time an open conflict of interests developed between the companies and the dominant groups in Chilean society who, by then, were demanding a larger share of the surplus generated by copper exports.

A new conflict arose in 1949 when post-war inflation gave way to recession. There was a serious drop in copper prices which led the companies to reduce production by 30% without consulting the Chilean authorities. The conflict took a critical turn when the Korean War started. In June 1950, again without consulting the Chilean Government, the U.S. Government and the copper companies decided to fix a maximum price of $0.245 per pound, which was significantly lower than the free European price on the London Metal Exchange. They also decided to establish a quota system through which countries involved in the war effort would benefit from the low fixed price. As in 1943, the companies were heavily subsidized by the U.S. Government through loans, long-term contracts and tax concessions. It has been estimated that as a result of these decisions, Chile lost some $300 million.[4]

The strong reaction from the Chilean public that ensued forced the Chilean Government to negotiate a copper agreement with the U.S. Government. This resulted in the Washington Agreement, which was signed in March 1951 and provided for a rise of $0.3 per pound in the copper price and authorized the Chilean Government to sell 20% of copper production on the open market provided it did not sell to the socialist countries. The Agreement was to last for one year. At the end of that period the Chilean Government and the National Congress refused to renew it. Thereafter, the Chilean Government decreed a state monopoly on all sales of copper and proceeded to buy copper from the companies at the set maximum price, only to sell it at the free European price. The copper companies and the U.S. Government reacted strongly to this attempt by Chile to become an independent seller. Not only did they put pressure on individual countries to dissuade them from buying

Chilean copper, but they also informed countries showing an interest in Chilean copper at free market prices that any Chilean purchases would be deducted from their quota, but at the higher price. Furthermore, the demand for copper decreased when the war ended, and Chile lacked experience on the international copper market. Lastly, the Chilean Government did not particularly want to sell to the socialist countries who were in the market for copper at that time, and given Chile's political dependence on the United States, such transactions might in any case have proved impossible. All of these factors combined to frustrate Chile's attempt as an independent seller, and stocks began to accumulate.[5]

In view of this, the dominant sectors in Chile decided to bring the independent marketing experiment to an abrupt end and to return to an orthodox policy of attracting U.S. capital. A new copper law, known as the New Deal for Copper (*Nuevo Trato al Cobre*), adopted in May 1955, defined the regime under which the Gran Minería was to operate.

The essential aspects of this legislation were:

(1) The basic tax rate on profits was set at 50%, plus an additional variable 25% tax; for the latter, the tax rate diminished as production increased in relation to an agreed base figure, so that the rate would reach zero when production doubled. The base figure was set at 95% of the average of production from 1949 to 1953. There were two periods in the course of these five years (1949-50 and 1953 respectively) during which production levels were low due to a recession in the U.S. economy, the depletion of the Potrerillos mine and the change from oxide to sulphide ores in Chuquicamata. On the other hand, these five years also included a period of high production levels due to the Korean War. On the whole, however, the base figure was low and the companies had no difficulty in keeping the variable rate down to some 10% without having to make any new investments.

(2) The system of partial 'returned value' was maintained and the companies were authorized to convert dollars from copper sales at the current bank rate. In practice, this meant a savings on costs of $0.05 per pound of copper.

(3) New regulations provided for accelerated depreciation, for generous estimates of reserves for mine development and for tax exemptions on imports of certain categories of equipment, machinery and spare parts.

(4) The companies regained full control of copper marketing.

These measures were designed to provide incentives to the companies so that they would increase their investments and raise the level of local production and refining. The results, in terms of company profits, were dramatic: while the average annual profits were $26.7 million in 1950-54, they soared to $50.3 million annually during the 1955-59 period – an increase of almost 90%. During the 1955-59 period price increases amounted to 35%. At the same time, reserves for depreciation, which are a part of the companies' real income, were tripled. Yet the hoped-for new investments did not materialize. During this period Kennecott's subsidiary, the Braden Copper Company, which operated the El Teniente mine, invested almost nothing in its Chilean operations. Between 1955 and 1959 Anaconda's investments in its subsidiary, Chile Exploration Company (Chilex), and the Chuquicamata mine scarcely rose above 40% of the annual average for 1950-54. Anaconda did invest $100 million in its other subsidiary, Andes Copper Mining Company (Andes), to bring the new El Salvador mine into operation to replace the Potrerillos deposits that had been depleted. However, depreciation was so rapid that over 25% of the investment had been recovered within two years. Production increases were only sufficient to return to pre-war levels. Not only was there no expansion of refining capacity in Chile but the percentage of copper refined in the country dropped from 89% in 1951 to 45% in 1961. 'Returned value' was reduced not only in relative terms – it was $183.1 million in 1959 compared with $228.0 million in 1955 – but also in absolute terms: as a percentage of the value of sales, average annual 'returned values' dropped from 70% during 1946-54 to 60% during 1955-64.[6]

Thus the new legislation failed on many crucial points. A further indication of this failure is that the conservative Alessandri Government (1958-64), which was usually on friendly terms with the U.S. companies, saw fit to raise taxes on the Gran Minería to 60% for the basic rate and 26.25% for the variable rate. This increase affected mainly Braden, which had made no new investments since 1955 and whose production level in 1962 was, as a result, only 10% above the base figure that had been set for tax purposes; the company therefore had to pay taxes at the rate of 80% of its gross profits. Its net profits during the 1962-66 period were 40% less than those of the 1955-59 period. The other companies were not as badly affected because either production had increased sufficiently, as in the case of Chilex, or, as in the case of Andes, the accelerated depreciation of its investment in the El Salvador mine allowed the company to show no book profits for the 1962-66 period. Depreciation was of the order of 20% of the value of sales. At the end of the period during which the El Salvador mine was being put into operation, accelerated depreciation stopped and the company's profits were multiplied fifteen times, reaching a level of 21% of the value of sales.[7]

As the 1964 presidential elections approached, it seemed clear that the objectives of the New Deal legislation had been frustrated, at least as far as Chilean interests were concerned. The companies, on the other hand, had derived maximum advantage from the concessions and their profits had soared during the 1955-59 period. But by 1963 the higher tax rate affecting mainly Kennecott led company executives to begin to think of ways to change the situation. At the same time a similar exercise was being undertaken by the sectors whose candidate ultimately won the 1964 presidential elections.

1.2. *Progress by Contract: Chileanization and Nationalization by Agreement*[8]

The two main candidates in the 1964 elections advocated a change in Chilean policy *vis-à-vis* the copper companies. Salvador Allende, the candidate for the left, argued for nationalization; Eduardo Frei, the Christian Democratic Party candidate who was ultimately elected with right-wing support, stood for state participation in the copper industry but not for total nationalization.

It has been fairly well established that the idea of Chile acquiring a majority interest in the El Teniente mine came from Kennecott, which in fact started negotiating on the matter with the new Government even before President-elect Frei was inaugurated. On the one hand, Kennecott urgently wanted changes as its tax position was very unfavourable because of the company's lack of investment during the 1950s; on the other hand, its Chilean operations did not account for a significant part of the company's worldwide operations (in 1963 the Chilean mines accounted for only 11% of Kennecott's worldwide profits). It was therefore possible for Kennecott to allow a majority Chilean interest in the company in exchange for tax privileges which, in practice, would have the effect of increasing the company's profits. Finally, Kennecott was aware that the Frei Government needed to show quick and spectacular results in implementing its copper policy (Frei himself had stated that the change in the copper regime was the basis of his economic policy). To do this, the Government needed the cooperation of the copper companies since Frei had already rejected unilateral nationalization as a possible solution. Thus Kennecott was entering the negotiations with a clear tactical advantage.

The policy of 'Chileanization', which was made public in December 1966, had the following objectives: increasing the Gran Minería's production so that it would double by 1972; giving the state equity participation in the companies; increasing the amount of copper refined in Chile; integrating the copper industry into the Chilean economy and giving the state an active role in marketing copper throughout the world. The key element of this policy was the agreement that had been negotiated with Kennecott in 1964; in 1966 a law authorized the Executive to set up joint ventures with the companies and to grant tax concessions to the newly formed companies.

The agreement with Kennecott provided for the creation of a new Chilean stock company, the *Sociedad Minera El Teniente* [El Teniente Mining Corporation]. All of Braden's Chilean assets and liabilities were transferred to the new company; at the same time, Braden became the owner of all of the shares. Subsequently, Braden sold 51% of these shares to CODELCO, which was acting on behalf of the Chilean Government. The first item on the negotiators' agenda was the price of this 51%. In 1966, the book value of Braden was $67 million. However, Kennecott maintained that this figure did not correspond to the real value of the company's assets and demanded a revaluation. Chilean observers of various political persuasions argued that if the book value of the company was less than its real value, this was either because the depreciation allowed on machinery was greater than its real decrease in value, or because capital investments had been treated as operational costs and thus did not show up in the assets. The result in both cases would be to reduce the level of profits subject to taxation by artificially inflating costs. Moreover in the second instance, the capitalization tax would be avoided completely. It would be somewhat surprising, therefore, that a company that had benefitted from such accounting procedures for many years could discard them in order to maximize the price it could get when selling the company's shares. Nevertheless, Kennecott stood firm and even argued that if the book value was too low, the new company would find it very difficult to obtain foreign credit to expand its operations. The Chilean Government's negotiators accepted this argument and agreed that another U.S. firm, the American Appraisal Company, should make an estimate of Braden's assets. American Appraisal calculated a value of $239 million, which increased the book value to $285 million. However, because of the political climate at that time, it would have been very difficult for the Government to pay more than $100 million for the 51%. It was therefore decided to impute only $160 million as capital and the rest as reserves so that the value of 51% of the equity would come down to $80 million. The revaluation was exempted from capitalization tax and the $80 million were paid immediately.

In addition, the agreement with Kennecott included the following provisions:

(1) The new company was to launch an expansion programme designed to raise production by 50% in 1971. The $230 million which the programme would cost was to be financed by a loan of $110 million from the Export-Import Bank (Eximbank) – which was repayable over fifteen years starting in 1972 – and through a $27.5 million loan from the Chilean Government. In addition, Braden would lend to the new company the $80 million paid by Chile, plus the interest due between 1967 and 1971, which amounted to $12.7 million and was also repayable over fifteen years starting in 1972. In practice, this formula meant that Kennecott had no need to put any of its own capital into the expansion programme (both the Eximbank loan and the loan from Braden were guaranteed by the Chilean Government).

(2) New tax arrangements, much more attractive from the company's viewpoint, were established. As a result of these arrangements Braden, as minority shareholder, saw its tax bill reduced by 45%. Moreover, the Government decreed that taxes would not be raised for at least twenty years.

(3) Braden was to take charge of managing the new company for a period of at least twelve years, and Kennecott Sales Corporation was appointed exclusive marketing agents for a period of ten years.

The idea behind this policy of privileged treatment was to offer Kennecott a 'reasonable' return on its investments as a way of inducing the company to continue operating in Chile. But the Chilean negotiators made a surprising mistake on this point: when calculating this 'reasonable' return, they made projections using the average price of copper during the 1961-63 period, namely $0.29 per pound, as a base figure. Yet, when the legislation authorizing President Frei to set up the joint ventures was still being discussed in the National Congress in 1965, Chile was selling its copper at $0.37 per pound, while the average price on the London Metal Exchange was $0.58. In April 1966 the price of Chilean copper rose to $0.62 per pound. As a result of this mistake Kennecott's profits in 1967 and 1968 soared to a level that had never been anticipated: during these two years, profits on Braden's 49% of shares were higher than Braden's total profits during the six preceding years (when it owned the entire company). This situation led Kennecott to agree, in 1969, to the introduction of a preferential dividend in favour of the Chilean state to be paid out whenever the copper price rose above $0.40 per pound. Even so, Braden's overall profits in 1969, based on ownership of 49% of shares, were six times higher than its 1966 profits, when it held 100% of shares.

For Anaconda the situation was quite different. Anaconda's Chilean operations accounted for 73% of its worldwide profits in 1963 and, as we saw earlier, its tax position was more favourable than Kennecott's. Consequently, Anaconda made it clear to the Frei Government from the very beginning that it had no desire to sell any part of its interests either in Chilex or in Andes to the state. Instead Anaconda proposed a conventional investment programme of over $100 million, and offered to increase this amount out of its own resources. Additionally, in order to preserve the image of state participation and also to take advantage of the tax regime for new mines, a part of the Chuquicamata deposits was formally separated to create a new mine called Exótica, which was to be exploited by a joint venture in which Anaconda would hold 75% of the shares and the state the remaining 25%. In tax terms, the agreement with Anaconda led to an 11% tax reduction for Chilex. This, plus the high copper price in 1967-69, meant that Anaconda's profits were spectacular, as shown in Table 6.1.

It was precisely this situation that led the Frei Government to decide on the policy of *nacionalización pactada* or 'nationalization by agreement'. This was an agreement with Anaconda to set up joint ventures for operating the Chuquicamata and El Salvador mines. As in the case of Braden, the new companies were to be 51% owned by the Chilean state, bought at the 1969 book value and paid in twenty-four six-monthly installments beginning on 30 June 1970. To guarantee repayment CODELCO issued promissory notes corresponding to each of the installments. Anaconda was appointed manager and sales agent of the two new companies for variable periods of time, with the stipulation that this agreement could not be terminated before Chile had repaid at least 60% of the total purchase price of 51% of the shares. In addition, it was agreed that

Chile had an option to buy the remaining 49% after having paid at least 60% of the initial 51% of shares at a price based on the profitability of the joint ventures.

This was the situation of Gran Minería when Salvador Allende was elected President of Chile in 1970.

2. NATIONALIZATION OF COPPER IN 1971

2.1. *The Process and Scope of Nationalization*

Before starting to discuss the effects of the copper nationalization carried out by the Allende Government and the problems mentioned at the beginning of this chapter, it may be useful to summarize the main features of the Constitutional amendment through which copper was nationalized and the subsequent decisions on the question of compensating the companies.[9]

Copper was nationalized through a Constitutional amendment for two main reasons: first, to emphasize the great significance of the measure being adopted and second, to help solve certain legal and technical problems deriving from the copper agreements made by the Frei Government. The amendment was submitted to the National Congress by the Executive in December 1970. After being debated in Congress for seven months, it was finally adopted in July 1971 with the support of all of the political parties in Congress.

The nationalization measure applied to the companies that made up Gran Minería plus a smaller company, the *Sociedad Minera Andina* (Andina) [Andina Mining Corporation], that had been set up jointly in 1967 by the U.S. Cerro de Pasco Corporation and the Chilean state (which held 70% and 30% of the shares respectively) to mine the Rio Blanco deposits. Although by 1970 Andina's productive capacity was not sufficient to include it in Gran Minería, it already had an expansion programme that would raise productive capacity above the required minimum level, and it was therefore decided that it should be included in the nationalization plans.

Nationalization affected the companies as a whole and, as they were legal entities, it included both their assets and their liabilities. It was decided that the companies to be nationalized would have the right to be compensated on the basis of their book value as of 31 December 1970, minus the following deductions:

(1) Any revaluations made by the companies (or by them in a previous legal status) after 31 December 1964. This clause specifically referred to the revaluation of Braden's assets (discussed above) which was set aside when calculating the level of compensation.

(2) The value of the rights to the mineral deposits. According to Chilean mining laws, the state is always the sole owner of the deposits and it merely

grants concessions to private interests; there was thus no need for the state to pay compensation upon termination of the concessions.
(3) Assets received by the state in defective condition or without access to service, repairs or spare parts.

The Constitutional amendment also authorized the President to deduct from the amount of compensation all or part of the excess profits realized by the companies since the New Deal legislation had gone into effect. Criteria were laid down for determining excess profits, including the companies' overall profitability in their worldwide operations, but these criteria were not mandatory for the President. The decision on the amount of compensation was to be made by an independent official – the Comptroller-General – whose main function was to assess the legality of Executive decisions. A Special Tribunal, made up of three superior court judges, the President of the Central Bank of Chile and the Director of the Internal Revenue Service, was set up to hear appeals from the companies. The President of the Republic was authorized to determine the period, interest rate and method of payment of the compensation. The term could not be more than thirty years and the interest rate not less than 3% per year. The amount of compensation thus determined superseded any previous obligation resulting from the agreements for equity transactions described above. The President was also authorized to decide whether the capital obtained through the debts had been usefully invested; if it had not, the state would not assume responsibility for such debts.

As can be appreciated, the question of excess profits was a crucial point in determining the amount of compensation that the companies would ultimately receive. In order to establish a criterion for what constituted normal profits, the President asked CODELCO to undertake a series of studies whose objective was to compare the profitability of the companies' Chilean operations with that of their operations in the rest of the world. Profitability was calculated in relation to book value in each case. The results are summarized in Table 6.2.

The results of this and of other studies led President Allende to choose a figure of 12% of the book value *per annum* as a criterion for normal profitability and to order that all profits exceeding this figure be deducted from the amount of compensation. The final calculation made by the Comptroller-General yielded the results shown in Table 6.3.

The U.S. companies appealed the Comptroller's decision and objected to all aspects of the calculation, including the determination of book value, the revaluation (in the case of Braden), the deduction of assets in defective condition, and the deduction of excess profits. The state also objected to some aspects of the determination of book value and to the way in which deductions were made. On the question of excess profits, the position of the Council for the Defence of the State was that the text of the Constitutional amendment gave the President exclusive power to make deductions under the excess profits clause, and that consequently the Special Tribunal was not competent to pass on this question. In the face of this argument, the U.S. companies asked the Tribunal to decide, previous to further judgment, whether or not it was competent to alter the deductions made under the excess profits clause.[10]

Meanwhile, on 31 December 1971, another set of promissory notes to Anaconda for the purchase of 51% of Chuquicamata and El Salvador expired (the Allende Government had paid the installments due up to 30 June 1971 since the nationalization proposals had not yet become law). In anticipation of this, CODELCO and the Council for the Defence of the State petitioned the Special Tribunal to order suspension of payments until the question of the amount of compensation had been resolved, for the Constitutional amendment established that compensation took the place of any previous obligations emanating from share purchases. For its part, Anaconda maintained that the notes were abstract commercial documents, independent of the share transaction, and that consequently the Special Tribunal was not competent to order the suspension of these payments on the basis of the nationalization legislation. The state had deposited with the Tribunal a sum in Chilean currency equivalent to the value of the notes that had become due as a way of guaranteeing payment if the judgment went against it; the Tribunal agreed with the state's argument and ordered the suspension of payments. On the basis of that decision the notes were not paid when they became due. Anaconda responded in February 1972 by obtaining a writ of attachment before the Federal Court of the Second District of New York. The writ was executed against the goods and current accounts of CODELCO and the *Corporación de Fomento de la Producción* (CORFO) [Corporation for Production Development], which had guaranteed the notes.

In September 1972, the Special Tribunal announced its decision on the previous judgment and declared itself incompetent to deal with challenges to the excess profits clause. It ruled that deductions made on the basis of the excess profits clause fell within the exclusive jurisdiction of the President of the Republic. At that point Kennecott decided to withdraw from the proceedings before the Special Tribunal, arguing that, given the amount of the deductions that were to be excluded from the Tribunal's jurisdiction, it no longer had any economic interest in the Tribunal's final ruling. It further stated that it reserved the right to claim ownership of the copper from El Teniente or the proceeds of its sale before the courts of other countries; this statement was circulated among European purchasers of copper from the El Teniente mine.[11]

2.2. *The International Conflict: Chile's Evaluation of the Options*

The conflict with the copper companies thus became open in September 1972; however, as early as the first few months of the Allende Government it was increasingly clear that nationalization of Gran Minería would bring the Chilean and U.S. Governments into conflict. In the preface to a book on expropriations written in June 1971 (that is, before the Constitutional amendment for nationalization was voted on by the National Congres), former U.S. Secretary of State William Rogers discussed the Chilean nationalization proposals and stated the U.S. Government's policy in the following terms:

> The United States Government is dragging its feet on fresh unilateral development lending to the offending countries. And it is doing what it can to slow down loans by the World Bank and the Inter-American Development Bank until the valuation questions are settled.[12]

There is no doubt that the conflict with the United States, whose President at that time was Richard Nixon, had deeper roots.[13] Salvador Allende's campaign platform very clearly stated the need to reduce Chile's economic, political, diplomatic and military dependence on the United States; more specifically Allende had denounced the Organization of American States (OAS) – and in fact the very concept of pan-Americanism – as an instrument of U.S. domination of the subcontinent. He had advocated setting up a Latin American organization, without U.S. participation, to negotiate with the United States on a bilateral basis. One of Allende's first foreign policy decisions was to re-establish diplomatic relations with Cuba. Moreover, the Nixon Administration was deeply disturbed by the fact that the Chilean Communist Party was participating in the Allende Government; more generally, the domestic structural changes advocated in the UP Government Programme could only be regarded as a threat to those groups in Chile that had been the United States' traditional allies. There is no doubt, however, that nationalizing the copper companies – particularly in the manner in which it was done – could not but exacerbate the conflict; it also provided the U.S. Government and the companies involved with a pretext for initiating the kind of direct economic blockade which would have been very difficult to set up under normal circumstances.

Before assessing the consequences of the conflict for the copper industry and for the Chilean economy, it seems fit to raise the question anticipated at the beginning of this chapter: how necessary was it to nationalize the copper industry (and to deduct excess profits from the amount of compensation) in terms of the Allende Government's programme of socio-economic transformations?

On the question of nationalization as such, the answer is clear: the Allende Government had no alternative – either political or economic – to a policy of outright nationalization of the copper industry. As we indicated earlier, in 1970 Gran Minería accounted for 80% of Chilean copper production and almost 60% of hard currency earnings. The foreign share in Gran Minería meant that the surplus available for domestic development was reduced by the amount of profits repatriated by the foreign partner. Perhaps even more important, it also meant that production, marketing and investment policy were all controlled by two U.S. transnational companies. It is difficult to imagine that a process of socialist transformation of the economy and of Chilean society as a whole could take place without first changing this situation of recurrent loss of resources and of foreign control over the country's most important industry. Moreover, in 1970-71, the political climate in Chile made it impossible to delay the fulfillment of the election promise to nationalize copper. At the time of the 1970 elections, both Allende and Radomiro Tomic, the Christian Democratic candidate, put forward an electoral programme which included the complete nationalization of the copper industry. It can therefore be said that the idea of nationalization was supported by two thirds of the electorate. The parties who made up the UP, especially the Socialists and the Communists who were the largest components, had been struggling for complete nationalization for the previous twenty years; they felt that nationalizing copper was a prerequisite to greater political and economic independence for the country. Thus it was the sectors that comprised the basis of support for the Allende Government that demanded complete nationalization, and in fact it appears that neither the President nor the parties that were in the Government ever contemplated any policy other than the immediate nationalization of the copper industry.[14]

However, as mentioned earlier, it was not nationalization as such which gave rise to the conflict, but rather the question of compensation. There are those who maintain that the conflict could have been avoided by paying the companies a 'reasonable' compensation, but this apparently simple solution raises a number of difficult problems. In the first place, it is not at all certain that an offer of reasonable compensation would have been sufficient to avert the conflict. To be sure, both the U.S. Government and the companies maintained that they recognized Chile's right as a sovereign state to nationalize its main natural resource; on the other hand, the companies also emphasized the fact that only three years earlier, the Chilean Government had signed an agreement with them which precluded unilateral nationalization.[15] Under these conditions, had the Allende Government agreed to pay a 'reasonable' price for the companies' assets, it might have been faced with claims for compensation for both the termination of the service contracts and cancellation of the 1967-69 agreements.

At a less speculative level, the idea that nationalization would have been possible without conflict presents some serious difficulties. The most obvious one is, of course, the question of what would have constituted 'reasonable' compensation. Because of the history of very high profits made by the companies, particularly during the 1967-70 period, a substantial additional compensation was politically very difficult. The majority party within the UP coalition, the Socialist Party, went on record as opposing any compensation at all, a position also shared by important sectors within the powerful *Central*

Unica de Trabajadores (CUT) [Trade Unions' Confederation]. By contrast, the companies initially put forward claims that amounted to $2 thousand million, although Kennecott stated that it would be satisfied with the payment of 49% of El Teniente's revalued book value – that is, approximately $176 million – instead of the $1 thousand million resulting from the capitalization of earnings.[16] Anaconda also reduced its initial estimation of $1 thousand million[17] to $474 million when it wrote off its losses for U.S. tax purposes in 1972.[18] All things considered, a figure of about $70 million a year for ten years appears to be a plausible estimate of the cost of satisfying the companies at that point in time.[19] As mentioned, this was politically unthinkable; furthermore, a compensation of that magnitude would have considerably reduced the immediate economic benefits of nationalization: it amounted to about one third of the companies' average annual profits for the preceding four years, when the copper price had been abnormally high.

Let us digress briefly to comment on an aspect of this problem that has given rise to many contradictory statements. It is the question of whether the 1971 nationalization allowed for real compensation to be paid to the companies. On the basis of the figures summarized in Table 6.3 the companies concluded that they would not receive any compensation. While this assertion by the companies received widespread publicity, it is in fact incorrect. To begin with, Kennecott continued to receive payments for the $92 million loan contracted in 1967. As was indicated earlier, this constituted payment for 51% of El Teniente, plus interest for the first three years. This figure was only $8 million less than the total book value of El Teniente in 1970, excluding revaluation. While it is true that Anaconda received only some $36 million in 1970-71 for the purchase of 51% of Chuquicamata and El Salvador, if Chile had assumed responsibility for the debts of all nationalized companies, this would have amounted to paying compensation amounting to 49% of the debts. In the case of El Teniente, liabilities amounted to 75% of the gross value of assets, excluding revaluation, and 45% if revaluation is taken into account. In the cases of Chuquicamata and El Salvador, the debts amounted to 43% of the gross value of assets.[20] Moreover, the Government was prepared to pay compensation for Exótica and for Andina, neither of which had realized excess profits.

As was to be expected, these arguments convinced neither the companies nor the U.S. Government, so that when the Allende Government decided on the course of action described above it knew that it was heading for a conflict with both of them.

Let us now turn to discussing how the conflict, and its possible consequences for the national economy, were perceived in 1971, and how the Chilean Government hoped to face them.

2.2.1. *Possible Responses from the Companies*

The first aspect of the conflict involved a confrontation with the companies themselves. Here the companies could presumably make use of the usual array of reprisals available to transnational companies in situations of this kind, which included: technological reprisals (withdrawing technicians, directly or indirectly cutting off the supply of spare parts or inputs needed in the production process); commercial reprisals (closing marketing channels, putting pressure on purchasers of Chilean copper); and legal reprisals (embargoes and claims on the ownership of the nationalized copper before the courts of various countries).

While these measures did represent a threat, it was thought that the possibility of their causing insuperable problems was rather remote. A set of factors having to do with the way in which Chilean copper was produced and marketed, as well as international legal theory and practice, clearly favoured the Chilean position.

1. Chile had already acquired the technical capacity to take over production operations without any reduction in efficiency. In fact at the time of nationalization, there was only a small group of foreigners doing technical work in the mines and thus the companies were in no position to disrupt production by withdrawing technical personnel on a large scale.[21] There was the separate problem of the degree of loyalty which the state could expect from the Chilean technical and administrative personnel. Under foreign ownership of the mines, these employees had enjoyed special privileges (they were, for example, paid in dollars). However, this problem had much more to do with these employees' working conditions under the new management and with more general political considerations than with the question of compensating the companies.

As far as machinery, spare parts and imported raw materials were concerned, the Gran Minería operations were highly dependent on U.S. suppliers. It has been estimated that 90% of imported inputs for the mines came from the United States; still, the copper companies had no direct control over the flow of imported inputs although, by using their commercial contacts and their buying power, they could always try to disrupt relations between the traditional suppliers of the Chilean mining industry and the Chilean state as new owner of the mines. Simultaneously, a difficult situation was created by the fact that CODELCO, which became the main shareholder of the nationalized companies, had little experience in purchasing inputs for the mines from foreign suppliers; the purchasing departments of the copper companies had more experience in this area than the state agency and they also were, on the whole, staffed by Chilean personnel who enjoyed special privileges. The whole area of purchasing was therefore a potentially dangerous one.

2. As to the problem of marketing Chilean copper throughout the world, in 1970 the bulk of Chilean copper production was sold to Western European

countries; the amount sold to the United States was relatively small and the percentage acquired by other subsidiaries of the U.S. companies to be refined and sold in Europe was virtually negligible (see Table 6.4).

In view of this situation it was unlikely that the companies could have persuaded dozens of European firms which normally purchased Chilean copper to change their supplier. Chilean copper accounted for approximately 15% of the world's total copper production, excluding the socialist countries; while there was a certain amount of surplus production in relation to world demand, it was unrealistic to think that the Western economies could be deprived of a substantial part of the Chilean copper, which they needed as a result of an economic blockade orchestrated by the U.S. companies.

It was therefore generally believed that by taking reasonable precautions, the Chilean Government could continue to operate the mines and to market its copper throughout the world despite the companies' threat of reprisals. This meant organizing an international network of buying agents to purchase inputs, possibly from companies located in various countries, and looking into the possibility of buying in those markets, other than the United States, where similar items could be obtained. Countries such as Great Britain, Canada, Japan, Australia and New Zealand seemed to be the most promising, since subsidiaries of the original U.S. suppliers operated in them and they were likely to be less vulnerable to commercial and legal pressures from Anaconda and Kennecott. On the marketing side, it was decided at an early stage to make use of the experience gained by CODELCO during the 'Chileanization' period, when the staff of its Sales Department had an opportunity to be exposed to international negotiations. It was also decided that a network of sales agents would be located in Europe and would be responsible for managing the annual contracts or setting up equivalent ones.

3. From the legal viewpoint as well, it was assumed that Chile would be in a strong position to deal with possible attacks from the companies. The evolution of international law during the previous twenty years had strengthened the concept of national sovereignty over natural resources; evidence of this trend is provided by the adoption of United Nations Resolution 1803 in 1962 and, one year later, by the U.S. Supreme Court's decision in the Sabbatino case, which dealt with the nationalization of the sugar industry in Cuba.[22] The effect of UN Resolution 1803 was clearly and succinctly described by U.S. specialist in international law:

> ... under the resolutions adopted by the United Nations, nationalization of property constituting natural wealth or resources can never be illegal. The failure to pay 'appropriate' compensation under the Resolution of 1962 would not convert an otherwise sanctioned or legal act into an illegal one. The transfer of ownership is thus legal without regard to the observance of the payment of compensation.[23]

Thus the trend in international law had been towards depriving companies which were being nationalized of their most effective legal weapon: the possibility of claiming property rights over the nationalized goods and of trying to regain possession of these goods regardless of where they are located. The U.S. Supreme Court decision in the Sabbatino case recognized the validity of the Cuban nationalizations, despite the fact that no compensation had been paid, on the basis of the 'act of state' doctrine. According to this principle, the courts of one country cannot judge the validity of an action taken by any other sovereign power within the latter's own territory. It is true that shortly after the Sabbatino decision was handed down, the U.S. Congress passed the so-called Hickenlooper Amendment which, in practice, had the effect of revoking by legislation the doctrine that had been established by the Supreme Court; but even then, the Hickenlooper Amendment only applied to companies in which U.S. interests had a share of at least 50%.

In the context of this general evolution of international law on nationalization, the technical and legal strategy of nationalization was worked out with the aim of reducing Chile's vulnerability to attacks from the U.S. copper companies.[24] In particular, the legal advisers to the Chilean Government conducted a study of U.S. court decisions on the question of sovereign immunity, that is, the theory that, in the courts of a given state, neither another state nor its assets can be the object of legal proceedings. It was thought – rightly, as it later turned out – that this would be a crucial aspect of any judicial confrontation concerning the promissory notes for 51% of Anaconda's operations, which Chile had purchased in 1969; these notes, it will be remembered, were cancelled by the nationalization.[25]

As will be seen below, the Chilean Government's understanding of the general nature and significance of the legal conflict with the companies was basically correct; however, on specific aspects of the conflict events took a course which had not been anticipated with any degree of precision. One area in particular had not been examined adequately: there had, in the past, been legal proceedings in certain European countries in which the validity of nationalizations had been challenged; when the nationalization in question had taken place in a former colony of a particular country and had affected the interests of that country's citizens, the courts of that country had decided against the nationalizing state, thus creating an unfavourable precedent for the Chilean position. This was the case in France and the Netherlands as a result of nationalizations that had taken place in Algeria and Indonesia, respectively. The precise extent of the threat presented by this situation was not realized by the Chilean Government until Kennecott actually initiated proceedings on this basis in France and the Netherlands in September 1972.

2.2.2. *The Evaluation of the Other Possible Effects*

A second area where problems might have arisen was the effect that nationalization would have on the flow of capital and technology, both into the copper industry and into the economy as a whole. Since the Allende Government's general policy was to discourage direct foreign investment, the impact of nationalization on investment of this type was not a cause for concern. But the possible effects of nationalization on flows of credit and other sources of financing that were not linked with foreign ownership of companies in Chile was quite another matter. Initially, it was felt that such flows need not be affected by nationalization, particularly those coming from the private sector in Europe and Japan. And obviously the socialist countries provided another possible source of capital. A similar reasoning was deemed applicable to the flow of technology; in the copper industry there was the additional advantage that extraction and refining technologies were fairly widely diffused and there had not been recent technological changes of any importance.

There is no doubt that the most potentially dangerous area was that of commercial and financial relations with the United States – relations which would involve the U.S. Government itself, the international financial agencies dominated by the United States, and even the U.S. private sector if the U.S. Government were to decide to block all economic relations with Chile. An extreme example of this kind of measure had been the U.S. decision, at the time of the conflict with Cuba,[26] to invoke the Trade with the Enemy Act. It was quite possible that such a move on by the U.S. Government would influence the governments and private sectors in other Western countries.

In 1970, the Chilean economy was highly dependent on that of the United States. Almost 40% of total Chilean imports originated in the United States, including – as mentioned earlier – some 90% of supplies for copper mining; other areas where U.S. imports were substantial were automobile parts and petroleum. Petroleum was not imported directly from the United States, but 60% of imported crude oil came from U.S. companies.[27] All of this trade was based on a network of financial arrangements in which private U.S. banks provided lines of credit to the importers via Chilean banks and the main suppliers themselves extended direct credits – often guaranteed by the Eximbank. Short-term credit to Chile from private U.S. banks amounted to $220 million in 1970 and loans from the World Bank and the Inter-American Development Bank (IDB) – both dominated by the United States – averaged $50 million a year during the 1965-70 period.[28] Also, the United States was Chile's main international public creditor, accounting for a full 50% of Chile's huge external debt, which was passed on to the Allende Government in 1970.

To be sure, one of Allende's basic objectives was to reduce this dependence, but it was clear that a sharp break in economic relations between Chile and the United States could not but create serious difficulties for the Allende Government. This was particularly so considering that certain issues tended to increase the external vulnerability of the Chilean economy. The domestic, social and economic transformations which the Government intended to carry out were undoubtedly going to put pressures on the balance of payments since a more progressive distribution of income had to result in an increase in imports of intermediate and consumer goods. At the same time, the creation of an *Area de Propiedad Social* (APS) [Area of Social Property] as well as the acceleration of the agrarian reform would probably lead, at least initially, to a reduction in production levels and thus increase the pressures on the balance of payments. Finally, international copper prices were exceptionally low and no significant rise was expected during 1971-72.

These were the factors which pointed to the dangers and risks of a conflict over compensation; the total picture was, however, not so negative. To begin with, it was felt among Chilean decision-makers that a Cuban-type blockade was unlikely. As long as the UP Government's foreign policy did not provide excuses for taking extreme measures, the impression was that the political costs of a blockade of this kind for the U.S. Government would be very high, given the political climate in Latin America and throughout the world. It was also expected that if an open conflict with the United States could be avoided, short-term credits from Western Europe and Japan would remain unaffected, while at the same time Chile could re-direct its imports from the United States to those countries. This possibility remained open because of the way in which the international system was evolving: conflicting tendencies within the advanced capitalist world were emerging and would lead to increasing capitalist competition. In addition, it was hoped that the socialist countries would make a substantial contribution and that this would help mitigate the effects of the U.S. economic blockade.

The preceding is not meant to imply that the decision on the question of compensating the copper companies was based solely on a purely rational evaluation of costs and benefits. A decision as important as this, taken in the context of a revolutionary process, must be influenced by a variety of factors – some of them not rational – and the decision on compensation was no exception. For one thing, all sectors in the UP coalition felt that, in all justice, the companies had no right to substantial compensation. The companies' Chilean operations had, over the years, yielded such extraordinary profits that, in the words of the decree which provided for the deduction of excess profits, the situation called for an 'historical rectification'.

Beyond that the positions of the various political groupings and technical experts within the UP did not coincide completely. As indicated above, the Socialist Party maintained from the beginning that no compensation should be paid, as a matter of principle, and that the Government should be prepared to face the consequences of such a policy, whatever they might be. Moreover, there was no agreement on how serious such consequences might be. Some of the UP experts thought in fact that the external sector would increase the range of freedom in the Government's economic strategy; this misconception was based on an overestimation of future copper production, and in certain cases on the belief that the U.S. Government would be unable to elicit the cooperation of the multilateral lending agencies in organizing an economic blockade against Chile. On the other hand, there were those who believed that the probability of a clash with the U.S. Government was not essentially dependent upon Chile's attitude toward the copper companies, but upon the threat which the UP experiment represented for the U.S. Government's desire to perpetuate its economic and political domination of the continent. It was, therefore, thought that trying to avert the conflict by compromising on the compensation question was no solution at all: the conflict would occur in any case, though other pretexts might have to be used to trigger it.

Thus it was a complex interplay of different political attitudes and factual assessments of various groups within the UP coalition which resulted in the approach ultimately taken on the question of compensating the U.S. copper companies.

3. THE DEVELOPMENT OF THE INTERNATIONAL CONFLICT ON CHILEAN COPPER: THE CAUSES AND CONSEQUENCES

3.1. *The Impact of Nationalization on the Gran Minería*

Before discussing the development of the international conflict on Chilean copper we must examine the impact of nationalization on Gran Minería operations. As we shall see further on, there was, in fact, no sharp distinction between the 'domestic' and the 'international' aspects of the copper question. Nevertheless this section will focus on the relationship between, on the one hand, the change of management in the copper industry and the new policies that emerged from it and, on the other, the performance of the industry in the areas of production and marketing.

Generally speaking, the main objective of the Government policy on the newly nationalized Gran Minería was to keep the industry operating in a normal manner in order to ensure that the flow of foreign exchange, necessary to support the overall economic changes introduced by the UP, would not be interrupted. Consequently, no bold and risky measures were proposed on matters of production and marketing. Changes were only introduced whenever they appeared necessary to correct faulty policies, or to deal with new situations emerging as a result of nationalization.

If one looks at the impact of nationalization on production the first thing one notices is that production levels did not collapse as a result of the U.S. companies' withdrawal; there was, however, a drop in the combined production of the three largest mines (see Table 6.5).

The reasons for this decrease are complex and certainly not associated solely with nationalization. A significant proportion of this drop in production can be attributed to technical problems created while the U.S. companies were still managing the mines. In the case of El Teniente, the main problems derived from an insufficient supply of water for the new concentrator installed at Colan and from the difficulties involved in putting a new and untried method of fusion in the converters into operation. In both cases, the responsibility could be assigned to those who set up the expansion programme. In Chuquicamata, the management decided in mid-1969 to drastically reduce the removal of overburden and to apply high-grading methods, whereby only those sections of the mine with high copper content are exploited intensively. The problem with this method is that after some time access to other parts of the mine becomes very difficult and the accumulated overburden must be removed at great cost. Two technical missions, one from France and one from the Soviet Union, which studied the condition of the mines after Allende came to power, criticized Anaconda's extraction methods in Chuquicamata and more generally their low standards of management.[29]

These and other technical problems would have affected the level of production even if the mines had not been nationalized. Of course, there were also difficulties associated with the process of nationalization itself. To begin with, a certain number of U.S. and Chilean technicians resigned during the first two years because, among other things, certain privileges which they had enjoyed until then, such as being paid in dollars, were discontinued. But as had been anticipated, the impact of losing these technicians was in fact not significant. There were difficulties in some areas but on the whole, the employees who stayed on, together with those who joined the companies after nationalization, were perfectly capable of continuing mining operations in a normal way. Evidence of this comes from the El Teniente mine, where production figures in 1972 were the highest in the mine's history. As for the areas in which difficulties arose, in most cases the Government was able to find the technicians that were needed in Eastern or Western Europe, and in some cases U.S. personnel stayed on. As mentioned earlier, another negative factor was that the supervisory personnel who stayed on at the mines became increasingly hostile to the Government and to the mines' management. These were not only technicians but also administrative personnel who had been recruited by the U.S. managements essentially on the basis of their loyalty to the company. The nontechnical employees stayed on because there were few employment opportunities for them in other countries, but they remained hostile to the Government. As political forces in Chile became increasingly polarized, these employees were responsible for growing labour problems and even for sabotage.

Labour discipline also became a problem. When the Chilean state took over the mines the elaborate system of rewards and sanctions designed by the companies to ensure discipline and maintain productivity was done away with.

The new management wanted to introduce a totally different system based on the workers' participation and awareness, but the transformation was slow and difficult and labour problems developed. In Chuquicamata, there were forty-six strikes in 1972, compared with thirty-nine in 1971, which led to a loss of 6,048 work shifts in 1972 compared with 4,193 in 1971. At El Salvador, a two-week strike in 1971 resulted in a loss of production equivalent to half of the total production lost through strikes in the whole of the year before.[30] Finally at El Teniente, a political strike based to some extent on economic grievances – which lasted from the end of April to the end of June 1973 – led to a drastic reduction in the previously high level of average production there.[31]

On the marketing side, CODELCO became the sales agent for the nationalized companies and essentially maintained the existing marketing system; this included appointing sub-agents in the major marketing areas who would be responsible for dealing with annual sales contracts negotiated by CODELCO, for handling paper-work and for supervising payments. The markets for Chilean copper did not change in any substantial way. Sales to Western Europe dropped slightly, although they still accounted for over half of total world sales in 1971-72. Sales to the United States also dropped from 15% to 10% of total Chilean copper exports between 1970 and 1972, while there was an increase in sales to Japan, Latin America and the socialist countries, particularly China.

As for the terms of sales, Chile played an active role within the Intergovernmental Council of Copper-Exporting Countries (CIPEC, the members of which were Chile, Peru, Zaire and Zambia) in a policy of price support. The world market for copper went through a period of recession in 1971-72 as a result of a general slowdown in economic activity in Europe and the United States. On the supply side, new mines began production in Canada and in Papua New Guinea; plans for these operations had been made by Rio Tinto Zinc in 1967-68, when copper prices seemed to have a more promising future from the producers' viewpoint.[32] In this situation, Chile argued that joint action was necessary to stabilize copper prices and to work towards price increases. However, this initiative did not succeed because of disagreements, particularly involving Zaire, over questions of markets and prices, and no united action on the part of the producing countries was possible. For its part, Chile decided not to take unilateral action as this would have entailed serious risks.

Generally speaking, the net result of nationalization was positive in terms of the objectives the policy was meant to achieve. Since dividends were no longer paid out to foreign companies, the amount of foreign currency generated by the mines that was retained in Chile rose by about 25% a year. Moreover, a larger proportion of inputs were purchased in Chile; this resulted in a reduction of expenditures in foreign currency and thus had beneficial effects on the industrial sector. In addition, the concentration of copper resources and the centralized control which Chile exercised over them gave the country certain financial advantages. These included the use of copper shipments as a basis for obtaining credit from private European banks: by the end of 1973 such credits amounted to about $20 million. Finally, it became possible to integrate the copper industry more rationally into overall economic planning and to transfer surplus generated by the mining sector to the rest of the economy through the manipulation of exchange rates.

An examination of the effects of the international conflict which arose as a result of nationalizing copper does not substantially alter this positive picture. In the sections that follow, we shall see how the conflict developed and we shall distinguish the direct conflict with the companies from the effects that nationalizing copper might have had on relations with the U.S. Government.

3.2. *The Conflict with the Companies*

The most overt expression of this conflict was in fact the reprisals from the companies. There was, however, a difference in the way the two companies reacted. As mentioned earlier, Kennecott had derived substantial benefits from the 'Chileanization' agreement and its economic investment in Chile was less substantial than Anaconda's. It chose a strategy based on open confrontation and on using every opportunity for taking reprisals against Chile anywhere in the world.[33] More specifically, its tactic was to try to quickly obtain writs of attachment on copper and on the proceeds from its sale in various European countries as a way of disrupting normal trade in El Teniente copper and creating chaos which would force the Allende Government to negotiate. To this end the company obtained writs of attachment in France, the Netherlands and the Federal Republic of Germany between September 1972 and January 1973. Similar attempts in Sweden and Italy did not succeed. Kennecott did not extend this strategy to Great Britain, even though that country was the second largest purchaser of Chilean copper, because the British legal system did not allow for quick attachments in cases of this type and also because existing court precedents in nationalization cases were clearly favourable to the Chilean position.

The French embargo was lifted at the end of November by a higher civil court (*tribunale grande instance*) in Paris, although Chile's main defence – sovereign immunity – was rejected. The Dutch attachment was lifted unilaterally by Kennecott since it applied to a shipment of copper whose value had already been attached in France; the German attachment was lifted unconditionally by the Hamburg District Court in mid-January.[34] In other words, Kennecott did not achieve its tactical objective. To be sure, its action did create difficulties *vis-à-vis* marketing Chilean copper in Europe: sales of rather small amounts of El Teniente copper were suspended in France and Sweden and in other cases shipping routes had to be changed, which involved extra costs. But the fact is that Kennecott was unable to block the sale of El Teniente copper in Europe. Far from forcing the Allende Government to negotiate, Kennecott's offensive strengthened the Government's resolve not to compromise. Moreover, the reprisals helped mobilize support within Chile for the Government's policy on this question and gave rise to a wave of international solidarity with Chile which culminated in a special meeting of ministers of the CIPEC countries in November 1972 in Santiago, where Kennecott's action was condemned and a plan for defending and supporting Chile was agreed on.[35]

Anaconda's tactics and strategy were completely different. Rather than seeking to establish its rights over its 49% of the nationalized companies, Anaconda concentrated on obtaining the U.S. courts' recognition of its claim to payment for the 51% purchased by the Frei Government. If Anaconda succeeded in doing this, it could try to attach funds and goods (not only copper) belonging to CODELCO and CORFO in various Western countries as a way of paying off the debt. This strategy was being used successfully in New York, where the defence which Chile presented – sovereign immunity – had been rejected in the first instance at the time of the military *coup d'état* in 1973.[36] It therefore represented a far more serious threat than Kennecott's action, even though the problem posed by Anaconda was only a medium-term one and Chile's liability was limited to the value of the promissory notes. Moreover, the precautionary writ of attachment granted by the New York court extended to all materials purchased by CODELCO for use in the mines; in practice, this meant that New York and its port could no longer be used as a source of inputs. This gave rise to a technical problem of some importance since certain inputs could only be obtained in the United States, and although they could be shipped from other U.S. ports, there was always the possibility that Anaconda might try to take legal action in other states in the United States. In order to overcome this problem CODELCO launched a vigorous campaign to find new suppliers in Canada, Western Europe, Japan, Australia and New Zealand. In general, Chile had no apparent problems in making purchases in those countries (the same was true in the United States although U.S. suppliers demanded very strict terms of sale such as cash payment and deposits at the time of ordering). But problems still remained. Some of the materials, particularly spare parts, could only be obtained from certain U.S. companies; there were no substitutes from other sources. In some cases not even subsidiaries of U.S. firms could provide certain types of products, so that requests sent to a Canadian or a European subsidiary were simply referred to the head office in the United States. Costs were considerably higher when material was purchased from Canadian subsidiaries. Altogether in 1972, Chile managed to divert a high proportion of its U.S.-imported inputs to Canada (which began to account for about 50% of total purchases) and to London (about 20%).[37]

In addition to taking legal reprisals, the U.S. companies tried to use their influence to damage the commercial prospects of the nationalized companies. Kennecott tried to apply pressure on European purchasers of El Teniente copper, but the results were meager: only one Swedish company was persuaded to stop buying Chilean copper. It has also been said that Anaconda tried to persuade those companies in the United States which were major suppliers to the Chilean mines to stop selling to Chile. Although that was not achieved, Anaconda's action may have contributed to the U.S. suppliers' insistence on the very strict terms of sale that have been mentioned earlier. Finally, Anaconda participated actively in meetings of the so-called '*Ad Hoc* Committee on Chile' which were held in January 1971 – that is, before nationalization. This was a committee set up by U.S. companies with interests in Chile to press the U.S. Government to take a hard line *vis-à-vis* the Allende Government; the objective was to prevent a massive nationalization of U.S. capital in Chile, or at least to make it more difficult. Kennecott sent a representative to the first meeting, but not to subsequent ones. The group ceased to function shortly thereafter. In general, there is no evidence that Anaconda or Kennecott participated actively in the efforts to 'destabilize' the Allende Government, which were directed by the CIA and involved the International Telephone and Telegraph Corporation (ITT).[38]

To summarize, the direct conflict with the companies did not create insuperable difficulties for the Allende Government. The costs to Chile can well be regarded as a reasonable price to pay to regain the ownership and control of the country's basic source of wealth, and to do so in a manner compatible with the nation's interests and dignity.

3.3. *The Conflict with the U.S. Government*

The situation was quite different when it came to coping with reprisals taken by the U.S. Government. It had been expected that an open blockade of the type used during the Cuban conflict was unlikely to take place and this was indeed the case. Inter-American relations and the international situation as a whole had changed sufficiently to make the political cost of such a measure too high. But without reaching the level of open warfare, the measures taken by the U.S. Government – quietly but systematically – constituted a crucial element in the process which decided the ultimate fate of the UP experiment.

The Nixon Administration's policy *vis-à-vis* Chile involved what has been called a 'triad' of approaches.[39] First, as we have just indicated, measures of the type that had been used against Cuba were avoided; the official attitude was characterized as 'cool but correct'. Second, there was an economic blockade which included the following measures directed against Chile: suspension of all bilateral aid – except military aid – as well as of loans and guarantees from the Eximbank; opposition to loans being granted to Chile by the World Bank and by the IDB; pressure on private banks in the United States to reduce their lines of credit to Chile; and refusal to renegotiate the Chilean external debt. Finally, a systematic campaign of covert action was launched by the CIA with the aim, first, of preventing Allende's election and second, of preventing the consolidation of his regime. These covert measures included a $1 million propaganda campaign conducted before the elections and an unsuccessful attempt to stage a military *coup* to prevent Allende from being confirmed by the National Congress after his election (the first economic reprisals were taken at that time in order to create favourable conditions for the *coup*). Moreover, throughout the 1971-73 period the U.S. Government spent some $7 million in support of right-wing political parties and publications, and of civilian groups in the extreme right that were linked with terrorist and other subversive activities such as the lockouts of 1972 and 1973. In addition, close contact was maintained with military groups who were known to favour a *coup d'état*, including the group which staged the *coup d'état* of September 1973.

The vast amount of documentary material which emerged from the U.S. Senate's investigation into CIA activities in Chile reveals that the U.S. Government's overall objective in Chile during this period was to prevent the consolidation of the Allende Government. More specifically, the purpose was, at the very least, to reduce the Chilean Government's effectiveness in carrying out the UP programme and in introducing irreversible changes, and at best to bring the entire UP experiment to an early end, either by constitutional means (such as impeachment or resignation) or by means of violence. As we shall see below, obtaining compensation for the copper companies was a secondary objective.

There will be no attempt in this chapter to discuss in detail the effects which U.S. intervention had on Chile under the UP Government and on the final demise of the experience: that question is dealt with in other chapters in this volume. Briefly, I feel that U.S. intervention taken as a whole was a very important element in that experiment's failure. The economic blockade created serious balance of payments problems which, in turn, affected the availability of consumer and intermediate goods for the industrial sector. However, the economic blockade in itself did not constitute an insuperable obstacle for the Allende Government. Around mid-1973, the copper price had gone up considerably and Chile had managed to find new sources of short-term financing – the area worst affected by the blockade – in Europe and Japan. To be sure, there were still serious imbalances in the economy and politically, the destabilizing effects of the difficulties encountered until then were considerable. However, had it been possible for the Government to consolidate politically, it might have been in a position to deal with the economic blockade. The possibility of such political consolidation had been clearly established at the time of the congressional elections in March 1973, when the Government obtained 44% of the vote, an increase of almost 23% over the corresponding figure for the 1970 presidential election. But at the same time this consolidation was being undermined by CIA covert action. There is no doubt that the basic dynamic of subversion in Chile under Allende stemmed from the class struggle within Chilean society and the reaction of the dominant sectors of that society to the UP's political programme – a programme which these sectors regarded as fundamentally harmful to their interests. But it is also quite clear that the subversive elements inside the country received decisive help through the intervention of the CIA, which provided technical capability, financing and political support.[40] Thus the combined effects of the economic blockade and of political subversion, which were mutually reinforcing, ensured that the Allende experiment would not be viable.

3.3.1. *The Conflict over Nationalizing Copper and the U.S. Government's Policy*

To what extent did the conflict over nationalizing copper influence the formulation and implementation of the U.S. policy of intervention in Chile? The answer to this question is complicated because irrational and subjective elements within the U.S. Government blurred the logic behind their actions, and because, moreover, the role of the compensation issue within U.S. policy-making remained quite ambiguous.

It seems clear that U.S. policy was not a response to the way in which the nationalization of copper was carried out; as we have indicated, the U.S. Government's campaign against Allende was initiated before he was inaugurated. To be sure, Allende had clearly expressed his intention to nationalize the copper industry; furthermore, the UP programme and the political orientation of its constituent parties indicated that copper would probably be nationalized in a way which would be regarded by the companies as harmful to their interests. However, it is a fact that President Richard M. Nixon's instruction to the Director of the CIA at the time, Richard Helms, to organize a *coup d'état* in Chile was issued quite some time before any of the specific problems that have been mentioned in relation to copper nationalization – including the idea of a retroactive deduction of excess profits – had arisen. Moreover, it was explicitly stated at this stage that the U.S. Government's main concern was the potential repercussions in Latin America of a democratically elected marxist government successfully carrying out its programme of change in Chile.[41] While such statements are not always a reliable source about real attitudes, they were, in some cases, made under the cloak of confidentiality and are thus probably closer to the truth. The UP experiment had implications for U.S. hegemony in the Western hemisphere: it was the United States' basic rejection of these implications which governed their policy towards Chile, the objective of which was to ensure that the experiment would not succeed.

Of course, in the formulation of this objective U.S. economic interests in Chile – including not only the copper companies but also the substantial ITT investments – were not ignored. It can be argued that Allende's policy towards the U.S. companies helped to harden the initial position of the U.S. Government. It was also clear from the outset that ensuring that the companies should receive 'adequate' compensation was one of the objectives of U.S. policy – though, as indicated below, not a central one. Later on, when the question of excess profits arose, another U.S. policy objective appeared, namely preventing the establishment of a precedent which would be harmful to U.S. investors in general. Finally, the decision that was ultimately taken on deducting excess profits had the effect of further strengthening the opposition to Allende[42] in the United States.

Throughout the process, the U.S. Government openly linked the question of compensating the copper companies with certain aspects of the economic blockade; more specifically, with the votes of U.S. representatives to the World Bank and the IDB and with renegotiation of Chile's external debt. As to the first question, the U.S. Government always eschewed responsibility for the international agencies' refusal to grant credits to Chile and claimed not to have the power to manipulate them; but it made no secret of the fact that the United States would vote against these agencies extending loans to Chile as long as the problem of compensating the copper companies was unresolved. This attitude[43] became an official policy of the Nixon Administration in January 1972 and was made law two months later, when the U.S. Congress passed the so-called Gonzales Amendment.

The U.S. Government also linked the question of compensating the copper companies with the renegotiation of Chile's external debt. In April 1971, at a meeting of the Club of Paris (which is made up of the Western creditor nations plus Japan), the United States opposed a plan for scheduling Chile's external debt unless the Allende Government promised to pay adequate compensation to the nationalized companies. The Chilean Government refused to do so. In the end, as a result of the intervention of several Western European governments, a compromise solution was reached: Chile accepted 'the principles of payment of a just compensation for all nationalizations in conformity with Chilean law and international law'. This was an ambiguous formulation because, according to Chilean legislation, the companies had no right to compensation.[44] Nevertheless, the problem for Chile was not resolved by the Club of Paris agreement, which only set minimum guidelines for the bilateral negotiations with each creditor nation. The U.S. Government refused to renegotiate its part of the Chilean external debt (which, as mentioned above, amounted to 50% of the total) unless the Allende Government committed itself more concretely on the compensation question. This went on until the Allende Government was overthrown and it provided a justification for continuing other aspects of the blockade such as the suspension of credits and guarantees from the Eximbank.

This explicit linking by the United States of the compensation question to the economic sanctions mentioned above can be interpreted either as an attempt to legitimize the blockade internationally, or as the creation of a limited confrontation designed to resolve the compensation question even if the global strategy failed. On the other hand, the evidence collected by the U.S. Senate shows that decision-makers in the U.S. Government felt that the economic blockade in itself could not significantly alter the Allende Government's policies. As a result, it is probable that a third course of action, designed at least to avoid setting a precedent on the question of deducting excess profits, was adopted by the U.S. Government. There has been speculation to the effect that the U.S. Government might have proposed ending the economic blockade in return for an arrangement with the Allende Government providing for nominal compensation, or for substantial compensation indirectly financed by the U.S. Government itself.[45] Although none of the purported offers had been established it is possible that they might have been made either as part of a multi-purpose, coordinated strategy designed, among other things, to enable the United States to retain a degree of influence over the Allende Government in case the latter succeeded in consolidating its position, or more probably on the basis of the personal initiative of certain U.S. officials. In any case, it is not impossible that certain groups in the U.S. Government considered these types of solutions as a way of diminishing their losses, should the rest of the strategy fail.

3.3.2. *The Economic Blockade and the Allende Government's Policy on the Compensation Question*

If the description in the preceding section is accurate, then the question of compensating the copper companies was neither the principal motive nor the central objective of the U.S. Government's general strategy. It was, however, a secondary objective and it gave rise to a sub-strategy which was linked with certain specific aspects of the economic blockade. Whether or not this strategy might have succeeded if the political situation in Chile became stabilized must remain a matter for speculation; nevertheless it appears, on the basis of the available information, that there was in fact little chance of bringing about a substantial change in the Chilean Government's position on the compensation question.

There is no doubt that the U.S. economic blockade created difficulties for the Allende Government; and while one group within the Government felt that U.S. hostility would not be abated by finding a solution to the copper problem, the Government as a whole chose to work on the basis of the opposite hypothesis: that a solution to the copper problem which would be acceptable to the United States could bring about the truce in the economic war launched by the U.S. Government. Nevertheless, the Allende Government was not prepared to deviate from the criteria for compensation laid down by the Constitutional amendment; in any case, this was not legally possible except through another Constitutional amendment. Thus, irrespective of the hypothesis chosen at the beginning, the situation tended to move towards an impasse. In order to break the deadlock, Chile proposed in December 1972 that the procedure established by the treaty for the settlement of disputes, and signed by both countries in 1914, should be implemented. This treaty stated that differences or conflicts between the two countries that could not be resolved through direct negotiations should be investigated and reported on by an International Commission made up of two members nominated by each of the parties and a fifth member nominated by common agreement. The countries had to make available to the Commission all the information necessary for making a decision and the Commission had to submit its report within one year. Once the report had been issued, the governments concerned had to try, within six months, to reach an agreement on the basis of the recommendations contained in the report. If that was not possible, the dispute had to be submitted to the Permanent Arbitration Tribunal in The Hague unless it affected 'the sovereignty, honour or vital interests of either of the two countries, the provisions of their respective constitutions or the interests of a third power'.[46] Chile proposed that the investigation should not be limited to the question of compensating the copper companies but should also cover the more general question of the economic relations between Chile and the United States, and more specifically the attitude of the U.S. Government in the international financial agencies.

The United States opposed the Chilean proposal for two reasons: first, because the 1914 treaty could not, in this case, lead to a decision that would be binding on both parties since both governments would have to give their consent before the arbitration phase could begin and Chile was not, at that time, in a position to give such consent; second, because it felt that inclusion of questions other than the copper dispute would go beyond the terms of the treaty. The United States proposed that a simple arbitration procedure should be used, that the award should be binding and that the subject of arbitration should be limited to the question of whether the copper companies were entitled to compensation and how much it should be.

During talks held in June and August 1973, Chilean representatives pointed out that legally, the U.S. proposal would require a new Constitutional amendment or, at least, new legislation. Thus there was no possibility for the Executive to commit itself on this point since it had no authority in the legislative field. The Chileans submitted new proposals based on the provisions of the 1914 treaty but taking U.S. objections into account. These proposals were being considered by the U.S. Government when the *coup d'état* took place in Chile in September 1973.

During the negotiations, the Chilean Government's approach was to try to reach a general agreement which could lead to a *modus vivendi* with the United

States – without, however, altering the principles upon which copper nationalization was based, in particular the criteria for deducting excess profits. The idea behind this policy was that the U.S. Government would, at some point, recognize that maintaining normal relations with Chile had a higher priority than defending the private interests of the copper companies. On these bases it should have been possible to negotiate a general agreement which would have also taken the companies' interests into account, as long as such an agreement was compatible with the essential aspects of nationalization. But this, in turn, required that the Allende Government be perceived by the United States as moving towards consolidation – as in fact the results of the March 1973 congressional elections suggested. On the other hand, two factors threatened to halt this trend towards consolidation: first, the cumulative effects of the U.S. economic blockade and, second, the fact that while talks were taking place between the two governments, the United States was intervening directly in Chile in support of groups dedicated to violently overthrowing the Allende Government.

4. CONCLUSIONS

The conclusions that can be drawn from this analysis of the interaction between internal and external factors in the Chilean copper nationalization, and its significance for the ultimate fate of the Allende Government, have already been advanced in the preceding pages. However, it is still useful to summarize them here:

(1) Copper nationalization, as part of the UP's programme of basic changes, was an economic and political necessity which could not be avoided; therefore the Allende Government had no real alternative to nationalization.

(2) The possibility of finding a nonconflictive solution to the problem of compensating the copper companies was minimal, except by agreeing to concessions that would have rendered the entire exercise nonviable or economically self-defeating.

(3) The conflict with the United States, which stemmed from a variety of political and economic factors at national and international levels, and became more acute as a result of copper nationalization, was anticipated by those responsible for the Allende Government's economic policy. But it was felt that the risk of conflict with the copper companies was an acceptable one, and that – though potentially more serious – the risk of direct confrontation with the U.S. Government could be diminished by other aspects of Chilean foreign policy and international economic relations.

(4) Chilean assumptions on the importance of the conflict with the companies proved to be basically correct in that no insuperable difficulties in the production or sale of Chilean copper occurred as a result of the direct reprisals taken by Anaconda and Kennecott.

(5) However, the conflict with the United States, which the U.S. Government attributed to copper nationalization, was more serious in that it gave rise to a financial blockade against Chile by private and public banks in the United States and by the international lending agencies dominated by the U.S. Government.

(6) Nevertheless, it is not at all clear whether the U.S. economic blockade was essentially a function of the copper nationalization conflict. It has been clearly established that U.S. official actions against the Allende Government started even before the confirmation of Allende's election by the National Congress, and that they were motivated by a variety of factors. It is probable that copper nationalization increased the United States' determination to make sure that the UP experiment should fail. It is also possible that a 'satisfactory' solution to the conflict with the companies would have led to a reduction in the economic aggression against Chile. However, it is unlikely that this kind of solution would have altered the U.S. Government's basic resolve to 'destabilize' the Allende Government in the hope of, at least, ensuring its defeat in 1976 and, at best, provoking its overthrow before 1976.

(7) The U.S. economic blockade was an important factor in the rapid deterioration of the Chilean economy in 1973 insofar as it led to a marginally decisive reduction in the supply of foreign exchange, especially that required to purchase U.S. goods which were indispensable for the functioning of Chilean industry. Inasmuch as the economic difficulties were one of the factors which caused the opposition to become more radical and ultimately caused the *coup d'état*, it can be argued that the U.S. economic blockade contributed to the Allende Government's overthrow. (The much more decisive impact of the CIA's subversive activities must, of course, not be forgotten.)

(8) Nevertheless, the marginal character of the impact of the U.S. economic blockade does not support the thesis that the Allende Government was necessarily doomed unless it gave in to U.S. demands. The effects of the blockade could have been minimized through a moderate increase in the level of financial support provided by the Western European and socialist countries; the blockade would also have lost much of its impact had the increase in copper prices, which did not benefit Chile until the second quarter of 1973, occurred much earlier. There is no evidence that the low international copper price during 1971-72 was the result of manoeuvres on the part of the companies or the U.S. Government. But the question arises of whether the existence of a mechanism designed to guarantee to Third World countries minimum revenues for their exports might not have provided Allende with a crucial element of support. Even then, the *coup d'état* might still have taken place, but at least it would have been more difficult for the Chilean monopolistic bourgeoisie, the fascist elements in the armed forces and U.S. imperialism to put an end to Allende's socialist experiment and, ultimately, to democracy in Chile.

NOTES

1. This includes companies with a productive capacity of at least 75,000 metric tons per year, namely those operating the mines of Chuquicamata and El Salvador (49% Anaconda), El Teniente (49% Kennecott) and Exótica (75% Anaconda). Also nationalized was the Andina Company (70% Cerro Corporation) which was contemplating expanding beyond the 75,000 tons mark within the next few years. Altogether the five mines accounted, in 1970, for about 80% of total copper production in Chile and about 60% of the total value of Chilean exports. See R. Corvalan Vera, *Indicadores económicos y financieros 1970-76* [Finance and Economic Indicators 1970-76] (Santiago de Chile, Economic and Financial Survey, 1976), 46.

2. M. Wilkins, *The Emergence of Multinational Enterprise: American Business Abroad from the Colonial Era to 1914* (Cambridge, Mass., Harvard University Press, 1970), 184.

3. C.W. Reynolds, 'Development Problems of an Export Economy. The Case of Chile and Copper' in M. Mamalakis and C.W. Reynolds, *Essays on the Chilean Economy* (Chicago, R.D. Irwin, 1965), 226.

4. T.H. Moran, *El cobre es chileno. 'Dependencia' e 'independencia' en la economía política internacional del cobre chileno 1940-70* [The Copper is Chilean. 'Dependence' and 'Independence' in the International Political Economy of Chilean Copper, 1940-70] (Santiago de Chile, Universidad de Chile, 1970), 59; and P. Nudelman, *La compensación a las companías del cobre nacionalizadas por el Gobierno de Chile* [The Chilean Government's Compensation to the Nationalized Copper Companies] (Santiago de Chile, CODELCO, 1973), 4.

5. R. Tomić, 'Primeros pasos hacia la recuperación del cobre: el Convenio de Washington de 1951' [First Steps towards the Recovery of Copper: the Washington Agreement of 1951], in R. French-Davis and E. Tironi (eds), *El cobre en el desarrollo nacional* [Copper in National Development] (Santiago de Chile, Ediciones Nueva Universidad, 1974), 131-157.

6. C.W. Reynolds, 'Development Problems...', 375; M. Mamalakis, 'Contribution of Copper to Chilean Economic Development, 1920-67: Profile of a Foreign Owned Export Sector', in R.F. Mikesell, *et. al., Foreign Investment in the Petroleum and Mineral Industries. Case Studies of Investor-Host Country Relations* (Baltimore, Johns Hopkins University Press, 1971), 416-417.

7. These figures are taken from annual balance sheet of Andes.

8. See N. Girvan, *Copper in Chile: A Study in Conflict between Corporate and National Economy* (Jamaica, University of the West Indies, 1972); K. Griffin, *Underdevelopment in Spanish America* (London, George Allen and Unwin, 1969); Moran, *El cobre es chileno...*; Moran, *Multinational Corporations and the Politics of Dependence* (Princeton, Princeton University Press, 1974); R. Novoa, *La batalla por el cobre* [The Struggle for Copper] (Santiago de Chile, Editorial Quimantú, 1972); M. Vera, *La política económica del cobre en Chile* [The Economic Policy for Copper in Chile] (Santiago de Chile, Ediciones de la Universidad de Chile, 1961).

9. An English translation of the complete text of the constitutional amendment has been published in *International Legal Materials*, 10 (1971), 1067.

10. Details of the litigation on Chilean copper can be found in Novoa, *La batalla...*, especially 297ff.

11. Kennecott Copper Corporation, *Expropriation of El Teniente. The Largest Underground Copper Mine* (New York, 1971).

12. William P. Rogers, 'Preface' in R.B. Lillich (ed), *The Valuation of Nationalized Property in International Law* (Charlottesville, University of Virginia Press, 1972).

13. See C. Fortin, 'Principled Pragmatism in the Face of External Pressure: The Foreign Policy of the Allende Government', in R. Hellman and H.J. Rodenbaum (eds), *Latin America: The Search for a New International Role* (New York, Halsted Press, 1975), 217-245; and J. Petras and R. LaPorte, Jr., 'U.S. Response to Economic Nationalism in Chile', in J. Petras (ed), *Latin America: From Dependence to Revolution* (New York, John Wiley and Sons, 1973), 195-230.

14. Novoa, *La batalla...*, 120-130.

15. Kennecott in fact explicitly used the 1965-67 agreements to question the validity of the nationalization in legal proceedings undertaken in Sweden. See Kennecott Copper Corporation, *Expropriation of El Teniente...*, 10-11.
16. Kennecott Copper Corporation, *Expropriation of El Teniente...*, 84 and 92.
17. Anaconda Company, *Confiscation of Anaconda Property by the Chilean Government* (New York, 1971), 1.
18. *The Wall Street Journal* (25 July 1974).
19. The bases for this estimate are presented in the paper I have written entitled 'Nationalization of Natural Resource Industries and Multinational Corporations: Reflections on the Case of Chilean Copper', which was submitted to the Cambridge Symposium on Foreign Investment and External Finance in Latin America in June 1974. In July and October of that year the Chilean military junta announced that it had reached an agreement on compensation with Anaconda and Kennecott respectively. The agreement included an immediate payment of $85 million and average annual payments of about $55 million beginning in 1975 and extending over ten years (this figure includes the capitalized value of a tax exemption of $54 million). Capitalizing the down payment at 6% a year, the compensation amounts to about $66 million over ten years. See Carlos Fortin, 'Compensating the Multinationals: Chile and United States Copper Companies', *IDS Bulletin*, 7.1 (1975), 23-29.
20. These figures are taken from the companies' Financial Accounts for 1970.
21. Kennecott Copper Corporation, *Expropriation of El Teniente...*, 14; and M. Molff, 'Los problemas básicos del cobre' [The Basic Problems of Copper], in G. Martner (ed), *El pensamiento económico del Gobierno de Allende* [The Economic Thought of Allende's Government] (Santiago de Chile, Editorial Universitaria, 1971), 176.
22. *Banco Nacional de Cuba* [National Bank of Cuba] *vs. Sabbatino*, 376 (U.S.) 398.
23. N.R. Doman, 'New Developments in the Field of Nationalization', *New York University Journal of International Law and Politics*, 3 (1970), 318.
24. Novoa, *La batalla..., passim*.
25. Novoa, *La batalla...*, 330-339.
26. O.B. Miranda, *Las nacionalizaciones cubanas, los tribunales norte-americanos y la enmienda Hickenlooper* [The Cuban Nationalizations, the U.S. Tribunals and the Hickenlooper Amendment] (La Habana, Ministerio de Relaciones Exteriores, 1971).
27. Secretaría Ejecutiva de Relaciones Económicas Externas del Gobierno de Chile (SEREX) [Foreign Trade Department of the Central Bank], *Análisis de las vinculaciones comerciales con los Estados Unidos* [Analysis of the Commercial Relationships with the U.S.] (Santiago de Chile, 1972).
28. These figures are taken from the annual reports of the IDB and the World Bank.
29. L. Geller and J. Estevez, 'La nationalización del cobre' [The Nationalization of Copper], in: Instituto de Economía [Institute of Economics], *La economía chilena en 1971* [The Chilean Economy in 1971] (Santiago de Chile, Universidad de Chile, 1972), 557-558.
30. Instituto de Economía, *La economía chilena...*, 570-571.
31. See *Chile hoy* [Chile Today] 49 (1973) (Santiago de Chile).
32. R.F. Mikesell, *Foreign Investment in Copper Mining. Case Studies of Mines in Peru and Papua New Guinea* (Baltimore, The Johns Hopkins Press for Resources for the Future, 1975), chapters 6-10.
33. 'Kennecott Declares War', *The Times* (6 November 1972).
34. Some of the documents related to the legal proceedings in Europe are reproduced in Kennecott Copper Corporation, *Expropriation of El Teniente...*, Supplements 2-4.
35. The resolutions included breaking commercial relations with Kennecott and the commitment not to replace any Chilean copper that might be excluded from certain markets as a result of Kennecott's action.
36. Novoa, *La batalla...*, 338.
37. These figures were provided by CODELCO's Supplies Department (July 1973).
38. *Multinational Corporations and United States Foreign Policy. Hearings before the Subcommittee on Multinational Corporations of the Committee on Foreign Relations*, 93rd Congress, 1st Session, 2 April 1973 (Washington D.C., The U.S. Government Printing Office, 1973).

39. *Covert Action in Chile, 1963-73. Staff Report of the Select Committee to Study Governmental Operations with Respect to Intelligence Activities* (Washington D.C., The U.S. Government Printing Office, 1975), 28.
40. The last Minister of Defense in the Allende Government, Orlando Letelier – who was assassinated in Washington D.C. in September 1976 – stated in a lecture at Oxford University in June of that year that there was mounting evidence of direct involvement of the United States' Defense Intelligence Agency (the military counterpart of the CIA) in the preparing and executing of the *coup d'état* in Chile. In his view, this was not brought out by the U.S. Senate investigation because the Ford Administration made their cooperation with the Church Committee conditional to the Committee refraining from any probing into the activities of the Defense Intelligence Agency.
41. *Covert Action in Chile*..., 27.
42. According to the information obtained by *The New York Times*, the CIA contribution to financing and planning opposition activities against Allende increased in October 1971. Informants indicated that this increase was related to the announcement in September 1971 that there would be no compensation for the copper companies, to the arrival of Soviet technicians at the mines and to reports received in Washington D.C. about the shipment of Cuban arms to Chile. See *The New York Times* (24 September 1974).
43. Rogers, 'Preface' to Lillich (ed), *The Valuation....*
44. Central Bank, *Economic News*, 19 (30 April 1972), 4.
45. See, for instance, the testimony of Professor John Strasma to the U.S. House of Representatives in *The United States and Chile during the Allende Years. Hearings before the Subcommittee on Inter-American Affairs of the Committee on Foreign Affairs*, 18 September 1974 (Washington D.C., The U.S. Government Printing Office, 1975), 268-269. Former U.S. Ambassador to Chile Edward M. Korry has referred repeatedly to an offer which he made to Allende in September 1971 but has given contradictory accounts of the authority under which he acted and of the specific terms offered. See U.S. House of Representatives, *The United States and Chile*..., 641 and 651; and *Hearings before the Select Committee to Study Governmental Operations with Respect to Intelligence Activities of the United States Senate*, 94th Congress, 1st Session, Volume 7, *Covert Action* (Washington D.C., The U.S. Government Printing Office, 1976), 130-134.
46. The full text of this Treaty was published in *Diario oficial* [Official Diary] No. 11,397 (17 February 1916) (Santiago de Chile).

Table 6.1. *Profits and Prices in the Gran Minería, 1961-69 (profits in millions of dollars; prices in dollars per pound)*

	Profits		Effective Prices
	Anaconda	*Kennecott*	
1961	26.1	9.3	0.285
1962	33.3	10.0	0.293
1963	33.2	6.4	0.293
1964	35.2	12.9	0.312
1965	35.4	8.5	0.357
1966	59.7	22.1	0.467
1967	92.1	37.8	0.485
1968	102.3	38.4	0.517
1969	130.7	49.1	0.662

Source: CODELCO (Santiago de Chile).

Table 6.2. *Net Annual Profits of the Gran Minería in Percentage of Book Value, 1955–70*

	In Chile	*Outside Chile*	*Overall*
Anaconda	20.2 [a]	3.5	7.2
Kennecott	34.8	10.0	11.6

[a] Chile Exploration Company.

Source: CODELCO.

Table 6.3. *Calculation of Compensation for the Nationalized Companies in the Gran Minería, 1971 (in millions of dollars)*

	Chuqui-camata	*El Salvador*	*Exótica*	*El Teniente*	*Andina*
Book value	241.96	68.37	14.81	318.80	20.14
Deductions for:					
Mining rights	–5.40	–0.35	–0.25	–0.22	–1.53
Defective assets	–13.06	–5.60	–4.55	–20.52	–0.34
Revaluation	–0.00	–0.00	–0.00	–198.58	–0.00
Compensation	223.50	62.42	10.01	99.58	18.27
Deduction for excess profits	300.00	64.00	0.00	410.00	0.00

Source: Comptroller-General of the Republic of Chile.

Table 6.4. *Chilean Copper Exports, 1970*

Country of destination	%
Federal Republic of Germany	25.3
United Kingdom	14.8
Italy	10.0
France	6.9
Sweden	4.0
Other Western European countries	9.0
United States	15.2
Japan	9.4
Latin America	5.3

Source: CODELCO.

Table 6.5. *Production of the Gran Minería and Andina (in thousands of metric tons)*

	1969	*1970*	*1971*	*1972*
Chuquicamata	283.4	263.0	250.2	234.6
El Salvador	77.1	93.0	84.9	82.8
El Teniente	179.9	176.6	147.3	190.6
Exótica	–	1.9	35.3	31.3
Andina	–	5.0	53.6	53.9
Total	495.4	540.5	571.4	593.2

Source: CODELCO.

7

ALBERTO MARTÍNEZ

THE INDUSTRIAL SECTOR: AREAS OF SOCIAL AND MIXED PROPERTY IN CHILE

INTRODUCTION

The purpose of this chapter is to analyze various aspects of the expropriation policy implemented by the *Unidad Popular* (UP) Government. The principal goal of this policy was the expropriation of industrial companies and the formation of a new social and economic sector of production, known as the *Areas de Propiedad Social y Mixta* (APSM) [Areas of Social and Mixed Property].

This analysis focuses upon four central points: (1) the need for the formation of the APSM; (2) the project's aims and scope; (3) the timing and mode of the project's implementation; and (4) the extent to which the aims were achieved and the causes of the successes and shortcomings. In connection with the latter point, stress is placed on external pressures and on some of the ways in which these pressures were reduced. The first two points, of necessity, require an analysis of the structural tendencies of the urban-industrial complex. For this reason a brief survey of the main features of its development before 1970 will be given. The third point is directly concerned with the specific circumstances under which the UP's Basic Programme had to be implemented. The fourth point discusses the internal dynamics of the APSM, referring, of course, to the influence of outside circumstances and to the interdependence of the two aspects.

Even though an attempt has been made throughout this chapter to take into account two essential features that were peculiar to what happened in Chile, it seems appropriate to draw special attention to them in this introduction. They are:

(1) The whole series of transformations and the problems which were encountered took place within the framework of an intense struggle for political power between antagonistic social forces, forces which were an important factor in the outcome of the struggle.

Footnotes, tables and the Appendix to this chapter may be found on pp. 255-274.

(2) The experiment we are dealing with is an unfinished one; it was interrupted when the new elements were just beginning to show their strengths and, also, some of their weaknesses.

The first feature means that, unlike in other cases, implementing the programme was subjected to a multiplicity of pressures that prevented it from following a previously determined and well defined course. These various pressures produced both advances and retreats, as well as some inconsistencies. The course of events was in constant danger of being diverted not only by the competing forces but also by mistakes.

The second feature implies that in any conclusion which is made, one should take care not to go beyond that which actual social practice allows. In a more complete experiment, many of the difficulties and successes might have turned out to be purely circumstantial and, conversely, others might have been more permanent.

The information used in this chapter is taken from data and analyses which have been widely published in the press, as well as from specialized works. The experiences of many of the people involved have also served as important sources of information. In the latter case, an attempt has been made whenever possible to substantiate the facts with documentary evidence. Unfortunately, the data, particularly the quantitative and qualitative parameters of the APSM's behaviour, are not as systematic as might be desired. (This should be kept in mind when studying the tables in the Appendix to this chapter.) In such cases an attempt has been made to use some indirect indicators or hypotheses which seem plausible. Finally, it should be pointed out that much of the information and the legal decrees refer to the industrial, commercial and financial APSM as a whole. This, together with the need to make comparisons, makes it necessary to refer not only to the core of the industrial sector, but also to the remaining sectors, even though it might be only tangentially.

1. NATIONAL AND FOREIGN-OWNED MONOPOLIES IN THE URBAN-INDUSTRIAL SYSTEM

It is well known that the urban-industrial complex was the most dynamic part of the Chilean economy from the crisis during the 1930s onwards.[1]

The sectors and subsectors of production, trade and finance embraced a network of activities at differing stages of development. These differences lay in the total volume of capital used as well as in the capital used per unit of production, in the degree of technical complexity, in the levels of productivity, in the wage levels, and in the amounts of surplus obtained. The system was dominated by a small number of groups who not only wielded great economic power, but also had interests in a number of companies engaged in a variety of activities. Each sector had, in turn, a markedly monopolistic or oligopolistic structure.

The most important sector, the manufacturing industry, had the highest level of concentration of ownership. A few enterprises controlled a decisive proportion of the jobs available, the value added, the capital and the gross surplus from production (see Table I.A in the Appendix to this chapter). This phenomenon involved more than just the technical relationships between the size of the relatively modern units of production and their considerable importance in a small market. The largest companies owned several plants. Moreover, their boards of directors were dominated by a small group of people. The structure of the other sectors showed the same level of concentration, although in a less marked form (see Table I.B in the Appendix to this chapter). The principle companies were dominated by the same groups.[2] This multi-sectoral spread of the cores of economic power allowed for exceptional mobility. If there was some difficulty in one company or in a group of companies, resources could quickly be switched to others in a different branch or sector.

The base of the industrial monopolies system was the production, circulation and consumption of such products as coal and steel, machinery, textile fibres, cellulose and paper, rubber and plastics, wood, oil, footwear, beverages, tobacco and others (see Table I.C in this chapter's Appendix). Through the provision of these goods and the management of financial resources, the monopolies established complete domination over small and medium-sized industries. The latter, however, played an important role in the system. First, as was to be expected, they transferred an important part of their surplus to the monopolistic core. Second, because of the low level of the productive forces at their disposal, they had to exploit the labour force under their control to a greater extent. Moreover, they constituted a protective barrier which absorbed the greatest fluctuations in the market. In addition they served as the main pressure group in such matters as pricing policy, wages, taxes and state support. Thus the whole constituted a single system with interdependent elements, dominated by the monopolistic core. These links were reinforced by professional and personal ties. When it was working normally and expanding, the system's cohesion tended to overcome its internal contradictions. It was only when the whole social formation began to show signs of exhaustion that conflicts began to arise with increasing force and eventually developed into a crisis in the 1960s.

Although these features had become more pronounced in the years immediately preceeding 1970, it cannot be said that they were a recent development. Even in 1937, when the process of import substitution was fully underway, such concentration was apparent.[3] Although information on the years previous to 1937 is insufficient, everything seems to indicate that the Chilean economy never had any other kind of structure. Throughout the entire process of capitalist development through industrialization, there was never a period in which competition prevailed. This structure, with its highly concentrated ownership of property and of production, developed within a framework of heavy protection from outside competition. It could hardly have been possible otherwise, given its low level of development in relation to industry in the advanced capitalist countries.

It is understandable that a system of this kind should lack the incentive to expand for the most important factors necessary for accumulation and therefore for expansion of the domestic market were lacking: competition, growth of industrial exports, domestic production of capital goods, a broad base of energetic small producers, etc. The weakness of the purely private industrialization process necessitated the development, from 1940 onwards, of a strong state sector in basic industries: electrical energy, the production and refining of oil, steel and others. At the same time, the state developed a large network of supports for private economic and financial activities, particularly for the monopolies. The system became one of state-monopoly capitalism, in which the state increasingly took on responsibility for the reproduction and expansion of the system, by means of direct and indirect investments. The importance of the public sector in industrial accumulation became more and more decisive in the 1960s (see Table I.F in this chapter's Appendix).

State participation was, however, unsuccessful in bringing about a higher rate of investment. It was only with difficulty that the state was able to compensate for the drop in investments by the private sector. This decrease cannot be explained by a reduction in surpluses in the private sector. In fact, the private sector's share in industrial value added – which can be represented in index form through the so-called payments made to sectors other than labour – tended to increase in the 1960-70 period, also in relation to earlier periods (see Table I.F). On the other hand, the rise in public spending, in which funds earmarked for investment played an important role, became increasingly difficult to finance because of resistance from those sectors which appropriated the greater part of the generated income.

A way out of this conflict was sought by opening up industrial activities to foreign private investment. In 1960 a new legal status was devised for this type of capital.[4] During the following ten years foreign investments increased to about five times their 1959 level. These funds were channeled into creating subsidiaries of and partnerships with existing companies which controlled the market (see Table 7.1).

In this way the established companies secured for themselves a comfortable monopoly or a leading position within the oligopolies in the various branches of industry.

Investments were made primarily in the fastest growing sectors of the economy: canned fish and seafood, wood, paper and cellulose, chemicals and certain kinds of machinery (see Table I.E in this chapter's Appendix). Although the majority of these goods were for the domestic market, the increase in exports strongly influenced the rate of growth, particularly in sectors such as canned fish and seafood, paper and cellulose, chemicals and certain types of machinery (Table I.E). Apparently interest was not only focused on exploiting certain natural resources, such as marine products, wood, cellulose and copper, but also on making use of the possibilities offered by the Andean Pact agreements to develop particular sectors, such as chemicals, certain types of machinery and transport equipment.

The growing presence of foreign investment in domestic industrial production not only increased dependence on foreign capital but also limited the private accumulation of capital (see Table I.D in the Appendix). At the same time it accentuated the most negative aspects of the traditional industrialization process.

In the first place, the relatively low rate of investment, together with increasing capital intensity,[5] tended to generate only a very slow rise in the rate of employment. The pressure of unemployment prevented wages from increasing in relation to productivity increases and reinforced the existing concentration of income (see Table I.F in the Appendix). On the other hand, the great differences between the use of new equipment in the most dynamic sectors and its use in the most backward branches of industry accounted for considerable wage discrepancies. Furthermore, the greatest discrepancies were between large and small companies within the same branch. In 1968, 45% of all workers earned less than the minimum wage, while 1.5% earned between 4 and 6.5 times the minimum wage. There was a ratio of 1 to 6.5 between the average wages of the most extreme cases.[6] The pressures that arose because of these differences became particularly difficult to control during the UP Government period.

In the second place, the domestic market grew slowly at a time when the bulk of production was aimed at precisely that market.[7] A low rate of accumulation, together with a high proportion of imported equipment, eliminated one of the most important elements in the expansion of domestic demand. The growing participation of foreign companies tended to perpetrate this situation. Basically, the bulk of their equipment and input needs were satisfied by their head offices. It does not appear to have been in the interest of these companies to undertake any significant import substituting, except on a minimal level. Because of other structural features of the economic system – the foreign capital enclave and the backward system of social relations in the rural sector – the market received very weak stimuli. The foreign capital enclave, because it was highly organized, imported practically all its inputs and accounted for a small and continually decreasing number of jobs. The lack of dynamism in the rural sector had similar consequences. In order to compensate for this weakness in the expansion mechanisms, the state apparatus had to support the market by supporting construction activities, particularly the construction of housing. Nonetheless there was a permanent tendency to underuse existing capacity.[8]

In the third place, production in general basically depended on the capacity to import. The system of import substitution had in the preceeding decades reduced the relative importance of nonfood consumer goods. Apart from food, a majority of the imported items consisted of intermediate goods and capital goods for industry (see Table I.C in the Appendix). The ratio between production and exports became an increasingly rigid relationship determined by technical considerations. Production could not develop, or even sustain itself, without a guaranteed export level; any decrease could well have resulted in a considerable decline in income. External resources consisted, for more than 80%, of copper sales.

These circumstances meant that domestic activity came to be regarded as a function of the availability of foreign exchange, and certainly the amount of foreign exchange available was a limiting factor. However, how the economy moved within that framework was determined by a few internal aspects of the urban industrial complex, particularly the level and composition of investment, public expenditure and income distribution. A simple increase in foreign exchange income certainly did not automatically lead to a similar increase in output. There were contradictory trends, such as an increase in consumer goods imports, which worked to the detriment of some branches of production. On the other hand, the decrease in foreign exchange income would lead to an increase in the external debt, given that the aim was to maintain the level of economic activity. During earlier periods – for example, during the 1930s and World War II – similar decreases favoured the import substitution process. Later on, this effect grew weaker and weaker. The possibilities for replacing imported goods had been reduced to some intermediate and capital goods. But any change of growth which they might have had clashed with the system's 'rationality', with its existing structure and underlying characteristics. As these possibilities diminished, the development of an urban-industrial complex increasingly came to depend on a greater, or at least continuously sustained, increase in the capacity to import.

2. THE APSM IN INDUSTRY

The UP programme denounced foreign domination of the economy and the structural deformations produced by domestic and foreign monopolies. In order to prevent the further development of this process and the consequent modifications in the existing situation, the UP argued the need to expropriate the monopolies and to create the *Area de Propiedad Social* (APS) [Area of Social Property] for basic mining resources and for industry, as well as for other nonagricultural sectors.

The process of transformation of our society begins with a policy designed to build up a dominant state sector, made up of companies currently in the hands of the state plus any companies that are expropriated.[9]

In considering this proposal, the question might be asked of whether it was not possible to modify the pattern and rhythm of development by limiting nationalization to basic resources and making use of a series of more conventional measures, such as strict controls on foreign trade, appropriate exchange rate management, changes in the pricing system and in credit and fiscal policies, and use of the remaining measures available for stimulating production. In other words, was there no way of eliminating the economy's most pernicious features other than by expropriating the monopolies in the urban-industrial complex? The answer is necessarily negative, if one takes into account the following points.

(1) There was a complete decline in the private monopolies' capacity to increase the rate of surplus accumulation for productive purposes. This incapacity was in direct opposition to the need for substantial increases in medium- and long-term rates of investment. Foreign capital did not bring in a significant amount of resources; on the contrary, it made increasing use of the resources locally available (see Table I.D in the Appendix).

(2) A privileged position in the investment structure which had been accorded to the final stages of consumer goods production was aimed at high income sectors with a large import component. Given this situation it was necessary to develop production of basic intermediate and capital goods, production which required heavy initial expenditures and which produced very low returns, or no returns at all, for long periods in almost any market conditions.

(3) In almost all cases, the techniques used corresponded to availability on the world market; they ruled out possibilities for domestic production and technological development and made the unemployment problem even more acute.

(4) Declared surpluses greatly underestimated the real amounts; this was due to the use of such well known methods as overvaluing imports, undervaluing exports, unjustified padding of costs, uninvoiced sales, etc.

(5) Not only was there no change whatsoever in the regressive distribution of income between employers, technicians and workers, but there was also no change within each of these groups. On the other hand, there was the need to achieve, within a fairly short period, a more even income distribution.

(6) Any attempt to make purely cosmetic changes in the existing structure would have implied such an array of controls and restrictions on prices, taxation, foreign trade, incomes and other fields, that it would have differed little from direct intervention. Under these circumstances it was impossible to infuse a new dynamism into the monopolistic system. The political reactions which such an attempt would have caused would not have been different and it would not have been possible to harness the energies of the other social strata, particularly the workers.

The basic premise underlying the expropriation of the core of economic power, and the formation of the APS in industry, commerce and finance was, therefore, that the existing structures had exhausted their possibilities. It was not a purely subjective desire to nationalize and to begin construction of a new, socialist system of relations of production. It was, in fact, a necessary step given the great contradictions in the system.

In any case, the measure was to affect only a small group of companies. Most of the rest of the economy was to remain in the private sector, or *Area de Propiedad Privada* (APP) [Area of Private Property]. The state would provide technical, economic and financial support to this sector, which would then have to function within the general framework outlined by Government policies.

Between the APS and APP, an *Area de Propiedad Mixta* (APM) [Area of Mixed Property] was to be organized whose basic feature was association between state and private capital, either domestic or foreign. It was envisaged that this arrangement would prove to be very useful for cases in which the expropriation of a company was not necessary, but where the state had to lend a great deal of support. In these cases, the resources brought in could take the form of shared capital. The concept involved the idea of individual agreements with the owners since it implied some sort of contribution from both sides. In this sense, the presence of a certain proportion of private shares in a company was not enough for it to be classified as an APM company. A minority holding of this kind, however large, in a state-owned limited company, did not necessary imply any real degree of association. In many cases it merely demonstrated the fact that it was not necessary to hold 100% of a company's capital in order to exercise control over it. From this viewpoint there is no justification for classifying companies in the APS or APM by referring only to a particular percentage of participation. The APM in fact merged into the APS, except a few foreign industrial concerns. In the latter cases, the agreement was to take the form of a continuing supply of inputs, technological back-up and some management functions. Such a company had, for its part, to guarantee a given level of profits on the private capital invested in it.

The new organization of the economic system, together with the traditional policy instruments – control of foreign trade, credit, prices and wages – were to constitute the basis for a national planning system. Basically, the main aims to be achieved were: (1) to free the country from its dependence on foreign capital in order to establish new conditions of operation for the foreign capital that was not to be expropriated, and to obtain the greatest possible independence in technological development, trade and foreign financing; (2) to ensure a type of economic development that made maximum use of country's human, natural, financial and technical resources; (3) to solve the more urgent problems of the majority of Chileans by increasing the production of essential consumer items and reducing the production of superfluous goods through a change in the use of resources, particularly of installed capacity; (4) to ensure rapid growth in employment through adopting a type of technological development appropriate to the need for using domestic resources; (5) to combat inflation by means of the above-mentioned structural changes, orderly monetary and credit policies, rationalization of trade, and price controls.

The new economic areas encompassed by the APSM were to play a decisive role in achieving these aims. Their dominant role meant that the development and mode of operation in these areas would influence the entire economy, as the monopolies had done in the past. This dominance was to involve: (1) serving as a centre for state investments, which made up the majority of the national savings, and therefore being the most rapidly growing social sector; (2) undertaking indigenous technical development and forming a national structure of investments; (3) serving as the centre for the expansion of the new relations of production.

On the short term, the APSM were to: (1) provide a basic lever for implementing the Government's plans for the economy as a whole; (2) constitute a decisive mechanism for channelling additional surpluses into the public sector; (3) compensate for the deficiencies in production which might arise in the APP.

The size which the APSM were originally envisaged to acquire could be precisely established for several sectors, first of all for basic resources. In mining production it included more than 90% of total copper sales since the small mines' processing plants belonged to the APS; it also included around 80% of iron ore, 100% of nitrates, and a little less than 80% of coal. Oil production was already entirely controlled by the state. In this way about 90% of exports would be brought into the APS.

As for the urban-industrial complex, all the companies involved in financial services, basic utilities (water, generation and distribution of electricity, and gas), and rail, sea and air transport were to be included.[10] Freight transport by road was hardly taken into account, even though in 1969 it already accounted for about 70% of the domestic movement of goods, excluding minerals and fuel.[11]

It is difficult to determine the role initially played by the APSM in the manufacturing industry and in domestic commerce. The UP Basic Programme took into account only monopolies and large strategic enterprises which conditioned the country's economic and social development, i.e. the steel, cement, basic chemical, cellulose and paper industries. However, it is possible to guess the magnitude of this role on the basis of a statement made in the UP Programme about the degree of industrial concentration: '... in 1967, of 30,500 existing enterprises, only 150 monopolistically controlled all markets, appropriating all Government aid and banking credits'.

These 150 major industrial enterprises accounted for about 40% of the production value and 30% of the jobs in factories employing more than five workers (see Tables II.A, II.B and II.C in the Appendix). There is no data for commercial enterprises, but it was known that twelve major enterprises controlled 43% of wholesale trade.[12]

A lack of clear criteria for determining what was meant by monopolistic or strategic activity and the subsequent attempts to find definitions caused much dissent within the UP. Furthermore, this lack of clear criteria was often used to fight against Government policy. Naturally, the problem was particularly complex and needed to be approached from various angles. First, from a strictly political viewpoint, it was necessary to establish the dividing line between enemies and possible allies, or at least sectors which could be neutralized. Second, the activities of power groups, from a strictly technical point of view, extended to the monopolistic and oligopolistic areas as well as to those areas where a certain degree of competition existed. Therefore, an additional criterion was required in order to fix a general demarcation line. Thus the dominant character which was postulated for the APS implied control over the principal centres of the structure of production and circulation, from which the rest of private enterprise could be guided. This was the case within those sectors of the economy in which, in spite of the existence of some very important production units, capital was dispersed to a much greater degree. Obviously in this situation dominance by the APSM could not lead to the expropriation of medium-sized or even small capitalist enterprises; therefore, the question of how to find new organizational forms for them was raised. Finally, the medium- and long-term development of the economy made it essential to select some concerns which should be brought within the APSM for technological reasons – for example, certain engineering works which could be the basis for a national machine industry. Clearly, to adequately define the problem it was necessary not only to analyze the structure of the different sectors, of the circulation within the industrial complex and of the activities which should constitute the basis for future development, but also to analyze the political restrictions which implementing the programme might encounter as it was implemented.

Throughout the first year, the Government acted on the basis of some of these general considerations. Only towards the end of 1971 were precise criteria laid down for defining companies that might be taken over in the various sectors.[13] These were companies which, as of 31 December 1969, had assets valued in 1971 at E° 14 million.[14]

This definition embraced more than 200 companies, however, several groups had to be excluded from it: those which already belonged to the state or had been legally transferred to it as of that date; the newpapers and other mass media; some financial services; construction companies, etc. Finally, ninety additional companies were to become part of the APS or APM, the breakdown of which is shown in Table 7.2.

Of course, a definition of any kind eliminated much of the confusion that had arisen. Nevertheless, its purely quantitative nature, and its reference to only one parameter – capital – left some aspects unresolved, for example, how to control some basic activities despite their relatively dispersed capital structure, since they could be the bases for longer-term development.

Nonetheless, the plan encountered strong opposition and was discussed for a long time in the National Congress. The Government was thus obliged to continue operating in 1972 and 1973 under the same conditions as previously. At the same time, the sharpening political and economic conflicts forced the Government to intervene in a number of cases which fell outside the limitation proposed in 1971. It was particularly in the industrial sector that such situations arose. For this reason, in the studies on the size of the planned APSM, which were made in different periods, the numbers of companies involved differ.[15] Nevertheless, the overall figures on their relative importance in the fields of production or sales, and in employment, are strikingly similar: in production or sales, two studies coincide in putting the size of the planned APSM at between 43% and 44% of the total number of units employing more than five workers. The third study, which puts the number at 31.7%, is not strictly comparable because the chosen field of study includes the production of establishments with less than five workers (see Table II.B in the Appendix). The difference, however, is in the magnitude of handicraft production, which is around 30%. This conclusion is reinforced by the fact that the number of workers involved coincides: the two cases where information on this number is included put the figure at around 23% (see Table II.C in the Appendix). These points of agreement, despite the differences in the number of companies, seem to indicate the decisive importance of about 180 companies with great productive potential. Additional units would make very little difference to the overall quantitative significance of the areas, even though they might affect some particular branch of production.

Studies on the proposed distribution of the APSM between different groups of industries show similar trends. There is a noticeably higher incidence in basic intermediate goods (see Table II.A in the Appendix): textiles (23), paper and cellulose (27), chemicals (30, 31 and 32), nonmetal mineral products (33) and basic metals (34). In the areas of metal products and machinery the importance of the project varies substantially depending on whether or not the semi-handicraft sector is included. This is logical, given the incipient character of this line of production. It also shows that planned control of production could not be implemented on the basis of the expropriated sector alone, in light of the fact that a substantial part of this branch of industry was highly dispersed geographically. Under these circumstances, it would have been essential to seek viable forms of organization for small businessmen and independent producers. In the remaining groups concerned with normal consumer goods – including food products (20), drinks (21), clothing and footwear (24), furniture (26) and printing (28) – the importance of the planned APSM was less, and considerably less important if the handicrafts sector is included (see Table II.A). It should be noted, however, that important differences would have arisen within the food products group. In some sectors where there was highly concentrated ownership – as in sugar, pasta, oil and canned fish and seafood – the APSM would be decisive. Where this was not the case, the APSM would be insignificant.

Of the studies mentioned, only one investigates the APSM's scope in other fields such as foreign trade and the share of foreign capital.[16] As for the former, it turned out that 68.3% of industrial exports and 67.3% of industrial imports were made by companies belonging to the new sector. As for the latter, the plan implied reducing the share of foreign capital in the total number of industrial limited companies from the 20.3% it represented in 1969 to approximately 1·1% (see Table II.D in the Appendix).

There are no adequate figures for evaluating the significance of the APSM in the domestic wholesale trade. It must, of course, have been greater than in production. The components of the APSM exerted their influence here as both sellers and buyers. In addition there were commercial marketing units which increased the previous volume of goods. In any case, on the basis of an overall figure of 32% of production, it can be seen that the significance of the APSM in this sector would still be limited. It was envisaged that almost all retail trade would remain in private hands.

It was expected that the project would establish a new set of regulations to control the continued presence of foreign capital. Although there was no precise plan for accomplishing this, it was at least possible to find satisfactory provisional solutions in the form of joint ventures in which state participation was dominant. The continuing presence of foreign interests under these conditions implied recognition of the need both to bring their operations under domestic control, and to maintain the technical link that was essential to maintaining production throughout a large part of the industrial apparatus. This ensured that any eventual break would have to be the result of some concrete action by the foreign companies and not of ill-considered positions by the Government. Only the development of new external relations and of domestic technological ability would enable this dependence to be effectively reduced and finally eliminated.

All of the above evidence confirms the high degree of concentration of ownership and of control of the fundamental means of production. Under these circumstances, the APSM's formation directly affected only a small group of companies and individuals. Moreover, the fact that these were the activities which, relatively speaking, had the highest technical development and level of productivity implied that only a small proportion of the workers would benefit directly from modifying the production relations within these companies. Not more than 20% of nonagricultural blue- and white-collar workers in the APSM as a whole, and not more than 30% in the industrial sector, were affected.[17] On the other hand, there were an exceptionally large number of economic units and workers, particularly in industry and commerce, that would remain in the private sector.

The programmes that were drawn up did not include definitions of clear operational guidelines for companies in the private sector. Given their numbers and the fact that they were highly dispersed geographically, it would have been essential to propose modes of operation and development which were appropriate to their importance and their social and economic characteristics. The definitions should have included some principles that would have offered guidelines for such aspects as: ways of participating in the management and planning of the various branches and sectors of the economy; forms of internal organization and links with the various levels of the APSM; and ways of taking part in setting up price, wage, income and investment policies.

Of course, the mere absence of these guidelines was not the main cause of the difficulties which were encountered. It does, however, indicate that attention was being focused almost exclusively on the monopolistic core; very little attention was being given to analyzing the importance of, and the policy to be followed towards, the economy's future private sector, which was an essential and inseparable part of the urban-industrial complex. Another related consequence was vagueness about what role that sector of the working class which was linked to these companies was to play in the structural transformations in the economy's new way of functioning. This shortcoming must have contributed to the workers' tendency to demand either higher wages and/or more fringe benefits, or indiscriminate expropriations.

The plan for setting up the APSM as a whole clearly indicated the measures to be taken with respect to the monopolies, and also the objectives which the new social sector should achieve. Two important aspects, however, remained unclear: first, the criteria by which the range of companies liable to come within this area were to be defined, and second, the features necessary for articulating the private sector within the new economy's functioning and management.

3. THE FORMATION OF THE APSM IN INDUSTRY

The section of the UP's Basic Programme on expropriations did not specify when, during the Government's term of office, the expropriations were to take place. Therefore, we must raise the question of when the circumstances would have been tactically most appropriate for expropriation – although in fact the turn of events did not leave many alternatives open. From the outset the immediate tasks that the new Government had set for itself, and the ways in which the threatened sectors began to use their power, meant that top priority had to be given to the formation of the APS in the urban-industrial complex.

In the years immediately preceding 1970 the structural problems had grown increasingly more serious. Towards the end of 1970 the economy slumped towards depression. Under these circumstances the immediate problems of the level of economic activity, unemployment and inflation were uppermost in the minds of the new Government officials. In order to deal with these problems a programme for immediate action was drawn up. The essential features of this programme were as follows: wage increases to compensate for the loss of purchasing power during the previous year, with a substantial improvement in minimum wages and pensions; a special programme of investments in public works and housing, and increases in social expenditure; a new system of contracts and credits to stimulate companies' production while reactivating demand; and finally, a system of strict price controls and of increases in fiscal revenue. This series of measures was designed to produce a quick increase in production. A wealth of unused resources were available to achieve this end, particularly productive capacity, labour and foreign exchange reserves – despite considerable medium- and long-term external debts.

Use of the state apparatus's entire range of control was necessary for implementing this project. But from the moment elections took place it could be seen that the traditional levers of economic policy would be insufficient. The power groups immediately began to use their influence in the financial system and in the large production and distribution companies, etc., to create difficulties for the new Government. Under the prevailing conditions, the sectors whose interests were being threatened subordinated their 'economic logic' to their 'political logic'. In fact, economic interests soon revealed their true nature as expressions of the social relations which constitute their essence.

In the case of Chile this true nature of economic interests became evident from the behaviour of the monopolistic cores as early as September 1970, and systematically grew more intense. In addition to subordinating any economic initiatives to the need to recover their political preeminence, these threatened sectors interrupted the normal operations of the production cycle and tried to turn all of their assets into liquid resources. The latter action was both a way of protecting as much as possible of what they owned from expropriation, and of creating economic difficulties for the Government. All this was manifested in various ways: obstacles were created which would prevent a rise in economic activities, inasmuch as such a rise would involve increasing employment or using additional capital; inventories of raw materials, particularly imported ones, were diminished to critically low levels; illegal currency transactions were made; foreign currency fled abroad; liquid capital was used for speculative purposes; and exaggeratedly high wage increases were encouraged in order to break the price control policies. Naturally, each company used these actions for varying lengths of time and in varying degrees of intensity. All of these activities were justified in terms of a lack of confidence as a result of the new political conditions. In addition to their immediate economic impact, they brought pressure to bear on the Government and intimidated other social groups.

It is not possible to detect any differences between the attitudes of the most important non-monopolistic entrepreneurs and the behaviour described above. Exceptions were, perhaps, the demands for prompt guarantees against expropriation, improvements in rates of profit, and a definition of the types of production in which private initiative was possible.[18]

The foreign companies linked to the urban system adopted a similar – though in most cases more prudent – attitude. A good proportion of them were willing to negotiate with the Government for the sale of their assets, or a part of them. Only a small number, especially such U.S. companies as International Telephone and Telegraph (ITT), Ford, Dow Chemical, Ralston-Purina and others, followed a policy of openly breaking with the Government. Another group of companies were interested in reaching new agreements that would guarantee them markets and international profit levels. The majority apparently followed dual tactics: on the one hand, these companies either tried not to relinguish their position in the country, or in some cases to improve it; on the other, they supported – directly or indirectly – the tactics of the domestic monopolies.

Implementing the series of immediate measures caused swift reactivation of the economy and some effective income redistribution. The negative repercussions arising from exceeding the limits originally set did not become evident until towards the end of 1971. In order to achieve results, the Government had to force production to respond in the face of resistance from the major business interests. Depending on the companies involved the Government followed various courses, ranging from traditional economic supports to expropriation. This reflects the close interrelationship between the plans for structural changes and the immediate actions taken by the Government. In fact, the short-term aims increasingly required more far-reaching instruments of state control in all sectors.

The expropriation of basic resources was carried out quickly by means of a constitutional reform, through which almost 90% of total exports passed into state hands.

As far as the urban-industrial system was concerned, the Government proceeded to expropriate, and to take over management in domestically owned monopolies, whenever it was possible to apply legal decrees, to reach agreements on transferring their assets, or to buy shares on the market. The most notable example of buying shares on the market was the acquisition of almost the entire banking system through the voluntary sale of stocks by the shareholders. Most of these stocks were undervalued and were paid for in installments over a period of up to seven years, depending on the amount held by each holder on a particular date. Relatively small numbers of stocks were paid for in cash, enabling the small shareholders to be properly compensated. By November 1971 this process had been virtually completed.[19] Subsidiaries of foreign banks – e.g. the Bank of America, the First National City Bank, the Bank of London and South America and the Banque Française et Italienne – were acquired by direct negotiations.

In the case of monopolies in industry, commerce and basic services, the process was much more complicated and drawn out. On the one hand, the causes for expropriation, state take-over of management or requisition were dependent on evidence that production was being impaired in various ways or that the sale of goods was needed by the population. On the other hand, application of these measures needed to have the support of the workers in the company in question, both to be able to carry them out and to guarantee an increase in production under the company's future administration. Finally, it was in the industrial and commercial sectors that the affected groups offered the greatest resistance after the first measures had been taken, not only on the ideological and legal levels but also in practice. In several companies specialized personnel were brought in to organize physical resistance. A case in point is the Compañía Manufacturera de Papeles y Cartones (paper products), the largest of the private monopolies, which organized 'take-overs' designed to prevent Government take-overs of management in the factories, using both specialized people and loyal workers to do so.

The general approach with respect to foreign capital which was linked to domestic monopolies was to try to reach agreements. The essential principle underlying these agreements was that there would be Government control by means of the total or partial transfer of stock at an agreed price, with continued technical support and supplies from the head office. When a mixed company was established, the foreign part of it was guaranteed a certain level of remittable profits. Almost all the mixed companies were, properly speaking, in this category. The most important agreements in this category were reached with International Business Machines (IBM), Coates (thread), the Record Company of America (RCA) (electronics), the automobile manufacturers (Renault, Fiat, Pegaso and others), and engineering companies. The need to maintain the technical links for as long as might be necessary, in order to avoid hampering production, was obvious. The individual agreements with companies reflect the need to distinguish between two aspects of their behaviour one with regard to their particular interests, and the other with regard to the general framework of the system of international relations. It was particularly in the second field that there was a high degree of hostility and opposition towards the Government, as was later demonstrated by the difficulties encountered in securing external resources.

In 1971, 116 industrial companies were brought under state control. Of this number, fifty were on the so-called 'list of ninety', and approximately another twenty-five were covered by the broader plan sent to the National Congress in October 1971 (see pp. 230-231 of this chapter and Table III.A in the

Appendix). All these actions were carried out using existing legal instruments, although they were applied in a strict way. In most cases, only a change in management and not a transfer of ownership was envisaged. In these circumstances, the Government had to begin negotiations with the owners in order to acquire their assets and establish the company's new legal position. The decisive factor in the discussions was, of course, the correlation of forces – whether economic, financial or political – which was established in each case. Here the position of the workers who were directly affected played a fundamental role. The terms for compensation offered to the Chilean owners were in keeping with the formulas that would subsequently be generalized in the draft legislation mentioned above. The amount of the compensation was the book value of the previous financial year, payable primarily in medium- and long-term bonds linked to the price index; this solution assured small shareholders of full compensation and larger shareholders of proportionally less compensation. These bonds could be redeemed immediately if the proceeds were to be invested in certain activities designated by the Government.[20]

The APSM's rapid expansion was undoubtedly one of the most important factors in increasing the workers' support for the Government. The opposition, however, managed to convince many people that the methods used were of very dubious legality. In particular, they succeeded in making a large number of small and medium-sized entrepreneurs believe that the Government intended to carry out massive and indiscriminate expropriations because it was not acting in accordance with any specific law. Towards the end of 1971, when the bill on expropriations was sent to the National Congress, the opposing positions had already become fairly well entrenched. The opposition presented another bill on expropriation, known as the Hamilton-Fuentealba Bill, at almost the same time: its principal objectives were to reduce the APSM to a substantially smaller number of companies than the Government had proposed, to submit each separate case of expropriation to congressional control, and to introduce a fourth social sector of a cooperative nature which would be known as 'workers' companies'. This presupposed such a substantial limiting of the APSM in the urban-industrial complex that it would, in fact, prevent the APSM from taking shape at all. Hereafter the legal, social and economic conflicts grew increasingly bitter. All efforts to reach an agreement, particularly the agreement proposed by the President Allende and the President of the Christian Democratic Party in June 1972, failed. In the latter case the opposition came from the right-wing faction among the Christian Democrats, which had already begun to exert a decisive influence.

It might be asked to what extent an agreement, even a partial one, might have been possible before this period – that is, more precisely, during the first half of 1971, when the more progressive element within the Christian Democratic Party was still in control of the party and the popular movement was on the upsurge. It seems clear that this would have meant subjecting the project to very wide-ranging discussion not only with representatives of small and medium-sized businesses, but also with the political groups with an interest in the projected transformations. This would, of course, have involved seeking a certain consensus, and would to some extent have delayed the overall implementation of the plan. It would not, however, have prevented the Government from taking over management whenever necessary. In fact, while there is no guarantee that sufficiently satisfactory results would have been forthcoming in the first half of 1971 it is, on the other hand, fairly clear that this was a much more favourable juncture for negotiated settlements than mid-1972.

During 1972 and 1973 the conflict sharpened. The formation of the APSM was increasingly threatened by conflicting forces. Despite this, it continued to grow rapidly but departed more and more from the original plan.

In the first half of 1972, the APSM in industry had grown substantially. By the end of the first half of 1972 approximately 70% of the APSM had been established (see Table III.B in the Appendix). The industrial plants that were to be incorporated into this sector but were still in private hands were producers of food products, tobacco, footwear and clothing, paper and cellulose and chemical products. The figures from the study carried out at the end of 1972 show that this situation had been maintained with few changes, despite the addition of a number of other companies. By that date twenty-five of the seventy-six industrial companies on the 'list of ninety' still remained outside the APSM. Of this group, six companies accounted for 6.6% of overall industrial production (see Table III.C in the Appendix). These units constituted a fundamental part of the above-mentioned branches of production. Their inclusion would have brought the APSM up to more than 90% of its target size, and up to more than 80% in each of its subdivisions.

On the other hand, the increase in the number of industrial companies under state control in 1972, without any appreciable increase in production (or sales), confirms that the APSM had continued to depart from the limits that had been projected for it. Towards the end of 1972 the total number of components incorporated during the whole period reached 197 (see Table III.A). The process continued during 1973, affecting a further 100 companies. This brought the total to approximately 300 which, when added to the forty-five state industrial concerns in existence at the end of 1970, totaled 350 components in the APSM.[21]

Various factors were responsible for the departure from the limits originally projected for the APSM.

In 1971 two main factors were responsible for this departure. First, some businessmen abandoned their factories because of insoluble financial problems. The Government was thus forced to take over these factories to maintain levels of production and employment. Second, there were a certain number of labour conflicts over salaries which dragged on indefinitely and which demanded management take-overs. Of a total of sixty-six companies affected in 1971 and not returned, in spite of the fact that they were not covered by the original projects, the management of fifty-one of them came under Government control through action of the Ministry of Labour. Despite the fact that this situation was largely beyond the Government's control and affected a relatively small number of components, it served as the basis for an enormous propaganda campaign with far-reaching ideological consequences.

A significant proportion of the management take-overs in 1972 and 1973 resulted from workers' intervention in response to sabotage by the owners during the lock-out in October 1972 and the attempted *coup* in June 1973.

Even without taking into account the companies not returned by the end of 1972 and in 1973, the APSM had been established to a large extent in most industrial activities. The precariousness of the legal aspects of the take-overs in many cases created difficulties in management. Despite this, in most of the precarious cases (industries) the means existed for controlling the companies' productive and financial affairs. An important part of this control mechanism had already been established in the first half of 1972. In other words, state control of the economy had grown to a much higher proportion than what had been considered necessary. Nevertheless, it was not possible for the state to dominate all the macroeconomic variables. Despite the advances made by the APSM in bringing about workers' participation in the management and organization of production, it could not play – either totally or partially – some of the important roles it had been assigned for the time being, namely accumulating the surplus, complementing the array of controls needed for the orderly functioning of the economy, and supervising the productive and financial management of the private sector.

4. THE APSM AND DOMESTIC FINANCIAL PROBLEMS

Implementation of a programme of immediate action exceeded the limits that had initially been envisaged. Moreover, the degree of Government control over the flow of capital was not adequate enough to carry out the necessary income transfers. On the one hand, wage increases were higher than authorized; on the other, non-wage-earning sectors managed to retain a large part of their monetary income, preventing sufficiently large transfers to the wage earners and the public sector. In this situation the APSM were, to a greater or lesser extent, unable to achieve some of their objectives.

A large majority of workers strongly supported the Government's policies. Their strong organization into a single labour confederation, the *Central Unica de Trabajadores* (CUT) [Trade Unions' Confederation], enabled them to act with exceptional forcefulness in implementing the programme of structural transformations and short-term policies. Increases in production achieved in the nationalized concerns were principally dependent on the capacity to keep the productive process both functioning and developing; increases in production in those firms remaining in the private sector were largely due to the staunch attitudes of the workers in these matters.

The loss of bargaining power by private businessmen, and the new correlation of forces in the state apparatus, enabled wage earners to consistently put pressure on employers for higher wages. In several cases their demands went beyond the possibilities the companies had within the framework of the envisaged pricing policy. This was due in part to the marked wage discrepancies both in various industries and within each company (see the discussion on p.225 of this chapter). The attempts to reduce these discrepancies took the form of considerable increases in the general wage levels. It was extremely difficult for the unions to resist these pressures which, moreover, were also brought to bear by Christian Democratic leaders, by extreme leftists on several occasions, and even by UP leaders in some cases.

The APSM's piecemeal formation meant that workers' participation in the management of companies could be developed to varying degrees. While participation by the workers had an appreciable effect on their understanding of the management process, it was not sufficient to reduce their demands for increased wages. In addition, for some time there was no clear effort to develop new ways of organizing work and wages; had such changes been instituted the demands for wage increases might have been curbed. Furthermore, wage increases went far beyond what the Government had envisaged: between October 1970 and October 1971 they rose more than 50%. The average wage and salary indices rose by 48.5% and 55%, respectively,[22] 8.5% and 15% more than the limit set at the end of 1970. However, this nominal increase in wages represented an increased purchasing power of only about 20%, since the consumer price index rose by 22.1% during the same period.

On the other hand, the increase in production brought about a substantial drop in unemployment. The overall unemployment level in greater Santiago was 5.5% in 1971, but for the month of December 1971 alone it was only 3.8%. This is particularly striking when compared to the level in December 1970 of 8.3% (see the Statistical Appendix following Chapter 2, Table III).

Despite these improvements, demands for wage increases continued during 1972. The highest level was reached between October 1972 and January 1973, when wage and salaries indices rose to a level of almost 35% above that of the consumer price index, taking September 1970 as the base (see Table IV.A in this chapter's Appendix).

Wage increases are usually regarded as inflationary *per se*. This implies that, given a total income, profits and rents from property are irreducible. In reality the situation is different. There seem to be two limits, one economic and social limit, and another 'technical and productive' limit, which mark these increases as inflationary. The former is determined by the effective capacity that exists to raise wages and reduce other forms of income. The latter is reached when profits and rents have disappeared or have been reduced to the minimum consumption level of the people receiving them and thus begin to affect the simple reproduction needs of the system. In the particular cases with which we are concerned, the former limit had already been surpassed in 1971, when implicit redistribution was less than in 1972.

As has been pointed out, the measures which were implemented made possible a considerable increase of the GDP (Gross Domestic Product) by 7.7% in 1971. However, wage and public finance needs required approximately double that amount.[23] These needs raised particularly complex problems for the Government's financial policy.

Strict application of the system of conventional controls, as well as growing support for the APSM, limited increases in consumer prices to only 22.1% between December 1970 and December 1971. Companies were able to absorb a considerable proportion of the wage increases by reducing their profits, which was partially compensated for by increased sales. Naturally, the situation was not the same in all companies, since the ratio between sales and wages varied from one sector to another, and demanded changes of varying degrees. In some cases, increased turnover compensated for raising wages; in other cases, however, the result was quite the reverse. These circumstances affected companies in the APSM as well, but for these companies the situation was more serious. Since the Government's aim was to keep consumer prices at the lowest possible levels, authorized price increases were in many cases lower than average. An additional factor was the exchange rate, which may be regarded as an index for the price of copper – that is, of the nationalized mining sector – given its single foreign price. Some of these inequalities can be seen in Table 7.3.

Such inequalities produced a considerable increase in the APSM's deficits. The greatest impact seems to have been on those traditional state enterprises which were producing the most widely used inputs (electricity, fuel and others) and, consequently, influencing the greatest number of prices. This phenomenon in fact merely aggravated the long-standing problem in this group of enterprises, particularly with respect to the financing of their investments. However, on the whole the new enterprises brought into the APSM did not show a deficit, despite the decrease in their surpluses. In other words, these 'new enterprises' helped to reduce the overall deficit (see Table IV.B in the Appendix to this chapter). In any case, there was an appreciable transfer of resources from the APSM to wages and to the private sector. As a result the APSM were unable to perform the task it had been allocated of accumulating surpluses; instead they in fact became instruments for distributing resources.

Throughout 1970-73 financial problems were particularly severe in the public sector. In the first place, compared to 1970, wage and social security payments increased in 1971 by 59% and 77% respectively. In real terms this meant an increase of approximately 44% in current budget expenditures and an increase of 4.7% in its share in GDP expenditures (see the Statistical Appendix to Chapter 2, Tables X and XII).

From the viewpoint of redistribution, increasing revenues and financing the deficit were the greatest problems. The most important single problem was the decrease in the tax payments from the large copper mining sector, due to the drop in the copper price, a decrease which amounted to E°2,300 million, or about 1.5% of GDP expenditures. Deficit financing came mainly from internal credits. Foreign credits, which in 1970 represented 45% of the total requirements, disappeared in 1971. Credits from the Central Bank had to be increased to seven times their 1970 levels. Thus it is clear that, as early in 1971, external problems were already beginning to have a significant effect on the public sector's budget (see the Statistical Appendix following Chapter 2, Table XI).

In 1972 the most serious additional financial problems arose from a decrease in the fiscal budget's real current income and increases – albeit smaller than the decreases in income – in expenditures. These two factors together meant a 4.7% increase in the deficit. In addition, the APSM incurred further losses (see Table IV.B in this chapter's Appendix and the Statistical Appendix at the end of Chapter 2, Tables X and XI). In 1973 there was a general drop in income and expenditure, but the magnitude of the deficit remained unchanged. The deficit was financed almost exclusively by credits from the Central Bank. Foreign loans did not return to their 1970 levels.

Not only the consolidated deficit of the public sector, but also credits granted to (1) organizations created by agrarian reform and (2) the private sector, resulted in the large-scale printing of paper money. In December 1971 the quantity of money in the private sector was nearly E°11,400 million, or 114% higher than in December 1970 (see Table IV.A in this chapter's Appendix and the Statistical Appendix following Chapter 2). It is estimated that this figure meant an excess of at least E°5,00 million over the amount that the economy could have absorbed that year, given the increase in the number of transactions, in prices and in other liquidity requirements.[24] By the end of 1972 the quantity of money had increased again, this time by 150% in comparison with 1971.

The public sector's financial difficulties reflected, in a nutshell, what we have generally called an insufficient degree of control over financial flows, and this restricted income redistribution to certain limits. This concept can be clarified by noting some of the principal manifestations of this lack of control. First, political and institutional opposition in the National Congress prevented the tax system from being changed and modernized. Second, effective authority over the traditional bureaucratic apparatus was lacking, and it was this bureaucratic apparatus which supervised the most important financial transactions. In addition, the banking system failed to become an efficient instrument for social control over the circulation of financial resources. To these objective limitations should be added the initial underestimation by the UP's economic leadership of the significance of the domestic financial shortfall. The UP leadership also failed to utilize available methods for cushioning the impact of the shortfall in 1971, particularly in relation to (1) relative price levels in the APSM and (2) supervision of taxes and credit. As to the first point, it seems that an appreciable improvement would have been possible, even though consumer prices might have risen. Inflation could have been brought under control by price increases of approximately 30% (instead of only 22%) particularly in view of the 35% increase in 1970. Conditions in 1971 – when the social situation was under control and the market was relatively normal – certainly made this a perfectly feasible course of action. While a quantitative estimate is difficult, it is clear that tax avoidance and nonpayment on social security did not diminish significantly, nor was credit more strictly regulated. Both actions were possible, within certain limits, despite the objective impediments.

In 1972 the UP Government was faced with new conditions, that is conditions which had not been evident the previous year. The increasingly sharp social tensions led the private sector to increasingly evade state controls. An excess of liquidity, reduction in investments and liquidation of stocks contributed to the rapid formation of a pool of speculative capital. Black market transactions became the rule for a sizable number of economic agents. In 1972 financial problems became more acute mainly because of a decline in public revenues (see the Statistical Appendix following Chapter 2, Tables X and XI).

The explosive increase in the money supply began to cause general confusion in the market from the beginning of 1972. These circumstances had, as far as the APSM were concerned, two important series of consequences: the internal ones and the external ones. Supply problems hampered efforts to reorganize all facets of production: structure, distribution of productive functions among the different components, organization of inventories, development of investment projects, and so on; in addition, there were administrative difficulties created by the perpetual search for solutions to pressing financial problems; finally, the political and social conflicts sharpened. These problems completely absorbed the attention of the various departments of the ministries involved, as well as of the great majority of workers, thereby preventing them from supervising and organizing the private sector. However, the private sector could not see sufficient progress being made towards the solution of its most pressing problems – supplies of basic raw materials, at the right time and the right price and in sufficient quantities – or towards the creation of a coherent system for dealing with its more general problems. The APSM could not manage to organize itself internally, nor could it direct private sector production.

In this way, overstepping the financial limits outlined in the short-term programme ended up by blocking or hampering the immediate tasks assigned to the APSM – accumulation of surpluses, management of the private sector, and development of its own capabilities.

Given these circumstances it is worth considering whether, once financial disarray had become general, as it had by 1972, it might have been possible for the APSM to decisively contribute to bringing the situation back under control. Whether, in other words, the sheer size of the APSM constituted an adequate additional lever for controlling the economy, meaning that the mistakes lay in the way it was being managed; or alternatively, whether the APSM's capacity had been overestimated, meaning that it was impossible for these areas to carry out these tasks.

The actions which the APSM could have taken for this purpose were: modification of its relative prices with respect both to private sector prices and to salaries; greater efficiency, particularly in relation to productivity; and an increase in production while still making profits. These tasks, quantitatively speaking, involved eliminating not only the APSM's financial deficit but also that of the public sector, which, respectively, amounted to 22% and 110% of the APSM's income.[25] Given the size of the deficit, the efficiency and production aspects – which were fundamental from the immediate political viewpoint and, in the medium and long run, at an economic level – could have no direct and decisive financial significance at that time. Improvements in productivity are slow, even under normal conditions, and increases in production depended to a great extent on factors beyond the APSM's control, particularly in the case of foreign resources. In this sense it seems that a different management of the wage and price system would have been the best immediate possibility.

This aspect can be clarified without too much difficulty if the excess of liquidity and the market's disorganization are borne in mind. Any increase in the prices in the APSM (and in the type of exchange rate) that affected the costs of private companies could, for the most part, be transferred to their own price levels without much difficulty. Traditional direct controls turned out to be less and less effective, particularly in the many small and medium-sized manufacturing and marketing companies. In this context, therefore, it was difficult to bring about a differentiated increase in prices in order to transfer income from the private sector to the APSM without such action having a great impact on wages. Any improvement in the APSM's profitability necessarily meant that the workers had to bear the consequences. The mechanisms for direct supervision could only have regained their partial effectiveness if the excess of liquidity had been absorbed in this way, and the market had returned to normal. From that moment on it would have been possible to begin making significant transfers from the private sector to the APSM.

However, this possibility clashed with the Government's social priorities. Besides, the political situation at that time, approximately mid-1972, made it impossible for corrective measures to be coordinated. In addition, any attempt to put such schemes into practice while trying to maintain the level of real wages was contradictory. A vicious circle would develop whose only consequence would be an acceleration of the rate of inflation and of the disarray prevailing in the market. In fact, the attempt made during August and September of 1972 had precisely that effect: at that time the exchange rate was raised considerably, with the result that the prices of imported products rose; this was followed immediately by a general wage readjustment, the consequence of which was an acceleration in all the imbalances, in the deficit, and in the issuance and distribution of money (see Table IV.A of this chapter's Appendix).

On the other hand, a purely quantitative and indiscriminate increase in the size of the APSM would probably not have succeeded in solving the problems either. By the end of 1972 the APSM effectively controlled 20% of total industrial production[26] and a slightly higher percentage of domestic marketing. A large increase to, say, 40% would probably not have made any qualitative difference in the difficulties analyzed above. Moreover, in the case of domestic marketing the APSM would have had to take in a considerable number of medium-sized industries, which would have been difficult to sustain; this would have upset the basic plan for political and social alliances. It was, however, possible to enlarge the APSM's scope quite significantly with regard to financial and production flows without broadening its productive base. This was done by maximally increasing control over wholesale distribution. For this purpose the Government exercised indirect control over all imports and had the capacity to rapidly increase direct controls over a large number of intermediate and finished goods, both of domestic and foreign origin. This instrument was to have (1) permitted control over a significant proportion of the inputs and outputs of the private sector, (2) made it possible to follow a discriminating pricing policy, and (3) exercised considerable influence over the structure of production. In fact, control over the wholesale trade of a sector or subsector of production makes it possible, for example, to fix equilibrium prices for state and private producers, allocate production programmes more rationally among the various production units, and control the flow of goods. Moreover, it made possible a retail pricing policy which ensured that increases were effectively concentrated within to the marketing system. Development of this procedure only began around the middle of 1973. It was put into practice in the home appliances sector with satisfactory initial results. It may be expected that its extension to other sectors would have permitted a considerable increase in the effectiveness of the mechanisms for directing and controlling the private sector.

In the abstract, this scheme may be regarded as another alternative for bringing the APSM closer to its desired role. There can be no doubt that advancing on this front was less difficult than broadening the APSM's productive base. However, it is not clear whether sufficient political strength existed to extend it to complete control over the distribution of industrial products.

In sum, the APSM companies could have, to a limited degree, helped to improve the general economic situation in several respects: internal organization, relative prices, control of marketing, etc. However, it could not, by itself, change the fundamentals of the financial situation. Also, its further development would have involved regaining control over the processes of production and distribution. This in turn would have required a substantive increase in the political and social forces at the Government's disposal, and concerted economic action at all levels.

5. THE INTERNAL ORGANIZATION OF THE APSM IN INDUSTRY

The internal organization of the APSM enterprises suffered both delays and setbacks. At first, in 1971, this was because efforts were concentrated on expropriating the economic components that were to comprise the area. Thereafter, in 1972 and 1973, it was because of external difficulties, financial problems and the disorganized state of the market. Despite all this, it was possible to develop several important aspects. For example, the organization of workers' management and participation was given a particular boost. However, other aspects, such as new forms of management, the reorganization of work and wages, as well as the planning of relations between different enterprises, all suffered delays.

Clearly it was precisely the latter aspects that were most affected by the growing inflation and disorganization in distribution and supplies. From this viewpoint it cannot really be said that new production relations were attained in the APSM. The complex process of socialization that follows the establishment of state property was begun on only the most limited scale. It is, of course, debatable whether such a process can develop fully before the working class and the people have taken control of social and political life. Nevertheless, it seems possible to prepare the way for the subsequent completion of the process by using such methods as democratization of administration, new organization of work and wages, and the development of planning procedures in the production units. On the other hand, it is clearly difficult to remove the relations between enterprises from the pressures of the still dominant traditional capitalist market; this is even more difficult if these pre-existing relations are increasingly disrupted – as they were – and have a negative impact on efforts to reorganize the functioning of state enterprises.

The first task undertaken was setting up central control mechanisms which were appropriate to the APSM's new character and size. Four main areas can be identified: large-scale copper mining, which was in the hands of CODELCO, the state agency responsible for supervising the U.S. companies; the banking system, directed by the Ministry of the Treasury and the Central Bank; domestic marketing activities, controlled by an *ad hoc* secretariat; and the whole system of industrial and energy-related enterprises, under the control of the *Corporacíon de Fomento de la Producción* (CORFO) [Corporation for Production Development], the state agency for increasing production.

The overall problem of creating a new organic structure was all-pervasive, though the form it took naturally varied from one place to another. However, the most pervasive difficulties seemed to have been in the industrial area. The most important point was that a large number of companies and workers were involved, and they had widely varying technical levels and many different ways of organizing production, distribution and wages as well as widely differing financial circumstances. Intermediate bodies, known as sectoral committees, were established in order to (1) find a common approach to many of these problems, (2) reduce the supervisory responsibilities of the upper bureaucratic levels, and (3) concentrate managerial and technical talents. In legal terms, these committees were administrative units of CORFO; their responsibilities extended to the state and private companies of, more or less, a particular branch of the industrial or services sector (see Table V.A of the Appendix). Their main tasks consisted of establishing basic guidelines for the way production was to be carried out by APSM companies, distributing basic resources among them, drawing up development programmes for each branch, coordinating technical cooperation, and supervising the execution of allotted tasks. The development of wholesale distribution networks, foreign exchange agencies and construction units was also their responsibility. In addition, they were to exert economic control over the private sector. To perform these tasks it was necessary to set up technical and managerial committees which would fulfill these functions. In general, the attention of these committees was absorbed by immediate problems connected with both the initial organization and subsequent management of companies. The APSM's external responsibilities only began to receive some attention in 1973. A similar situation developed with the reorganization of production. Study of the problems of specialization by enterprises, of changes in the structure of goods, and of quality control only began after the end of 1972.

The basis of management continued to be, almost without exception, the same company as that which the Government expropriated or in which it had taken over management. In other words, the same set of basic means of production, as well as the same workers, became the unit of economic calculation within the APSM. Management of these companies had, of course, to fit in with the aims and allocations of resources by the appropriate sectoral committee. When they had been fully developed, these aims and allocations became the guidelines which were to constitute the sector's plan. These companies maintained traditional market relationships with other companies, whether in the social or the private sector. The problems of profitability described above prevented the principle of financial autonomy from being put into practice. As is well known, this principle plays a fundamental role in the organization of state companies in most economies which are moving towards socialism. This is one of the areas in which different conceptions of the nature and character of economic relations within the state sector become apparent. In this particular case, the fact that this principle was not applied was more the result of a *de facto* situation than of a particular conception. It cannot be said that a significant discussion of these problems ever took place.

The normal functioning of these new structures was, however, hampered by a number of difficulties. In the first place there was, on the domestic level, insufficient coordination between the individual bodies responsible for the different aspects of the APSM's activities: the Ministry of the Treasury and the Central Bank in domestic financial matters; the Central Bank's Foreign Trade Department (SEREX) in questions concerning the use of foreign exchange; the Ministry of Labour in matters of labour organization and the system of wages; and, finally, CORFO in the APSM's overall management. In the second place, within the committees and the enterprises themselves there were divergent views on important aspects of production management. These problems were essentially the expression of a greater weakness in the system as a whole, namely the lack of a single economic authority to establish a consistent policy which outlined operations, responsibilities and methods necessary to resolve eventual conflicts. Despite this, the experience that managerial participation gave the workers, technicians and supervisors indicated that some progress was made towards achieving the Government's basic aims.

The most important aspect to be developed in the APSM companies was democratizing management through the participation process. The terms of a general agreement made at the end of 1970 between the Government and the CUT clearly stated the principles of this new initiative. Essentially, the agreement asserted that the state-controlled components would be managed, within the guidelines of the national economic plan, by a council consisting of five representatives of the workers, directly elected, and six representatives designated by higher authorities, one of whom was to function as managing director. The representatives of the collective were to include an individual from the technical level and another from the administrative level. Besides being included in immediate managerial responsibilities, the workers were to elect committees at the different levels of internal organization: the departments, sections, etc. These committees were to function as technical bodies alongside the individual in charge in each case. Delegates from these committees were to form sectoral committees and, finally, committees on the national level.

Initially this scheme was applied in a rather bureaucratic way. It was only when the experiment got underway that it began to take on any real meaning.

New work methods began to come into use and the workers' influence began to grow rapidly. The most advanced manifestation of this process was the workers' assemblies set up by sectors of production, in which representatives of all the factories were involved – including, on several occasions, representatives from the private sector. In these assemblies basic production problems and the Government's proposed plans were discussed, and directives concerning subsequent developments were drafted.[27]

It is difficult to extract any generally valid conclusions on a number of important aspects of these experiments, such as relations between unions and the participation organizations, and between the workers and the technical staff. The few provisional documents available[28] give no indication of any general tendencies with regard to these problems. On the other hand, the documents clearly show that democratization of labour relations and the disappearance of the traditional despotic discipline were double-edged. On the one hand, there was a considerable increase in the initiative taken by the workers in all fields: cultural, ideological and, above all, with regard to production. There were many observations forthcoming on such matters as technical support for the more backward companies, savings of foreign exchange, improvement and control of production and so on. On the other hand, there is evidence of a certain amount of labour disorder: absenteeism, unjustified work stoppages and failure to perform the allotted tasks.

The documents mentioned above do not indicate any interest in a completely different initiative which was proposed by the Christian Democrats, the 'workers companies'. This formula is not concerned with a different way of organizing participation within the framework of a state entity, but with the very concept of the company itself. As is well known, it basically proposed a cooperative form of management. Apparently, before this time confrontation generally occurred on the level of general political concepts rather than on actual social practice.[29] An abstract discussion of the problem, apart from being very familiar, would be outside the scope of this chapter. But it is important to remember in this connection that, in the thwarted agreement between President Allende and Senator Fuentealba of June 1972, the principle of creating this type of company in a certain number of components was accepted.

By 1973 workers' participation had been organized in a majority of companies in the APSM, though with rather diverse and, in general, inadequate levels of maturity. The fundamental causes were delays in the reorganization of certain key relations of work and wages and inadequate planning of the work to be done. It is easy to understand that, without these factors, it was impossible to increase social control over individual and collective tasks to a satisfactory level. The lack of progress in these areas, which only began to receive systematic attention at the end of 1972, also retarded the economic strengthening of the APSM, preventing it from exercising more decisive influence over the economy as a whole.

In the first place, the absence of any data concerning real labour requirements and production targets precluded adequate control of productivity. It also meant that a significant number of companies took on unnecessary personnel. Of course, the structural unemployment which had been passed on from before 1970 constituted an additional pressure. While it was possible to overcome this problem completely in 1971, when an exceptional rise in production permitted a rapid increase in labour output, this was not the case in 1972, when the increase in economic activity was lower. Nevertheless, despite the drop in productivity, it was still above the 1970 level. The fall in production, which resulted from external restrictions and the sharpening of internal problems, meant a considerable drop in productivity in 1973. It should be borne in mind that, in this last case, it would have been practically impossible, in almost any circumstances, to prevent a drop. There is no doubt that employment is much more rigid when faced with a drop in production than when faced with an increase in production. Changes in the indicator can be seen in Table 7.4.

Unfortunately, there are no figures which distinguish the APSM from the private sectors. But, even if one supposes a much more unfavourable situation in the state sector, the drop in production could not have become very serious in 1972.[30] It is important to emphasize that problems of internal efficiency did not have a decisive impact on the APSM's financial situation (see p. 244 of this chapter).

In the second place no reorganization of the wage structure was achieved. In addition to the vast differences in salary levels noted earlier, there was a different wage system in each company, made worse by an extraordinary diversity in the companies' internal structures. Under these circumstances it was particularly difficult to establish any kind of link between increases in real wages and productivity. The wage readjustments that followed price increases brought chaotic rises in the level of real wages. Wage increases were in fact still being made in accordance with an earlier tradition.

Finally, these deficiencies prevented the establishment of a rigorous planning system; but despite this it was possible to begin developing some of the most important elements: control of production and allocation of some particularly scarce resources, such as foreign exchange. The most important actions, designed to ensure that companies operated in accordance with the system, were not implemented until 1973. Of particular significance was the preparation of an annual plan for 1974. The essential aims of this plan can be summarized as follows: (1) to reorganize production with the basis being extreme rigidity in the capacity to import, giving priority to the most widely used consumer goods; and (2) to raise the level of productive investments, giving priority to those connected with the processing of agricultural products or those which already had their financing guaranteed by foreign credits. The basic idea was to make maximum use of foreign resources by all possible means, namely: reduction of imported inputs per unit of production by modifying the range of items produced and eventual elimination of sophisticated goods, changes in the types of products made, increased exports and import substitution. The plan got as far as being discussed by the workers in a large number of state enterprises and was accepted by a considerable number of the most important enterprises in the private sector. Preparation of the plan itself showed the possibilities for considerable improvement in the relationships with the private sector and for greater efficiency in the use of foreign exchange.

In summary, the APSM's internal organization had only just begun in the second half of 1972. Several of its most important aspects did not reach the development stage and others were severely delayed by the general disorganization of finances and production. For this reason – and despite the rapid progress made in democratizing management – the essential elements of a new system for production relations were not created within this sector. These difficulties prevented the APSM from functioning more efficiently and from playing a more important role in production as a whole. Despite this, the few programmes that were implemented, párticularly workers' participation, gave rise to an exceptional increase in production in 1971 and a somewhat smaller increase in 1972. In 1973, foreign pressure caused a considerable drop in production.

6. INDUSTRIAL PRODUCTION IN THE APSM AND EXTERNAL DIFFICULTIES

Wage increases, social expenditures and special building programmes substantially raised overall domestic demand. In addition, the changes in income distribution modified the demand structure, creating a proportionately greater increase in the need for basic consumer goods. In most sectors production responded adequately to these demands in 1971. The rigid attitudes of the most powerful business groups were overcome by the workers' actions and by Government measures. Overall growth, which was very marked in the first year, was slower in 1972 and declined in 1973 (see Table VI.A in this chapter's Appendix). Increases in both domestic social opposition and in foreign pressures were the main causes of these fluctuations. Almost all of the difficulties encountered by industry were due to this increase in foreign pressures. This was particularly significant since this sector represented about 45% of the value added in material production in 1970.

As noted above, there are no separate systematic sets of statistics for each social area. It is possible, however, to determine that the most important physical production, which was controlled totally or partially by the APSM, followed the overall trend (see Table VI.B in the Appendix). On the other hand, it is striking that some items produced by the large private companies, such as paper, cellulose and detergents, showed a decline in production in 1972 (Table VI.B). Of course, a broader sample is needed to make a more definitive statement on divergences between the two sectors.

One of the factors which accounted for the rise in production in 1971 was the increased use of installed capacity. Indeed this was one of the major reasons for almost all the production increases in 1972. It is important to emphasize that, despite what has usually been maintained, difficulties in this sphere were most decisive in limiting production. In fact, one study shows that productive potential in 1971 was nearly 20% higher than the actual levels reached (see Table VI.C in this chapter's Appendix). The method of calculation, moreover, seems to underestimate some possibilities, for it is based on an analysis of the best averages in the past, when there was a systematic underuse of installed capacity. Of course, in relations between different industries, perfect adjustments between differing capacities did not exist. This meant that efficient use of installed capacity could result in problems with delivery dates. Under these circumstances, only a few bottlenecks were enough to lead to a halt in the overall increase in producing a final product; in fact most such bottlenecks led instead to a steady rise in the quantity of imported inputs per unit of production. This was the case, for example, when there was a difference between spinning and weaving capacities, with the latter exceeding the former. Once the possibilities for domestic production of thread were exhausted, weaving could only continue to expand by using imported supplies. It appears that extreme situations were only reached in a few sectors (e.g. cement, certain kinds of steel, some chemical products and certain synthetic fibres) towards the end of 1972. To be sure, the above calculations do not take into account possibilities for short-term increases in capacity by eliminating bottlenecks. In 1972 and 1973, in fact, some small projects designed along these lines had been planned, and in several cases begun. However, this problem was not attacked directly, despite its being one of the most important aspects outlined in the guidelines for the economy.

The decline in production in 1973 also bears no relation to capacity levels. Nevertheless, in several places problems caused by inadequate maintenance had already begun to reduce potential output. To be sure, this situation was closely linked to difficulties with the supply of imported spare parts. The problems in 1973 were directly influenced by other factors: on the one hand, the extreme political actions of the sectors opposed to the UP affected such fundamental services as transport for long periods; on the other, the operating stocks of companies, particularly of imported raw materials and spare parts, had reached critically low levels. Hoarding on a massive scale made this an extremely acute problem. It is well known that under these circumstances, continuing processes suffer frequent interruptions that seriously affect their performance levels.

It is evident from the available material that continuing increases in production in 1972 and 1973 were prevented by the limited supply of agricultural products and imported inputs. The former is reflected by an increase of only 7.7% in the food sector in 1971, which was considerably below the industrial average, followed by decreases in 1972 and 1973. It is thus understandable that the first shortages occurred in agricultural products. In addition, given the redistribution of incomes, these were the products for which there was the greatest increase in demand. The increases in imports for this sector were unable to compensate for the deficiencies in domestic supplies.

The difficulties with imported inputs affected the entire agricultural sector. If the supplies of these products in 1970 are taken as normal, then requirements in 1971 and 1972 increased in value by 21% and 30%, respectively. These increased requirements could be explained by increases in production by 16% and 20% in comparison to 1970, and by increases in import prices of 4% and 8% (see Table VI.D of this chapter's Appendix). It could be estimated that effective imports were considerably lower than requirements in each of the years mentioned (Table VI.D). These resources were obtained from stocks of raw materials, intermediate goods and spare parts which had been imported before 1970.

As in the past, the growth in production was principally designed to satisfy increased domestic demands. Everyday consumer goods, except food, and intermediate goods moved in the way as the rest. In 1971 durable consumer goods increased in the same way, spurred by the indiscriminate growth of demand and production. In 1972 and 1973, however, a more restricted allocation of resources had to suffice. The few capital goods that were made in Chile, mainly in categories 35, 36 and 38, grew systematically, even in 1973, due to a new policy for stimulating their development.

Production for export, which grew markedly in 1971, returned to its pre-1970 levels in the following years (see Table VI.E in this chapter's Appendix). The idea that the exchange rate was responsible for discouraging exports does not appear to be borne out by empirical evidence. This can be explained as follows: sales of copper, which accounted for more than 85% of total exports, were more dependent on the world situation than on competitiveness, which was assured by low wages and a high level of technology. Besides, there was a growing tendency to divide the market among the large producers. As far as industrial exports were concerned, it can be seen that they too relied fundamentally on the use of certain natural resources. Here difficulties were almost invariably encountered in finding foreign markets, which are normally monopolistically controlled and heavily protected, rather than in competitiveness. On the other hand, examination of the exchange rates indicates that the time when they were most unfavourable, in 1971, was also the time when the largest volume of industrial products were exported (see Table VI.F of this chapter's Appendix). Without prejudicing the above observation, it is necessary to point out that, in any case, a policy of strong differentiation was started in 1972 to stimulate other marginal industrial exports (Table VI.F). The need to support these initiatives by fixing the price of foreign exchange at an appropriate level must not be confused with the idea that this expendient can be used to drastically modify the balance of trade situation of an economy such as that of Chile.[31]

It may thus be concluded that in 1972, and even more in 1973, there was potential in industry that was not used, primarily because of external restrictions. Many aspects could have been developed in a fairly short period, but in order to accomplish this it was necessary to have additional imported resources and to concentrate efforts on making some technical modifications.

In the first place, further industrial exports to the socialist countries and to Latin America could have been developed. In fact some experiments were started; for example, an agreement was signed with Bulgaria for steel sheets worth a total of about $2 million; these were to be paid for in home appliances, for which there was abundant unused productive capacity. This kind of arrangement could have been repeated in various parts of the industrial apparatus.

A second possibility was to eliminate products which require large amounts of foreign exchange. These were normally nonessential goods. When the 1974 plan was being drawn up, it was found that the suppression of a few electrical appliances could reduce the average imported inputs per unit by more than half. In the same area, there were possibilities for small, short-term expansion which would have enabled substitution of a series of intermediate goods. For example, by importing relatively inexpensive machinery, it would have been possible to replace some leather inputs by synthetics in manufacturing footwear. Another most important initiative was the search for short-term credit lines which could allow acquisition of intermediate goods for specific industries such as electronics, transport vehicles, etc.

Finally, it seems that it might have been possible to implement some important restructuring in some parts of the industrial apparatus in a reasonably short time. Certainly, the fundamental structure could only be substantially modified over a longer period. There was, of course, the experiment aimed at transforming the Ford and General Motors plants into assembly lines for Fiat lorries, using a reasonable percentage of domestic inputs. It was also possible to consider a much greater use of domestic capacity for production of simple capital goods and certain kinds of spare parts. The underuse of these lines was substantial (see Table VI.C of this chapter's Appendix). To make the most of these possibilities, however, broad foreign technical support was needed, which involved both the planning and the application of appropriate production technologies.

In summary, the potential of industry was by no means exhausted in 1972. There were several aspects which were only just being explored in that year, and in 1973. For these aspects to be developed, however, greater availability of foreign exchange, technical support and a much broader and more experienced international trade organization were essential. Although this foreign support might have been important for increasing production and helping to reduce pressure on many points, it could not change the essential situation, which was that domestic economic imbalances existed because there was no political force strong enough to overcome them. Only a substantial change in that situation – one favourable to the transformations already implemented – could have made it possible to restructure the whole process, strengthen and develop the APSM into a dominant force and thereby enable adequate use to be made of both internal and external resources.

NOTES

1. Among many other works on this subject, the following should be mentioned: A. Pinto, *Chile, un caso de desarrollo frustrado* [Chile, A Case of Frustrated Development] (Santiago de Chile, Editorial Universitaria, 1959); A. Pinto, *Chile, una economía difícil* [Chile, A Difficult Economy] (Mexico City, Fondo de Cultura Económica, 1964); R. Lagos, *La industria en Chile. Antecedentes estructurales* [Industry in Chile. Structural Antecedents] (Santiago de Chile, Instituto de Economía, Universidad de Chile, 1966); J. Cademártori, *La economía chilena* [The Chilean Economy] (Santiago de Chile, Editorial Universitaria, 1968); A.G. Frank, *Chile, el desarrollo del subdesarrollo* [Chile, The Development of Underdevelopment] (New York, Monthly Review Press, special edition, 1967); A.G. Frank, *Capitalisme et sous-développement en Amérique Latine* [Capitalism and Underdevelopment in Latin America] (Paris, Maspero, 1968); O. Garretón and Y. Cisternas, *Algunas características de la toma de decisiones en la gran empresa* [Some Characteristics of Decision-Making in the Large Enterprises] (Santiago de Chile, Servicio de Cooperación Técnica, March 1970); H. Ramírez, *Historia del imperialismo en Chile* [A History of Imperialism in Chile] (Santiago, Editorial Universitaria, 1968); Centro de Estudios Socio-economicos (CESO) [Socio-economic Studies Centre], *Chile hoy* [Chile Today] (Mexico City, Siglo XXI, 1970); S. Ramos, *Chile, una economía de transición?* [Chile, A Transition Economy?] (Santiago de Chile, Prensa Latinoamericana, 1972). The best collection of statistical data on the most recent period is ODEPLAN, *Antecedentes sobre el desarrollo chileno 1960-70* [Antecedents on the Chilean Development 1960-70], Series I, no. 1, *Planes semestrales. Plan de la economía nacional 1971-76* [Half Yearly Plans. Plans of the National Economy for 1971-76] (Santiago de Chile, 1971).

2. The E. Matte group could be cited as an example. It controlled, among other things, Cemento Melón (cement), Aceros Andes (steel), Compañía Manufacturera de Papeles y Cartones (paper products), and other industries, Sochile (a commercial distribution company), the Banco Sud Americano (The Bank of South America) and other financial and service companies. See Garretón and Cisternas, *Algunas características...*, for a general attempt at identifying the economic power groups.

3. See CESO, *Chile hoy*, 68-69.

4. The Foreign Investor's Statute (1960) and Articles 14 and 16 of Decree 1272 of the Ministry of Economics (1961).

5. Imports of equipment for industry rose from some $9,000 to $18,400 for each additional person employed during the five year periods from 1960 to 1965 and from 1965 to 1970. See ODEPLAN, *Antecedentes sobre el desarrollo chileno...*, 180 and 182.

6. ODEPLAN, *Antecedentes sobre el desarrollo chileno...*, xxxii.

7. Although industrial exports practically tripled during the 1960-70 period, they amounted to not even 5% of the gross value of the sector's production in 1968, or 10% of total exports.

8. ODEPLAN, *Plan Anual 1971* [Annual Plan, 1971] (Santiago de Chile, 1971), 6, quoted in S. Ramos, *Chile, una economía...*, 104.

9. *Programa básico de la Unidad Popular* [Basic Programme of the UP]. An Englisch translation of this is published in J. Ann Zammit, *The Chilean Road to Socialism* (Brighton, England, Institute of Development Studies, University of Sussex, 1973), 255-284. The Spanish version is available in *Chile, Peru, Bolivia, documentos de tres procesos Latinoamericanos*. Bibliteca fundamental del Hombre Moderno (Buenos Aires, Centro Editor de America Latina S.A., 1977).
10. The majority of railways and airlines were already in state hands.
11. ODEPLAN, *Antecedentes sobre el desarrollo...*, 192.
12. *Encuesta continua de comercio y servicios* [Permanent Survey of Trade and Services] Dirección Nacional de Estadísticas [National Office of Statistics], quoted in S. Ramos, *Chile, una economía...*, 68.
13. The bill was proposed to create areas in the economy and was presented by the UP Government in October 1971.
14. This was roughly equivalent to $1.5 million, given the exchange rate which was current at that time.
15. The studies are S. Bitar, 'Efectos de las Areas de Propiedad Social y Mixta en la industria chilena' [Effects of the APS and APM on Chilean Industry], *Trimestre económico* [Economic Quarterly], 163 (1974); A. Bardón, 'Control directo del estado en la industria manufacturera' [Direct State Control on the Manufacturing Industry], in *Comentarios sobre la situación económica, 1er semestre de 1972* [Statement on the Economic Situation, 1st Quarter of 1972] (Santiago de Chile, Universidad de Chile, Facultad de Ciencias Económicas [University of Chile, Faculty of Economic Studies 1972]; Instituto de Economía y Planificación [Institute of Economics and Planning], *La economía chilena en 1972* [The Chilean Economy in 1972] (Santiago de Chile, 1973). See Table II.A in the Appendix.
16. S. Bitar, 'Efectos de las Areas...', 552 and 554.
17. In both cases self-employed producers are excluded from the figures.
18. The Ministry of Economics organized a series of meetings with representatives of the different sections of the employers' association, the *Sociedad de Fomento Fabril* (SOFOFA) [Industrial Development Society] (metal-working, industry, wood, construction materials, leather and footwear, plastics, etc.) in the first weeks of 1971. It could be seen in these meetings that the majority of the entrepreneurs were from medium-sized sectors rather than from monopolistic groups. The general trend at these meetings was that the entrepreneurs demanded the formulation of guarantees which would be offered to the medium-sized entrepreneurs. No written records exist of these meetings.
19. The only important bank not incorporated was the Bank of Chile.
20. This formula for compensation had a very similar precedent in the Agrarian Reform Law passed in 1967.
21. This figure was given by the military junta in República de Chile, *Un año de reconstrucción* [A Year of Reconstruction] (Santiago de Chile, 1974). Only companies in the industrial committees are included.
22. See the Central Bank, *Boletín mensual* [Monthly Bulletin] (March 1975), 461; and the Statistical Appendix which appears at the end of Chapter 2, Table V.
23. The wage increase amounted to approximately 8% of GNP expenditure, while the budget deficit amounted to 8.4%. See the Statistical Appendix following Chapter 2, Table XII.
24. Prices increased by 22.1% and there was a 7.7% increase in GDP expenditure and possibly more in transactions. The difference implies a drop of approximately 20% in the velocity of circulation.
25. These are annual figures for 1972; see Table IV.B in this chapter's Appendix and the Statistical Appendix following Chapter 2, Table XIII. Copper mining is not included; if it were, the percentages would be approximately 23% and 90%.
26. See Instituto de Economía y Planificación, *La economía chilena....*
27. One of the most important assemblies took place in the textile sector in order to discuss the 1974 plans.
28. These are interviews with workers and supervisors in three large textile mills and one engineering works.

29. It is possible that this observation is distorted by the great influence of the marxist parties in the textile factories. However, the same happened in engineering, where the marxist parties' influence was minimal.
30. This is an extreme hypothesis which assumes that an increase in employment mainly in the state sector and similar growth in production in both areas would result in a decrease of less than 10% in productivity.
31. The military junta, which currently controls the Government, claims to have achieved this effect by means of rapid devaluation. In fact what has happened is that, by means of a drastic drop in purchasing power in Chile, it has created exportable surpluses of essential consumer goods, particularly food.

Table 7.1. *Share of Foreign Capital in the Largest Industrial Companies*

	None		*Less than 30%*		*Between 30 and 50%*		*More than 50%*	
	Number	*%*	*Number*	*%*	*Number*	*%*	*Number*	*%*
In the 261 largest	142	54.4	42	16.1	22	8.4	55	21.1
In the 160 largest	78	48.7	28	17.5	17	10.6	37	23.2
In the 100 largest	39	39.0	21	21.0	12	12.0	28	28.0

Source: E. Acevedo and H. Vergara, 'Concentración y capital extranjero en la industria chilena' [Concentration and Foreign Capital in the Chilean Industry], *Economía y administración* [Economy and Administration], 15 (1970), 27-53 (Concepción, Chile).

Table 7.2. *Characteristics of the 'Ninety New Companies'*

Sectors	*Number of companies*	*% of employment*	*% of capital of limited companies*	*% belonging to the largest shareholders*	*% of foreign capital*
Industry	74	10	42.4	59.7	22.9
Commerce	6	1	15.5	52.5	27.2
Transport and communications	6	4	75.7	81.8	66.3
Electricity (distribution)	4	...	8.0	26.4	0.9

Source: *Panorama económico* [Economic Panorama], 270 (1972) (Santiago de Chile).

Table 7.3. *Price Indices for Some State Companies (annual averages; base: 1970 = 100)*

	1971	*1972*	*1973*[b]
Petroleum derivates	100.9	142.6	255.0
Electricity (Endesa)	105.5	122.6	122.6
Railways	120.6	205.3	500.7
Exchange rate[a]	107.2	153.9	175.6
Imported products (wholesale)	122.2	190.9	358.0
Industrial products (wholesale)	113.9	189.3	392.3

[a] Exchange rate for copper exports.
[b] Only until June.

Source: World Bank, *Special Report on the Chilean Economic Outlook* (Washington, D.C., October 1974), Vol. III, tables 9.8 and 3.11 and Tables VI and VIII in the Statistical Appendix following Chapter 2.

Table 7.4. *Industrial Production (base: 1970 = 100)*

	1971	*1972*	*1973*
A	106.6	104.9	92.7
B	106.5	103.7	. . .

A: The industrial employment index is for greater Santiago and the Lota-Coronel and Taleahuaho-Concepción areas, which cover almost 40% of the economically active population. The production index was made by the Instituto Nacional de Estadistícas [National Institute of Statistics] (Santiago de Chile).

B: Calculated by the World Bank.

Sources: Table VI.A in this chapter's Appendix, the Statistical Appendix following Chapter 2, Tables III and IV, and the World Bank, *Special Report* . . ., Vol. III, table 2.2.

APPENDIX

Table I.A. *Concentration of Ownership in the Manufacturing Industry, 1963 (percentage)*

	Number of plants	*Employment*	*Capital*	*Value added*	*Gross surplus*[a]
Large industries (plants of 200 people or more)	3	44	58	51	52
Medium-sized industries (from 20 to 199 people)	30	40	35	38	38
Small industries (from 5 to 19 people)	67	16	7	11	10

[a] The gross surplus is defined as the value added less remunerations to labour, including the employer's payments to social security. Since the remunerations also include payments to executives and directors, the value of the gross surplus is underestimated, particularly in medium-sized and large industries.

Source: CESO, *Chile hoy* [Chile Today] (Mexico City, Siglo XXI, 1970), 70. Data supplied by CORFO (Santiago de Chile).

Table I.B. *Concentration of Ownership in Commerce, 1967*[a]

	Companies		*Sales*	*Employment*	
	Number	*%*	*%*	*Number*	*%*
1. Wholesale trade					
Large companies	70	2.7	76.1	20,300	52.9
Medium-sized companies	856	32.7	19.2	10,170	26.5
Small companies	1,689	64.6	4.7	7,900	20.6
2. Retail trade					
Large companies	30	...	5.5	...	...
Medium-sized companies	4,800	4.6	20.6	44,900	14.8
Small companies	100,000	95.4	73.9	258,100	85.2

[a] The size of the companies is not indicated in the source.

Source: S. Ramos, *Chile, una economía de transición?* [Chile, An Economy in Transition?] (Santiago de Chile, Prensa Latinoamerica, 1972), 69. Data from the Instituto de Estadísticas [Institute of Statistics], *Encuesta permanente de comercio y servicios* [Recurring Survey of Trade and Services] (Santiago de Chile).

Table I.C. *Concentration of Ownership in Industry, by Industrial Sector, 1968*

	Number of plants [a]	*Large industry*		*% of sales*
		Number of plants	*%*	
20 Food products	1,344	64	4.8	43.7
21 Beverages	141	14	9.9	55.2
22 Tobacco	3	1	33.3	100.0
23 Textiles	541	28	5.2	47.8
24 Footwear and clothing	744	23	3.1	44.3
25 Wood	1,037	5	0.5	12.3
26 Furniture and accessories	250	1	0.4	17.4
27 Paper and cellulose	63	3	4.8	94.4
28 Printing and publishing	243	...	...	...
29 Leather	118	...	...	...
30 Rubber	45	2	4.4	88.1
31 Chemical products	265	34	12.8	48.9
32 Petroleum and coal derivates	14	...	...	...
33 Nonmetallic minerals	212	12	5.7	63.6
34 Basic metals	92	...	...	...
35 Metal products	478	16	3.3	31.0
36 Nonelectrical machinery	196	5	2.6	44.0
37 Electrical machinery	129	15	11.6	61.7
38 Transport equipment	519	18	3.5	55.8
39 Various industries	231	6	2.6	31.4
Total	6,248	247	4.0	48.7

[a] Only plants with ten or more workers. 26,701 units of less than ten workers are excluded.
[b] Large industries are defined those with annual sales of more than E°100 million in 1968, which was the equivalent of roughly $15 million at that time.

Source: E. Acevedo and H. Vergara, 'Concentración y capital extranjero en la industria chilena' [Concentration and Foreign Capital in the Chilean Industry], *Economía y administración* [Economy and Administration], 15 (1970), 27-53 (Concepción, Chile).

Table I.D. *Gross Domestic Investment in Fixed Capital in the Manufacturing Industry (percentage of value added per sector)*

	Total	*Private investment* [a]	*Public investment*		
			Total	*Direct*	*Indirect*
1960	13.8	...	...	...	...
1961	10.5	9.1	1.4	0.9	0.5
1962	8.8	7.7	1.1	0.5	0.6
1963	8.3	6.8	2.0	1.5	0.8
1964	9.3	5.4	3.9	3.1	0.6
1965	10.2	5.9	4.3	3.7	0.6
1966	11.1	6.7	4.4	3.8	0.6
1967	8.7	5.1	3.6	1.7	1.9
1968	8.5	5.3	3.2	1.1	2.1
1969	...	...	5.1	2.3	2.8

[a] Includes foreign private investment, estimated at 20% of the total for the period.

Source: ODEPLAN, *Antecedentes sobre el desarrollo chileno 1960-70* [Antecedents on the Chilean Development 1960-70] Series I, no. 1, *Planes semestrales Plan de la economía nacional 1971-76* [Half-Yearly Plans, Plan of the National Economy for 1971-76]. (Santiago de Chile, 1971), 155, 157, 177 and 178. Calculations are based on data found at 155, 157, 177 and 178.

Table I.E. *Annual Rate of Growth, Structure of Exports and Distribution of Foreign Investments in Industry*

	Annual % of growth 1960-70	*% distribution of industrial exports, 1970*	*% distribution of foreign investments 1960-69*[a]	*% share of foreign investment in total capital, 1969*
Food industries	5.1	6.8[b]	25.6	9.0
(Canned fish and seafood)	(14.7)	...	(21.6)	...
Wood and cork	7.6	10.9	7.3	2.0
Paper and cellulose	12.4	37.4	26.3	16.4
Rubber	7.7	...	...	45.1
Chemicals	8.8	8.5	4.4	38.3
Metal products	10.2	...	...	13.5
Nonelectrical machinery and equipment	7.8	...	...	14.7
Electrical machinery and equipment	9.4	...	...	59.9
Transport materials and equipment	11.1	...	11.0	43.8
Total manufacturing industry	5.5	100.0	100.0	20.3
Beverages	2.7	...	...	24.6[c]
Tobacco	2.2	...	...	58.6[c]
Basic metals	2.1	35.2	13.5[d]	18.4

[a] This includes only investments and credits in accordance with two legal instruments; it excludes inflows by means of a noncontrollable regulation and investments using local resources.
[b] Mainly canned fish and seafood and their by-products.
[c] Refers to investments before 1960.
[d] Mainly semi-manufactured copper.

Source: Rates of growth and distribution of exports from ODEPLAN, *Antecedentes sobre el desarrollo* . . . , 117, 157 and 160; distribution and share of foreign capital from S. Bitar, 'Efectos de las Areas de Propiedad Social y Mixta en la industria chilena' [Effects of the Areas of Social Property and Mixed Property on Chilean Industry], *Trimestre económico* [Economic Quarterly], 163 (1974), 250, 259 (Mexico City).

Table I.F. *Distribution of Value Added in the Manufacturing Industry*

	Salaries [a]	*Wages*	*Social security payments*	*Total payments to labour*	*Payments to other factors of production* [b]
1950-54	12.6	32.4	3.0	48.0	52.0
1960	11.3	23.1	7.8	42.2	57.8
1961	11.3	23.0	8.0	42.3	57.7
1962	10.9	21.2	7.1	39.2	60.8
1963	11.0	20.5	6.7	38.2	61.8
1964	10.7	19.3	6.6	36.3	63.7
1965	11.3	19.5	7.6	38.4	61.6
1966	12.0	19.7	8.3	40.0	60.6
1967	12.0	19.9	7.8	39.7	60.3
1968	11.0	18.5	7.0	36.5	63.5
1969	34.2		...	...	...

[a] Includes payments to executives and directors.
[b] Includes rents, interests, earnings and income of self-employed workers. The income of self-employed workers has decreased in importance.

Source: CESO, *Chile hoy*, Table 10, 52. Data from CORFO, *Contabilidad nacional 1940-68* [National Accounts 1940-68] (Santiago de Chile); and ODEPLAN, *Distribución y cuentas de producción, 1960-68* [Distribution and Production, 1960-68], Vol. IV (Santiago de Chile); ODEPLAN, *Antecedentes sobre el desarrollo . . .*, 186.

Table I.G. *Structure of the Importation of Goods (percentage)*

	1965	*1966*	*1967*	*1968*	*1969*	*1970*
Food	23	21	22	19	18	17
Other consumer goods	7	7	7	9	9	10
Petroleum	3	4	4	3	4	3
Other raw materials and unfinished products	41	40	37	35	43	41
Capital goods	26	29	30	34	26	29

Source: World Bank, *Special Report on the Chilean Economic Outlook* (Washington, D.C., October 1974), Vol. III, Table 32.

Table II.A. *Number of Companies in the Industrial APSM*

	December 1970		*December 1972*		*Planned*	
	A	B	C	A	B	C
20 Food products	19		49	41		57
21 Beverages	1		3	4		4
22 Tobacco	0		0	1		1
23 Textiles	0		18	17		18
24 Clothing and footwear	1		3	8		8
25 Wood	4		13	11		13
26 Furniture (except metal)	0		4	4		4
27 Paper and cellulose	3		3	5		6
28 Printing	1		1	4		1
29 Leather	0		0	0		0
30 Rubber	0		2	1		2
31 Chemical industries	4		14	17		20
32 Petroleum and coal derivates	1		1	2		1
33 Nonmetal mineral products	1		17	11		18
34 Basic metal industries	1		13	12		16
35 Metal products	2		22	21		22
36 Nonelectrical machinery	3		7	7		7
37 Electrical machinery	1		23	12		25
38 Transport equipment	3		9	12		12
39 Others	0		0	0		
Total	45	43	202	190	173	235

Source: A: A. Bardón, 'Control directo del estado en la industria manufactura' [Direct State Control in the Manufacturing Industry], in *Comentarios sobre la situación económica 1*[er] *semestre de 1972* [Statement on the Economic Situation, 1st Quarter of 1972] (Santiago de Chile, Universidad de Chile, Facultad de Ciencias Económicas [University of Chile, Faculty of Economic Studies], (1972), 155-171. Included in the planned ASPM are companies under state control in 1970, those that had come under state control by May 1970, and those included in the group of the so-called '90 companies' still in private hands. Four companies in the large copper mining sector (copper smelting) that had originally been included were left out. A coal mining company remains under 32 and another is duplicated under 31.

B: S. Bitar, 'Efectos de las Areas . . .'. The planned APSM includes companies under state control in 1970, those that had come under state control by December 1972, and those included in the group of the so-called '90 companies' still in private hands. It excludes an undefined number of companies under state control, which are regarded as less important, and the large copper mining companies.

C: Instituto de Economía y Planificación [Institute of Economics and Planning], *La economía chilena en 1972* [The Chilean Economy in 1972] (Santiago de Chile, 1973). The planned APSM includes all companies under state control by December 1972 and those which had officially been designated to come under state control but which were still in private hands. The large copper mining sector is excluded.

Table II.B. *Production (or Sales) of the APSM in the Manufacturing Industry (percentage)*

	December 1970			*Planned*			
	A	B	C	A	B	C	D
20 Food products			13.8			30.4	29.3
21 Beverages	12.5	10.9	1.5	35.2	34.9	33.6	27.4
22 Tobacco			0.0			100.0	91.3
23 Textiles			0.0			38.5	48.8
	0.4	0.0		29.5	28.3		
24 Footwear and clothing			0.0			18.3	16.6
25 Wood and cork			5.3			18.5	5.8
	2.2	4.0		16.1	18.6		
26 Furniture (nonmetal)			0.0			18.7	2.0
27 Paper and cellulose			10.7			85.0	80.6
	8.2	6.2		77.2	46.7		
28 Printing			2.3			14.3	3.0
29 Leather			...			8.0	...
30 Rubber			...			75.3	67.0
31 Chemicals	25.0	39.3	12.3	48.1	73.9	49.0	34.9
32 Petroleum and coal derivates			80.9			96.5	100.0
33 Nonmetallic mineral products	2.3	0.3	0.3	72.0	68.8	68.8	76.3
34 Basic metal industries	27.8	26.7	26.7	49.5	83.9	83.9	60.3
35 Metal products			1.9			33.0	15.9
36 Electrical machinery	10.6	11.9	14.4			44.8	11.4
				64.0	58.6		
37 Nonelectrical machinery			0.4			46.5	58.4
38 Transport equipment			21.2			97.2	3.9
39 Others	0.0	10.9	10.9	0.0	10.9	10.9	...
Total	12.6	11.8	11.8	43.5	43.9	43.9	31.7

Source: A: A. Bardón, 'Control directo del estado . . .'. Calculated on the basis of sales of companies with more than five workers according to the 1967 manufacturing census, projected to 1970; in several cases these are estimates. Companies in the large copper-mining sector are excluded.

B: Weighted average for production in each sector according to the 1967 manufacturing census, based on the data from S. Bitar and A. Mackenna, *Panorama económico* [Economic Panorama], 278 (June/July 1974) (Santiago de Chile).

C: Bitar and Mackenna, *Panorama económico*...'. Calculated on the basis of production of companies with more than five workers using data from the 1967 manufacturing census. Companies in the large copper-mining sector are excluded. In Bitar's 'Efectos de las Areas . . . ' the figures are not broken down by branches. A previous publication by Bitar in *Panorama económico* gives the same table with a total similar to the study in *Trimestre económico* [Economic Quarterly]. The former is the one that has been used here.

D: Instituto de Economía y Planificación [Institute of Economics and Planning]. Calculated on the basis of estimates by ODEPLAN for total industrial production in 1972 (including units with less than five workers) at 1971 prices.

Table II.C. *Role of the Industrial APSM in Total Employment in Industry (percentage)*

	December 1970 A	*Projected* A	B
In all industries	6.5	22.2	23.6
In industries with less than 5 workers per establishment	9.5	33.0	–

Source: A: S. Bitar, 'Efectos de las Areas . . .'.
B: Instituto de Economía y Planificación, *La economía chilena* . . . .

Table II.D. *Foreign Share in the Capital of Industrial Limited Companies*

	1969	*After establishment of projected APSM*
20 Food products	9.0	5.2
21 Beverages	24.6	23.1
22 Tobacco	58.6	40.0
23 Textiles	9.9	5.4
24 Footwear and clothing	18.7	9.3
25 Wood and cork	6.7	2.2
26 Furniture (nonmetal)	16.4	8.1
27 Paper and cellulose	15.2	9.5
28 Printing and publishing	2.2	2.1
29 Leather	2.0	1.4
30 Rubber	45.1	25.0
31 Chemical industries	38.3	22.8
32 Petroleum and coal derivates	0.6	3.6
33 Nonmetalic minerals	24.7	18.1
34 Basic metals	13.6	6.0
35 Metal products	18.4	18.8
36 Nonelectrical machinery	14.7	8.7
37 Electrical machinery	59.9	16.2
38 Transport equipment	43.8	10.6
39 Others	18.9	21.0
Total (weighted average)	20.3	11.0

Source: S. Bitar, 'La presencia de la empresa extranjera en la industria chilena' [The Presence of Foreign Enterprise in the Chilean Economy], *Desarrollo económico* [Economic Development], 50 (1972) (Buenos Aires).

Table III.A. *Number of Industrial Companies Affected by Expropriations, Requisitions and Management Take-Overs by the Government* [a]

		Total	*APSM according to 'list of 90'*	*Companies retained, not included in 'the list of 90'*	*Companies returned*
Expropriations and requisitions	1970	1	1	–	–
Total	1971	137	49	66	22
Expropriations and requisitions	1971	33	17	15	1
Government take-over of management	1971	104	32	51	21
Total	1972	102	40	41	21
Expropriations and requisitions	1972	50	25	24	1
Government take-over of management	1972	52	15	17	20
Companies brought into the APSM by decisions taken after 'the list of 90' project			+67	−67	
Total up to December	1972	240	157	40	43

[a] Expropriations and requisitions were carried out using the legal instruments of the Ministry of Economics. Government take-overs of management were done through the Ministry of Labour.

Source: Instituto de Economía y Planificación, *La economía chilena* . . . , 96, 97, 98 and 135.

Table III.B. *Progress in the Formation of the Industrial APSM (number of companies, percentage of sales and of planned size)*

	June 1972 A				*December 1972* B			
	Companies		*Sales*		*Companies*		*Sales*	
	No.	*% of plan*	*% of sector*	*% of plan*	*No.*	*% of plan*	*% of sector*	*% of plan*
20 Food products	31	76			49	86	17.3	59
21 Beverages	2	50	18.8	53	3	75	26.0	95
22 Tobacco	0	0			0	0	0.0	0
23 Textiles	17	100			18	100	48.8	100
24 Footwear and clothing	1	12	22.9	78	3	38	1.3	8
25 Wood and cork	11	100			13	100	4.8	83
			16.1	100				
26 Furniture (non-metal)	4	100			4	100	2.0	100
27 Paper and cellulose	3	60			3	50	2.1	3
			34.4	45				
28 Printing	4	100			1	100	3.0	100
29 Leather	–	–			–	–	–	–

	June 1972 A				*December 1972* B			
	Companies		*Sales*		*Companies*		*Sales*	
	No.	*% of plan*	*% of sector*	*% of plan*	*No.*	*% of plan*	*% of sector*	*% of plan*
30 Rubber	1	100			2	100	67.0	100
31 Chemical industries	10	59	37.7	78	14	70	19.4	56
32 Petroleum and coal derivates	1	50			1	100	100.0	100
33 Nonmetal mineral products	6	55	39.3	55	17	94	63.6	83
34 Basic metals	9	75	41.5	84	13	81	52.5	87
35 Metal products	15	71			22	100	15.9	100
36 Nonelectrical machinery	7	100	51.8	81	7	100	11.4	100
37 Electrical machinery	6	50			23	48	45.2	77
38 Transport equipment	12	100			9	75	3.9	100
39 Others	–	–	–	–	–	–	–	–
Total	140	74	29.7	68	202	86	21.9	69

(In June 1972, the sales figures 37.7 and 78 are bracketed for items 30–32, and 51.8 and 81 for items 35–38.)

Source: A: According to Bardón, 'Control directo del estado . . .'.
B: According to Instituto de Economía y Planificación, *La economía chilena* . . . .

Table III.C. *Importance of Six Large Industrial Companies Not Brought into the APSM*

	% of total production of the sector	*% of projected APSM shares for the sector*
20 Chiprodal (dairy products)	5.4	18.4
20 CRAV (sugar)	2.8	9.5
22 Compañía Chilena de Tobacos (tobacco)	91.3	100.0
24 CATECU (footwear)	10.0	60.0
27 Compañía Manufacturera de Papeles y Cartones (paper)	64.0	92.0
31 Indus Lever (chemical products)	11.0	28.0
Total industry	6.6	21.0

Source: Instituto de Economía y Planificación, *La economía chilena* . . . , 155.

Table IV.A. *Indices of Prices, Wages and Salaries, Money and Exchange Rates*

		Exchange rate [a]	*Consumer prices* [b]	*Wholesale prices* [b]	*Wages and salaries* [b,c]	*Money in the private sector*
1970	September	100	100.0	100.0	100.0	100.0
	December	100	101.5	101.0	112.1	114.0
1971	March	100	104.9	105.9	132.7	150.5
	June	100	112.7	110.8	144.0	172.9
	September	100	115.5	113.9	151.8	202.5
	December	129.4	123.9	122.7	169.1	243.7
1972	March	129.4	140.6	140.6	186.2	283.2
	June	129.4	158.2	156.9	208.7	319.9
	September	204.7	247.8	230.6	336.0	367.0
	December	204.7	326.6	298.3	461.6	614.4
1973	March	204.7	398.4	371.5	514.2	830.5
	June	409.0	606.2	493.4	740.6	1,179.5
	September		956.4	716.8	905.4	1,844.1
	December	2,811.0	1,985.4 [d]	3,723.8	2,515.8	3,183.7

[a] From December 1971 onwards this is an average for several areas.
[b] These figures are from official indices of the Instituto Nacional de Estadísticas [National Institute of Statistics] (Santiago de Chile).
[c] These figures refer to the month immediately after the one indicated.
[d] After the *coup d'état* in September 1973, the basis and methodology for the calculations were changed. All the sources estimate its true value to be around 3,200, which is more in keeping with the wholesale price index and the money supply.

Table IV.B. *Financial Balances of the APSM Companies* [a] *(percentage of expenditure of the GDP)*

	1971		*1972*		*1973*	
	Total APSM	A	*Total APSM*	A	*Total APSM*	A
Current income	...	(4.5)	21.3	(3.9)	19.2	(5.9)
Current expenditure	...	(6.3)	22.8	(6.1)	22.0	(12.4)[b]
Savings on current account	...	(–1.8)	–1.5	(–2.2)	–2.8	(–6.5)[b]
Capital expenditure	...	(2.5)	3.9	(3.2)	3.7	(1.9)
Capital income	...	–	0.7	(–)	0.3	(–)
Deficit	...	(4.3)	4.7	(5.4)	6.2	(8.4)

A: Companies which were owned by the state previous to 1970.

[a] Excludes large copper mines, which in 1972 and 1973 only covered their current expenditure.
[b] There appears to be an error in the data referring to purchases of goods and services.

Source: World Bank, *Special Report* . . . , Vol. III, table 5.3 and the Central Bank, *Boletín mensual* [Monthly Bulletin] (Santiago de Chile, December 1975), 1447.

Table V.A. *Sectoral Grouping of APSM Committees and their Enterprises as of September 1973* [a]

	Number of companies
Agro-industrial products	50
Textiles and clothing	41
Fishing	22
Natural fibres	3
Leather and footwear	3
Pharmaceuticals	6
Forestry	25
Construction materials	21
Mining industry	6
Light chemicals	18
Copper products	3
Light engineering	19
Agricultural mechanization	9
Electrical and electronics	20
Automobiles	19
Heavy chemicals	5
Steel and other metal-working	46
Energy and fuels [b]	22
Total	335

[a] The heading 'other industries' is not included here. Generally it did not include industrial activities.
[b] This includes only three enterprises from the industrial sector: one oil refinery and two gas companies.

Source: República de Chile, *Un año de reconstrucción* [A Year of Reconstruction] (Santiago de Chile, September 1974).

Table VI.A. *Production Indices for the Manufacturing Industry (1968 = 100)*

	1970	*1971*	*1972*	*1973*
Food products	99.6	107.7	105.9	102.0
Beverages	91.1	114.9	123.3	134.3
Tobacco	97.7	123.1	126.3	131.3
Textiles	96.0	110.1	113.1	101.5
Footwear and clothing	104.8	118.9	123.5	117.1
Wood, except furniture	108.1	131.7	146.7	93.1
Furniture	113.4	109.1	155.6	120.8
Cellulose and paper	88.3	91.8	90.1	104.5
Printing and publishing	109.5	173.8	126.4	96.0
Leather products, except footwear	103.9	119.7	90.0	85.8
Rubber products	111.0	135.5	138.8	127.5
Chemical products	120.9	144.0	150.4	147.6
Petroleum and coal derivates	105.4	128.6	138.5	129.9

Table VI.A (continued)

	1970	*1971*	*1972*	*1973*
Nonmetallic minerals	102.9	120.9	123.2	126.5
Basic metal industries	108.0	116.7	124.2	119.7
Metal products, except machinery	98.6	109.1	117.8	121.4
Nonelectrical machinery	94.2	126.3	151.5	189.3
Electrical appliances	99.5	113.3	104.2	89.1
Transport equipment	127.0	111.9	120.3	140.8
Various	81.0	108.0	123.1	119.0
Total	104.0	119.3	122.6	117.3

Source: Instituto Nacional de Estadísticas, *Indice de producción industrial* [Industrial Production Index] (Santiago de Chile, 1974).

Table VI.B. *Physical Production and the APSM Share by Sector (end of 1972)*

	Unit	*1970*	*1971*	*1972*	*1973*	*% in APSM*
A: Steel ingots	1000 T	547	610	581	508	100
Cement	1000 T	1349	1370	1408	1372	100
Flat glass	1000 m^2	2559	2667	2355	3426	100
Copper wire	Ton	15170	15940	21948	22336	100
Petroleum derivates	1000 m^3	3215	3944	4290	3964	100
Tyres	1000 s	676	791	805	766	100
Paper	1000 T	224	222	223	227	2.1 (Paper and Cellulose)
Cellulose	1000 T	210	210	172	154	
Refined sugar	1000 T	282	316	325	285	55
Electrical energy for industry	1000 KWH	845	928	992	948	100
B: Beer	1000 L	...	219	229	206	100
Cigarettes	1,000,000	...	8312	8515	8368	0
Rayon thread	Ton	...	1551	1974	1695	100
Detergents	Ton	...	46225	43306	45999	0
C: Textiles	1000 T	...	103	106	...	48
Refrigerators	1000 s	...	69	71	...	94
Cookers	1000 s	...	210	245	...	80
Heaters	1000 s	...	255	263	...	80

Sources: A: Central Bank, *Boletín mensual* (September 1975).
B: Instituto Nacional de Estadísticas, *Indice de producción* . . . .
C: Instituto de Economía y Planificación, *La economía chilena* . . . .

Table VI.C. *Estimate of the Industrial Growth Potential for 1972 (index of production)*

	Annual average		*% variation*
	Actual 1971	*Potential 1972*	
Personal consumption industries	116.4	132.3	+13.6
20 Food products	107.7	113.6	+ 5.5
21 Beverages	114.9	132.2	+15.1
22 Tobacco	123.1	140.3	+14.0
23 Textiles	110.1	125.9	+14.4
24 Footwear	118.9	133.9	+12.6
26 Furniture	109.1	157.9	+44.7
28 Printing	173.8	196.1	+12.8
29 Leather	119.7	186.8	+56.1
39 Others	108.6	126.7	+16.7
Light engineering industries	113.2	147.8	+30.5
35 Metal products	109.1	128.3	+17.6
36 Nonelectrical machinery	126.3	216.3	+71.3
37 Electrical machinery	113.3	142.0	+25.3
38 Transport material	111.9	143.7	+28.4
Basic primary industries	121.3	152.0	+25.3
25 Wood	131.7	151.7	+15.2
33 Nonmetallic minerals	120.9	136.6	+13.0
34 Basic metals	116.7	158.4	+35.7
Various intermediate industries	133.2	150.3	+12.8
27 Paper and cellulose	91.8	109.7	+19.5
30 Rubber	135.5	177.3	+30.8
31 Chemicals	144.0	154.8	+ 7.5
32 Petroleum and coal derivates	128.6	143.0	+11.2
Total	119.3	141.5	+18.6

Source: Ardras Uthoff in *Comentarios sobre la situación económica, 1er semestre de 1972* [Statement on the Economic Situation, 1st Quarter of 1972] (Santiago de Chile, Universidad de Chile, Facultad de Ciencias Económicas [University of Chile, Faculty of Economic Studies], 1972), 15-38. The data is from the Instituto Nacional de Estadísticas.

Table VI.D. *Estimate of Imports and Requirements for Intermediate Goods for the Non-food Industries*

	1969	*1970*	*1971*	*1972*	*1973* [a]
Total imports of goods ($m)	927	956	1015	1103	1608 [a]
Nonfood intermediate goods [b] ($m)	...	445	485	460	664
Nonfood industrial production [c]	100	100	116	120	114
Physical import requirements [c]	...	100	121	130	148
External price [c]	...	100	104	108	130
Requirements for imported products ($m)		445	538	579	659
Deficit (–) ($m)		–	–53	–119	+5

[a] The figure for imports estimated by the Central Bank is $510 million higher than the figure given by the *Superintendencia de Aduanas* [Superintendence of Customs]. A similar overestimation had already been made in previous publications for 1971 and 1972.

[b] See the Statistical Appendix at the end of Chapter 2, Table XIV.

[c] Index of the unit value of imports. See the Statistical Appendix at the end of Chapter 2, Table XV.

Source: Central Bank, *Boletín mensual* (September 1975) and Instituto Nacional de Estadísticas, *Indice de producción . . . .*

Table VI.E. *Industrial Exports (in millions of dollars)*

	1969	*1970*	*1971*	*1972*	*1973*
Semi-processed copper	8	15	16	20	28
Paper and cellulose	28	32	32	24	30
Chemical products	8	11	12	8	7
Canned fish and seafood [a]	24	24	39	19	19
Total	104	129	143	105	111

[a] Including fishmeal.

Source: World Bank, *Special Report . . . .* , Vol. III, table 3.3.

Table VI.F. *Index of Exchange Rates for Industrial Goods and Wholesale Prices*

	Exchange rates for industrial exports	*Exchange rates for imported raw materials*	*Wholesale prices*
September 1970	100.0	100.0	100.0
September 1971	100.0	100.0	115.5
December 1971	129.4	129.4	122.7
June 1972	129.4	129.4	156.4
September 1972	245.7	204.7	230.6
March 1973	245.7	204.7	371.5
June 1973	819.0	204.7	493.4

Source: See the Statistical Appendix at the end of Chapter 2, Table VIII.

8

ALFONSO INOSTROZA

NATIONALIZATION OF THE BANKING SYSTEM IN CHILE

In a broadcast to the nation on 30 December 1970, the President of the Republic of Chile, Dr. Salvador Allende, announced the decision to nationalize the Chilean banking system. This decision, an important aspect of the UP Government's policy, in fact constituted one of the basic elements in the strategy of the left-wing Government, along with the nationalization of copper mining, the creation of an *Area de Propiedad Social* (APS) [Area of Social Property], the acceleration of agrarian reform and the nationalization of foreign trade.

While the bill which was to set the nationalization procedure into motion was being prepared and sent to the National Congress, it was decided that the *Corporación de Fomento de la Producción* (CORFO) [Corporation for Production Development][1] should be authorized to buy bank shares from small shareholders so as to create an option which would be favourable to them.

It was in this form that a direct attack was launched against a powerful and vital enclave which was controlled by pressure groups connected with Chile's traditional ruling classes: the landowners and the leaders of monopoly industry. For nearly three years the UP Government sustained a dramatic struggle to gain control of this decisive means of power – the management of currency and credit; its struggle was similar to that undertaken in order to nationalize copper.

1. CHARACTERISTICS OF THE BANKING AND FINANCIAL SYSTEM IN 1970

1.1. *The System's Institutions*

When the UP Government assumed power on 4 November 1970, the Chilean banking system was organized along the lines of the model typical which is of

Footnotes to this chapter may be found on pp. 311-312.

Western countries. It consisted of a widespread network of national and foreign banks with branches and agencies throughout the length and breadth of the country, operating services in apparent and relative competition with a total labour force of about 22,000 employees. At various times previous to 1970 it had been realized that banking in general had become overgrown, given the state the country and its economic structure was in. On the basis of such views, which were widespread, the most recent reform of the legal code for banking in 1960 had set severe limitations on creating and establishing new banking organizations, whether they were national or foreign.

The institutions which made up the banking system were: (1) the Central Bank [Banco Central]; (2) the State Bank [Banco de Estado], the capital of which was entirely state property; (3) twenty-one private commercial banks, of which eleven were of a regional nature; and (4) five foreign banks. All of these organizations were subject to the supervision of the *Superintendencia de Bancos* (SB) [Bank Superintendence].

The nonbanking finance sector was composed of (1) *Corporación Vivienda* (CORVI) [the Housing Corporation],[2] a state organization; (2) savings and credit associations led by the *Caja Central de Ahorros y Prestamos* [Central Fund of Savings and Credit]; (3) two mortgage banks; (4) some mutual funds; (5) the insurance companies.

In the nonbanking finance sector, besides the specific tasks for which it existed, deposits of public funds were often made; this created close links between the various parts of the financial system. The savings and credit associations, which were private organizations created in 1960 to acquire private savings and channel them into housing construction, had acquired considerable importance because of the amount of resources they mobilized; they became very influential owing to their close connection with entrepreneurial groups in the construction sector and with certain private banks, so that within a short time an important economic pressure group had been organized. These associations were not nationalized.

Investment and mutual funds, which did not achieve any significant expansion during their short existence, declined after 1970 – ostensibly as a result of the slump in the Stock Exchange and the financial speculation activities during the period of UP Government.

The insurance companies, which were long established in Chile and highly developed, maintained their normal activities after the Government made public its decision not to include them in its initial nationalization programme. These companies also belonged to the private sector and maintained close links with the commercial banks; their interests were closely bound together through cross participation in their equity capital.

1.2. *Principal Characteristics of the Banking System*

The Chilean banking system has a long tradition dating back to the previous century. The first banking institutions were established between 1830 and 1840. With the country's vigorous economic and political growth from the middle of the nineteenth century onwards, the banks were strengthened not only commercially but also through their relationship with the agricultural, mining and infant industrial sectors. The right to issue banknotes gave private banking institutions special power and influence over the country's economic resourses. A powerful and influencial socioeconomic sector began to emerge; it was structured around the banking business and had direct connections in the governing political parties (principally conservative and liberal) at the leadership level. During this century the banks grew even more, especially after World War II. The financial sector underwent a marked expansion, which was reflected in the number of new banking institutions created, in the extent of credit operations, and in the growing links with industrial enterprise and insurance, transport and distribution organizations through the banks' participation in the capital of these enterprises. The financial system's economic and political leanings thus acquired considerable impact and began to constitute a power block of the national bourgeoisie. The creation of the Central Bank and of the SB in 1925 arose out of the state's decision to regulate and control the activities of the banks in accordance with commonly accepted principles in Western countries. However, the structure and powers transferred to the monetary authorities did not prevent the influence of the private banks in Chile's economic progress from continuing and increasing.

1.2.1. *Ownership of Capital*

The structure of banking capital varied according to the type of institutions included in the system. The shares of the Central Bank (whose capital is composed in a way which is curious and unique for this type of institution) were (1) those that belong to the state (a minority proportion), which entitle the holders to appoint four directors or members (of a total of eleven members) of the Directorate or the Administrative Council; (2) shares subscribed for by national and foreign banks, which make up the major part of the Bank's capital and give holders the right to nominate only three directors; (3) shares subscribed for by the public, which form a relatively small percentage of the capital and empower nomination of only one director. The remaining three directors are nominated by nonbanking institutions which do not participate in the equity capital. Their representation is as follows: (1) a director representing workers and employees, elected by union throughout the country; (2) a director appointed by the Chamber of Commerce; and (3) a director representing the *Sociedad de Fomento Fabril* (SOFOFA) [Industrial Development Society] and the *Sociedad Nacional de Agricultura* [National Agricultural Society].

This structure corresponds to a formula originally proposed by the Kemmerer Commission, which was in charge of the studies which led to the creation of the Central Bank. The purpose of the formula was to preserve a relative balance between the different strengths and leanings of interests represented in the Directorate, and thereby to guarantee that the country's monetary policy would be relatively independently managed. An attempt was made to avoid a polarization of forces and an overly strong influence on decision-making either by the state on the one hand, or by private interests on the other. This is not the place to analyze in depth the aims which the Kemmerer Commission has pursued since 1925, but it is worth noting that at the time the UP Government came to power, the financial bourgeoisie's growing influence in all fields of the state apparatus had clearly shifted the balance of forces within the Directorate of the Central Bank in favour of the private sector or entrepreneurial class.

1.2.2. *The State Bank*

The State Bank was created in 1953. Its capital was entirely state owned and arose from a merger of the National Savings Bank, the Agricultural Bank, the Industrial Bank and the Mortgage Credit Bank. It was a commercial bank which carried out transactions in national and foreign currency (as any private bank does) and at the same time promoted and developed various economic sectors. Its Directorate included representatives of associations or groups of entrepreneurs working in the country's principal economic activities.

1.2.3. *National, Private and Commercial Banks*

These (twenty-one of them) and the mortgage banks were established as limited companies. Their capital was subscribed for by private investors – either individuals or legal entities – for the most part resident in the country; however, in certain cases a percentage of shares was in fact held by non-residents. While a basic feature of this type of institution was that large numbers of shares were distributed among numerous investors, significant holdings of shares were subscribed for by individuals, associations or investment groups in order to ensure control of the company's policy and decisions taken within the Directorate or Administrative Council. The Bank of Chile, the principal bank in the country, perhaps presented a special case in this respect: ownership of its shares was widely spread in the population but a feeling of class interest nevertheless united many of the shareholders – as will be explained later.

1.2.4. *Foreign Banks*

The First National City Bank, the Bank of America, the Bank of London and South America, the French and Italian Bank (Sudameris) and the Bank of Brazil were established in accordance with Chilean banking law as branch offices or agencies of their main banking houses; their capital therefore entered the country in the form of foreign inflow. The Bank of Brazil is a special case, as it was a branch of an official bank established in the country to promote trade between Chile and Brazil, but at the same time it carried out all the transactions of a banking institution.

The system of subscribing for shares described above, and particularly the form in which specific pressure groups acted in order to preserve their control of decisions, constituted a complicated mechanism which through the years brought about the intermingling and linking of different power groups to the extent that they came to constitute a real elite.[3] This elite, sustained by the power generated through the control of money and credit, gradually extended its influence not just to the major companies and monopolies of the industrial, commercial, retailing, insurance and services sectors but also, and markedly, to the political arena. It was active in the National Congress and also in the state structure through the nomination of representatives to the boards of directors of numerous organizations which formulated and implemented policies, as for instance in the Central Bank and State Bank. Moreover, these interest groups were linked with foreign capital, especially from the end of World War II onwards; this link was clearly defined in the field of banking.

Existing legal arrangements allowed the banks to invest in the capital of commercial and industrial limited companies; this made it possible for banking representatives to serve on the boards of directors of many different companies. There was, in turn, nothing to prevent leading personalities of the centre and the right from similarly taking on such positions as directors of companies and banks, thus completing the cycle of mutual reinforcement and consolidation of power.

The economic concentration resulting from this situation was one of the most notable features in the Chilean economy's structure, and one of the aspects most denounced by the left-wing parties; the result was that the UP Government's programme contained long-debated policies and immediate measures to attach the bases of this monopolistic concentration.

Socioeconomic studies and research carried out in the 1960s in various Chilean universities had described these relationships and had established that no fewer than ten economic and financial power clans, which were structured around the banking institutions and were the cores of their operation, were controlling the vital centres of Chilean economic life by means of monopolistic management of the volume of industrial production and foreign trade, running distributive companies and the mass communications media and the press – not to mention their close association with the large landlords.

In this way, the commercial banks served as an essential instrument in constructing this enormous monopolistic system and supplied the necessary resources for its expansion and consolidation. In addition, the private banks acted as an excellent means of forming relations with international banks, notably those of the United States, and obtaining financial resources destined for the principal Chilean companies. Control and supervision by the monetary authorities did not prevent these exchanges of favours and illicit financial operations.

The U.S. banks dominated the supply of resources for financing foreign trade operations. This took place through the extension of credit lines, the opening of new credit sources and many other financial transactions. These U.S. financing flows were channeled through the Chilean commercial banks as well as through branches of the First National City Bank and the Bank of America in Chile. The amount of financing which originated from European banks was always relatively small in comparison and was basically restricted to a few British, French, West German, and to a lesser extent Italian and Dutch, institutions.

The U.S. banks' influence went beyond the bounds of private banking as such. The recurrent deficits in Chile's balance of payments had forced many previous Governments – in particular those of Ibañez (1952-58), Alessandri (1958-64) and Frei (1964-70) – to seek short-term credit from the New York currency market. Previous understandings and the signing of stand-by agreements with the International Monetary Fund (IMF) established a 'pool' of private U.S. banks which supplied the loans needed in combination with funds from the U.S. Treasury and the IMF itself.

Therefore, the role played by the U.S. banks in Chile should be understood as it related to the moment at which the UP Government initiated its reform programme and began to sever the bonds which tied the country to the multinational companies and to the huge U.S. financial consortia.

1.3. *Origins of the Banking System's Resources and Operations*

There were numerous sources of finance which the banking institutions had at their disposal for developing their lines of credit. The economic policies applied over the years, and the various alternatives that the Chilean economy had experimented with, determined in each case the extent to which such sources were used. These sources can be summarized as follows:

(1) Acquisition of deposits: this was traditionally the most important method employed by the private banks.

(2) Re-discounts and special credits from the Central Bank: these instruments of monetary policy were in widespread use until 1967, at which time their use decreased appreciably, owing to the Frei Government's monetary policy, until 1970. The latter Government preferred the use of other elements related to the management of international monetary reserves,[4] the movement of private foreign capital and short-term indebtedness through the banking system.

(3) Financial operations with international private banks: a special characteristic of Chile's monetary market had been the intense demand from the private sector for banking credit in order to finance industrial production, foreign trade and speculation in goods and real estate and in private consumption. Determining the interest rate was not an element that was capable of containing and directing this demand, and for this reason the policy of the Government and the Central Bank was permanently oriented towards restricting credit by a wide range of measures.

The recurrent deficit of the fiscal budget, which was financed by the issue of bonds, was another factor which caused the Central Bank to maintain permanent limitations on the overall expansion of credit.

These were the aspects underlying the emphasis placed by the Frei Government on the policy of controlling credit in the private sector, so as to allow for an improvement in the foreign sector and an increase of international reserves. The private's sector need for finance in Chilean currency could therefore not be met through the usual channels and other sources had to be sought, using the means provided for in Decree 1272 of Article 14, which establishes how foreign capital in foreign currency is to be acquired. All the companies began to use this means: a considerable amount of foreign currency entered the country through Article 14 and was converted into Chilean currency. The credit control arrangements were thereby avoided and the Central Bank's international monetary reserves were swollen with this foreign currency. The critical moment occurred when, as a result of the change of government, the administration of these capital flows changed and the Allende Government's finance authorities demonstrated that these flows were nothing more than credit operations, negotiated mainly with U.S. banks (a very low percentage was with Western European banks) under the guarantees made by the Chilean commercial banks.[5]

A volume of about $400 million represented the agreed amount that could be obtained on a short-term basis by the Central Bank from the international banking system until November 1970, entered not as liabilities but simply as nominal responsibility in the operation account of the Central Bank's general balance sheet. At this date the Central Bank's international credits amounted to some $450 million.[6] The repercussions of this particular aspect of monetary policy on the Central Bank's management, particularly on financing, were incalculably great and the damage incurred will be examined in section 2 of this chapter.

Besides all of the foregoing, the monetary and credit policies followed up to 1970 suffered from other defects, shortcomings and limitations. Credit directed through private banks, even if it was limited by the regulations laid down by the Central Bank, was controlled only in quantitative terms, and not qualitative terms. Ceilings were imposed generally and from bank to bank by the Central Bank, but they involved minimal controls aimed at keeping these banks within the basic objectives of a policy of credit restrictions. The series of regulations were designed to attract credit for specific priorities but they did not have any significant effect. Nor did selectivity prevent the concentration of credit among a limited number or debtors, and the many internal memoranda of the Central Bank and the SB did not prevent the geographical concentration of credit resources. It is worth noting that the provinces of Santiago and Valparaiso together cornered about 80% of all credit.

The State Bank, which on many occasions was used by the monetary authorities to improve the distribution of credit resources, was unable to significantly prevent the effects of this phenomenon because, to a large extent, of the obvious interference of private interests in its Directorate. In December 1970, 45.6% of credit was concentrated in the hands of 1.3% of the banking system's debtors.[7]

Another factor which is indicative of the concentration in banking is the excessively large share of certain banks in banking activities as a whole. Thus, for example, the Bank of Chile constituted the most important single institution amongst the private banks: it had 27.6% of the system's deposits at its disposal, controlled 28.6% of allocations and obtained 30% of the banking system's profits.[8]

From this description it can be deduced that the private banks constituted an essential instrument in establishing and strengthening a capitalist system which was characterized by a high degree of monopolistic concentration. The private banks acted as a strong binding force for the entrepreneurial class and various power groups were formed around the different banking institutions: in these groups family, social and economic interests were fused and were oriented towards the control of strategic sectors of domestic production, foreign trade, financial services, the national radio and the press. Such power groups exercised considerable influence over the state apparatus and in certain governments had succeeded in controlling key institutions in the public sector by nominating their own representatives to manage them.

It was in reaction to this state of affairs, and with the aim of curtailing the harmful influence of such monopolistic groups and of such socioeconomic development in Chile, that a thorough reform of the banking system was initiated as soon as President Salvador Allende took power.

2. THE UP GOVERNMENT'S POLICY OF NATIONALIZING BANKS

In this chapter the concept of nationalization refers to two aspects of one process: (1) the Government policy of transferring *private* domestic equity capital of commercial banks to the state or to the *Area de Propiedad Social* (APS) [Area of Social Property]; (2) the earmarking of private *foreign* equity interests for incorporation in state ownership.

The Government policy for banking reform was to be executed in various stages, each of which was to take place in accordance with each new situation which arose in the course of replanning the economy, so that it would be appropriate to the new conditions created by implementing other proposed reforms in the Government's economic, political and social programme.

These different stages are listed below; the order in which they are given does not necessarily imply that they became effective in that chronological order.

(1) Nationalization of Chilean commercial banks.
(2) Nationalization of foreign banks operating in Chile.
(3) Reform of the general banking law, including the law on the SB's authority and functions, to adapt it to the new concepts and relationships of the social transformation.
(4) Reform of the Central Bank's legal charter to replace the Directorate with a Monetary Group which was designated by the Government; this was done to broaden the Central Bank's scope with respect to formulating and executing of monetary policy, principally as regards financing the APS and foreign financing, and to endow the bank with special powers for planning, controlling, conducting and renegotiating Chile's external debt.
(5) Reform of the State Bank's legal charter regarding (i) the composition of its directorate; (ii) specific authorization to design and apply a new credit policy for the reformed sector of agriculture; (iii) the reorganization of development activities; (iv) a definitive statute for the nationalized banks.

The interruption of this process of democratic transformation of Chilean society by the military *coup d'état* in September 1973 left unfinished the tasks outlined by the banking reform; only stages (1) and (2) had been implemented.

2.1. *Purposes of the Banking Reform*

As has already been indicated, one of the main aims was to eliminate economic concentration by divesting the controlling group of their mainstay, control of the banks. Studies carried out by UP experts had concluded that the concentration of economic power in the hands of a few oligarchic groups, and the problem of external dependency, were different aspects of the same basic issue: the effect exercised by the few on the political, social and economic growth of the whole country.

The UP postulated that only a series of basic reforms – nationalization of mineral resources, agrarian reform, nationalization of the banks and of the strategic manufacturing industry, and control of foreign trade – would place the country on the path to progress which would lead to effectively establishing the basis for a truly socialist society.

The banking reform similarly aimed at eradicating two vices which were deeply rooted in credit policy: the concentration of credit resources in the hands of a few creditors and the creditors' geographic concentration in the two main provinces of the country. These degrees of centralization had been resented throughout the country for a long time because of the distortions they produced in the production structure.

The organization of banking policy by the UP Government reflected two major concepts for mobilizing the full potential of the labour force:
(1) Democratization of credit in the sense of breaking down the privileged clique in order that the vast number of small and medium-sized entrepreneurs, handicraftsmen and peasants would benefit from the resources thus made

available. These sectors had been continually excluded from an effective national credit policy. To this end it was necessary to formulate and implement a policy for creating institutions and finding personnel which were genuinely convinced of the UP's aims and the need for these structural changes.

(2) Decentralization of credit in the sense of mobilizing monetary resources for regions with a great potential for production in terms of human and material resources, thereby enabling the necessary response to planning requirements and less uneven development.

Profits of the commercial banks in the private sector had always been the highest and this had induced the proliferation of private banks. Half-yearly statements always showed percentages of considerable profits, despite the inveterate inflation process which held sway in the country. Trade and exchange operations secured a substantial part of these profits. The acquisition of surpluses for national investment priorities, either through budgetary or any other policy, was another objective of the reform. Originally it was stipulated that a proportion of these profits would be used to pay the cost of nationalization, and the balance would be used in accordance with the objectives indicated above. The basic aim was to transfer the surpluses of some sectors to others in accordance with a scheme of national requirements and priorities, to maximize operational efficiency, to reduce costs and maintain or reduce the level of the interest rate, as far as possible, as a contribution to the fight against inflation. These were short- and medium-term objectives which were considered to be compatible but which needed to be applied rapidly, given the political and economic conditions which existed at the beginning of 1971.

Another aspect of the reform which was to be implemented in the banking sector was the effective unification and centralization of the formulation and execution of monetary policy. This also had often been impaired by the interference and influence of the private banks, whose interests did not coincide with those of the nation as a whole or with any actual forces in production and commerce. Many valuable and positive initiatives in the national credit policy were stifled because they were unlikely to contribute to strengthening certain banks and because they threatened to reduce the hoped-for profit margins.

In the field of foreign exchange operations the private banks had always proved to be very suspicious of any control or regulation of their transactions; they had ensured that they had sufficient freedom to manoeuvre in selecting banking agencies, sources of finance, control of foreign currency deposits, use of credit lines for financing nonessential imports, renewal of agreements, opening and extension of credit lines, and debt levels. This freedom to manoeuvre involved the role of the Central Bank and made it difficult to apply a more planned national policy for foreign exchange and trade.

Consequently, as explained above, one of the urgent proposals in banking reform was to rapidly reorganize the bank's functioning. The aim was to centralize foreign financial operations and establish the basic requisites which would enable the application of a standard for regulating a foreign exchange budget for imports and exports, which would be valid for the whole country. The proposal was to also include a working account in foreign currency, an account for financing and debts with banks and foreign institutions, and, in general, a collection of instruments designed to deal with the economic conditions current in November 1970, especially with the new concepts in the UP Government's Programme and with the predicted political conditions at the national and international level. To give an illustration: the lack of confidence in domestic and foreign economic and financial circles was immediately shown in the period after the presidential election of 4 September 1970. On 7 September (the first working day after the election) four U.S. banks hastened to announce the closure of their credit lines, and this was the beginning of a process which continued until 4 November and even after that. This in turn accentuated the flight of capital, as reflected in the price of the dollar on the unofficial foreign exchange market, that is the black market. Within Chile a psychological campaign was begun to provoke financial panic and pressure the public into making massive withdrawals of deposits from the banks and from the public and private nonfinancial sector, in order to create a crisis in the financial system which would have political repercussions.[9]

This series of events created a high level of awareness among the Chilean public, particularly in the production, trade and financial sectors. Everyone hastened to take the necessary safeguards against the immediate future and an atmosphere of tense expectancy was produced while the new Government was initiating its action. From the outset, the political leadership of the UP parties was aware of the difficult situation that it had to overcome. This situation included the lack of confidence expressed in economic and financial circles and the strategies that the political opposition was developing and intensifying in its desire to obstruct the reform programme. Above all the UP was faced with delicate international financial problems which were the product of the attitude taken by the great majority of U.S. banks. Other institutions, such as the World Bank and the Inter-American Development Bank, later joined in on this form of boycott.

It must therefore be considered perfectly natural that from the outset the new authorities were preparing themselves to fight a difficult battle. They were attempting to gain possession of the minimum resources necessary to confront the existing emergency situation and at the same time set up bases for longer-term action. An exhaustive analysis of the legal guidelines and regulations which governed the banks, foreign trade and foreign exchange provided the first series of instruments to combat the most acute problems. It must not be forgotten that UP had decided for political reasons to maintain the strictest respect for the existing legal system and to implement at least the bare minimum of structural reforms. It was in this context that the process of nationalizing the private banks in Chile took place.

2.2. *Legal Alternatives Which Could Have Been Implemented*

Several alternatives for implementing the reform of the banking system were considered and discussed.

(1) The first alternative was implementation of the existing regulations of the Commercial Code, which permitted the Treasury to acquire ownership by payment resulting from mutual agreement. In the case of private banks it was impossible to implement these regulations because of the thousands of shareholders.

(2) Beyond this alternative, it was felt that the Constitution allowed the acquisition of private property without the owner's consent, that is, the Constitution would allow for expropriation with compensation provided that a special law, based on the Constitution, was passed to fix the conditions for such expropriation. Since the Government's intention was to compensate the largest shareholders over a relatively long-term period – fifteen years in non-readjustable amounts with a 5% annual interest – the passing of a law seemed to be the most apt alternative.

However, political analysis indicated that this course presented numerous obstacles which would unnecessarily delay this urgently needed reform. Therefore, legal proceedings were arranged in order to begin the process of nationalization.

(3) This procedure of transition basically led to the favouring of holders of a relatively small number of shares, for they fixed conditions which were clearly favourable because of the buying price. This procedure, which was well within the existing legal framework, allowed for state purchase of bank shares so long as the total number that each shareholder owned – not just a part – was purchased. These shares had to be acquired at the average price that they had yielded on the Stock Exchange in the first half of 1970. It is worth noting that owing to the result of the presidential election on 4 September, the value of bank shares had greatly decreased. Deliberately, no advantage was taken of these circumstances, as doing so would have caused obvious damage to the small shareholders.

Therefore, the offer announced by President Allende actually was an exceptional opportunity. Aware of the political aspect of the slump in stock exchange values, the Government did not want to damage the small saver who had invested in bank shares to protect himself against inflation. It was clearly established in the official announcement that, at the end of the buying operations, private individuals who still owned shares would fall under the terms of payment that the law prescribed, that is to say, compensation over a fifteen-year period.

(4) As for foreign banks, the Government decided after a careful study of each case and, given the general banking law, to negotiate bilaterally with the banks' home offices in order to stipulate the terms of purchase for each branch. Foreign banks influenced by the Government's decision agreed to negotiate the

sale of offices in Chile and designated special delegates to do so. The negotiations took place in Santiago and were led by Central Bank authorities. The principle guiding the Government's representatives was to obtain total nationalization without any concessions, with delayed payment and low interest rates, while trying to maintain credit lines for the Chilean banking system at competitive rates. This proposal would be especially important in the event of a closure of credit lines and the realization of an international economic blockade. To fulfill both the objective of nationalization and to break the economic blockade, known as the 'invisible blockade', constituted an inordinate problem.

2.3. *The Instruments of Nationalization*

In order to acquire shares in national private banks, a buying procedure was created whose main facets were as follows:

(1) It was recommended to CORFO that the power to buy bank shares should be exercised through a clear agreement on this specific point with its Directorate or Administrative Council. This Council was made up of twenty-one members who were mainly representatives of the public sector, but there was also representation from the private sector (five council members altogether). The agreement was adopted without the private representatives being present.

(2) CORFO delegated to the State Bank the specific task of arranging the agreement, of receiving the shares offered by shareholders and of completing the transactions by making the payments agreed upon. The State Bank, with its vast network of agencies and offices throughout the country, facilitated all the tasks involved in the transaction.

(3) The conditions for buying, fixed in the CORFO agreement, were that: (a) CORFO would acquire the total amount of shares held by each shareholder at the time of selling; (b) the buying price of each share would be the average of the price on the Stock Exchange in the first half of 1970. This average was calculated by the SB for each bank; (c) sales of stocks up to the amount of E°10,000[10] would be paid in cash; (d) amounts from sales of between E°10,000 and E°50,000 would be paid in *Certificados de Ahorro Reajustables* (CAR) [Readjustable Savings Certificates], type A, issued by the Central Bank, which were to mature in two years; (e) amounts of sales greater than E°50,000 would be paid by a type B CAR, which were to mature in seven years; (f) state purchase was allowed from 15 January to 15 March 1971; (g) shares not sold during this period would be acquired through the expropriation law.

Control and inspection of each of the stages of the transactions originating from the CORFO agreement were the SB's responsibility because of the particular legal attributes which the SB had. The Central Bank, through the clear specifications given by the Economic Council of Ministers, had complete control of the bank reform process (that is, the way each of its distinct stages was carried out), as well as of the formulation of pertinent policies for the transition period, the organization of the new banking system, and also the final realization of the country's new banking structure.

The formula for payment described above involved certain inconveniences for the Government, but for the shareholders it was advantageous because its terms – mainly the seven-year payment period – were much better than those proposed by the Government in the bill which was to be sent to the National Congress.

Of course, the small shareholders immediately converted their certificates up to E°10,000 into cash. It is worth noting that the purchasing power of the escudo remained stable during 1971 as that year was characterized by a relatively moderate increase in the consumer price index (23%). The issuing of CARs to larger shareholders also involved some significant advantages. The CARs were issued by the Central Bank, which was empowered to do this in 1960, when its statutes were reformed. They were conceived as an instrument for capturing liquidity and designed to serve normal objectives on the money market, for which purpose they were given special advantages, such as a 7% interest rate, biannual payment of interest and principle readjustability of both according to the annual variation in the Consumer Price Index (CPI), exemptions from tax on their interest and readjustments and the possibility of immediately reselling the certificate to the Central Bank. These were all exceptionally attractive conditions for private investors, especially as the CARs were also guaranteed by the Central Bank. CARs were issued in two series: 'A' with a two-year maturity and 'B' with a seven-year maturity. As time passed the CARs were converted into an instrument of saving against domestic inflation and competed with other certificates issued by central Government institutions or by independent state institutions.

The decision to give those holding shares amounting to more than E°10,000 such advantageous certificates as the CARs did not fail to attract criticism and objections from the UP stalwarts. They felt that more favourable treatment was being given to those groups which had traditionally had more power and privileges.

The amount of cash payments made to shareholders was estimated to amount to about E°110 million, while some E°300 million was paid through issuing A and B type CARs. Financing these amounts was done through the Central Bank, whose Directorate adopted an agreement which arranged for a loan to CORFO for E°400 million, which was designed to meet nationalization costs. CORFO was to pay back this amount within a period of one year, but this period could be extended if necessary. CORFO, in turn, would obtain the resources needed from the banking institutions' biannual profits. In this way, it was established that the banks themselves would pay for the state take-over in a period which was calculated so as to take into account the development of bank operations and the level of bank profits.

After the first days of a natural mood of expectancy, marked by an extensive campaign in the press, radio, and television mounted by the groups who controlled banking capital and were opposed to the nationalization process, the small shareholders began to approach the offices of the State Bank in order to sell their shares. This started off a process which increasingly involved the holders of a medium number of shares as well, to such a point that the closing date for state purchase of shares had to be postponed. The political situation was also, by then, inducing further delays which will be explained later. Gradually the sale of shares acquired a broader character and many of the large shareholders also began to offer their shares to the State Bank. Many of these large shareholders sought direct contact with the Government authorities with the aim of attempting special negotiations which would allow them to obtain additional advantages beyond those stipulated in the agreement made by CORFO's Council. The Government representatives categorically rebuffed these propositions and clearly stated that they would abide by the terms of the original offer.

Despite this negative response, some of the large shareholders kept trying to find better terms within the CORFO arrangement so that the CARs could be used for nonspeculative investments. With the approval of the Economic Council of Ministers, some of these propositions started to be considered and criteria were defined for deciding on each of the proposals presented. Amongst the criteria established, the following were emphasized: (1) investment was to be limited to three specific fields: nonluxury construction through the CORVI housing plans or through savings and loans associations, promotion and export of nontraditional products and national tourism; (2) credit institutions were to advance funds with the CAR being used as collateral, but only for a proportion of this collateral according to the maturity period; (3) plans for investment and for continuation of projects realized were to be supervised by the credit institutions' technical departments; (4) liquidity collected by the banks was to be handled and channeled according to the system of 'credit based on cash budget' so as to maintain control over these financial flows. Various agreements were worked out in this way and put into effect in the course of 1971. After the first of these agreements was reached, new shareholders began to show interest in this type of guided investment. However, the arrangements which they sought would have further distorted the scope and criteria of the agreements and the Government stuck to what it had already decided.

By the middle of 1971 CORFO had already succeeded in obtaining a majority of capital shareholdings in some eleven banks; this constituted 31% of the total deposits in private banks. If the State Bank is taken into account, then about 63% of the total deposits in the commercial banking system was in banks under state control. At the end of 1971 the state controlled the majority of the commercial banks with the exception of the Bank of Chile, in which CORFO owned 47% of shares; it also controlled two banks in Santiago in which the state had taken over management through the SB, and two small banks which the state had also taken over. Altogether this allowed the consolidation of the system so that consideration could now be given to how to reorganize the traditional structure.

Agreements made with foreign banks were the result of extensive negotiations, some of which were more complex than others. Government representatives had negotiated directly with the authorities of each bank concerned, without official or meddlesome interference from other levels – except in dealing with the Bank of Brazil. Because the latter was an official bank, talks with the Brazilians were carried out by both countries' Ministries of Foreign Affairs. After the first contacts, the Ministries decided that, given the objectives of both banks, given the extensive transactions between these banks, and finally, given the existent arrangements for regional integration, possibilities should be found for creating a special statute for the Bank of Brazil's office in Santiago and reinforcing banking links through opening of a similar office of the State Bank of Chile in Brazil. This decision facilitated trade with Brazil, particularly in foodstuffs of Brazilian origin, at times when the international economic blockade was most acute and the scarcity of credit lines created severe financial problems for the Central Bank authorities.

The agreements reached with the branches of private foreign banks displayed an appreciable degree of uniformity, reflecting the common approach maintained during negotiations with them. Naturally, some clauses demonstrated the special conditions of each discussion and the attitude of each foreign banking institution *vis-à-vis* the nationalization process, the development of the Chilean experiment and the existing links with specific economic interests, both national and international. The basic conditions presented in the negotiations with the foreign banks consisted of the following elements:

(1) Acquisition under terms of purchase to be established according to the most recent general balance sheet of the branch, on the basis of detailed auditing by a specialized team organized by the SB and the Central Bank. Auditing was carried out on each entry in the general account, with special emphasis on the portfolio of debtors, creditors, etc. The same was done with the gains and losses account.

(2) Evidence of fulfilment of all tax and social security obligations. Especially commissioned inspectors were entrusted with checking that this had been done.

(3) Evidence of the source and receipt of the capital used to establish the branch in Chile, and of additional capital inflows.

(4) Payment in the form of five to seven years credit, with a grace period of at least twelve months; thus no cash payment was made.

(5) Calculation of the credit in U.S. dollars, with the likely appreciation of European currencies against the dollar in mind.[11]

(6) A maximum interest rate of 6% for all contracts. The average interest rate of all the agreements was rather less: one contract stipulated a rate of 0%.

(7) At the request of some delegations a general criterion was established for authorizing foreign banks to maintain their representation offices to promote and finance business and trade. These offices could not carry out banking operations of any kind, but channeled them through one of the national banks which acted as its agent.
(8) It was established that Chilean courts would have final jurisdiction in all the legal problems that might arise from implementing these contracts.
(9) The principal offices agreed to maintain their foreign personnel as long as ongoing operations were being transferred to the new executives and national personnel responsible for them.

Of the elements for which there was no uniformity in the various agreements, the most important one to emphasize was the extension of the credit lines for the current financing of Chilean imports.

The European banks involved in negotiation (basically the British and the French) accepted the Chilean standpoint in that they maintained credit lines from their home offices to the banks in general and to the nationalized offices in Chile. Some of these banks not only maintained previous financing levels but also increased them significantly.

The U.S. banks, on the other hand, reacted in an absolutely negative way and although they adapted themselves to most of the changes they maintained an inflexible attitude as to providing finance to the nationalized Chilean banks. This position was in line with attitudes prevailing at that time in New York banking circles and in the U.S. Government. There were a few exceptions which will be mentioned later. Representatives of two U.S. banks offered more advantageous conditions with respect to periods and rates of interest in order to counterbalance the general U.S. financing attitude.

The compensation level agreed upon with foreign banks came close to $16 million and the quotas were paid punctually so long as the UP Government remained in power.

2.4. *Some Considerations on the Nationalization Process*

The political parties in the opposition sustained their continual and unrestricted propaganda campaign throughout the 1971-73 period. They claimed that President Allende and the parties in the left coalition had never intended to actually submit the bill for reforming banking through state control and nationalization to the National Congress.

This claim is not valid. In making this accusation the opposition groups were doing no more than finding arguments to demonstrate the leftist Government's inclination to work outside the legal framework or to remain only marginally within the Constitution. This chapter is not the place to discuss this point, but is appropriate to emphasize the following here: (1) nationalizing copper was carried out through a law and a constitutional commission proposed by the Government and approved unanimously by the National Congress; (2) accelerating agrarian reform was carried out according to the law passed under the previous Government; (3) formation of the APS in industry had been proposed in another bill. Therefore, the announcement that the state would purchase bank shares, and the submission thereafter of a bill to the National Congress which would provide for completion of the reform, were steps taken by the Government as part of its overall strategy.

Meanwhile, the success achieved by CORFO in buying bank shares, the response of the small shareholders, and also of the medium-sized and some of the large shareholders, had provoked a state of alarm among the financial and industrial bourgeoisie. These powerful groups began to mobilize to neutralize the negative reaction of public opinion which was already very sensitive to the financial manipulation of the Stock Exchange. In recent years, there had been many examples of national limited companies whose shares had been subject to all types of speculation and who had consequently had no option but to declare themselves bankrupt. All this had shown the small shareholders the lack of protection their savings had because of the way transactions on the Stock Exchange worked. Random speculation during the presidential election, the accentuated slump in stock values, the apparent losses incurred by literally thousands of private investors, while banks and companies alike continued to increase their gains, had convinced an important proportion of the public that it was necessary to support substantial economic changes.

The opposition's belligerent attitude left no room for doubt as to what would happen to the bill if it were sent to the National Congress. Moreover, it should be borne in mind that discussion of such delicate matters as money and banks, given an atmosphere of political strife and in a framework of formal debate, could take months.[12] Very serious monetary disturbances were predicted (withdrawal of deposits, speculation, price rises) to the extent that economic policy and political stability could be undermined. It was for these reasons (and others which cannot be enumerated here) that the Government postponed sending the proposals for bank nationalization to Congress. The political situation at that time, and the success achieved by acquiring shares in the manner described above, were influential in this decision.

The opposition employed a variety of weapons, the more so as the nationalization programme advanced and the irreversibility of the process became increasingly evident. The campaign organized by the press and the mass media was part of the scheme. At the same time, the Minister of the Treasury kept being questioned by the National Congress, which later established committees to which members of the Government, representatives of private interests and the universities, etc., agreed to testify.

This provided an opportunity to set the Anti-Trust Commission in motion, which had been created at the beginning of 1960[13] in one of the paradoxical postures of public image-making towards which the reactionary forces in Chile were inclined. This Commission was practically inoperative, but was unearthed and chosen by the opposition to establish a tribunal which would prosecute the Government for its banking reform, claiming that the Government's actual intention was to install a marginally legal banking monopoly. Before long the inconsistency of this claim became obvious; the Anti-Trust Commission failed completely and the opposition was frustrated anew.

With the failure of all these manoeuvres, the opposition resorted to using the Chilean constitutional impeachment procedure against the Minister of the Treasury. After a sharp political debate, impeachment was approved by a narrow majority. The Minister had to resign.

The opposition continued fighting with renewed vigour, concerning itself not only with nationalizing the banks but also with the whole range of political relationships. All of these activities were efforts towards 'destabilization' by the internal and external opposition, which was trying to drive a wedge into the advance of the reforms.

The transfer of power in the banking sector had at the end of 1971 been realized to such an extent that CORFO had the controlling share of the capital of the national banks, despite all the attempts to prevent this from happening. The state controlled 95% of investments and deposits. In the course of 1972 this control was reinforced by the successful conclusion of negotiations with foreign banks. The resultant situation is as follows:

1. Banks with a central office in Santiago (a total of ten banks)
   a. in which the state owned the majority of shares: seven banks, with a variable proportion of capital under CORFO control above 55%
   b. in which management had been taken over by the Government: two banks
   c. with a private majority holding: the Bank of Chile (CORFO had acquired only 47% of shares)
2. Banks with a central office in the provinces (a total of eleven banks)
   a. in which the state owned the majority of shares: eight banks, with a variable percentage of capital under CORFO control above 55%
   b. in which management had been taken over by the Government: two banks
   c. a special situation: one bank in which a volume of operations was managed by the Government but was in the process of being purchased
3. Foreign banks
   a. nationalized: four banks
   b. without statutory change: one bank which had a special Government agreement

From this situation it can be deduced that the Government had practically achieved its objective for the first two stages of nationalization; from here on it gradually reorganized the system, introducing a monetary policy which was in line with the new situation.

The advance of nationalization had profound repercussions in Chilean public opinion. The opposition's manoeuvres and campaign against the banking reforms did not succeed in hiding the opinions of a large majority of Chileans, who considered the Government's policy to be a new demonstration of the determination to make changes, as stated in the Government programme. Together with nationalizing copper, forming the APS and accelerating agrarian reform, the UP's basis for action was broadened. Management of the country's financial system constituted a vital instrument for economic planning and for the herculean task of expanding national investment.

These measures produced different reactions in foreign economic and financial circles. In the United States, the Government and the banks considered it to be a further demonstration of the Chilean Government's socialist policy. This coincided, moreover, with the existing prognosis on the 'Chilean case'. The hegemonic centre perceived that this satelite country was indeed slipping away from the U.S. sphere of influence. Nevertheless the scheme for nationalizing the banks did not in principle trouble these groups: they were primarily preoccupied with the principle of compensation involved in any nationalization policy. This preoccupation was not so much with the banks themselves as with what was happening to the companies' investments in copper and with everything which had to do with the method of compensation and deductions for excess profits; this controversial matter dominated Chile's international policy and the decisions made during the 1971-73 period.

In the Western European countries, financial circles reacted with reserve, for this measure was neither unknown nor even out of the ordinary, given the evolution of the economic relations on the Continent during this century, particularly since World War II. The tone of nationalization agreements signed with European banks was seen in these circles as a concrete demonstration of the Chilean Government's intent to proceed in good faith as regards foreign interests and to respect contracted agreements, while acting decisively on its unquestionable right to nationalize those economic sectors where this was considered expedient.

In the United States as well as in Europe there were obvious doubts as to the ability of state bodies to manage the banks, and it was feared that international payments and foreign currency transactions could be disturbed, causing considerable harm to the Government's prestige and the country's economy.

General opinion, together with the decision to renegotiate the external debt, which was taken at the end of 1971, made the foreign finance problem on both the short and the long term even more difficult to deal with.

3. HOW THE NATIONALIZED SYSTEM WORKED

It is not possible to fix an exact date for the beginning of the banking system's functioning under the new capital ownership. From the time that the acquisition of shares was initiated in January 1971 and CORFO began to gain control of the shares, modifications had to be made in the directorate of the banks in order to take the new balance of forces into account.

In fact, throughout the first buying period, the nationalized banks operated together with the predominantly private banks. The monetary authorities found themselves faced with new situations and with problems which had to be resolved immediately and pragmatically, with the obvious risk of making errors and bad judgments. These circumstances involved difficulties in that the banking law was quite specific and uniform, while the situations to which it had to be applied were diverse and general.

In this transitional period, the effect of nationalization was further complicated by the international blockade, the acute crisis in the balance of payments, renegotiating the external debt, the search for new sources of foreign credit and by the rigidity of domestic conditions.

3.1. *How the Transition Period was Organized*

Under the new banking policy, the Central Bank came to play a leading role in the financial system. It is necessary to point out that its statutes gave it the functions which all such organizations normally have, namely: (1) dictating and implementing foreign trade policy; (2) regulating foreign capital flows; (3) making and applying regulations for invisible trade, including foreign exchange controls on royalties, trade marks and patents; (4) submitting propositions for tariff policy to the Ministry of the Treasury through the appropriate commission in the Central Bank. In addition, during the period of the UP Government the Central Bank was entrusted with the responsibility for chairing the committee for renegotiating the external debt.

An institution which has this amount of responsibility and power naturally has great influence on the country's economy. Responsibility for organizing and running the nationalized banks placed it at the top of a very broadly based pyramid, yet it was handicapped by having to work out new policies on the basis of statutes written for other conditions.

Consequently, the Central Bank had to proceed pragmatically with the formulation and application of monetary policy during the transitional period, operating in accordance with how the process of buying shares advanced and how the forces in control of the banks' capital shifted.

As CORFO gained control of shares, the SB, in accordance with each bank's statutes, called special sessions of the Directorate or Administrative Council in each of the banks under its supervision. It is worth noting that in each institution, at the beginning of the process a managing director had been designated by the SB, with the Central Bank's approval, who was responsible for the transfer of authority from the former Directorate to the new one.

At no point did any bank suspend operations. Withdrawals of deposits did not occur, foreign operations were not interrupted or set back and, in general, day-to-day functions continued to be carried out quite normally. The first step of banking reform – nationalization – did not provoke the collapse of the country's financial system, as the experts and spokesmen of the internal and external opposition had predicted.

The members of the new directorates came from various sectors: they included professional people (principally economists and lawyers), Government officials and executives in state-owned companies, representatives from trade associations for medium-sized and small businesses, and the banks' own clients. During this transitional period these people were selected from lists of candidates specially prepared by the Central Bank. The presidents or managing directors of the nationalized banks were similarly carefully selected and nominated by the Central Bank. In some cases, those who had previously been directors came to occupy these positions. A similar procedure was used to fill corresponding positions in the nationalized foreign banks.

Employment was guaranteed to all bank personnel and in all cases the benefits and concessions which the workers had obtained through the years were maintained. The existing regulations for contracting and promoting personnel were strictly respected and any kind of irregular practice was strictly avoided, since this could alienate the support of the banks' employees for the nationalization process.

In the Central Bank a special department was created for dealing with all aspects of banking reform; a council of presidents of the state-controlled banks met periodically (weekly or fortnightly) under the Central Bank's chairmanship to discuss and analyze problems relating to banking policy and to recommend appropriate measures. Such measures were then adopted by the Directorate and the Executive Committee of the Bank and became operative.

In a handful of national banks, which did not represent any substantial proportion of the total banking operations, management was taken over by the state and put under SB responsibility. The take-over of management was an emergency measure which the monetary authorities could take in the face of abnormal functioning of banks.[14] The incumbent executives were suspended from their functions and a new manager was nominated by the SB.

Two of the state take-overs of management were decreed before nationalization began: both were cases of flagrant infringements of law for international transactions and involved fraudulent transfers of foreign exchange abroad.

3.2. *The Main Policies Implemented*

During the transition period, efforts were concentrated on implementing each of the propositions planned by the banking reform. Democratizing and decentralizing credit was therefore a top priority, in order to increase production directed to a large part of the population and, above all, to permanently increase the process of investment, and thus to transform the patterns of financing in an economy which had long been distorted. These were the essential aims which were pursued; under such circumstances monetary policy could be an effective instrument towards these aims.

Nevertheless, it is necessary to be aware of both the fact that these changes have their own dynamics, and the fact that it takes time to produce visible results. Credit policy has a rigid element which thwarts any policy change: credit institutions accumulate a given investment portfolio which reflects previous criteria, and a certain amount of time is required to modify this situation. Quick changes are only possible if new resources are injected into the economy.

Detailed arrangements were devised as follows:

(1) Specific regulations were included in agreements reached in given sectors: the reformed sector of agriculture, small and medium-sized industry (that is to say, those economic sectors which were traditionally backward but which had great potential in terms of production and employment).

(2) These credit arrangements would be reinforced by differentiated interest rates.

(3) Ceilings would be determined for each of the credit arrangements.

(4) The ceilings would be allocated regionally.

(5) These resources would be channeled through particular banks such that some banks would become specialized, thus reinforcing their position in a given field. The State Bank was to reinforce its position particularly as a bank dealing with agrarian reform.

(6) Collaboration with technical assistance organizations, such as CORFO's technical cooperation service, would be set up in order to implement these arrangements and make the best use of resources.

(7) Credit insurance would be organized so as to make it easier for small entrepreneurs to get credit. This proved to be an essential support element for stimulating the democratization of credit, even though the measures did not last for very long.

Another aspect which demanded attention was initiating a policy of merging banks. The large number of banks and their geographic dispersion on the one hand, and the policy of lowering the interest rate as part of the anti-inflation policy on the other, made it difficult for the small banks to finance operating costs, largely because these costs were fixed. As has been noted, it was thought that there were too many banks, and that this was partly responsible for the high interest rate in November 1970.[15] As is the case in highly concentrated capitalist economies, the least efficient marginal unit determines the market price, so that the most efficient unit obtains exceptional profits, thus reinforcing its position.

The aims of this policy of merging banks were to lower costs, increase efficiency and guarantee stability to employees. The Central Bank and the SB together carried out studies and set up a merger programme which included primarily incorporating the four branches of the foreign banks into certain national banks. In the first stages, attempts were made to consolidate the twenty-six banks into no more than ten large banks in order to transform them at a later date into even fewer institutions.

The general guideline for banking reform was to maintain the stable functioning of the nationalized banks. With the exception of a few executives who preferred to go into retirement, the majority of the personnel were kept on in their positions and new personnel was contracted only when vacant posts had to be filled.

3.3. *Centralizing Banking Operations*

The banking reform thus allowed the implementation of a series of measures to centralize and coordinate monetary policy, foreign exchange, imports and foreign finance.

This monetary policy, and the resulting budget, was designed to serve as an effective planning instrument in order to organize, identify and quantify the issuing of money in relation to programmes of production, investment, foreign trade and income distribution; it also served to assign priorities to credit programmes for the financing of the public sector and for private monetary circulation.

Managing this budget was not only the responsibility of the Central Bank; it was also supervised by the Monetary Committee (a branch of the Ministry of Treasury) which was intended to link up all public spending policies.

Two important instruments were used to implement credit policy in the economy's public (APS) and private sector:

(1) There were two methods for assigning credit to the APS enterprises: (i) directly to the enterprise as a 'credit through cash budget', either through a bank or through State Bank or Central Bank mediation;[16] (ii) through CORFO, which in turn transferred the credit to the enterprise in question.[17]

(2) In order to channel credit to the private sector, monthly expansion maxima were fixed within which the banks were to meet their clients' demands. The 'cash budget' system was considerably expanded in firms and its use was stimulated.

The 'cash budget' credit system had been set up several years earlier but was not extensively used. It was a good system for facilitating the planning of resources at the firm level because it allowed for allocating and guaranteeing a previously calculated sum. Payment was made on a periodic basis directly to the creditors through an established payment programme. The system was promoted widely under the new policy and was extended to state enterprises as well as to the social sector.

Although it had not been used for many years (since 1955), an imports budget was worked out once again to take into account the Chilean economy's great need for imports and its scarcity of foreign exchange. The Central Bank had introducéd import permits, and these permits were approved by the department concerned in accordance with the budget, which consisted of an item-by-item list of permitted imports. Certain items were put on a list of prohibited imports.

The probable monthly demand for foreign currency was estimated according to these basic needs and, on this basis, a cash budget for foreign exchange was drawn up which included all the requirements of the whole country, from those of the state to those of individuals, firms, etc., as well as the probable disposable incomes arising from exports and other sources, including foreign credit. This budget regulation, which was applied very strictly by the Allende Government, required that the Central Bank give its approval for each transfer. As had been the case in the past, the critical payments situation, which was pointed out earlier, completely justified this procedure.

This whole regulatory system could be satisfactorily implemented through the nationalized banking system as this was a system which facilitated the optimal use of these means and responded to the urgent need for concentrating all financial resources, deploying them efficiently in emergency situations and thus ensuring that payments to foreign suppliers and the banking agencies could always be made.

A whole new structure of relations emerged for foreign financing as a result of nationalizing the banks. It was a new experience and was approached pragmatically: its forms and structures became consolidated through actual day-to-day events. The combination of the U.S. banks' economic blockade, which was increasingly effective as the months passed, and the banking reform produced a natural lack of confidence abroad and a 'wait and see' attitude from international banking which was expressed in so many words by certain European bankers. The executives of various Chilean nationalized banks negotiated in various ways with the branches of foreign banks to arrange new reserve credit lines, but such efforts failed completely. Yet a new situation had emerged on the financial scene: it was no longer the banks which maintained a direct relationship with the international banking system; it was the state itself which acquired a significant relationship, so that when international credit was forthcoming, the recipient and responsible body was the state.

The effects of the blockade were reflected in the fall in international reserves. The situation then worsened because of the drop in the international copper price and because the Ministry of the Treasury did not collect some of the 1970-71 taxes which were due from the copper companies on time. About $200 million had to be provided by the Central Bank in the form of loans to the Treasury to finance the expenditures in the foreign currency budget. These and many other factors steadily built up and put pressure on the Government's economic policy, threatening its ability to carry out its programme.

The Central Bank was given the task of breaking the 'invisible blockade' and did so through a wide variety of negotiations with the European banks, the Eastern European socialist countries, the Latin American countries, Japan and Australia.

The foreign banks demanded that the Central Bank guarantee all the financing which they provided. Following acceptance of this procedure, credit lines were extended to the Central Bank, which then distributed them among the nationalized banks to provide openings for and/or confirmation of credits or other forms of financing.

This new procedure modified the national banking system's relations with international banking, and the Central Bank found that it possessed a new instrument for planning, namely the distribution of short-term credit and its allocation to objectives to which the Government had given priority.

By 1973 the Central Bank had, from a quantitative viewpoint, practically reconstructed short-term financing and had surpassed the level of $300 million available in November 1970 in the U.S. banks. By 30 June 1973 lines of credit totalled almost $600 million[18] and had the additional advantage that the creditor countries were geographically more dispersed, as had also become the case in the structure of foreign trade. At the same time, however, more of the credit was bilateral. Of the total, 50% came from Western Europe and about 25% came from Latin American countries.

In general terms as far as it affected short-term credit, the blockade was momentarily broken, although the worsening of the domestic political situation made the future very uncertain. The problem of multilateral short-term financing, and of medium- and long-term loans, remained. Renegotiating the debt and the policy for compensating the large copper companies played a key role in this.

4. THE FEATURES OF NATIONALIZED BANKING IN CHILE

Different conclusions can be drawn from this nationalization process, which was only in its initial stages and still had many difficulties to overcome. Analysis of this brief experience must be made in the context of the political events which interfered in the process, taking into account the internal and external obstruction to which the Government was subjected, as well as its own policies and the mistakes which were indeed committed during the Government's three-year period in power.

The Chilean process has made clear that in a programme of substantial reforms leading to a country's economic and social transformation, state control of money and credit is essential to implementing such reforms.

The kind of nationalization applied in Chile was relatively simple and well within the Chilean legal system. Furthermore, it has been shown that nationalization generally did not provoke unsurmountable upheavals, nor did it lead to the financial collapse of countries like Chile. On the contrary, it was seen to produce undeniable benefits and advantages.

4.1. *Nationalization of the Banking System in the Context of Economic Policy*

The UP Government's basic policies were undertaken within the first months after the UP came to power. The combined influence of various reform measures had a powerful impact and generated mutual effects which worked to strengthen the implacable political opposition.

The effects of banking reform were stronger on domestic interests than on multinational enterprises. When the foreign banks were nationalized, because adequate compensation was negotiated with them in the contracts, criticism from them was eliminated, although they would have preferred to maintain their profitable operations in Chile. Through maintaining credit lines to the state-owned bank, foreign banking could continue to reap its profits, although on a somewhat smaller scale. It was for these reasons that the strongest and most adamant opposition to nationalizing the banks came from within the country.

At first the success in CORFO's purchases of bank shares created the impression that the domestic financial bourgeoisie was going to accept state control in the commercial banks as an irreversible fact. But, in fact, this was only an impression. The bourgeoisie thought that the Government would fail in its attempt to apply a capitalist mechanism in socializing a sector of the economy; it therefore had not yet prepared its counterattack and had not recovered from the overall effects of the Government's programme.

It is an accepted and often proved fact that new governments have their greatest force, authority, and support for carrying out their plans in their initial stage. During this stage the opposition generally adopts an observant attitude. Furthermore, one has to recognize that banking shares were spread among a great many holders, and this made the creation of united opposition difficult on the short term, so that the issue of state purchase of shares did not arouse any real oppositional fervour. The large shareholders preferred to protect their investment and tried to negotiate before launching a direct attack. The low price of shares on the Stock Exchange was another factor which induced holders to get rid of their shares, especially when confronted with the undeniable advantages of the Government's offer.

However, the power groups showed that they had not lost their capacity to react and slowly began to reorganize. The fight for control of the Bank of Chile, which was the most important private commercial bank (it had offices throughout the country and only the State Bank had comparable power), was determinant in the outcome of the struggle, and it became a symbol for the bourgeoisie's elite.

Class consciousness and economic and political survival were expressed through the fight over the Bank of Chile. At the end of almost three years of struggle CORFO succeeded in obtaining 47% of the capital, through which it exercised control within the Directorate. The Government was able to name a president and various directors. However, errors in evaluation and some weaknesses in the Government's assessment of certain situations were to prevent it from exercising more complete control over the Bank. Time was on the side of the opposition and soon the struggle which had been concentrated in the Bank of Chile came to involve the whole foreign and domestic oppositional front.

Meanwhile the big bourgeoisie was looking for other sectors in which to establish its influence in order to make up for losing the banks and to find new sources for financing its activities. It found these in trade, in transport, and in savings and loan societies. Furthermore, it had an advantage through the abundant liquidity resulting from the agricultural expropriations, from the sale of banks and businesses, and from the economy.

This new liquidity led the fiscal authorities to strictly limit the expansion of credit. The fact that they could count on a greater control of banking as a result of the nationalizations facilitated the implementation of new and more selective credit regulations.

However, the demand for more credit by the APS enterprises continued to increase and became stronger as the process of incorporating enterprises into the APS accelerated, thus revealing the APS's lack of finance. In that there was no substantial modification in either the official pricing policy or in the planning of production and costs, banking credit became the essential means for financing.

Thus it was in a situation of excess liquidity, and during substantial transformations in the economic system – principally in the industrial and agricultural ownership structure – that banking reform and the efforts to restructure the banking system took place.

The application of the UP's programme modified the economic framework and the business climate so that perspectives for development opened up and the economy reacted accordingly. At first, the response of private business was to take advantage of this opportunity and the exceptional conditions which, to the surprise of the oligarchy in the various sectors, the Allende Government provided.

The new liquidity also modified the traditional means for financing firms and the current commercial practices, transforming the market into a buyers' market. Firms began to sell their accumulated stocks and arranged new conditions of sale for their products. All discounts to wholesalers and retailers were abolished, terms of payment were strictly on a cash basis and in many cases payment had to be made in advance, so that buying by means of any kind of credit was completely eliminated.[19] In this way the cash flow of firms improved. They began to pay off their creditors and were able to reduce the need to resort to bank credit in order to obtain working capital.

In the wake of these changes the Central Bank modified the monetary and credit policy. Dealing with such a complex situation was particularly difficult because of the explosive liquidity which could neither be localized, controlled nor reduced, for the traditional system was structured precisely so as not to interfere with such market forces and consequently was completely inadequate. The National Congress refused to pass measures which would have allowed the monetary structure to be managed more efficiently. On the other hand the foreign currency reserves did not allow any room for manoeuvre either.

At no time, however, did the regulations issued by the Central Bank and the SB for determining monetary and credit policy and monitoring the functioning of the nationalized banks obstruct business between private firms and the banks. These regulations were also never used for purposes of political pressure. Naturally the reformed banking system did not make any concessions in terms of preferential treatment or consumer credits to specific social or political groups. It also eliminated all credit for speculation in real estate or on the Stock Exchange, as well as all credit to be used in hoarding consumer goods, particularly foodstuffs.

Since the paramount objective of the Government's programme was increased production of goods and services, maximum use of installed capacity and increased productivity, the measures adopted by the monetary authorities were precisely those which would channel resources towards those objectives, thus integrating monetary and production planning.

The new resources which were injected into the system were directed primarily towards firms producing goods and services which were essential to the Government's plans, regardless of whether these firms were in private hands or in the APS. But in fact the channeling of funds to private firms was already diminishing due to the transformations, outlined above, which occurred in the money market and in transactions in commodities.

This policy of close links between banking and the enterprises helped to fulfill a further objective: part of the economic surplus was to be captured by the nationalized banks in the form of interests. This surplus was later transferred to the Government's budget or to other administrative bodies which were singled out by the Government. This objective could only be accomplished to a minimum extent during the period of UP Government, owing to a number of factors which included: (1) a lowering of the banks' interest rate, which led to a decrease in income from commercial banks; (2) wage increases and other costs which diminished the surplus in the nationalized banks; (3) the decrease in bank financing required by private enterprise, because their cash position was strengthened as explained above; (4) the increased role of APS enterprises in distributing credit which, while seeming to increase the banks' interest earnings, actually did not constitute any real surplus transfer. The debts of the APS enterprises to the banking system increased to such an extent that they became a heavy burden to the APS's economic and financial management. The Government administrators (*interventores*), who were responsible for carrying out the measures adopted by the Cabinet and improving the returns from the nationalized industries, searched laboriously for ways of freeing the industries from the financial burden which repaying and servicing these debts represented. Through a resolution approved by the Economic Council of Ministers, these debts were passed on to CORFO which capitalized the total amount of the debt for each enterprise and then established a credit with the Central Bank for the whole amount.

This resolution did not in any way change the firms' financial situation since it did not remove the real causes of the lack of finance. From the viewpoint of bookkeeping it provided temporary relief in each case, but it did not alter the deficit problem as a whole.

It should be pointed out, however, that through the increased concentration of transactions in the Central Bank – which is understandable in this period of transition and reorganization of the system – the Bank recorded a higher level of profits; as required by the Bank's statutes, these profits were either handed over to the Ministry of the Treasury or used towards reducing the public debt.

Thus new criteria for distributing credit was established and was gradually applied through the nationalized banking system to the extent that the banks were integrated into the APS.

In accordance with the production plan, a monetary budget was set up in 1972 which comprised two fundamental, interrelated parts: one budget for each sector of production and the various enterprises, and another for the different geographical regions. Simultaneously the mechanisms governing the transfer of resources were strengthened. For this purpose the system of credits based on cash budgets was redesigned and enlarged. All the banks were instructed to channel most of their resources into this system of credits and the aim was to include both private firms as well as those in the APS. In the cases of large firms whose requirements exceeded the commercial banks' legal capacity, the Central Bank guaranteed the contracts which provided the funds.

Use of this credit system provoked a whole range of reactions among the executives of the APS companies, who felt that under existing circumstances it would be better not to put their firms under such control. This initiated a period of much discussion during which momentum was gathered (but never sufficiently developed) for studying the experiences and theories of the socialist states and those mixed economies in which the state played an important role.

For the medium-sized and small firms, which lacked capital and the facilities for self-finance, an active programme of credit support was continued. This programme's aim was to obtain a significant increase in production, given that a buyers' market prevailed. The nationalized banking system allowed for greater efficiency and effectiveness in contacting those in need of finance. It also had succeeded in decentralizing management to the provincial level, where a significant revitalization occurred in small and medium-sized production units that had for a long time been neglected. This was particularly the case in those provinces furthest away from Santiago.

The exogenous and endogenous factors indicated above made managing the economy extraordinarily complex. The excess liquidity complicated the task of the monetary authorities, who gradually lost control over the vast amount of money in circulation. This was undermining effective economic control at its most critical moments. The Central Bank's inability to counteract this dangerous situation did not improve matters. Measures to establish at least minimal planning through the monetary budget were inadequate and they broke down completely in the course of 1973. As the Government had not been able to impose limits on monetary flows in the beginning of its term in office, the system was not able to respond strongly enough later in the political and economic process.

The means used during this period to carry out the reform of the commercial banks were much hindered by contradictions in the management of monetary policy. The organization which was needed to effectively control monetary policy was hardly formed, and there was not enough time to demonstrate the advantages derived from such a transformation in the banking structure.

4.2. *Renegotiating the Debt with the U.S. Banks*

In the course of 1971 – the decisive year for the process of nationalizing the banks – the hostile attitude of the U.S. banks was reaffirmed while at the same time negotiations were begun with the European banks, on whose part there was little response at first. At the same time, the Central Bank had, with limited and precarious reserves,[20] to maintain the flow of foreign payments resulting from foreign trade, while servicing its short-, medium- and long-term debts.

As has been mentioned above, the debts of domestic companies to foreign banks (principally U.S. banks) totalled nearly $400 million in the form of short-term renewable credits that entered Chile as capital inflows (article 14 in the International Foreign Exchange Law). As these credits expired, the foreign banks began to demand repayment through the Chilean commercial banks, many of whom had guaranteed the loans. Following the established procedure, the Chilean commercial banks would solicit the Central Bank's authorization before proceeding with these capital transfers. Given the difficult foreign reserve situation, the Central Bank issued clear instructions that the commercial banks should seek the renewal of these credits, without paying or making concessions of any kind. The response of the foreign banks was not delayed for very long, but the principal means by which these (U.S.) banks could apply pressure was not open to them because the flow of credit that they could grant to Chilean commercial banks for financing foreign trade had already been cut or suspended. At this stage, tensions with the international banking community reached their highest and most critical point.

At the end of 1971 another measure was taken by the Allende Government which provoked a new series of events in the area of foreign finance: Allende announced that, in view of the balance of payments deficit and the economic blockade, the Government had decided to suspend the servicing of short- and medium-term foreign debts and was attempting to renegotiate its debts with foreign creditors. This measure made the efforts to open new lines of credit with European banks even more difficult, but at the same time this credit was desperately needed for financing the current imports necessary to maintain economic growth and domestic stability. All this demonstrated to the Government the harshness of the pressures applied to it when it attempted to defend its interests; it also clarified the obstacles that would have to be overcome if the Government was to carry out its programme.

Decisions made by President Allende and his Government *vis-à-vis* international finance persuaded the U.S. banks to avoid a total break with the Chilean Government, for this would have meant that they would have not been repaid. Amongst these credits were the loans advanced to the Anaconda and Braden copper companies by New York banks for investment programmes agreed upon under the Frei Government. These credits totalled approximately $700 million; the U.S. banks tried to negotiate a compromise formula for repayment of this amount.

The decision to accept the proposals for negotiation as presented by the Chilean Government reflected a peculiar situation that can only be properly analyzed by considering the following mixture of antecedents:

(1) The financing expected from the governments and banks of the socialist countries, although important, was not sufficient to meet the needs of foreign trade and national development as planned by the Government: a substantial proportion of the finance required would have to be forthcoming from European, Far Eastern and Latin American capitalist countries.

(2) By negotiating with, and obtaining an agreement from, the U.S. banks, a greater margin of manoeuvre would be won on the following fronts: (i) European banks in which U.S. capital was being held; (ii) negotiation of the external debt with the creditor countries in the Club of Paris, for discussions could be started from a better vantage point; (iii) expansion of the possibility of some U.S. banks to continue to operate within a nationalized banking system.

(3) Such international organizations as the World Bank (and its affiliated bodies, the International Development Association (IDA) and the International Finance Corporation (IFC)) and the Inter-American Development Bank (IDB), through their decision to discontinue loans to Chile, were indirectly influencing other sources of international credit, including the private international banking sector.

(4) The nationalization of copper (in July 1971) had resulted in counterattacks

from such U.S. companies as Kennecott and Anaconda, which were creating additional international finance problems.
(5) Foreign currency reserves were rapidly declining, for the restrictions and controls were not tight enough to halt the steady decrease in reserves due on the one hand to a considerably higher volume of spending, and on the other hand to a sharp interruption in the foreign credit flow that had been supporting the Chilean economy for more than twenty years.

It ought to be stressed that suspension of servicing of the external debt[21] did not effect payments for current foreign trade transactions, which continued punctually. Payment orders, bills of exchange, bank cheques, and all other types of obligations with respect to current transactions were promptly met by the nationalized commercial banks and the Central Bank. This was the only possible option open to the Government, given its need to have international credit flows into Chile re-opened.

The decision to renegotiate the external debt ought to have been taken much earlier, when the Government first came into office. The political impact of a democratically elected left-wing government, as well as the higher level of monetary reserves, would have provided a stronger position from which to negotiate. Criticism of the Allende Government on this point is valid.

Once the decision to enter into negotiations with the U.S. banks was adopted, as a means of clearing away the many obstacles that had accumulated, it was established that the basis for these negotiations would be the following: (1) assertion that the basic reforms being implemented were a direct expression of the country's sovereignty and strictly within existent constitutional and legal systems; (2) rejection of any financial agreement that was linked to negotiating a stand-by credit with the International Monetary Fund; (3) stipulation of repayment dates in the negotiated agreements that would contribute to a more rational structuring of the external debt, while facilitating a long-term solution to the recurrent balance of payments deficit; (4) exclusion of any clauses in the negotiated agreements that could interfere with the Chilean constitutional procedure for calculating compensation; (5) rejection of all attempts to suspend or alter the aims and means of Government's economic policies.

Negotiations with the U.S. bankers' consortium were completed in January 1972.[22] A preliminary agreement was reached by the two delegations and was ratified by both parties at the end of March. The stipulated interest rate was 6-7%, adjustable in relation to the Eurodollar market. The date of amortization was fixed at eight years, with one year of grace. When, in February 1972, the first round of the Club of Paris meetings started, the Chilean delegation used this preliminary agreement as a basis for renegotiating their debt.

While the agreement reached with the U.S. banks constituted a positive element in renegotiating the external debt, it was also an important step towards beginning negotiations with European and other banks for acquiring short-term credit. On the other hand the agreement did not modify the international policy of blockading the Chilean banks, except in the case of two or three New York banks which showed a more constructive attitude and, within limited margins, extended new financial facilities through their London offices. The embargo set up by the U.S. copper companies against Chilean assets in New York persuaded the Central Bank (and the Chilean banking community in general) to transfer its deposits and operations to the major European financial centres.

The centralization resulting from banking reform helped to facilitate the distribution of foreign currency working balances, depending on the amounts of financing obtained. However, the reduction of these balances, resulting from the decrease in monetary reserves, threatened to effect overall levels of finance. Nevertheless, another factor appeared which contributed to channeling important amounts of foreign currency into some Chilean banks. Various European banks agreed to make sources of finance available on the basis of the debts incurred through importing Chilean copper. This finance was to be put at the Central Bank's disposal. This source of liquidity, which before nationalization had been provided by U.S. companies in cooperation with the New York banks, opened up new possibilities in the struggle to break the economic blockade. But during 1972 (particularly in the second half), when Kennecott initiated legal procedures to set up embargoes in various European countries (Italy, France, Federal Republic of Germany and Sweden), the willingness of the European banks to disperse significant amounts of the negotiated credits was affected. More hopeful negotiations, which were being carried on at that time with various important European banks and would have allowed Chile recourse to the Eurodollar market for medium-term loans, also suffered as a result of Kennecott's embargoes.

In the course of 1973, when the danger of such embargoes had receded and normal copper trading began once again in Europe, the possibilities for short-term financing based on copper exports increased. Although loans were given more modestly, there was always the possibility that they would return to their former levels. However, the prevailing economic and political climate during the last period of the Allende Government impeded the realization of all medium-term borrowing in the international monetary markets.

The European international banking community took a sensible stance *vis-à-vis* the evolution of Chile's economy when determining credit (and risk) levels. Inflation, industrial and agricultural production, the size of currency reserves, money supply and the balance of payments were the dominant factors that they analyzed. Such matters as nationalization, agrarian reform and bank reform played a secondary role when making such decisions. On the other hand, the general impression is that the U.S. commercial banks were preoccupied to a far greater degree with considerations more closely related to the Allende Government's management of policies concerning the economic cycle.

4.3. *Workers' Participation*

It is also important to consider the process of workers' participation in running the banks. Throughout the whole nationalization process the banks' employees actively participated in every aspect of bank reform. Important demonstrations of support for nationalization were shown by the majority of workers, although there were other sectors that displayed opposition to the reform (especially during the last days of the UP Government). Altogether, the attitudes taken by the bank employees in the face of such profound political change were not uniform.

When examining these attitudes it is important to note that the social backgrounds of the banking employees were predominantly middle class. However, certain sectors of the upper middle class and the social elite were also represented and were especially influential in specific banks. The role that this sector of the banking community played in the lock-out of October 1972 and in later incidents of a similar nature clearly showed their class sympathies. These aspects should be taken into account when analyzing the attitudes of bank employees, for their understanding of the political process was extremely varied and consequently they expressed differing degree of support for the Government's policies.

At the beginning of bank nationalization the inclination of the majority of employees was to support the Government. The Banking Employees' Federation[23] showed clear support; over a period of nearly three years its leaders actively collaborated in both the bank reform and in fostering workers' participation while the reform was being carried out. On the one hand, the Government policy of maintaining the benefits which the employees had acquired after many years of struggle and of respecting the employees' ranks and functions, and on the other hand, the workers' effective participation in management and the desire to rationalize workers' functions and remunerations all contributed to create majority support from the employees for their representatives' favourable reaction towards bank nationalization. Because 'economicism' is usually accepted as a key feature of organizations dominated by a 'middle class' membership, it is appropriate to make note of the political initiatives undertaken by the Federation's leaders in order to win a base of support for a reform that affected the very core of the social, economic and political power structure in Chile. As a result of these activities, a statute of participation was drawn up and then ratified by the Government and the Federation.[24]

The gradual worsening of the general political situation, along with growing inflation and a shortage of food supplies, brought about an important erosion in the Government's support. This trend was also shown in the amount of support given by bank employees for the nationalization programme. Growing disagreements within the labour force were easily used by the Government's opponents to further weaken rank-and-file pro-Government sympathies; to do this end they created artificial conflicts and incited a lack of discipline so as to isolate and reduce the Federation's influence. As part of this general strategy, a parallel union organization was founded whose main object was opposition.

5. CONCLUSIONS

Nationalizing the banks was an important aspect of expanding social control over the economic process which was initiated by the UP Government. The reorientation of production, the absorption of nonutilized human and material resources and the revitalization of capital accumulation within a fundamental transformation in the ownership of the means of production, required that the state be able to manage the supply of money and the distribution of credit more decisively.

1. The method used to bring about bank nationalization remained strictly within the existent legal system. The transfer of ownership progressed smoothly and benefited not only the small shareholders but also the larger ones.

2. Nationalizing the branches of foreign banks operating in Chile was achieved through a process of direct negotiation, in the course of which these banks were adequately compensated. This policy facilitated obtaining financing from European and other banks for use in foreign trade. These banks showed a much more conciliatory attitude to the Allende Government than their U.S. rivals.

3. The transfer of the banks to the APS took place gradually without affecting their daily functioning. It did not cause upheavals in the economic life of Chile. Financial organizations did not collapse, as many opponents of the reform had predicted, and dealings with foreign banks were not interrupted. Furthermore, it should be mentioned that all commercial agreements and obligations were scrupulously honoured.

4. Nationalization permitted the Chilean monetary authorities to rationalize the financial system by hierarchically ordering the functioning of various bodies and centralizing the decision-making and implementation of monetary policy. Through recapturing control of the financial system the state was more able to initiate economic planning and to encourage and support an increase in the rate of national investment. The essential purpose of banking reform began to become apparent during 1971, with the democratization of credit and its geographical dispersion. These two goals led to a substantial and qualitative improvement in credit distribution.

One of the central problems for the authorities was to coordinate the monetary budget with the production plan in order to consistently distribute credit in accordance with the new targets laid down in the Government's programme. The upheavals produced within the traditional economic structure as a result of the thoroughness of the reforms, and also because of the explosion in liquidity during the second half of the Government's period in office, unfortunately reduced the positive effects of planning.

5. Despite these problems, a better policy of credit support for small and medium-sized businesses was developed through the preferential treatment given to these sectors. In this manner the traditional concentration of credit in the most powerful economic groups was effectively modified.

6. Bank nationalization had profound and positive repercussions on the mobilization of foreign currency. This was possible because legitimate foreign trade, the distribution of deposits in banks abroad and the volume of payments for budgeted transactions were all centralized.

7. A decisive change also occurred in the kind of short-term finance provided by international banks. The standard patterns of operation were changed, as was the way in which credit lines were negotiated and agreed upon with foreign commercial banks. Given that previous sources of financing were closed due to the 'invisible blockade', new sources of credit were used according to the priorities established in the budget for imports. However, while improvement in the geographical diversity of sources of short-term financing started to reflect the new trade pattern, the multilaterality of credit sources decreased.

8. Workers' participation during the nationalization process had many positive aspects and proved that the banking and credit policies were strengthened when the majority of banking employees were given the opportunity to participate and to represent their interests.

NOTES

1. CORFO was established in 1940 to promote the country's development. The broad scope and legal powers which its charter gave it allowed the UP Government to assign to it the task of purchasing companies in the private sector in order to incorporate them into the APS.

2. Concerned with coordinating and executing the Government's housing plans, CORVI was authorized by law to receive the payments which were due from all those who subscribed to the plan for housing construction. Funds received by CORVI in this way were deposited in a special account in the State Bank.

3. See Ricardo Lagos, *Industria en Chile. Antecedentes estructurales* [Industry in Chile. Structural Antecedents] (Santiago de Chile, Instituto de Económica, Universidad de Chile, 1966).

4. The increase in the international copper price was interpreted as an appreciable increment of foreign exchange income and of the Central Bank's international reserves.

5. Credits were obtainable on terms which fluctuated between six and twelve months renewability.

6. See the Statistical Appendix following Chapter 2, Tables XIV and XVI.

7. Quoted from a speech which President Allende made on 30 December 1970 to announce state control of the banking system. The figures correspond to regular statistics prepared by the SB.

8. These figures are from Eduardo Trabucco, *Chile and the Principal Problems of Short Term Finance During the Period 1970/73* (Bonn, Friedrich Ebert Foundation, 1974).

9. It should be realized that this plan was part of a vast and complex conspiracy, designed to prevent President Allende from taking office, which has been fully corroborated and of which there is wide knowledge. See the report of the U.S. Senate Committee chaired by Senator Church, which is entitled *Covert Action in Chile 1963-73. Staff Report of the Select Committee to Study Governmental Operations with Respect to Intelligence Activities* (Washington D.C., United States Senate, The U.S. Government Printing Office, 1975).
10. The exchange rate in the (official) brokers' market during this period was E°14 to the dollar, that is to say, the amount to be paid in cash was equivalent to $715.
11. This situation got worse on the European markets in 1973.
12. According to the regulations of the National Congress sufficient means existed for extending the discussion of a law for two or three months and, if necessary, for postponing a decision indefinitely.
13. It was created under Jorge Alessandri's Government (1958-64), which was elected by Chile's political and economic right.
14. One of the banks, the Edwards Bank, which was of long standing in Chile and was linked to one of the most important socioeconomic power groups, became involved in this type of illegal operation to the amount of nearly $8 million (approximately equivalent to the bank's capital). This produced additional complications with a group of ten U.S. banks in New York which appeared to be involved in a loan used for the illegal transaction of funds.
15. The interest rate at that time was 24%, of which 20% was the basic rate, while 4% was an authorized extra charge. The Allende Government lowered this rate to a maximum of 18% and maintained this rate for the duration of 1971.
16. In the General Banking Code it was stated that banks providing credits could grant them to companies or individuals; however, each loan to an individual was limited to less than 5% of the bank's capital.
17. This procedure was used in unexpropriated companies which ultimately were to be brought under state control by a legal statute which, at that time, had not yet been defined.
18. E. Trabucco, *Chile and the Principal Problems....*
19. Before 1971, sales through bills of exchange, through credit on current account, or through postdated cheques formed the majority of transactions.
20. In November 1970 the gross total of international reserves was $450 million, or the equivalent of four to five months imports at that time.
21. There were a few cases in which payment of debts was not suspended.
22. No fewer than sixty banking institutions, mainly based in New York, recorded forwarding credits to a variety of public and private Chilean companies.
23. This was the major union for bank employees and many of its leaders were militants in the parties that made up the UP, which explains their solid support for the Government's bank reform policy.
24. This sectoral agreement, which applied only to banking, was part of a broader arrangement at a national level between the Allende Government and *Central Unica de Trabajadores* (CUT); [Trade Unions' Confederation], that fixed the guidelines for workers' participation.

9

SERGIO RAMOS

INFLATION IN CHILE AND THE POLITICAL ECONOMY OF THE UNIDAD POPULAR GOVERNMENT

The evolution of the Chilean economy between 1971 and 1973 was characterized by the development of a deep and extended transformation process which affected the basic structure and customary patterns of the economy's operation. The liquidation of latifundia, the creation of the *Area de Propiedad Social* (APS) [Area of Social Property], the consequent weakening of the large monopolies, the restructuring of international economic relations so as to end economic dependence, together with an economic policy of direct and immediate benefit to the workers, are major characteristics of the period. Strong and growing inflation accompanied this evolution and at the same time serious supply problems developed in intermediate products as well as in commodities for final consumption. Inflation and supply were matters of great relevance in the economic situation in which the *Unidad Popular* (UP) Government found itself. Reflecting this situation, the economic policy drawn up and implemented by the Government had as one of its central objectives the 'fight against inflation'.

The advent of the UP Government was not the first time that there was inflation in Chile: its dominant presence goes back several decades. In fact, in 1970 Chile's experience with anti-inflationary policy was already much wider and more systematic than in the majority of Latin American countries, and it appeared to constitute an important starting-point for the policy that the UP Government was to implement. However, during the 1971-73 period the nature and causes of inflation were different, as much in policies applied as in the general orientation. On this point, as in practically all other aspects of economic life, the UP Government marked an historic change of direction in the traditional tendencies of dependent capitalist development.

The fundamental difference in nature of inflation during this period was due to the different content and significance of the disequilibria. The origins of inflation were recognized as, above all, part of an acute crisis in Chilean capitalist development which intensified enormously towards the end of the 1960s. In

---

Footnotes, tables and the figure to this chapter may be found on pp. 354-362.

order to overcome that crisis, which was defined by the Government's programme as 'structural', the popular movement proposed a series of transformations to establish new bases for subsequent economic development, so as to eliminate the situation's determinants on the economy's dependent capitalist structure and the corresponding system of political domination. Political resistance in the face of change, and the natural disruption provoked by transforming the basic parameters of an economy, led to new types of disequilibria, until then unknown in Chile, arising out of the structural transformations aimed at overcoming the existing crisis. Obviously, within this new framework, the distinct nature of the economic policy was determined as much by the basic changes themselves as by the general orientation of Government action in favour of new class interests, that is the workers and the majority.

This chapter attempts to analytically rank some of the major factors that determined the direction and magnitude of inflation during the 1971-73 period; it thus also presents the broad outline of the economic policy applied. A complete study of this question would require a more detailed analysis of all the economic measures of the period, for in fact the inflationary process is a consequence of more general measures. More precisely, it is one element in the global economic evolution and is dialectically conditioned to the movement of the whole politico-economic system; that is to say, it exercises a greater or lesser influence over the latter while being simultaneously determined by it. Consequently, while inflation is a component of that general movement, isolatable inflationary factors do not exist which could 'explain' it, even when elements or factors exist within the general economic evolution that directly and immediately determine the direction and magnitude of the inflationary process. It is precisely this double relation that, while not permitting explanation through isolated factors, enables analytical ranking of a certain hierarchy of determinant factors within a general movement.

Constructing such an analytical ranking is equivalent to clarifying the direction of the global economic evolution during the 1971-73 period and to pointing out some of its principal internal relations.

1. INFLATION AND ECONOMIC DISEQUILIBRIA

Every inflationary process is a result and a component of a disequilibrium in the economic system and is, therefore, an aspect of its general movement. In global terms, two types of disequilibria in the economic system can be distinguished: *functional* and *structural*. Both, in given conditions, provoke a lack of proportionality in the determined relations in the system; this leads to adjustment, principally although not only through variations in the absolute and relative levels of prices. To the extent that this adjustment process acquires a more or less permanent character – through the persistence of the disequilibria that gave rise to it and through the induced development of new imbalances – the system is confronted with inflation.

In order to pinpoint the causes of Chilean inflation during the 1971-73 period it is necessary to briefly describe the difference between these two types of disequilibria. The inflationary process was the result of the joint presence of both types of disequilibria and the combination of their effects.

1. We shall define *structural disequilibria* as a breakdown, of greater or lesser magnitude, in an economic system as a result of the transformation of that system's basic structural parameters; that is to say, a breakdown in those supports upon which the entire organizational edifice of economic activity is based. These basic structural parameters are (or, at least, were in the Chilean economy) the following: (1) the type of ownership (private or social) of the means of production and the degree of concentration; (2) the direct and indirect economic role of the state and its class character (which class interests and social sectors does the state serve?). The direct economic role of the state consists in its participation in economic activity as a direct producer, i.e. owner and administrator of the means of production. The indirect economic role consists in its power to intervene (*fiscalidad*) in the secondary distribution of surplus value and to take action over the conditions of its realization (direct state market, development of the infrastructure, price policy, etc.). The basic determinant of the state's economic role is its class character: not the intensity of intervention, but the direction that it takes.[1] (3) The third structural parameter is the relation of the domestic economic sectors with the international economic system (dependence/independence). When basic parameters of an economic system are transformed as a result of a revolutionary process, the class character of the state is radically changed and the organization and construction of a new economic system is embarked upon; this creates conditions for rapidly establishing a new type of economic operation. The disequilibria arising from such transformation can be quickly eliminated by the emergence of new dominant relations, the more so when these are established on the short term. But even more important in eliminating these disequilibria is the triumph of a revolutionary process, for this allows new dominant political forces to exercise all the weight and authority of an 'extra-economic force': the political force for controlling the disequilibria created by the social transformation process. In this way, the transition period between the breakdown of the old system and the domination by the new structural relations can be faced with a good probability of success. Such has been the experience of countries in which socialist revolution has triumphed.

However, another type of transformation could appear in the structural parameters of an economic system: when, as was the case with UP in Chile, the transformation is carried out in a *gradual* manner and the classes and social sectors that instigate it do not hold all the power strings, the result is the breakdown of the existing system – the crumbling of its base supports and of its operational logic – without either a new structural base or economic order being created. If, during this process, a minimum degree of reorganization upon new bases is not achieved, the breakdown of the existing system is followed by the *general anarchization of economic activity*.

In such conditions the structural disequilibria become permanent, at least during the period in which political power remains ill-defined. Practically all norms of economic behaviour which have so far prevailed are destroyed, as are the criteria for judging capitalist economic activity. In particular, the previously dominant objective of maximizing the profit rate is transformed into the immediate maximization of the mass of profits, especially through the development of speculative capital. The price system loses all its value as a means of resource allocation and as a guideline for the choice which the capitalist must repeatedly make between consumption and investment; the degree of uncertainty surrounding private ownership – intensified by the political struggle that is part of the structural transformation process – wipes out in one stroke economic considerations based on the previous criteria. The development of speculative capital and the greatly reduced significance of the price system are definitively translated into accelerated monetary depreciation. Inflation – among other economic phenomena – appears as the inevitable, necessary consequence of the permanence of disequilibria and at the same time constitutes a decisive element in the anarchization of the economy.

2. The second type of disequilibria, which we have called *functional*, is of a different nature from the structural disequilibria described above. We shall define *functional disequilibria* as those proportional realignments in the relationships between economic variables determined within an economic system whose structural parameters are not subject to change. That is to say, we are dealing here with maladjustments within a system and not, as in the previous case, with the rupture of the system.

The structure of a given economic system, with a certain level of development in the productive forces, determines its operational relations, including its different agents' established norms of conduct. Thus, for example, for a given degree of concentration in private ownership of the means of production and movements of surpluses abroad, and for a given level and direction of state intervention in the secondary redistribution of surplus value, there corresponds a certain structure of distribution of national income and a more or less stable composition of global demand (between social sectors and types of products) etc., that circumscribe a certain productive profile for the economy. Global supply and demand interact, moulding the stable operational relations of that system, within which the 'normal' or 'typical' economic behaviour of the different agents are especially important.[2] Such functional relationships are expressed largely through the quantitative proportionality between the different economic variables, particularly through the price level and the price system, which is a central indicator of economic activity. Relations such as the volume of money supply and the volume of production, domestic production and the foreign trade flow, the state budget and the level of employment, etc., normally present an easily visible stability in a given economy, without necessarily implying the existence of a global economic equilibrium but rather, at most, the maximum degree of disequilibrium which is compatible with a certain level and form of operation of the system.

However, when such relationships between the different variables are abruptly broken down, adjustment to a new level tends to occur and it operates in the fastest way possible; that is, it begins with modifications in the price level and system. But, if breakdown conditions persist and the system does not have the necessary flexibility and adaptability, adjustment through prices becomes a permanent process. For example, an increase in the means of payment which is proportionately greater than the volume of production at nominal prices presupposes, *ceteris paribus*, a tendency towards a general rise in price levels. To the extent that this is gradually and relatively small, the process could be realized through marginal adjustments to the price system; that is to say, allowing for free play in the capacity of adaptation (flexibility) of the productive structure and/or of the monetary system. This is true in the case of a maladjustment compatible with a certain level and pattern of operation of the economy, as mentioned above. If, on the other hand, both the magnitude of the breakdown, and the speed with which it is produced, is significant, then the tendency towards a rise in the level of prices will also be of greater magnitude and velocity and, what is more important, the breakdown in relative prices will be appreciable, reflecting different degrees of inflexibility in the various branches and sectors of the economy. The subsequent process of readjustment to the price system (impelled, above all, by the struggle to recreate the conditions which equalize the average rate of profits between each sector) finds its expression in a new tendency towards a rise in the level of prices and so on. Depending on the persistence of the disequilibrating elements (in this example, the more than proportional increase in the money supply) and the capacity of adaptation of the productive structure, the rise in the price level can trigger either an explosive process or a process of increasingly minor and controllable fluctuations.

3. The level and type of operations of the economy is determined through its basic structure within certain margins; the economic structure sets a certain latitude for manoeuvre compatible with the parameters that most directly influence economic operation. For example, a particular economic structure based on concentration of private ownership of the means of production generates a type of income distribution that is also characterized by concentration. However, the greater or lesser degree of appropriation of income by

a restricted group can fluctuate within certain limits. What cannot possibly happen, without contradicting the structure of the system, is that the income distribution be forced – at the level of economy's operation – into significant and permanent evolution towards a pattern of equality of income distribution. In other words, a process of income redistribution will encounter insurmountable constraints if the structure of the system does not change; the limits of income distribution that are compatible with the concentration of ownership will constitute a brake for those distributive efforts that affect the economic structure.

It is clear that even though there are structural limits to the modification of those parameters which most directly influence the level and type of operation of the economy, a particular margin of manoeuvrability can also be counted on. Structural limits for the operation of the economy are not absolute; the operation always presents a greater or lesser degree of *relative autonomy* in the face of the system's structural characteristics. Hence there is the (restricted) possibility of manipulating the economic system by means of acting upon determined key parameters such as the fiscal budget, the exchange rate, interest rates, etc. – action that is normally confused with *the* economic policy. If the immediate causes of an inflationary process lie in functional disequilibria, then action at the level of the parameters that determine those disequilibria is an evident necessity; otherwise, the inflationary process will continue to develop and indeed will probably increase. At the same time, if the disequilibria are combined with pressures arising from the structure of the system, a single policy of instrumental manipulation will be ineffective and will have to be complemented by appropriate structural transformations.

Consequently, starting from a given degree of development in the contradictions of the economic system, every anti-inflationary policy has to be a *combination* of more or less accelerated transformations of the economic structure and action upon determined parameters of its operations.

It is necessary here to give some attention to the nature and scope of the concept of economic policy that must be used in any analysis of the UP Government. The traditional concept of economic policy as being equivalent to instrumental manipulation is manifestly inadequate (and erroneous) in describing the type of actions that were taken in Chile. In fact, the distinctive characteristic of Chilean economic policy during the 1971-73 period was that it entailed, *simultaneously and integrally*, a transformation of the basic structure of the economy and an accelerated modification of the pattern of economic operation.

If economic policy is considered to be limited, as is usual if a government manipulates certain parameters (the interest rate, fiscal deficit, or money supply), this implicitly supposes that the structural characteristics of the system are constant. It is not necessary to develop a long argument to demonstrate the purely ideological character of this concept and the class character (defending the interests of the dominant classes) of the practical actions that derive from it. In reality every economic policy, that is, direct and conscious action by the system of political domination and its institutions on the economy, contemplates two types of measures: those that have as their object the parameters that determine the level and pattern of operations, and those directed towards acting upon the basic structure of the economy. In the latter case, such action could be aimed at modification (which we shall call structural transformation[3]) or at protection and preservation of the structure. The fundamental difference between a revolutionary economy policy and a reformist one – which *a fortiori* is conservative – lies in the magnitude and nature (that is, the class character) of the action that each carries out on the basic structure of the economic system.

The economic policy of the UP Government was characterized, as we have said, by the integration into a single movement of those measures aimed at structural transformation and those aimed at changing the immediate determinants of economic operation; this integration gave the policy its uniqueness and indivisibility. The first official statements by the UP Government clearly outlined these aims, as did the documents that the UP teams of experts had drawn up before President Allende took office. For example, in October 1970 it was stated:

> It is obvious that the short-term economic programme has to be in line with the Basic Programme of Popular Unity, so that it represents a first stage towards the latter's effective fulfillment. In the Basic Programme are found both a political undertaking and an economic necessity. A traditional scheme for economic management, even on the pretext of overcoming immediate problems, would harm our pledge and would not offer effective solutions to our problems.... We cannot aim at a first stage of purely conventional measures as a preliminary step to economic recovery, nor can we aim at a second stage in which we would again take up the Basic Programme's proposals; on the contrary, from the beginning we have to cover political and economic demands simultaneously.[4]

This indivisibility represented the difference between the revolutionary character of the UP Government and the reformist experiences of the past.

The same concept of indivisibility was formulated with regard to the anti-inflationary policy. This was the necessary consequence of realizing that anti-inflationary measures formed an integral part of global economic policy. The former could only be applied in the framework of the latter, which is but a reflection of the objective phenomenon pointed out earlier that inflation is a result and a component of the overall movement of the economic system. This concept is summed up in the 'First Statement' which Minister of the Treasury Americo Zorrilla presented to the National Congress a few weeks after the UP Government took office: '...the general direction of the anti-inflationary struggle on the long term is to initiate in-depth transformations of the Chilean economy. We shall act...with all the instruments and in all the fields that may be necessary.' And he added: 'The anti-inflationary struggle is a fundamental aspect of the Government's economic policy. It permeates each and every one of its measures.'[5]

Because of the indivisible character of the economic policy, the aim was to act simultaneously on the structural and operational parameters. It was this simultaneous action which defined the essential nature of the anti-inflationary policy as a component of general policy, while always being subordinate to the total policy.

It is therefore impossible to discuss either the anti-inflationary policy or the evolution of price movements without referring to the overall economic situation. Since the transformation of the system's basic parameters constituted a dominant feature of the situation, any such discussion must necessarily deal with the nature and forms of the political struggle for the revolutionary transformation of Chilean society.

2. DETERMINANTS OF THE ECONOMIC EVOLUTION DURING 1971-73

The Chilean inflationary process developed within the framework of a general economic movement in which three key phenomena were preeminent: (1) the power struggle and the forms that it assumed; (2) the structural transformations that were initiated; (3) the economic policy aimed at transforming the economy's customary patterns of operation. Essentially, these phenomena were the final determinants of the Chilean inflationary process; hence it is necessary to describe them before discussing the specific forms in which they acted.

2.1. *The Power Struggle and its Direct Effects on the Economic System*

The principal determinant of the Chilean economy's evolution, in direct and indirect terms, was the intense struggle by a popular movement – the proletariat and their allies – to win political power, and the fierce defence by the bourgeoisie and imperialism of their dominant positions. *Without some explanation of that struggle and of the forms that it assumed it is impossible to comprehend the economic movement of the 1971-73 period*. Hence an initial difficulty in analyzing the inflationary process: we should begin with a comprehensive and detailed study of the political struggle which goes far beyond the limits of this chapter. Nonetheless, recognizing the unavoidable risk that any less comprehensive description may be difficult to understand or unclear in details, we shall attempt to describe the power confrontation's principal features and its more immediate effects on the Chilean economic system.[6]

The struggle to win power to bring about a revolutionary transformation in Chilean society goes back many decades in the country's political history. But in 1970, with UP's electoral triumph and the subsequent accession of the Allende Govenment, the form and urgency of that struggle changed radically. Gaining political power, as an immediately practical, urgent and unavoidable task, was implanted into the Chilean popular movement as the guiding principle behind its activities in all fields of social life. The objective of economic transformation particularly played an extraordinarily important role in the strategy for gaining power. Moreover, as of 3 November 1970 – the date on which the UP Government took office – the forms of political struggle changed substantially, setting their mark on the entire historical period that was about to begin.

A distinctive feature was that of taking over the executive branch of government, for the Chilean popular movement came to control and to be in a position to use a formidable power apparatus and the important instruments in it for the actual transformation of Chilean society. This control, which normally results from a triumphant revolutionary process, was *partially* obtained before the popular movement's definitive break with the existing system. By the same token, the accession of the UP Government signified *the rupture of the hegemonous character of the existing system of domination* and, consequently, a new orientation in the political struggle of the sectors that hitherto had maintained such hegemony: the big national bourgeoisie and imperialism. For these two sectors the change in direction implied a transition from the defence of a system to offensive action aimed at re-taking lost positions, with a view to re-establishing a hegemonous role in the system of political domination which was disintegrating.

Because of this single fact, the political struggle reached a magnitude and violence which had never before been known in Chile. Given that the survival of the system was at stake, and with it all the roles and privileges that the dominant sector had, all forms and areas of struggle were 'legitimate', even if it was necessary to assail certain components of the social system which never before had constituted a forum for political struggle. The most evident example was the domestic reactionaries' determination to smash the old Chilean democracy if necessary – as indeed it turned out to be. Thus, given the need to defend the global survival of the system it was worth gambling the whole stake, regardless of the partial damage that might be sustained on the way. Economic activities in particular, being of enormous significance as a key aspect of the political struggle, were the victims of this attitude.

When the popular movement took over the executive branch of government it was in a position, and under the obligation, to advance the revolutionary process, making use of the new instruments that were now within its reach. Given the character of the social structure, the revolutionary forces considered the large monopolistic and landowning bourgeoisie to be their principle enemy, together with U.S. imperialism and domination of foreign capital within the country. Consequently, the principal tasks at this stage, as expressed in the Government Programme, were: '...the replacement of the present economic structure, putting an end to the power of national and foreign monopolistic capital and of the great landed estates, so as to begin the construction of socialism...'.[7] Breaking down the economic structure was therefore the key factor in every subsequent advance. Dismantling the Chilean capitalist system and its corresponding structures of social and political domination constituted a fundamental element of the 'assault on power'.[8] In every pre-revolutionary situation, the degree of disintegration of the existing system, its material and ideological weakening, is a decisive factor for the triumph of the revolutionary process, even in the Chilean case with its very distinctive characteristics.

At the same time, the popular movement and the Government had to be capable of turning to its advantage the balance of political forces, and of winning over the vast majority of the population to its policy of revolutionary transformation. While such a condition is valid for every revolutionary process, it was especially significant in Chile. The UP was running the Government but had not gained all the power: the class character of the state continued to dominate and the repressive apparatus (the armed forces and the police) in particular was not under UP control. So long as this was so, it was vital that the possible use of repressive force against the Government be *politically neutralized*. It was of the greatest importance that neutralization be achieved by having a balance of forces that was favourable to the UP or, at least, fully opposed to a *coup d'état*, given that the military balance was unfavourable to the UP. Although the accession to government yielded formidable instruments to the UP, it also brought it serious responsibilities. Among these, obviously, was that of ensuring the operation of certain minimum conditions for reproduction of the economic system. This was extremely important for all the sectors, ranging from those in the opposition to those which were neutral, including those who supported the Government but were not resolutely committed to the revolutionary process. Among them the armed forces were undoubtedly the decisive factor. To the extent that the system of transformations could function with a minimum of coherency and along viable lines, the armed forces could support (or more precisely, could not oppose by force) the evolution of the process. To the extent that the evolution led to radical disarticulation or disintegration of economic and social life, however, the political forces – whether in or outside the armed forces – which until then had opposed a *coup d'état* but were not revolutionaries, would reverse their attitude. That is to say, they would oppose with all available means the actions of a Government that not only appeared incapable of facing up to a global crisis but, even worse, also appeared to be responsible for that crisis. *The anarchization* of the country's economic and social life turned the balance of forces against the UP in the sense that it eliminated the political conditions which until then had made it possible to rule out the use of force.

In other words, the revolutionary movement was interested in accelerating the disintegration of the system while at the same time strengthening the power alternative which it represented. The opposition, however, was interested in exactly the reverse, that is transforming the disintegration of the system into pure anarchy, into a development that must inevitably lead to political isolation of the UP in the face of a solution by force which that anarchization made necessary.

The Chilean economy was a key battleground in developing these tendencies towards disintegration and anarchization. Neither the Government nor the opposition doubted that the evolution of the economic situation was of the utmost importance in the development and conclusion of the political struggle. If the disintegration of the existing economic structure were accompanied by the gradual consolidation of a new organization of economic activities, then optimal material conditions would be created for developing and strengthening the popular power alternative. If disintegration was transformed into generalized anarchy, conditions would be created under which the balance of forces could be turned against the Government, wiping out UP's political ability to neutralize the use of repressive force.

It is therefore valid to contend that *the economy was simultaneously a backdrop and a battlefield for political struggle*. The outcome in the balance of forces and, with it, the solution to the power struggle depended largely on the forms taken by the evolution of the economy.[9]

All this enables us to more easily understand the immediacy, amplitude and effects of political actions which were *directly and indirectly* expressed as economic actions (if it is still meaningful to maintain this dichotomy). It is not necessary here to give details of the many examples of such actions, particularly since they will appear throughout the following analysis. It is sufficient to mention the structural transformations carried out by the Government, the magnitude and intensity of U.S. imperialism's reaction in directly economic terms (trade fluctuations, the financial freeze, etc.), and the relentless economic action of the national bourgeoisie. The list of political actions is long: the near collapse in private capital, including reinvestment; the pillaging and subsequent abandonment of businesses; the flight of foreign currency; unbridled price speculation; cornering of the market in manufactured goods and raw materials, and the breakdown in the distribution systems of numerous black markets; the systematic use of enormous masses of speculative capital and foreign funds; direct sabotage of production and of the communication infrastructure, energy, roads, etc. What better example of these directly economic political actions is there than the two employers' lock-outs in October 1972 and between July and September 1973!

To sum up, it is impossible to understand the movement of the Chilean economy between 1971 and 1973, and *a fortiori* of the inflationary process, if we do not bear in mind the effects brought about by the struggle for political power. During 1971-73 a situation was created which we have defined as one of structural disequilibria, further worsened by conscious political action by the national bourgeoisie and imperialism in promoting the complete anarchization of the economic system. This was the fundamental cause of inflation in

Chile and the basic explanatory factor in the overall cycle of economic events during this period.

What strictly economic factors made these tendencies materialize? In what more specific forms did they facilitate the acceleration of inflation? Before answering these and other questions, it is necessary to point out two other principal factors that influenced the evolution of the Chilean economy.

2.2. *Structural Transformations*

The UP Programme consisted of realizing a combination of structural transformations whose nucleus was nationalization of the major domestic and foreign monopolies in practically all sectors and branches of economic activity. It is unnecessary to cite the Programme's well known propositions here: in synthesis, it proposed nationalization of basic wealth, mainly under the control of foreign imperialist capital in the major industrial monopolies, the banks and the entire financial sector, furthering of in-depth agrarian reform, nationalization of infrastructural sectors, of foreign trade, etc. In other words, it proposed an attack on private ownership of the means of production of such magnitude that the state sector had to become the dominant sector of the economy, as much through its direct control of strategic activities as through the (planned) type of relations which it maintained with the private sector, as well as through the development of an area of mixed ownership. In reality, a much more circumscribed attack on the basic pillar of the system – private ownership of the means of production – would have been sufficient to break down the economic organization which was prevalent at the time. In practice, the transition from private enterprise to state control extended further than the limits fixed in the Basic Programme, even though many of the large enterprises marked out for that sector were not actually transferred to the state.

In this transformation process two objectives were to be fulfilled: elimination of private ownership of the strategic sectors, and the dismantling of the material bases of the country's dependence on foreign capital and the international system of domination. Private ownership and dependence, two structural aspects of the system, were subjected to the strongest attack ever experienced in Chile, thus producing the disintegration of the existing system in practical terms.

Everything considered, although the dismantling process may have advanced at a fairly appreciable speed despite legal restrictions imposed by the judiciary under pressure from the opposition, the process of setting up and operating the state sector took a very different course. In effect, this sector never managed to entail a functional unity of a new type, nor was it effectively transformed into the dominant sector of the economy in the sense laid down in the UP Programme. Only from the quantitative viewpoint were the nationalized enterprises dominant in some sectors and branches. This was the case in mining, banking, communications and energy, and foreign trade; but this quantative domination was not achieved in the manufacturing industries, in the construction business, in commerce, in transport, and in the other service branches.

The truly decisive factor in this process was the inability to achieve a new type of operation within the state sector and, more important, to establish effective domination over the private sector. To play its role effectively, the state sector needed to ensure that at least two basic conditions were fulfilled: (1) effective and detailed planning of the functioning of each of its units and of the relations that were established between them; and (2) the introduction of a new form of management and control of those enterprises based on direct workers' participation. The objective of the state should have been to establish conditions that guaranteed the social orientation of the different economic units according to the general interests of UP, while also safeguarding their economic efficiency. Workers' participation was an important mechanism in developing and strengthening the popular power alternative and the route towards change in capitalist production relationships. Undoubtedly, workers' participation advanced more rapidly than state sector planning; this disequilibrium also seriously limited the effectiveness and extent of participation, which in certain cases was transformed into yet another bureaucratic hindrance to management of the state sector.[10]

The inability to adequately meet these two fundamental requirements for the state sector's operation, together with a series of restrictions of the economic policy, which will be analyzed later, resulted in a completely different type of economic behaviour. Actually, except in the individual cases of some productive units, the state sector did not play its envisaged role as collector of surpluses, did not achieve harmonious and coordinated internal operation, and did not serve as an instrument for controlling the private sector.

Through deficit financing, provoked as much by the fall in productivity and increases in costs (reflections to a great extent of the economy's internal disorganization) as by the price policy that was pursued, the state sector acted as a mechanism for the net transfer of surpluses *to* the private sector. The public sector deficit and the substantial expansion of internal credit implied a disproportionate increase in the means of payment which was rapidly transferred to the private sector, thus helping to augment the mass of speculative capital and the consequent inflationary pressures. This was the principal mechanism that permitted the emergence of many of the tendencies outlined above.

The state sector's behaviour was undoubtedly influenced by the fact that the capitalists stripped their enterprises in the material and financial sense before these could be transferred to state control; moreover, the agrarian reform process was hampered by restrictions that maintained the right of landowners to keep the best lands for themselves and impeded the expropriation of animals and machinery, etc. In this sense the anarchic character of the incorporation of enterprises into the state sector was important, for many incorporations had no economic significance except that of generating additional pressure on financing the public sector and increasing the complexity of managing of the APS.

A direct consequence of the lack of planning in the state sector's operations was its inability to dominate and guide the economic operation of the private sector. Relations between the state and private enterprises were individual, unsystematic and took place without any efficient general guidance from transaction to transaction, although the state sector had many instruments that should have enabled strict control of private companies. Had monopolistic control of certain intermediate inputs (iron, cement, etc.), energy resources, the operations of foreign trade, credit, etc. been utilized in a coordinated and planned fashion, it would have been sufficient to guarantee the most detailed control of private sector production. Some very well known examples of this include the canning industry (where the state monopoly in tin plate was decisive), the clothing companies (textile monopoly), the construction firms (iron and cement), and so on. These were never really under state control – despite the existence of all the necessary conditions – until the moment when they had to be requisitioned or audited. A global effect of the state sector's extension under these conditions was the net transfer of surpluses to the private sector which enjoyed a very extensive freedom of action, in view of the fact that its economic behaviour – directly determined by the political struggle and the process of structural transformation – broke not only with 'capitalist rationality'[11] but also with all the juridico-economic norms prevailing in the country. Speculation and black markets were the principal forms of expressing this freedom (particularly in commerce); they were also the fundamental activities towards which resources produced by the state sector, which was deficient in revenue, were directed. Inflationary pressures and supply problems thus expressed weaknesses in the structural transformation process within the new type of state sector, both in its internal operations and in its relations with the private sector.

2.3. *Changing the Customary Patterns of Economic Operation*

The third determinant factor in the economic movement during the 1971-73 period was the content and direction of the Government's economic policy regarding the most immediately determinant operational parameters of the level of economic activity.

This new direction in economic policy could be condensed into the catch phrase: 'solve the immediate problem of the large majority'; it was translated into a programme which, with the exception of the simultaneous structural transformation, could be classified as a Keynesian short-term reactivation plan for the benefit of the popular sectors. Its objective was to sharply increase the level of economic activity by rapidly raising global demand, on the basis of income redistribution in favour of the most deprived sectors of the population; a compensating global increase in supply was expected from underused productive capacity, the reserve labour force and existing foreign currency holdings.

Under such conditions, and using the available resources to its advantage, the Government's economic policy centred on increasing the workers' real income, rapidly absorbing underemployment and facilitating – through the free play of monetary, foreign and fiscal policy – the expansion of productive activity resulting from the increase in global demand. The whole policy was formulated within the framework of firm control of price movements in order to guarantee a real increase in workers' income and to oblige capitalists to lower their average profit rate, while maintaining or increasing absolute overall profits through the expected increase in production.

The results of this policy became apparent in the first months of 1971. The main effects were measured in terms of the central objectives: for example, production began to increase, underemployment diminished, popular consumption began to expand rapidly, etc. The quantitative results of this policy will be described later; for the moment we are interested in its general significance, the restrictions it subsequently faced and its social orientation. With respect to policy orientation there can be no doubt that its aims and achievements were in defence of the workers and the most rapid solution possible of their main problems. All UP Government actions – ranging from an incomes policy that implied real wage increases, to broadening and stabilizing employment, to a policy for housing, health, education, etc. that corresponded to both more immediate and long-term needs – were directed to serve class interests that were new to the country. Stated in more general terms, this policy implied strong pressure to change the customary *modus operandi* of the Chilean economy. The old 'concentrated and exclusive' pattern was substituted by exactly the opposite: redistribution of incomes, economic expansion, workers' participation not only in the fruits but in the control of their own productive activity. The UP Government thus brought about a substantial break with the traditional pattern of economic operations.

All these changes in the operation and direction of the economy could not be made without serious tension and contradictions being provoked between the structure and operation of the economy; this was expressed fundamentally as the *need to modify the mechanisms by which generated surpluses were collected and allocated*. In effect, unless such mechanisms were changed, that is, unless the Government and the workers were allowed to increase the amount of surplus collected, the stability and effectiveness of the expansive policy would be questionable. Success required that more resources be allocated to certain key tasks, among which changing the productive profile and expanding the 'social programmes' needed to be stressed.

The national economy's productive pattern had been shaped during many decades of activity aimed at satisfying the concentrated demand of small high income groups; that is, it was a type of demand that was quantitatively restricted and qualitatively diversified. Under the new conditions, the demand that had to be satisfied was oriented towards the less diverse basic consumption needs of the new sector whose increased incomes were beginning to lead to a quantitatively much more important demand in certain sectors (food, clothing, etc.). At the same time, the new political context required rapid solutions to the traditional problems of health, housing education, etc. These problems had implications for the productive structure which were the same as those previously mentioned: they required a very appreciable amount of short-term resources. The same short-term urgency existed in the need to change the productive profile of the economy, which implied: (1) an immediate change in the orientation of each productive unit; and (2) an immediate change in the relative availability of resources between different sectors (credit, raw materials, technical assistance, etc.). For example, if it became evident that the pattern of accumulation had to change in the medium and long run, then reinvestment, eliminating bottlenecks, broadening and modernization of the productive apparatus, etc. would from the very beginning have to be compatible with the new criteria.

The failure to bring about these changes led to the development of global and sectoral disequilibria which were proportionally related to the strength of the redistributive process and to the increased (individual and social) consumption by lower income groups; that is to say, strong inflationary pressures developed. Hence the policy of expansion in favour of the people needed to simultaneously transform the mechanisms for the collection and allocation of surpluses generated in the national economy. It required mainly, therefore: (1) the development of the state sector of the economy such that that sector would not only generate an increasing amount of surplus, but would also secure part of the surplus generated in the mixed and private sectors; in other words, the state sector's transformation into a dominant sector; (2) the elimination of the transfer of surplus abroad, which involved breaking down the existing dependency and setting up a new scheme of international economic relationships; (3) an increase in efficiency and a change in directing the mechanisms for secondary redistribution of surplus principally through the taxation system and subsidized prices. All these entailed a modification in the economic role.

To sum up, a policy whose aim was to benefit the people and expand their power demanded a transformation in the basic structural parameters of the Chilean economic system. The need to closely coordinate this transformation with implementation of this policy was prerequisite to avoiding the emergence and development of disequilibria in the system's operation and, with it, of inflationary pressures. The element of pressure implicit in the policy to expand the people's power was a third key determinant in the economic events of the period, especially since the transformation process, in terms of both its speed and its content, was lagging behind what was needed in this situation.

The combined results of these three phenomena was the development and expansion of the inflationary process, after an initial period of reduction in the rate of price increases. The two following sections present first a quantitative description of this inflationary process and thereafter a description of the main economic forms that those general phenomena assumed.

3. A DESCRIPTION OF THE INFLATIONARY PROCESS DURING 1971-73

The available statistics on Chilean inflation do not have the detail and reliability that would allow precise analysis of all the variations, but they are in the main sufficient to show the principal inflationary tendencies and magnitudes. Since that is the aim of this chapter, the use of the available indicators will suffice for our analysis.

The two basic indicators of price movements in Chile are the *Consumer Price Index* (CPI) and the Wholesale Price Index (WPI); while there are other indices of sectoral price trends (e.g. the building industry price index) they are of more limited usefulness. The aim of the CPI is, as its name indicates, to measure the level of prices at which people make their current expenditures in a given period; that is to say, it is supposed to measure the 'cost of living' of the 'average consumer'. The WPI is designed to measure the level of prices at which inter-industry transactions are made, as distinct from final consumption by individuals. Technically, both are Laspeyres indices, that is they measure price variations with respect to a constant structure of consumption in a base year. Therefore, variations in these indicators show the relation between prices at a given moment and those of a base year of comparison, assuming no change in the structure of expenditure, which is doubtful in periods of rapid economic change. As to the volume of the transactions covered, the WPI covers approximately two thirds of the total and the CPI the remaining third;[12] however, the importance of the latter is much greater from two points of view.

In the first place the CPI, by measuring the cost of living, is a principal indicator of the effects of the inflationary process on living conditions of the population, on movements in real income of workers, and on the effectiveness of incomes policy, etc. In other words, it is used as a principal indicator when studying economic policy. In the second place, in Chile the CPI acquired an economic role of great importance that went far beyond that of a simple statistical indicator: in fact, its variations were transformed into an objective economic phenomenon. The CPI came in practice to set the minimum required limits for the readjustment policy, for the revaluation of assets, etc., and for all those variables susceptible to the effects of inflation, without the Government being able to break those limits. A simple statistical indicator, based on a sampling, with all its defects and limitations, was transformed into an objective constraint on certain measures of economic policy. Moreover, the technical nature and mode of calculation of this index were fixed by law; hence, any attempt to modify it in order to be able to more adequately measure the movement of prices under the new conditions had to be approved by the National Congress that was controlled by the opposition. Naturally, this was not achieved. Yet to carry out a discriminatory wage and price policy, with the object of improving the living standards of low income groups and collecting surpluses for the state, it was necessary to modify the bases for calculating the CPI, giving greater consideration to movements in prices of popular consumption articles and less consideration to those of luxury goods.[13] To the extent that this change was not achieved, the CPI continued to provide information about the average consumer only, so that the economic policy's discriminatory capacity was restricted to the results of a limited statistical indicator.

As we have said, the reliability of CPI values throughout the 1971-73 period, and above all in its final phase, merits some discussion. In synthesis, given the type and method of calculation of this index, and its characteristic 'social average', the CPI showed general trends but hardly described detailed price movements. In fact, during periods of accelerated inflation and of important transformation in the economy, the structure of people's expenditure, the 'basket of goods', has a tendency to change rapidly. Even if one accepts that the relative distribution of incomes did not vary appreciably, the single fact of a generalized rise in consumption (e.g. to the detriment of investment) brings about changes in expenditure. Under these conditions, which were present in the Chilean economy, the use of an index based upon a predetermined constant structure of expenditure in a previous period (the base year of the CPI was 1969) necessarily limits the reliability of the resultant values. The definition of the 'average consumer' varied with time, but the index did not measure it.

In short, the estimation of the prices of each commodity or service that formed part of the index was compromised as the inflationary process accelerated, as speculation and the black market grew, and as the problems of partial supply became more generalized. Since the price of each product was determined by direct observations of a restricted sample, it was very probable that under the conditions described generalizations grew increasingly less valid. The great distortions provoked by speculation and by those who were cornering markets could not but restrict the validity of sample values for the totality of effective prices in each zone or region; moreover, this restriction differed for each type of product.[14]

Given the type of phenomena indicated, it is reasonable to assume that the CPI did not represent the trends in the general movement of prices and underestimated their magnitude, especially from the middle of 1972 onwards when the speed of the inflationary process was greater and when market cornering and speculation became a general and permanent phenomena.

This conclusion is reaffirmed if one considers the different estimates of the general level of consumer prices, which are indicated in Table 9.1. The trend described by all the estimates is one of growth in the inflation rate at an increasing rate, reaching extraordinarily elevated magnitudes in 1973. Until 1972, with small variations, the different estimates are quantitatively comparable, with the exception of those given by the World Bank, which in reality do not directly measure the level of prices but rather the variations in monetary supply, adjusted through variations of the gross product and through the velocity of circulation. In 1973, however, the quantities in question were quite different. This is due, on the one hand, to differences in estimated price increases between January and August of that year, that is to say, the period for which estimates have been made – these estimates being more relevant and valid. On the other hand, these different estimates reflect the upward movement which, beginning in September 1973, was caused by the policy of free prices applied by the military junta. The real inflationary explosion between September and December 1973 hinders a relatively homogenous calculation of the magnitude of price increases throughout 1973. Hence it is preferable, whenever possible, to refer to the values of the index up to August 1973, accepting that they probably undervalue the rise in prices but at least are relatively more comparable to previous magnitudes.[15]

Once these assumptions and limitations are accepted, it is possible to examine the general tendencies of the Chilean inflationary process in more detail.

1. It is worth pointing out, first, that during the UP Government's first year there was an appreciable reduction on the previous inflation rates and, even more significant, the accelerating inflationary trend was broken. In 1971 the average annual rate of increase in the CPI was 20.1%; in previous years the respective values had been: 1967, 18.1%; 1968, 26.6%; 1969, 30.7%; 1970, 32.5%.

Naturally, these figures hide political and economic realities which are fundamentally different. From this difference there usually arises an observation which should be kept in mind: while it is certain that the rate of price increases diminished in 1971, this was achieved thanks to an 'artificial' policy of controls and of use of international reserves which increased global disequilibria, the consequence of which was inevitably the subsequent reactivation of inflation. Those who maintain this point of view argue that the policy applied was limited to changing the forms in which inflation was expressed but did not halt its development. Put differently, an inflationary process is expressed not only through a rise in the price level but also in other ways, such as financing imports by spending reserves, or transitory changes in the velocity of money circulation that for a certain time absorb a disproportionate growth of the means of payment, etc. Although this kind of argument is pertinent, especially in the case of Chile, where these phenomena were in fact present, it is necessary to make two precise observations in this respect. In the first place, the *form* in which economic disequilibria become manifest consists in a rise of the general price level and changes in the system of prices; that is to say, the inflationary process as such provokes definite economic effects, different from those arising out of the *form* of, for example, a fall in international reserves. The behaviour and forecasts of economic agents, the profit rate in the different sectors, the distribution of personal income, etc. are affected in a different way depending on the form in which economic disequilibria are expressed. In general terms it can be said that, as components of a global economic movement, the manifest forms of economic disequilibria have different effects on its subsequent evolution; it is incorrect to extend the concept of inflation further than rises in the price level and changes in price relationships. The other forms of disequilibria can give rise to inflationary pressures or, if one likes, to a pre-inflationary situation, which is different (because of its effects) from an open inflationary process. In the second place, a study of the causes of the creation of inflationary pressures and of their *transformation* into an open inflationary process clarifies the movement of economic contradictions. Thus in the case of Chile, the causes of the transformation of inflationary pressures into price level rises opens a discussion of the causes which determined that evolution.

2. A second characteristic of the inflationary process during the period of UP Government was that, after the break with the tendencies already indicated, the price level rose increasingly until it reached extraordinarily elevated magnitudes, a probable prelude to a hyper-inflationary process. In Tables 9.2 and 9.4 the most significant magnitudes have been calculated as in Table 9.1 (see also Tables VI and VII of the Statistical Appendix following Chapter 2). In brief, the rate of the average increase in consumer prices was, in 1972, approximately four times greater than in 1971; between January and August 1973 it was 5.8 times greater than in the same period in 1972. The rate of average increase in the January-August period of each year was, respectively, 12.7% in 1971, 63.5% in 1972 and 150.5% in 1973. The whole sale price index showed similar behaviour (see Table 9.4). The extraordinary magnitude of the price increases, particularly during the last phases, can be appreciated by examining the tables.

3. A third characteristic of Chilean inflation was that the process of price increases comprised a series of fluctuations, the most important of which took place in August-October 1972 and in the months after March 1973, as shown in Table 9.3 and Figure 9.1. This type of price growth shows the effects of the anarchization of economic activities, effects more important than *those derived from a steadily growing rate of increase in the price level instead of growth at an increasing rate*, as was the case in Chile. In particular its effects are felt in a major *breakdown* of the relative price system.

It is possible to delimit certain stages and phases in the Chilean inflationary process (see Figure 9.1) by this type of fluctuation. The first stage extended from the beginning of 1971 to the middle of 1972 and ended in the most important inflationary explosion of the period. Within the first stage two phases can be distinguished; phase I was from the beginning of 1971 to September-October 1971; phase II was from November 1971 to July 1972. Phase I had relatively small variations in the price growth and gentle fluctuations in its development. During phase II the magnitude of the variations more than doubled and the amplitude of the fluctuations became greater. This first general stage reflects a certain success, although with increasing difficulty, in the policy of containing price increases. It can be said that during this stage the inflationary process was kept within certain limits which were comparable with its rate in the years immediately prior to the UP Government.

The second general stage extended from August 1972 to August 1973, the period during which inflation reached very high rates and underwent violent fluctuations. A third, fourth and fifth phase can be distinguished during this stage. Phase III was one of pure inflationary explosion between August and October 1972, the period during which the greatest price increases were produced. Phase IV extended from November 1972 to March 1973 and had an even higher level of price variation than in the first and second phases, but much lower than that reached in the third. During this fourth phase fluctuations in the rate of price increases were very pronounced. Finally, during phase V, which extended from April to August 1973, the very high rate of price increases continued. This was a phase of real 'sustained inflationary explosion' which one could suppose constituted the first manifestation of hyperinflation parallel to the intensification of the political struggle. As will be seen in section 4, the different phases coincided with important moments in the political situation and in economic policy. The following simple average monthly price variations characterized each phase:

Phase I	(January to October 1971)	1.48%
Phase II	(November 1971 to July 1972)	3.87%
Phase III	(August to October 1972)	20.00%
Phase IV	(November 1972 to March 1973)	6.90%
Phase V	(April to August 1973)	15.50%

4. A fourth general characteristic of the movement in prices, common to every inflationary process, was the distortion of the system of relative prices. This phenomenon was quite intense in Chile due to the simultaneous existence of a very extensive speculative movement and Government control and stipulation which, though effective, was uneven in the different sectors, branches and specific products. The examples of extreme distortion in relative prices are many and well known; by way of illustration we can quote a few which appeared above all from the middle of 1972 onwards, when inflation and specu-

lation increased. The price of a paperbag for cement, for example, became higher than that of the cement it contained; the price of the bag of cement became lower than that of a bag of sand, so that building was cheaper with pure cement than with concrete mixes. At times it was more economical to tie parcels with copper wire than with string, or to use wheat and milk as animal feed than to buy normal fodder; the price of a kilogram of bread was similar to that of an egg, etc. These examples, which could be endlessly multiplied, illustrate the degree of distortion in the price system and, undoubtedly, the enormous variations in profit rates among different branches and sectors. The efforts, whether through laws or otherwise, to permanently readjust the price system (and/or take advantage of existing distortions) in order to realign the rate of profit (and/or increase extra surpluses) constituted a permanent and significant inflationary impulse.

One of the most general expressions of this distortion was the difference between selling prices in the private sector and those in the state sector. This difference was due mainly to greater Government control over the prices in the APS and stricter adherence by firms in this sector (for example, in electricity, telephones, steel, cement, etc.) to official price policy. Hence, the difference of the relative price structure in the state from that of the private sector was an added help in transferring surpluses from the state to the private sector. This distortion provoked, when attempts were made to overcome it, real inflationary explosions.

Equally, the different components of the price indices (see Table 9.4 and Table II of the Statistical Appendix following Chapter 2) showed notable variations in their growth rates and, therefore, in their internal structure. These differences were as much a result of differing demand, arising from the global increase in consumption, as of variations in speculative pressures under conditions of supply difficulties. It is impossible to quantify the degree to which each of these factors influenced the differences: we are interested here only in pointing out the existence of the phenomenon. For example, the differing evolution of the prices of foodstuffs and clothing products in the CPI is notable. While in 1971 their evolution was comparable, in 1972 foodstuffs grew more rapidly than clothing; in 1973 (until August) this relation was inverted through the extraordinarily rapid increase in the price of clothing products. This suggests that speculative movements and the needs of the official policy of readjusting relative prices varied, in the different phases, among different branches and sectors, according to sectoral inflationary expectations and the prevailing supply situation.

Finally, while in 1971 and 1972 the CPI and the WPI showed comparable rates of growth, in the eight months preceding August 1973 the increase of consumer prices was much more rapid than the increase of wholesale prices. This difference can only be explained if we know the extent of speculation in the final phases of the UP Government and the size of the black market.

Both phenomena tended to speed up consumer price increases, while their impact on wholesale transactions was weaker, if only because a good part of the latter was determined by the prices and official tariffs of the state services. The difference in growth in both indices reflects the movement of speculative capital.[16]

4. THE DYNAMICS OF ECONOMIC DISEQUILIBRIA

In this section we present an overall view, necessarily schematic and summarized, of the application of the UP Government's economic policy and of the development of the inflationary process, bringing together the diverse phenomena already mentioned and describing the main issues.

We shall confine ourselves chiefly to 1971 for two reasons. In the first place, 1971 was the only year in which the economic policy had a certain degree of coherency in its conception and, more important, of consequence in its application. In the second place, with particular exceptions, the contradictions and tendencies that were to dominate economic developments during the period of UP Government were already manifest in 1971, to a greater or lesser extent.[17]

The economic policy applied during the first months of the UP Government had a dual aim of beginning a process of structural transformation and solving the most immediate problems of the majority of the population, both aims being intimately linked and mutually conditioned. Given that the Chilean economy was at that time going through an acute deflationary crisis (a product of the tendencies of the system's mode of operation and of a very tense pre- and post-electoral political climate), solving the most important short-term problems required a sharp rise in the level of economic activity and a simultaneous change in the social sector's patterns of participating in and benefitting from the fruits of that activity. This was an expansionary policy directed to increasing the benefit to the people.

The question of whether it would be possible to apply this policy depended on whether the will, and the necessary conditions, to carry out such a policy existed, that is to say, on whether the Government could gain control through new political and social forces whose class orientation was different from that of all previous Governments. As regards the specific conditions which the short-term expansional policy needed, it was based on the increasing use of productive reserves generated by the crisis situation. In the main, these reserves consisted in significant unused, installed productive capacity, the availability in abundance of a labour force, and a volume of international reserves that would finance more imports in anticipation of an increase in exports. In addition to the traditional and familiar latifundista underuse of land, the industrial manufacturing enterprises operated on the average at less than 70% of capacity, and in certain branches at less than 50%; the total unused labour force amounted to around 200,000 people; net international reserves at the end of 1970 totalled $343 million, equivalent to more than a third of annual imports. Naturally these are only estimates, but taken together they reaffirm the existence of immediately usable productive reserves when the UP Government took office. Such reserves or potentialities certainly did not constitute a 'legacy' which the UP Government had received and could use at its own free disposal. They were a result of the economic crisis and consequently were committed on the short term to the extent that the new economic policy was successful, or that the pressures that until then had been contained were unleashed against them. It is sufficient to compare the level of international reserves with the volume of external debt or with the amount of capital available on the short term in order to comprehend their true nature. In general, these 'resources' allowed the Government to embark at least technically upon an expansion of the level of economic activity.

Under these conditions, the economic policy was defined around two main axes: on the one hand, increase and change in the structure of global demand and, on the other hand, specific programmes designed to increase the flexibility of internal support and to facilitate greater use of productive resources. The sectoral and global equilibrium of supply and demand, as well as the objective of income redistribution, depended directly on the variations in the price system, which then became a key element in the expansionary policy.

Given the levels of consumption (or of underconsumption) by the popular sectors, the immense majority of the population, any income redistribution in their favour had to be translated into an expansion of global demand directly caused and indirectly induced by the increase of consumption. Starting from this basis, the Government initiated a process of increasing the real income of those sectors, acting mainly through three specific policies: incomes, prices and employment.

The *incomes policy* embodied in Law 17416, passed in early 1971, consisted of effecting readjustments in wages and salaries which were fully equivalent to the rise in the cost of living in 1970 (34.9%) for all workers not subject to special agreements (settlements, collective contracts, or labour tribunal rulings); in practice, these workers considered this amount of readjustment as a minimum in wage negotiations. For remunerations lower than the minimal living wage,[18] the readjustment had to be increased by five scales on the salary 'ladder', thus amounting to 39.9%, and for those groups earning between 1 and 2 living wages the amount of readjustment was increased by 3 salary scales, amounting to a 37.9% readjustment for all workers in this income bracket. The minimum wage was increased by 66%. Similarly, the wage policy included a more than proportional increase in family assistance benefits for low income groups, initiating a process of levelling off incomes, thus eliminating disparities between different supplementary schemes. In this way, the family allowances of public officials were increased by 76.5%, those of the armed forces and customs officers by 112.5%, and the working class allowances were increased 100%. The treatment of retirement pensions, social security and other similar payments followed comparable lines. Furthermore, the Government obtained exceptional means for benefitting public officials in the so-called 'ignored services': those which in previous years had seen their incomes diminish in relation to the average for state officials. In synthesis, this policy was designed to carry out a general readjustment in wages and additional loans which would compensate for the losses in purchasing power due to the previous year's inflation, ensuring a proportionally higher readjustment for the lower income groups.

An essential complement to the incomes policy was *control of the rise in prices*. While the readjustment of wage differentials enabled a redistribution within the salaried sectors, when combined with price control it signified a drop in the average rate of profit and, therefore, a net redistribution in favour of salary earners. Naturally it was not just a question of control of the general level of prices but also of their relative structure; in particular, the price of foodstuffs and other popular consumption goods and services had to be especially watched so as to safeguard the workers' real income gains.

The third important element in the expansion of global demand and in redistribution was the *employment policy*. The single fact of incorporating people who had been previously unemployed *en masse* into the active labour force, under the salary and price conditions described above, led to an increase in global demand. Moreover, in itself a reduction in unemployment constituted a central objective of economic policy; at the beginning of 1971 the great number of unemployed was a principal social and political problem (8.3% in December in greater Santiago).[19] The absorption of the unemployed was based on the general rise in the level of economic activity resulting from the expansionary policy, and on the effects of the 'mobilization programmes' described below. Among these programmes, those relating to the construction sector (housing and public works) were the most important for this objective, given the intensity of labour force engaged and the multiplier effect on the whole economy. In 1971, the increase in the amount of construction accounted for practically all of the increase in capital expenditure by the Treasury.

The *mobilization programmes* served to make domestic supply more flexible and gave a direct impetus to the rise in the level of economic activity. Five main mobilizing programmes were set up: housing, public works, industrial, agrarian, and export promotion.

The *housing programme* consisted of accelerated building of low-price housing and emergency housing, social centres, town planning, etc. In order to increase the multiplier effect on the industrial sector, plans were made to equip houses with minimal, standardized furniture, facilities, etc. This programme was complemented with a series of measures designed to price houses within the reach of lower income groups with the aid of credits, lowering the value of the installments and the level of interest, and also suspending the automatic readjustability of these payments. The public works programme ensured the growth of the activities of that sector through increases in public spending and a change in its structure. It tried to make the development of minor public works (irrigation, sewage, drinking water, etc.) a priority that would fulfil a double purpose: use of a greater proportion of the labour force, leading to an immediate increase in production (e.g. irrigation works) and a solution to serious problems in the popular sectors (e.g. drinking water).

The objective of the *industrial reactivation* programme was to complement, in the manufacturing industry, the expansionary effects of the population's demand and to increase construction activities. It dealt principally with such measures as the banking system's credit support for industrial firms and the establishment of 'production contracts', that is, contracts guaranteeing the buying and selling of products and intermediate goods between private and state firms or directly between the former and the Government. Similarly, in the agrarian sector a policy of technical and financial support was set up which, within the framework of the agrarian reform already in progress, would facilitate an increase of production in the reformed and private sectors. In addition, measures were planned to ensure that the state could buy from farmers at official prices in order that their profitability might be raised without affecting consumer prices, thus reducing excessive wholesale margins.

Finally, there was the *export incentives* programme (the weakest and least successful of all the mobilization programmes), based mainly on a new policy of opening up international economic relations and state monopolization of foreign trade operations. It was proposed to develop the capacity of the state to buy products intended for export in order to safeguard domestic product prices independently of the exchange rate which, due to the impact on internal price levels, the Government had to keep under control.

In sum, the programmes were designed to directly mobilize underused productive resources, mainly in the construction sector, and to ensure the flexibility of domestic supply, especially by mobilizing public financial resources. Together with these programmes, or forming part of them, foreign trade and monetary policies played a fundamental role.

The increase in *imports* and the change in their structure, which was immediately possible thanks to the volume of international reserves, constituted the key variable for increasing domestic supply at a rate comparable to the expansion of demand. There were various reasons for the decisive role of imports. In the first place, the Chilean economy had a high raw material and intermediate product import rate, such that any more or less rapid increase in domestic activity, particularly in the industrial sector, required a rapid increase of imports. Second, imports of foodstuffs were indispensable to satisfy the people's needs, even when agricultural production increased substantially. In

1971, with depressed consumer demand affecting much of the population, imports of foodstuffs reached $170 million, a reflection of the stagnation in agricultural production that had been evident for many years. In fact, given the mass-oriented expansionary policy, the Government's anti-inflationary drive depended largely on the equilibrium between the supply and demand of the basic consumer goods, especially foodstuffs. If the objective was to redistribute income towards groups whose basic spending was on foodstuffs, then the prices of those products served as the key to any policy of expansion through domestic demand. Third, the foreseeable change in the structure of global demand and the modifications which had to be introduced in the domestic productive profile required a short-term industrial adjustment. In immediate terms, this was expressed as the need to eliminate the internal bottlenecks suffered in some firms and in the development of sectors such as transport, which required a policy of accelerated import of certain capital goods and stocks that were not being produced domestically.

Simultaneous with this import policy the Government set out an *exchange policy* based on the maintenance of a fixed exchange rate in contrast to the practice in previous years of periodic devaluations following domestic price increases. The stability of the exchange rate was a very important element of the anti-inflationary policy because the price of imports constituted a major component of industrial costs and was a direct determinant of domestic food prices. This policy was applied for practically all of 1971 and only at the end of the year was the national currency devalued.

Lastly, to complete this push to mobilize productive resources, a 'flexible' monetary policy was defined, based on the increase of monetary supply in accordance with the requirements of economic expansion. Once more the Government reversed the guidelines that had prevailed in previous years, under which monetary supply had been restricted for fear of its inflationary effects. This new monetary policy materialized mainly in a change of credit policy, defined with a view to providing credit facilities for small and medium-sized producers and businesses, making it a priority in accordance with the policy of development, etc. In order to carry out this objective, specific credit lines were either widened or created, with undifferentiated rates of interest (since from the first year of UP Government they proved to be negative rates of real interest), whose operation was based on quantitative control by the Central Bank and on nationalization of the banking system. In the second half of 1970 the maximum rate of interest was 24%, but early in 1971 it was lowered to 18%, even less than the corresponding rate for certain specific credits. The same was done for small and medium-sized entrepreneurs on the basis of their cash flow budget and for integral agriculture credit to rural settlements and to farmers' cooperatives, whose interest rate was fixed at 12% in 1971.[20]

The effects of applying this policy began to show early in 1971; industrial production began to grow in March-April; unemployment in greater Santiago decreased by 5.2% in June (3.8% in December 1971); business sales increased, as did import licences, etc. All these tendencies to increase the level of economic activity persisted throughout 1971 and resulted in the largest GNP growth rate registered in many years: 7.7% at constant prices. Also, for the first time in many years, the production materials sectors grew at a faster rate than the service sectors: while the agrarian sector grew by 5.1%, the industrial sector grew by 13.7%, construction by 11.4%, and mining, affected by the fall in the copper price, by 2.0%. Electrical energy generation increased by 15%, and the National Petroleum Company's production by 30%. Educational services also expanded considerably: enrollment in basic education increased by 5.1%, in average arts education by 21.1%, in professional education by 37.1%, and in universities by 28%. In the public health sector the results were very significant. there was a reduction in infant mortality and an increase in such free assistance as school lunches, a half liter of milk per day for all children, etc. There was almost no sector of the economy in which levels of activity did not easily overtake the rates of expansion achieved in the recent past.[21]

This unprecedented increase in economic activity was accompanied by the simultaneous development of huge disequilibria. The short-term effectiveness of the reflationary policy was based on the initial creation of a disequilibrium in the form of an accelerated expansion of demand. It was assumed that this would gradually reach an equilibrium at a new level and with a new structure, thanks to the reserves available for the expansion of domestic demand and the process of income redistribution. On the other hand, disequilibria that led to transformations in property relations had to be compensated by the development and consolidation of a planned social ownership sector whose operation, together with the modifications to the tax system, etc., played a key role in transforming the mechanisms for collecting and allocating surpluses, which were capable of financing the initial disequilibria and ensuring the subsequent expansion of the economy.

Nevertheless, the magnitude of the forces that started the economic reactivation largely overcame the public sector's capacity for collecting surpluses, in such a way that the created disequilibria exceeded the estimated permissible limits. The result was that consumption increased more quickly than production, sustained in real terms by a decrease in inventories and an increase in imports, and financed on one hand by existing international reserves and on the other hand by an explosive growth in the means of payment. A brief description of the financial disequilibria both within Chile and abroad will help us to understand certain specific mechanisms of the operation of the expansionary economic policies in 1971.

One of the most significant phenomena during the first year of the UP Government was the very high rate of increase in the means of payment. Money supply in the private sector rose from E°9,192 million in December 1970 to E°20,131 million in December 1971, that is to say, an increase of

119%, which should be compared with the mere 30% growth of nominal GNP (see Tables 9.5 and 9.6). Even if one cannot accept the conclusions drawn in this respect by the so-called Chicago school (Milton Friedman and his colleagues), which are of importance in Chilean economic polemics, it is evident that the tremendous disparity between the growth of money and nominal GNP must lead to great inflationary pressure. In fact, this is what happened in Chile, particularly when expansion of the means of payment in the hands of the private sector reached even higher rates in subsequent years.

The origin of this increase in money supply was basically the public sector deficit and, more especially, the fiscal deficit.[22] In effect, given that the 'monetary multiplier' (measured as the increase of private money divided by the increase in that issued) was 1.06 in 1971, it can be said that the whole growth of private money originated in the increase of the Central Bank's primary issue.[23] In 1971 the issues increased by E°11,543 million. Three quarters of the issue originated in the operations of the Central Bank with the Treasury, made up essentially of credits for funding the financial deficit.[24] Domestic credits from the Central Bank to users apart from the Treasury accounted for 17.2% of issue; on the whole it was directed to financial support for public institutions (including state firms), while Central Bank credits to the banking system[25] and the private sector underwent a new contraction in 1971. Finally, exchange operations represented only 7.2% of issue. Therefore, any explanation of the increase of private money necessitates a study of the public sector's behaviour and of its policy in financing its deficit.

Similarly, the increase in credits endorsed by the banking system, about E°5,000 million, was mainly directed towards financing activities which were state controlled in one way or another. Of this, E°4,000 million corresponded to increases in State Bank investments destined mainly to finance agrarian reform and decentralized public institutions. The remaining E°1,000 million, representing the increase in investments of the rest of the banking system, were also directed towards the public sector in the form of credits to APS firms. In this case, the change in direction was due to the transfer of private firms to the APS and the easy access to credit that their new status as national firms gave them. A comparison sums up this evolution: in 1970, except for credit to the Treasury and the municipalities, the remaining credits of the monetary system were oriented towards the private sector, that is 61.4% of the total; in 1971 the public sector absorbed 78.2% of this volume of credit.[26]

This means that in 1971 financial phenomena were almost entirely determined by the state sector's behaviour. Moreover, having instituted a 'flexible monetary policy' from the beginning in order to financially support economic reactivation with the formation of the APS and agrarian reform, state institutions could count on exceptional access to credit facilities. The fall in interest rates, the widening of specific credit lines and of their volume of operations – in the framework of the nationalization of the banking system – were measures that contributed to the decisive role of the state sector in financial expansion. Private firms, for their part, made practically no use of banking credit for their current financing: as a result of reactivation and of the enormous expansion in the quantity of money, their own cash flow was sufficient. In other words, they were able to obtain increasing financial resources without recourse to the banking system; methods of payment changed drastically as a result of the increased liquidity of the economy.

This change in payments, with a predominance of cash payments in addition to increased demand for cash settlements by individuals and firms, characteristic of a period of uncertainty and transition, decreased the inflationary pressures derived from the increased quantity of money, at least during the period that we have characterized as the first phase of the inflationary process (September-October 1971).

Tables X and XI of the Statistical Appendix following Chapter 2 summarize the main items in the public sector and Treasury budget, expressed in constant currency for ease of comparison. The public sector deficit quadrupled in 1971 as compared with the previous year. While current income increased by 14.3%, current expenditure increased by the much greater rate of 41.1%; simultaneously, capital expenditure increased by 16.4%. The public sector deficit thus increased from E°2,891 million in 1970 to E°11,213 million in 1971, an absolute increase in constant currency terms of E°8,322 million. Two components of current expenditure, wages and salaries and social security payments, increased in the same year by E°8,453 million (see Table 9.7), an increase which is almost identical to the increase in the total deficit. The coincidence suggests an immediate correlation between the two; it is valid to say that a strict correlation exists between the financial mismanagement in the public sector and the resultant effects of the main measures of income redistribution applied by the Government (including the increase in contracts). This correlation is relevant when a second factor, the weak growth in current revenue, the incapacity of the public sector to gather resources that would allow it to finance programmes of expansion and reflation, is pointed out.

This is one of the main contradictions that determined the operations of the Chilean economy: a rapid growth of public expenditure, due to the wages and employment policies that were implemented, at the same time as a slow growth in revenue on current account. This contradiction can be observed when analyzing the expenditures and revenue of the Treasury (see Table X of the Statistical Appendix following Chapter 2). Central Government revenue grew by 7.4% at constant money value in 1971, while current expenditure grew by 43.8%. The latter percentage is almost entirely equivalent to the increase in expenditure on wages and social security payments, since we know that 90% of central Government transfers and subsidies to the rest of the public sector and to the private sector were allocated to these items. The slight increase in revenue was almost exclusively due to taxes arising out of reflation of the economy. While indirect taxes grew by 11.1% – a reflection basically of this greater level of activity – direct taxation fell by -9.9%, demonstrating that the tax system's traditionally restricted redistributive capacity was severely limited in that year. In other words, wages readjustment and the employment policy were not accomplished by reducing expenditure in the most viable sectors, but at the cost of the growing indebtedness of the Treasury with the Central Bank. Practically all deficit financing came out of domestic loans, while direct public foreign indebtedness was not significant; this policy was in line with the balance of payments situation, which will be described later.

This deficit financing, that was to be repeated and to worsen in the following years, hides two important problems. First, the fact that throughout the UP Government the readjustments in wages in the public and private sectors surpassed the limits set in the respective laws; the Government's wage policy was broken by the pressure of claims from the workers. The permanent discussion about the 'hopscotch' policy, that is, workers' claims for wages over and above Government policy (among which were claims initiated by the opposition), was constant during the whole UP period. Second, the control of the opposition's majority in the National Congress was translated into systematic rejection of all Executive initiatives for modifying the tax system, not only its complete reform but also all propositions to change taxation rates and to create new taxes on property and capital, etc. Apart from minor modifications resulting from Government programmes to alleviate the small contributors' tax burden or to introduce technical changes in collection (pay-as-you-earn system), all efforts by the Executive to improve the discriminatory capacity of the tax system by increasing taxation on high income firms and individuals were blocked by the National Congress.

The economic effects of this congressional opposition were of the greatest importance and were felt in practically all sectors and economic activities. One example, directly related to wage levels and financial mismanagement, is shown in Table 9.8. The significance of the congressional opposition was clearly manifested in the evolution of the deficit which, in general terms, meant the virtual impossibility of carrying out a coherent financial policy that could balance the Government's revenues and expenditures. The pressure and necessity to expand fiscal expenditure in order to complete the UP programme were accompanied by complete inability to reduce, by fiscal means, the incomes of the Chilean big bourgeoisie (because of tax evasion, blockage of new taxation, etc.).

In 1971, it was obvious that even while the real incomes of wage-earners rose, this was at the expense of an increase in total income which maintained real buying power.[27] In these conditions – which were to be aggravated in 1972 and 1973 – wage readjustments represented, together with an increase of employment, especially as the inflationary process accelerated, a net transfer of financial resources (public sector deficit) towards the Chilean bourgeoisie.

Excess liquidity in the economy was progressively concentrated in the hands of the social sector, which could use it as speculative capital once the phase of great demand for money motivated by caution and uncertainty had passed.

The second major disequilibrium created by the implementation of the UP's economic policy was that produced in external relations, resulting in the rapid shrinking of the country's international reserves. In 1971 the decrease in net international reserves was $323.2 million (of a reserves total of $340 million), a movement that continued in the following two years and reached extraordinarily high magnitudes: $327.6 million in 1972 and $248.8 million in 1973 (see Table XIV of the Statistical Appendix following Chapter 2).

Thus, implementation of the expansion policy in 1971 resulted in increased economic activity, sustained by the utilization of productive reserves and foreign exchange which the Government had counted on since the beginning of the year. However, the public sector could not gather the necessary surpluses to sustain the subsequent development of a relatively balanced economic expansion, and at the same time external economic relations accentuated deficits and the short-term expansion 'model' began to crumble rapidly. With respect to price movements, this depletion signified the end of the first inflationary phase in September-October 1971, a phase during which the inflation rate was kept low thanks to the use of available reserves. This was also a period during which the UP and the Government reached its highest political capacity for economic control, while the opposition was just beginning to re-group after its electoral defeat in September 1970.

The second phase of the inflationary process began in October 1971 and was characterized by much more rapid price rises and by the start of problems in the supply of consumer goods. From the political viewpoint the 'march of the empty saucepans' on 1 December 1971 marked a turning-point in the attitude of the Chilean bourgeoisie towards the UP Government. From a position of withdrawal and reorganization, taking advantage of the emerging economic situation, they proceeded *en masse* to take up a position of active and militant opposition, and one of their objectives was to intensify problems through a strategy of creating anarchy.

This second phase started with such economic policies as the first general devaluation, the establishment of multiple exchange, the suspension of external debt payments, and the request for a meeting of the Club of Paris – in other words, with an effort to control external disequilibria.

From the UP Government's inception, the exchange policy had been considered one of the most important control levers in the anti-inflationary struggle. The Government tried to use the exchange rate as a protective screen for the domestic economy in the face of fluctuations abroad to avoid the inflationary effects of international price movements as well as disequilibria in external relations. That policy was based on the fact that variations in the exchange rate represented one of the most important cost factors both in national production and in the prospects of a favourable balance of payments situation in the future. Minister of the Treasury Zorrilla stated in his 'First Statement' to the National Congress (November 1970) that:

> One of the main factors in the costs structure of firms is the exchange rate. We will not go back to the policy of periodic devaluation, especially since the favourable prospects for foreign trade and the balance of payments will generate, as in the past, autonomous inflation and will raise inflationary expectations.[28]

This policy was maintained during practically all of 1971 despite the fact that its basic conditions, that is, 'favourable prospects for foreign trade and the balance of payments', were not fulfilled. The maintenance of a fixed exchange rate during the period of great external deficits reached its limit at the end of the year and was expressed in the high propensity to import which the exchange rate encouraged (despite the proliferation of restrictions and of administrative controls), the growing price distortions between domestic and imported products, etc. In maintaining a fixed exchange rate – despite adverse circumstances – the 'political necessity' of distinguishing the new situation from that prevailing under the previous Government was an influential factor. Up to 1970, the Frei Government had sustained a policy of periodic devaluation as a mechanism of external adjustment, which was strongly criticized (and with good reason, given the conditions at that time) by the UP in view of its inflationary character. The result of maintaining a fixed exchange rate was, at the end of 1970, the significant and sudden devaluation of the escudo with the consequent need to readjust domestic prices.

The prime bank interest rate was maintained, from the middle of 1970 until 13 December 1971, at E°12.2 to the dollar.[29] On that date the first national monetary devaluation occurred and multiple exchange rates for differentiated exchange areas were established (see Table VIII of the Statistical Appendix following Chapter 2). The exchange rate was maintained at E°12.2 to the dollar for foodstuff and fuel imports (list A); the rate for capital goods and spare parts imports was E°19 to the dollar (list C); luxury goods (list D) were imported at E°25 to the dollar; for everything else, including raw materials and intermediate products (list B), the exchange rate was E°15.8 to the dollar. On the average, the exchange rate varied from E°12.21 to E°15.8 to the dollar, that is to say, a devaluation of 28.6%, practically equal to the rise in domestic consumer prices between June 1970 and November 1971. The rate for buying foreign exchange varied from E°12.2 to E°15.8 to the dollar.

Obviously the objective of introducing the multiple exchange rate was to selectively minimize the inflationary effects of unavoidable devaluation. The maintenance of the exchange rate for foodstuff and fuel imports and the devaluation on list B products were directed towards sustaining the domestic prices of those products with greater influence, direct or indirect, on popular consumption. Successive modifications of the exchange rate were made on the basis of the same criterion. Subsequent experience showed that such a policy of multiple exchanges, even when it minimizes potentially inflationary pressures on certain prices, tends to provoke an important distortion of domestic prices, obliging a re-ordering (inflationary) to the extent that pressures for new devaluation cannot be resisted. A multiple exchange policy, in order to be permanently effective, requires certain conditions that were not present in the Chilean economy.

In brief, it was once more a case of economic planning and the mechanisms for collecting surplus. A policy of multiple exchange rates requires much more than merely a large amount of administrative control: besides this it requires an import programme which is planned in great detail and which limits, in order to serve the economy's overall needs, the propensity to import, although that propensity has been raised by the exchange rate distortions. More than this, a mechanism of planned financial transfers among the different sectors (or firms) and between the public and private sector is required. Only in this way is it possible to prevent the transfer of the cost of subsidizing certain imports to the mass of consumers as state sector deficits. The control of domestic prices and the planned transfers of surpluses will sustain a policy of multiple exchange rates; otherwise, the result will be, as in Chile, an extraordinary bureaucratic complexity in the operation of foreign trade which in no way helps rational decisions on how to use foreign exchange. Only towards the end of the UP Government was there any advance towards establishing a foreign exchange budget that was relatively detailed. The last modifications of the exchange system, made during August and September 1973, were characterized by the simplification of the exchange markets: the number of nominal exchange rates was reduced to six, four for the buying exchange rate and two for selling; the two exchange markets were merged into one, etc. However, the least that can be said is that neither these modifications nor the foreign exchange budget were opportunely proposed.

During 1972 the Chilean economy showed a more marked development of the tendencies towards disequilibrium which were indicated in 1971. The GNP fell by 0.8% (a 0.1% fall in GNP expenditure), which was the most important variation which had occurred from one year to another. The quantity of private sector money increased by 138.8% and the total money supply by 164.9% (see Table 9.5). Again, with a monetary multiplier of less than one, the expansion of private money originated in the growth of the monetary mass induced directly by the financing of the public sector (see Table 9.6). It is interesting to note the change in the composition of issues in 1972 because of the increasing importance of domestic credit from the Central Bank to various Treasury accounts. This was due fundamentally to the increased credits to decentralized public institutions and to the APS, which absorbed more than three quarters of this type of credit (the remaining credits from the Central Bank were to the banking system). Similarly, on examining the public sector and the fiscal sector deficits, it appeared that while in 1971 the fiscal deficit accounted for 81.3% of the public sector deficit, in 1972 the percentage dropped to 55.6. In other words, quantitative development of the non-fiscal public sector, basically the industrial APS and agriculture, was translated into an increase of the deficit that had to be financed with an increase of issue and of banking credits to the APS. In 1972, consequently, from the viewpoint of global financial resources, the state sector's expansion signified a net shift of resources to the private sector for the second consecutive year. The inability of the state sector to capture the economy's surpluses became even more patently obvious.

In particular with regard to the Treasury, in the face of an increase in current expenditures due almost exclusively to wage increases, the Treasury's current incomes fell by 14.8% and its direct tax revenues fell by 26.6% in constant money terms. In that year two general wage adjustment laws were approved; these led to an increased deficit (see Table 9.8) because the opposition rejected the means of finance which the Executive had proposed together with the wage increases.

As to external relations, the balance of payments deficit was slightly larger during 1972 than in 1971 (see Table XIV of the Statistical Appendix following Chapter 2). Undoubtedly, the enormous growth of the trade deficit was the most important element; in the face of the increase in imports (18.6%), mostly determined by foodstuff purchases, total exports diminished for the second consecutive year (-15.0%). This decrease is explained by the slight drop in the copper price ($0.486 per pound in 1972), by the fall in copper shipments and by a general decline in other exports.

An important factor in attempts to explain the trade deficit is the evolution of international import prices and those of Chilean exports. While the former increased notably in 1971 and 1972, export prices greatly diminished, as can be seen in Table XV of the Statistical Appendix. The Chilean economy's terms of trade deteriorated as a consequence of the world inflationary process and of an evolution in copper prices, the causes of which deserve a detailed analysis that cannot be made here.

Financing the balance of payments deficit was achieved by two principal means.

(1) Renegotiation of the external debt with the Club of Paris, which implied a relief of $243 million, practically the whole of the amount renegotiated, since the 'delay' in signing the bilateral agreements that rounded off the renegotiations almost allowed a suspension of payment. Debts with U.S. creditors were also renegotiated ($79 million), and other debts were left unpaid ($44 million).

(2) The second means of financing was an additional indebtedness (an increase in liabilities of international reserves) of $255 million and the use of $55 million in reserves; that is, the composition of the decrease of international

reserves was completely revised compared to the previous year. As foreign exchange resources had been depleted, the policy of external indebtedness was imposed as a fundamental mechanism for financing external deficits. The degree of external inflexibility in the Chilean economy increased quantitatively and qualitatively.[30]

Under these political conditions, the bulk of financial resources in the hands of the private sector was poured into the market in the form of speculative capital. Contrary to what had been typical behaviour up to the last months of 1971, caution and uncertainty ceased to counteract the supply of money, especially as the inflation rate and inflationary expectations increased. The speculative process now became general and produced much more rapid growth in private sector prices than in those in the state sector. The degree of control in the state sector was much higher than in the private sector and respect for price policies was also much greater, hence the main reason for the increasing deficit of the public sector. Moreover, the Government kept prices down in the very important public sector firms, arguing that, since they were producers of widely dispersed intermediate products and/or goods and services for popular consumption, any increase in their prices would imply a sizeable inflationary impact.[31] The distortion of the relative price system was a dominant economic phenomenon in mid-1972 and its main consequence was to accelerate the transfer of resources from the state to the private sector.

Up to July-August 1972, there was a period in which the more marked financial disequilibria in and outside Chile added to the opposition's political offensive; this resulted in a phase of inflationary tension during which price levels rose at more than double the rate of the previous phase, the beneficiaries being the non-wage-earner in the private sector.

In August 1972 the Government decided to devalue the escudo and to restructure the relative price system between the private sector and the APS in order to achieve 'equilibrium at a new level'. The escudo was devalued, on the average, from E°15.8 to E°28.1 to the dollar; the exchange rate for list A (food and fuel) went from E°12.21 to E°20, that of list B (raw materials) from E°15.8 to E°25, that of list C (spare parts and capital goods) from E°19 to E°40, and that of list D (luxury goods) from E°25 to E°80 to the dollar. The average buying exchange rate was also raised and a system of multiple exchange was established that was designed to promote nontraditional exports. Similarly, the buying exchange rate for copper wire was raised from E°15.8 to E°20 to the dollar in order to lower the deficit in current money of the major mining companies of Gran Minería and the National Mining Corporation (ENAMI).

The effects of this devaluation, added to efforts to restructure the relative price system, when an enormous volume of money circulating in the hands of a speculative private sector, transformed the 'equilibrium at a new level' into a veritable price explosion. In short, the employers' lock-out in October was the last log added to the inflationary fire, giving full vent to speculation, market cornering, sabotage, etc. – all those well known mass actions of economic anarchy and political subversion. As a result, August, September and October experienced an average monthly 20% rise in the level of consumer prices.

Price increases from the end of December 1971 to September 1972 reached 99.8%. To counteract its effects on the wage-earners' living standards, the Government proposed and obtained (with the corresponding effect on deficits) a new readjustment law. Previously, during the month of September, all workers had been awarded 'compensatory bonuses' of E°500 and E°700. Law 17828 of October 1972 constituted a general readjustment of wages and salaries, that is an 100% raise for all public officials and for some workers in the private sector on the condition that they deferred all further requests for one year, while taking advantage of the law's benefits. Once more, because of the lack of finance, the result was an increase in the fiscal deficit and a consequent expansion in monetary supply without any compensatory increase in fiscal revenues.

It is difficult to say whether, from then on, the Government followed an economic policy of any sort whatever, for there was only a mixed bag of temporary measures without any degree of coordination, distinguished by growing conflict within the UP and the Government (with respect to, for example, definition of the APS, to measures to be taken in the distribution sphere, etc.). From November 1972 to March 1973 the entire economic and political evolution was dominated by two factors: the consequences of the October lock-out and the general legislative elections that were to be held in March. For the purposes of this discussion, two phenomena should be pointed out. First, the most important effect of the October lock-out from the viewpoint of the economy's operation – and the most difficult one to measure – was the depletion in stocks of raw materials and finished goods (more precisely, of the relative structure of stocks among different firms capable of maintaining uninterrupted production) in almost all productive and distributive units; this was particularly serious in the agricultural sector.[32] This complete reversion to anarchy in the productive apparatus was one of the major factors which determined the subsequent price increases and facilitated the enormous growth of speculation.

The breakdown in the distributive apparatus caused by the October lock-out deserves special mention. Until then, the management of wholesale trade had been notoriously weak in the state sector, where firms were highly inefficient and disorganized; from then on, however, there was an almost complete lack of control in wholesale distribution and retail trade.

It is difficult to give any precise indication of the enormous significance of this lack of control in creating anarchy in the general economy, and in developing the black market and speculation, without going into a detailed analysis which is outside the scope of this chapter. All in all, the simple statement of the problem is sufficient to show that it was a major cause of the inability to introduce the necessary changes in the mechanism for collecting the economic surplus, and specifically in the development of supply problems in popular consumer products.

Above all, the October lock-out initiated new forms of organization among the masses, significantly increasing the scope of the existing organizations, as in the case of the *Junta de Abastecimiento y Precios* (JAP) [Council for Control of Supplies and Prices], and provoked a new mystique of popular mobilization. Between October 1972 and March 1973, this popular mobilization was largely channelled into the fight against the black market and speculation, a political element of prime importance in the electoral campaign. It was predominantly this strengthening of official control and the control of the masses which permitted a reduction in inflationary pressure and in the effects of speculation. Altogether the average price increases throughout this phase approached 7% per month, while other pressures built up that were to explode early in April 1973.

Once the results of the March elections became known and the impossibility of constitutionally overthrowing the President of the Republic was recognized, the opposition's politics changed to pure and simple subversion. The last stumbling blocks to headlong speculation and widespread development of the black market – complete anarchy in the national economy – were pushed aside. From then on there were no political conditions for sustaining the badly needed economic policy; the political and institutional crisis became so dominant that it could only be determined by the solution of the power conflict.

The evolution of the economic and financial situation can be summarized in one phrase: extreme exacerbation of disequilibria and the breakdown of basic economic institutions. The characteristics of disequilibria were also exhibited at a higher level. The APS deficit spiralled rapidly as prices once more fell below the private sector averages. The public sector's deficit for the first time became the principal source of fiduciary issue (see Table 9.6). As to the fiscal situation, after long discussions in the National Congress, a law for readjusting wages was approved which was designed to cover the price increases from October 1972 through March 1973 (60.8%): this law was approved but its financing was reduced to only 10% of what was needed (see Table 9.8).[33] Between January and September 1973, the quantity of money in the hands of the private sector increased by 178.7% and fiduciary issue increased by 203.1%. The copper price increased in April 1973, but the balance of payments deficit and foreign reserves continued to be extremely critical. The significant devaluations in May, June and September 1973 and the efforts to rationalize the exchange structure did not lead to any important changes.

The enormous quantity of money in the hands of the national bourgeoisie, resulting from the deficit in the public sector at a time of enormous difficulties in the productive apparatus, of constant seditious agitation (the unsuccessful *coup* attempt in June), and of consciously intensified speculation which left the Government 'fenced in' and trammelled in its operations, could only result in uncontrollable price increases. This was the final phase of inflationary anarchy or, more precisely, of inflation which was irresistibly generated by the external political struggle.

Only a politico-economic action that was capable of almost instantaneously decreasing the financial power of the Chilean bourgeoisie (i.e. monetary reform and rationing) could have subsequently or simultaneously allowed a restructuring of the productive apparatus, the mechanisms of surplus collection, the domestic trade system, the wages policy, etc.; this would have involved radical reorganization of the economy without which, in 1973, any anti-inflationary policy seemed purely utopian. To the extent that political conditions for change were not forthcoming, nothing was capable of stopping inflation and the anarchic breakdown of the Chilean economy, which was a key precedent for the fascist *coup d'état* of September 1973.

These were the general lines along which the economic situation developed in its different stages. The dynamics and orientation of that development, basically generated in 1971, led to the explosive evolution of the inflationary process due to the nature and magnitude of the disequilibria that were created and accounting for the political limitations of the Government. The question naturally arises: was this the only possible course of events? Was the economy's deterioration into anarchy inevitable under the UP Government? As always, answering such questions would require the re-writing of history on the basis of an 'if'.

However, one cannot limit oneself to an analysis that merely confirms the forms and features which the course of events acquired. The determining factors were so many and so complex that it is impossible to maintain with any degree of certainty that they were inevitable. At each moment in those three years of profound social change, more than one alternative action was open to the people, individually or collectively, who constructed the concrete history of Chile. The features and rhythm of the Chilean revolution were not written in advance in the book of fate. The parties and mass organizations, the political leaders and even each individual always had an option when faced with specific alternatives, albeit options of degree and not of sentiment, though even the latter always were present.

In order not to extend the scope of this chapter, we shall examine the general orientation of economic policy.

Take, for example, the impact that would have been created if the suspension of external debt payments and the request for renegotiation had been made in November 1971 and not a year later. Given the time and the form that those negotiations take, suspending payments would have signified a reduction in foreign exchange expenditure of around $200 million. Alternative uses for that money could have simplified many foreign trade problems (e.g. raw material and foodstuff imports and stock-building) so as to combat, *inter alia*, the effects of pressures of domestic demand. Similarly, a firm political decision on wage problems (and a better understanding of their importance) would have allowed an important reduction of the fiscal deficit to the ultimate advantage of the workers. In the same area, a more decisive tax reform at the right moment – for example April-May 1971 – would have opened up the possibility of increasing fiscal revenues while reducing the bourgeoisie's incomes. The application at the right moment of certain executive powers in this area (for example, the transfer of taxes on a basis of a decree effective as of 1970) would have served the same purpose. It is not difficult to find other numerous examples in the monetary policy, prices, agrarian reform, etc. Besides this, mention must be made of the major political decisions (for instance, the option of a referendum in April 1971) that later were seen as missed chances.

All in all, in my opinion there can be no doubt that there was, inherent in the content of this social development, a basic questioning of the Chilean big bourgeoisie's control over political power: whatever forms the struggle might have taken, and whatever its phases might have been, its content was immutable. What could have been modified were the conditions under which the alliance materialized and its aims and scope; in other words, the conditions which were to contribute in various degrees to shaping the correlation of political forces. Indeed this was the decisive factor in the outcome of the struggle. It is therefore incorrect to state that the increasing class confrontation which had been building up in Chile inevitably had to result in the overthrow of the popular movement. What was inevitable was that the confrontation would end in setting up a new hegemony, that is, a political power capable of intensifying the disintegration of the old order. This disintegration was initiated by the formation of the UP Government and excluded every kind of reformism. Once on the revolutionary road there was no way back from class confrontation, but there were numerous ways through which, under different conditions, its culmination could be reached. In the same way, in the economic field in particular, other alternatives were to some extent available and, although they became increasingly narrower, they were always present. Study of these alternatives would permit the Chilean experience and the evolution of the economy during this period to be correctly analyzed and evaluated.

5. CONCLUSIONS

1. During the 1971-73 period the Chilean economy underwent an increasingly accelerated inflationary process which, in its final phase, reached an extraordinary magnitude.

2. This inflationary process was caused generally by the disequilibria and contradictions resulting from applying a revolutionary transformation policy to the economic system's basic structure and to its pattern of operation. The UP Government was unable, politically and economically, to overcome these

contradictions by liquidating the Chilean big bourgeoisie's power and neutralizing U.S. imperialism's attacks.

3. The immediate cause of the inflationary process was the growth of enormous financial deficits and the concentration in the hands of the big bourgeoisie of massive speculative capital; this capital made it possible for the opposition to carry out a strategy of creating economic chaos and thus to further the accelerating inflation.

4. The growing deficit in the balance of payments helped to accelerate domestic inflation because of (i) the rigidity in the domestic production and import structure and (ii) the impossibility of maintaining, with a negative balance of payments, a protective barrier against international price fluctuations by means of fixed exchange rates.

5. The entire evolution of the economic situation and, with it, of the inflationary process, involved a contradiction between the reorientation of the economy's pattern of operations in favour of the people's interests – a direct result of the class character of the UP Government – and the corresponding structural transformation that this necessitated. This reorientation required a simultaneous change in the mechanisms for collecting and allocating surplus in order to achieve real financing; this was not forthcoming. The state sector failed to transform itself into a dominant sector capable of collecting most of the surplus generated so that this surplus continued to move out of, rather than into, the state sector.

6. At first, the expansionary policy was successfully sustained thanks to the material and financial reserves which were then available. Soon thereafter, the necessary correspondence between the structure and the functioning of the economy was broken; this was expressed in the intensification of economic disequilibria, the climbing rate of inflation and the increasing dearth of supplies.

7. The increasing lack of correspondence between the functioning and the structure of the economy was further aggravated by the oppositional sector's seditious political offensive. The resultant break with all 'economic legality' allowed vast speculation and black markets to become dominant, which led to the final inflationary explosion.

8. Given its political orientation and its Programme, the UP Government had no choice but to apply an economic policy which would satisfy the short- and long-term necessities and aspirations of the people. The resultant economic evolution, and in particular the inflationary process, were generated not by the policy's application, as seemed to be the case, but by the insufficient revolutionary transformation of Chile's economic and social system.

NOTES

1. This is an obvious example of the class character which state ownership acquired. One can speak of social ownership (in the form of state ownership) if and only if the state represents the interests of workers, and in consequence, the vast majority of the people. If, on the contrary, the state represents the interests of the capitalists, then 'nationalization' is simply a particular form of capitalist development, that is, monopolistic state capitalism.

2. The strictly economic importance of the dominant ideology as to which values and norms are to be socially imposed – which strongly influences the typical behaviour of capitalists and workers – should, in light of the Chilean experience, be studied in more depth and with insight than so far has been the case.

3. The concept of structural transformation, widely used in all analyses of the Chilean experience, should be understood here as transformation of the above-mentioned basic structural characteristics of the economy. There is a tendency to speak of structural transformations when describing a completely different phenomenon, namely transformation in the pattern and productive profile of the economy. Thus, for example, one uses structural transformation as a term for the preferential development of some productive branches in relation to others, that is to say, the alteration of one sector's or a group of sectors' contribution to the total output. Obviously the two concepts, cloaked in the same words, reflect substantially different phenomena and should not be confused.

4. 'Orientaciones básicas del programa económico de corto plazo' [Basic Orientations of the Short-term Economic Programme], a typed confidential document that was presented by the UP teams of experts to presidential candidate Salvador Allende in October 1970.

5. Americo Zorrilla, *Exposición sobre la política económica del Gobierno y del estado de la hacienda pública* [Statement on Economic Policy of the Government and on Public Finance], presented to the 'Comisión Mixta de Presupuestos' [Mixed Commission on Budgets], 27 November 1970 (Santiago de Chile, Ministerio de Hacienda, Dirección de Presupuestos, 1970).

6. A more detailed analysis of the political struggle is found in my book, *Chile: una economía de transición?* [Chile: A Transition Economy?] (La Habana, Casa de las Américas, 1972). A revised version of this analysis, including more details and considerable modifications, will appear as my thesis at the University of Social Sciences, Grenoble, France, and is tentatively entitled 'The Evolution of the Chilean Economy and the Economic Policy of the Popular Government'.

7. *Programa básico de la Unidad Popular* [Basic Programme of the UP], various versions of which were distributed among the public during the 1970 presidential elections. An English translation of the Basic Programme may be found in J. Ann Zammit, *The Chilean Road to Socialism. Proceedings of an ODEPLAN-IDS Round Table* (Brighton, England, Institute of Development Studies, University of Sussex, 1973), 255-284. (The Spanish version is available in *Chile, Peru and Bolivia. Documentos de tres procesos latinoamericanos*. Biblioteca Fundamental del Hombre Moderno (Buenos Aires, Centro Editor de America Latina, S.A., 1977).)

8. In my *Chile: una economía...*, a relatively detailed analysis is made of dependent monopolistic capital in Chile at the end of the 1960s. Using such an analysis as a basis, one can demonstrate the revolutionary relevance of the propositions in the UP Programme.

9. It should be noted that this statement – which in my judgment is of essence – has nothing to do with such simplistic (and incorrect) interpretations as 'they tried to win over the people through their stomachs', or 'greater concessions would have won over more sectors to the UP policy', etc. Such interpretations are not correct either in terms of the country's economic capacity or, more importantly, in terms of their alleged 'political effects'.

10. An important discussion on the relationship between central economic planning and workers' participation developed in the middle of 1972 and culminated in May 1973 with the approval by the Economic Committee of Ministers of a 'Plan de la Economía' [Plan for the National Economy]. Interesting in this respect are certain Government documents, especially the last two 'Statements' of the Minister of the Treasury to the National Con-

gress and such political documents as the discussions held in March 1973 and in the Central Committee of the Communist and Socialist Parties. This discussion, although not concluded, is interesting with respect to re-defining the role that trade unions should play in the workers' participation structures in industry.

11. Strictly speaking, what was broken down was the kind of capitalist rationality which typifies a stable economic system. Due to the political situation it was replaced by a new attitude, which was perfectly adapted to maintaining the struggle which the capitalists were fighting to defend their own system.

12. Ricardo French-Davis, *Políticas económicas en Chile 1952-70* [Economic Policies in Chile 1952-70] (Santiago de Chile, Ediciones Nueva Universidad, 1973).

13. During the discussion in October 1972 on the readjustment law, the Government proposed a new form of calculating readjustment on the basis of the variation in prices of the average consumer's 'shopping bag of basic goods'. This was rejected by the National Congress, and consequently the economic policy's capacity to discriminate between various social groups on the basis of their income level continued to be very limited.

14. The consumer price index referred to here corresponds to that calculated for greater Santiago (approximately one third of the country's population). Undoubtedly there are differences between this index and those corresponding to other regions of the country, just as there are regional salary differences. In many areas of Santiago, for example, a given amount per area, called a zone allowance, was added to the salaries. On differences in regional prices see Andre Passicot, 'Evolución del Producto Geográfico Bruto en 1972 y perspectivas para 1973' [Evolution of the Gross Geographical Product in 1972 and Prospects for 1973], *Comentarios sobre la situación económica (Primer semestre 1973)* [Statement on the Economic Situation (First Half of 1973)] (Santiago de Chile, Departamento de Economía, Universidad de Chile, November 1973, Second Edition).

15. The other estimates of the evolution of prices in 1973 all show, despite their variations, the same tendencies. For an explanation of why the official price index compiled by the National Statistics Institute undervalues the rise in prices between September and December 1973 see Santiago Barrios, 'Restauration au Chili' [Restoration in Chile], *Le temps moderne* [Modern Times] (October 1974), 77-108. Despite the values given in the official index, the military junta recognized, towards the end of 1973, that there was a greater rise in prices than was indicated by the index. It is in fact stated, in the Letter of Intent of the Government of Chile to the International Monetary Fund, which accompanied the official request for stand-by credits at the end of 1973, that 'the present indications are that during 1973 the retail price increase has been of the order of 750% to 800%'. Quoted by Alberto Martínez, *Política económica de un fascismo dependiente* [Political Economy of Dependent Fascism] (Paris, Institut d'Études Économiques et Sociales, 1975).

16. See also Barrios, 'Restauration au Chile'.

17. My insistence on outlining the role of the economic policy has nothing to do with a 'voluntaristic' vision of the movement of the economy. On the contrary, by outlining the role played in Chile by the type, degree and orientation of intervention by the 'political authority' in the economic system, I emphasize the fact that this intervention was the determinant element in stopping the previous development tendencies and in establishing the new type of 'objective' economic dynamics at the beginning of 1971. From then on, the dynamics of the economy depended much more on the forces that had been liberated and brought into play by these policies (which realized a strategy of more general political change) than by pressures resulting from the policies themselves. In the ensuing stages of the process of change, the economic policy – subjected to great restrictions – was minimally effective and limited to isolated and relatively uncoordinated actions upon determined phenomena.

18. 'Living wage' and 'minimum salary' are terms used in Chilean legislation to define the minimum remunerations of workers and employees, their main purpose being to establish a certain uniformity in accounting wages and salaries. For details on the remunerations policy in 1971 see Zorrilla, *Exposición sobre la política económica...*, 24-26.

19. One measure of the importance of this problem was that early in 1971 the Government declared unemployment to be a 'national catastrophe', a legal expression that al-

lowed it to make use of additional resources to confront the problem. This was the first time that this executive capacity was used for purposes other than national disasters.

20. As long as the UP Government was in power special rates of interest were maintained for small- and medium-sized producers. For the examples mentioned, the rates were kept at 12% until the end of 1972.

21. ODEPLAN, 'La evolución de la economía chilena en 1971' [The Evolution of the Chilean Economy in 1971] published in the Central Bank's *Boletín mensual* [Monthly Bulletin], 529 (March 1972). See also Gonzalo Martner, 'Los problemas de la producción bajo la Unidad Popular en Chile' [The Problems of Production under the Popular Unity in Chile], *Trimestre económico* [Economic Quarterly], 167 (1973).

22. While the fiscal sector comprises the institutions of central Government (the ministries, the National Congress, and others), the public sector comprises the Treasury, decentralized institutions and state enterprises.

23. Alvaro Bardon, 'Situación monetaria e inflación' [The Monetary Situation and Inflation], *Comentarios sobre la situación económica (Segundo semestre 1973)* [Statement on the Economic Situation (Second Half of 1973)] (Santiago de Chile, Departamento de Economía, Universidad de Chile, 1974).

24. The proportions indicated here are taken from a table showing the monetary system's sources and use of funds which was prepared by the Research Department [*Departamento de Estudios*] of the Central Bank and included in a report to the Economic Committee of Ministers (May 1973).

25. The banking system comprises all commercial banks plus the State Bank. The monetary system comprises the banking system plus the Central Bank (the issuing body).

26. For a detailed analysis of the credit situation in 1971 see Fernando Cossio, 'La evolución del crédito en 1971' [The Evolution of Credit in 1971], in *La economía chilena en 1971* [The Chilean Economy in 1971] (Santiago de Chile, Instituto de Economía y Planificación, Universidad de Chile, 1972).

27. ODEPLAN, 'La evolución de la económia...'.

28. Zorrilla, *Exposición sobre la política económica...*, 28.

29. Two exchange markets existed in Chile. The most important (or official) one was the bank market, on which all commercial and invisible transactions were made, as well as some private and all governmental capital transactions. All other transactions were made on the brokers' market (a unique Chilean institution). Though the following analysis refers exclusively to the bank market, one must keep in mind that the brokers' market was affected by the same problems as the bank market, namely introduction of multiple exchange rates, extreme complexity in the application of differential tax rates, multiplication of quantitative controls, etc. The most important difference is that in the brokers' market devaluations took place at shorter intervals and the flexible exchange rate for certain types of transactions (e.g. tourism) was formally re-introduced.

30. Until August of 1973 the deficit was financed mainly through additional indebtedness and suspension of debt payments, for the Club of Paris had not given any answer to the Chilean Government's request for renegotiation of the external debt, which was to be paid that year.

31. For an approximate quantification of the differences in prices between state and private firms see the Inter-American Committee for the Alliance for Progress (CIAP), OAS, *Domestic Efforts and the Needs for External Financing for the Development of Chile* (Washington, D.C., OAS Series H/XIV, CIAP 1650, 28 January 1974).

32. The first attempt to evaluate the damage done by the October lock-out, which deals mainly with the financial effects, is given in Minister of the Treasury Zorrilla's *Exposición sobre el estado de la hacienda pública y de la política económica del Gobierno* [Statement on Public Finance and the Economic Policy of the Government], presented to the 'Comisión Mixta de Presupuestos' [Mixed Commission on Budgets], 15 November 1972 (Santiago de Chile, Ministerio de Hacienda, Dirección de Presupuestos, 1972).

33. It should be noted that in this case, the approved project differed from the original proposal not only in the amount of financing but also in the budgeted expenditures. This was because the Government had originally proposed to grant readjustment for no more than three living wages (or for the highest portion corresponding to the three first living

wages), excluding any readjustment for those receiving more than twenty living wages. The pressures of all kinds which were exercised on the Government, both internally and externally, were translated into a maximum increase from three to five living wages, without any exceptions. While in the original proposal only 58% of fiscal expenditure on wages and salaries was subject to readjustment, that percentage rose to 79% in the approved project.

Table 9.1. *Consumer Price Index (percentage variations)*

	1971	*1972*	*1973*
National Statistics Institute			
Annual average	20.1	77.8	352.8
December-December	22.1	163.4	508.1
Inter-American Committee for the Alliance for Progress (CIAP)			
Annual average	20.1	88.8	575.3
December-December	22.1	210.6	681.6
World Bank			
Annual average	–	–	–
December-December	37.8	285.5	405.0
International Monetary Fund			
Annual average	20.1	77.8	505.9
December-December	22.1	163.4	647.0
University of Chile, Department of Economics			
Annual average	29.2	107.5	442.0
December-December	–	173.7	616.6

Table 9.2. *Consumer and Wholesale Price Indices (percentage variations from December to December)*

	CPI	*WPI*
1971	22.1	21.4
1972	163.4	143.3
1973	508.1	1147.1
January-August 1973	303.6	217.1

Source: Instituto Nacional de Estadísticas [National Institute of Statistics] (Santiago

Table 9.3. *Consumer Price Index (percentage variations)*

		Month by month	*Running quarterly average*
1971	January	1.4	
	February	0.7	1.1
	March	1.2	1.5
	April	2.5	2.2
	May	2.8	2.4
	June	2.0	1.7
	July	0.3	1.1
	August	1.1	0.8
	September	1.1	1.3
	October	1.7	1.8
	November	2.7	2.4
	December	2.8	3.1
1972	January	3.7	4.3
	February	6.5	4.3
	March	2.7	5.0
	April	5.7	4.2
	May	4.3	4.0
	June	2.1	3.6
	July	4.4	9.7
	August	22.7	16.4
	September	22.2	20.0
	October	15.2	14.3
	November	5.6	9.7
	December	8.3	8.1
1973	January	10.3	7.6
	February	4.1	6.9
	March	6.2	6.8
	April	10.2	11.9
	May	19.4	15.1
	June	15.6	16.8
	July	15.3	16.0
	August	17.1	

Table 9.4. *Composition of the Consumer and Wholesale Index (average 1970 = 100)*

CPI

	Total	*Foodstuffs*	*Housing*	*Clothing*	*Miscellaneous*
1970	100	100	100	100	100
1971	120.1	123.8	116.4	126.0	112.5
1972	213.5	266.5	148.5	200.3	180.8
1973	966.6	1270.0	470.8	1074.3	785.0
August 1973	563.9	737.1	311.9	815.9	417.5

WPI

	Total	*National products*				*Imported products*
		Agricul-ture	*Mining*	*Industry*	*Total*	
1970	100	100	100	100	100	100
1971	117.9	125.5	132.8	113.9	116.7	122.2
1972	200.5	262.0	228.1	189.4	203.4	190.8
1973	1225.8	1383.7	1307.3	1092.0	1151.0	1244.3
August 1973	467.6	723.0	523.0	446.3	496.8	369.0

Table 9.5. *The Money Supply (in millions of escudos)*

	1970	*1971*	*1972*	*1973* [a]
Private sector money	9,192	20,131	48,073	133,990
Total money	11,266	24,390	64,611	175,560
Fiduciary issue	8,701	20,244	55,407	167,928

[a] Until September.

Table 9.6. *The Origin of Fiduciary Issue (percentage)*

	1971	*1972*	*1973* [a]
Exchange operations	7.2	–22.1	–2.7
Domestic credit, including Treasury	17.2	54.6	67.0
Treasury operations	75.6	67.5	35.7
Total	100	100	100

[a] Until September.

Source: Central Bank, Departamento de Estudios [Research Department], Report to the Economic Committee of Ministers, May 1973.

Table 9.7. *Current Expenditure in the Public Sector (consolidated in millions of 1970 escudos)*

	1970	*1971*	*1972*
Current expenditure	24,442.0	34,497.0	55,662.0
Wages and salaries	11,264.8	15,089.0	24,153.0
Social security	8,723.4	13,352.0	15,299.0
Subtotal (wages and salaries + social security)	19,988.2	28,441.0	40,152.0
Others	4,453.8	6,056.0	12,510.0

Table 9.8. *Financing for the Readjustments Laws (Annual Effect) (in millions of escudos)*

	January 1972		*October 1972*		*May 1973*	
	Original project	*Approved project*	*Original project*	*Approved project*	*Original project*	*Approved project*
Revenue	*7,866*	*4,471*	*12,540*	*6,120*	*24,370*	*2,890*
Income taxes	1,270	206	5,850	470	2,520	–
Property taxes	1,130	132	1,000	–	10,050	140
Sales and foreign trade taxes	3,446	1,933	5,690	5,650	5,800	2,750
Others	2,000	2,000	–	–	6,000	–
Expenditure	*10,456*	*10,456*	*10,773*	*10,773*	*28,890*	*46,800*
Wages and salaries	4,543	4,543	3,874	3,874	7,922	18,540
Social security	2,658	2,658	2,044	2,044	7,020	9,511
Transferences to the public sector	2,963	2,963	3,328	3,328	13,158	14,654
Miscellaneous	292	292	1,527	1,527	790	4,095
Deficit (–) or surplus (+)	*–2,590*	*–5,915*	*1,767*	*–4,653*	*–4,520*	*–43,910*

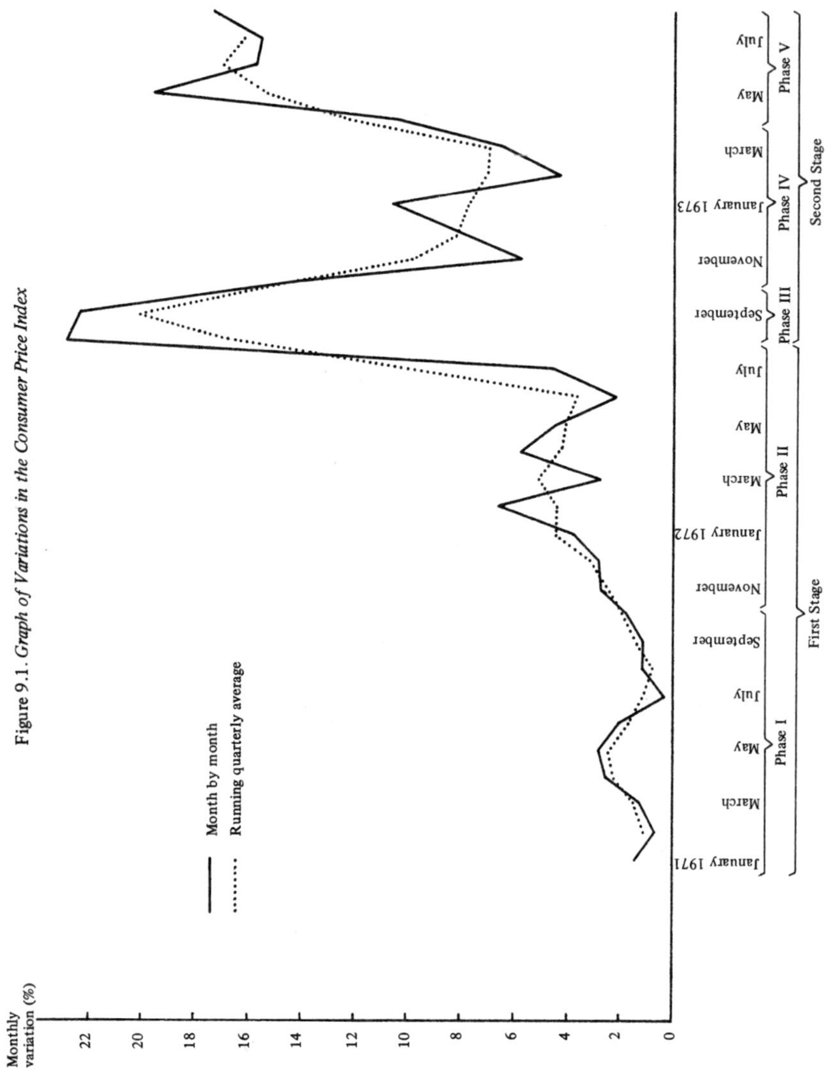

Figure 9.1. *Graph of Variations in the Consumer Price Index*

10

S. SIDERI

THE PROCESS OF TRANSFORMATION AND THE ROLE OF INTERNATIONAL COOPERATION: AN OBSERVER'S VIEW

> Our primary task is to do away with this constraining structure which only generates a deformed growth. Simultaneously we must build up our economy.
>
> S. Allende

> Salvador Allende died not because he was a socialist, but because he was an incompetent.
>
> P.N. Rosenstein-Rodan, 'Why Allende Failed', *Challenge* (May-June 1974)

1. THE UP'S ECONOMIC PROGRAMME

1.1. *Problems in the Chilean Economy*

The economic programme which contributed to the UP's electoral victory was based on a prognosis which was widely shared by economists and by most political groups; it identified the problems of the Chilean economy as follows:

(1) The rate of growth was slow, tending towards stagnation after the negative effects of import substitution became noticeable. It dropped from an annual average of 5.3% during the 1960-66 period to less than 3% during the last part of the 1970s.

(2) Monopolization was increasing due to both import substitution and the increasing importance of foreign capital. These were interrelated and tended to reinforce each other, and in 1969 20% of the industrial enterprises' capital was in foreign hands.[1]

(3) The unemployment rate was constant – no less than 6% – while an increasingly large proportion of new jobs – about two thirds – were being

Footnotes and the table to this chapter may be found on pp. 384-389.

created in the tertiary sector, which in 1970 absorbed 47% of the labour force.[2]

(4) Incomes were highly concentrated: 79% of the families received 47% of the national income, 90.9% of the families 66.5%, and 2% of the families 12.5%.[3]

(5) The rate of gross investment over GDP was constant – about 16% of GDP – and the public sector's share was increasing, so that it came to contribute about 70% of the investments in production and infrastructure.[4]

(6) The inflation rate was increasing.

(7) Agriculture was still dominated by latifundia and by minifundia: in 1965 2% of the total number of properties (254,000) held 55% of Chile's productive land while 80% was owned by 7.5% of the agricultural units. Consequently extensive cultivation prevailed and an increasing number of peasants were continuously pushed towards the urban areas, mainly Santiago which absorbed about 40% of the whole country's population. The supply of agricultural produce was less than the demand, and this necessitated large imports.[5]

(8) Except for food, imports of raw materials and capital goods increased as a result of the industrialization policy which in turn proved incapable of reducing the constraints resulting from the balance of payments situation.

(9) Finally, compared to other Latin American countries, Chile had a relatively high level of economic and social development but also more definite signs of stagnation and dependence.

Given this situation it is not at all surprising that there was a wide convergence between the UP programme's '40 measures' and the programme of the *Partido Democrático Cristiano* (PDC) which was propagated by R. Tomić,[6] who even recently emphasized that such similarity had its origins in the common awareness and the cooperation among the large majority of the Chileans. A short comparison of the two programmes demonstrates the similarity.

The PDC programme and the UP '40 measures' programme were both basically of the ECLA or *desarrollista* ('developmentalist') type, implying an acceptance of the need to limit the operation of the capitalist system,[7] but without realizing the implicit consequences of such action. For the UP all these measures were of course step forward towards socialism, although the duration of such a transitional phase was not specified – nor could it be. In the PDC as well the view that capitalism tends to some form of socialism was widely held. The creation of an egalitarian society was envisaged by both programmes. However, not even the UP programme conceptualized the need to change the values and priorities on which the structure of production and of demand was based, and to harmonize the short-term policies with those directed at creating structural changes.

The UP and PDC programmes agreed substantially on agrarian reform problems: in fact they even agreed with Alessandri's programme.

Thus, both programmes emphasized the leading role of the state in fostering a process of structural transformations in which large sectors of the population should increasingly and actively participate. Such changes were not contemplated by Alessandri.

Both programmes stressed the need to nationalize part of the industrial sector to create a new economy with a large non-private sector. This sector was to be composed of state-owned, worker-owned and state- and worker-owned industries. However, the size of the non-private sector contemplated by the UP was larger than that of the PDC. The UP wanted to include not only the large strategic industrial monopolies and the copper mines but also the larger nitrate mines, iron and steel, iodine and coal as well as the financial system (specifically private banks, whose nationalization Tomić also accepted) and the insurance companies,[8] foreign industrial monopolistic distribution enterprises and foreign trade. The creation of such a public sector did not imply the 'planning of a process of complete socialization of the Chilean economy', as was made clear in the UP programme and repeated by those directly responsible for the economic policy.[9]

Furthermore, a distinction was drawn between 'imperialist capital' and 'foreign capital': only the first was to be eliminated, while the second constituted no problem once regulated by specific criteria. Finally, the socialization process was restricted to the large monopolistic domestic and foreign enterprises. The fact that, in practice, this restriction was not always respected only shows the difficulty of monitoring structural changes; it is not related to the harmful initiatives of those who, in a desperate attempt to speed up the transitional period, unknowingly contributed to its demise.

Because the PDC's measures were more limited and mostly concerned with short-term policies, presenting them in a more specific manner was easier than in the case of the more general and far-reaching measures in the UP programme. Despite this, the PDC programme did not clearly define the extent of the social sector (*area social*) and the role and extent of the three types of ownerships which were to be incorporated in this sector. The UP failed, for its part – even when it was in office – to clarify the limits and nature of its aims. This was not only due to its programme's generality but more to the fact that a process of structural changes, once initiated, tends to produce its own dynamics. Such a process is easier to stop – and indeed it was stopped – than to carefully steer on a predetermined course at a given speed.

A further demonstration of the similarity between the PDC and UP measures was the nationalization of copper. This was done through a Constitutional amendment which was unanimously passed by the National Congress, in which the UP was in the minority. Substantial agreement also existed on the necessity to speed up the agrarian reform process which had been initiated, but very slowly implemented, by the Frei Government.

The two programmes stressed the need to revitalize the economy through a massive investment plan. Such an effort was expected to require the use and extension of price controls and the tax increases already adopted by the previous Government but opposed by Alessandri, who represented commercial interests. The general increase in production was considered by both programmes as a requirement for achieving a degree of income redistribution, increasing employment and simultaneously reducing the inflation rate.

It is in this respect that the *batalla por la producción* ('struggle for production') was an economic as well as a political necessity. What was not foreseen was the explosive effects of the demand increase, which was generated by a relatively small and short-lived income redistribution,[10] and the destabilizing effect that the fear for the structural changes described in the programme would cause to both demand and supply. While demand did in fact increase, although not necessarily because of an actual increase in consumption, income distribution tended to decline because of fear or deliberate unwillingness to cooperate and because of the unforeseen disruption created by the attempt to set up the new economy.

Important parts of the UP programme had actually been carried out by the end of 1971, but its disruptive effects did not appear until 1972 and continued during 1973. While in fact the Gross National Product (GDP) grew at a rate of 7.7% in 1971 (compared to only 3.7% in 1970), this rate was 1.4% in 1972 and dropped to -4.0% in 1973.[11]

1.2. *The Implementation of the UP Programme*

While practically all the measures described in the UP programme can be traced to the current development theory, to the recommendations of UN agencies and to most international declarations, the cumulative consequences of these measures have not always been fully understood. Nor has the (mis)use of their disruptive effects as an instrument to prevent further change been studied.

Inflation, together with stagnation, has been recognized to represent – at least in Latin America – one symptom of the failure to achieve an independent industrialization and to create an integrated and diversified economy.[12] The Pearson Report shared this view with respect to the Chilean economy's high inflation rate, but it also warned that changes 'can be reached only slowly if the economy is not to be severely disrupted'.[13] However, structural changes are intrinsically disruptive,[14] so that waiting until price stabilization has resulted from a long-term development programme leaves the problems posed by short-term inflation unresolved.

Inflation is in fact not only a symptom of the need for structural changes: it can easily and simultaneously become one of the main obstacles to realizing those changes, as was demonstrated in Chile by the growing inflation rate which followed Frei's reform attempts. In other words, inflation is an efficient instrument for delaying pervasive social reforms and institutional changes which, because they are the essence of development, are intrinsically disruptive and consequently inimical to a smooth transitional process. In order to assure a smooth transition the UP gave so much priority to reducing inflation that control over it was conceived almost as a prerequisite for implementing structural changes, instead of its being the result of the restructuring of the Chilean economy.

The disruptive effects of this restructuring were also enhanced by other problems. First was the refusal by the National Congress and part of the bureaucracy to allow and to carry out the necessary progressive tax reform,[15] which was intended to provide the means to increase investment. Second was the National Congress's opposition to a bill for nationalizing the industrial monopolies and to all legislation relative to the banking system. This forced the Government to either purchase enough shares on the market to gain control of these industries or to obtain shares more directly through disadvantageous contractual agreements.

Equally disruptive was the elimination of the latifundia and the implementation of the agrarian reform,[16] which was regulated in laws passed during the Frei Government. In fact 'history teaches us that land reform is seldom a tidy affair and is always time-consuming' and that 'short-run disruptions and conflicts arising from a programme of structural change in land ownership'[17] are quite natural. If a Government is to control such a complicated process it must have full power and be able to use a complicated series of instruments. This was not the case in Chile: in fact the disruption of agricultural production was less than could have been expected. This is especially remarkable considering the simultaneous rapid increase in demand which in agriculture was not met by the existing unused capacity, as was the case in industry during most of 1971. Consequently shortages started to appear after a while.

The conflict between some of the short-term measures and the long-term structural transformations – which was the most crucial problem in the UP economic policy – was due to the fact that the policy 'was part of a political strategy which was also short-term and which was basically aimed at dealing with two problems: the problem of reactivating the economy ... and the problem of increasing the 36 percent support obtained by the Left in the Presidential elections'.[18] At the end of 1971 the first problem had been dealt with: the GNP increased by 8%, industrial production rose by 12%, inflation was at its lowest (it dropped from 35% in 1970 to 22% in 1971) and employment was at its highest. The second problem had already been solved in April of 1971, when the UP got 49.7% of the votes in the Chilean elections, a percentage which it maintained until the last election in March 1973, when it got 43.9%.

However, the need for increasing success in the elections made the long-term structural changes dependent on the short-term objectives, for failure to achieve short-term objectives would reduce the popular support for the Government, which was committed to making changes within the bounds of the existing Constitution but lacked a majority both throughout the country and in National Congress, and thus would also make it politically more difficult for that Government to carry out structural changes. At the same time success with the short-term objectives made structural changes more difficult politically as well as economically. Politically it was not easy to make the masses accept a reduction in their recently improved situation. The middle class was similarly not willing to give up their demand structure, and maintenance of that structure had during 1971 made no small contribution to solidifying the UP gains in the elections – gains which, it was hoped, would lead to establishing majority rule.

Furthermore, economic expansion during 1971 increased business profits and so provided industrialists and merchants with the time and the means to reorganize and plan their defence.

The enlargement of the public sector (APS) in industry had not created 'a drastic change in the working modalities' of this sector either during 1971[19] or by the end of 1972, when 83% of the food industry was in private hands, as was 74% of beverages, 99% of footwear and clothing, 98% of furniture and household equipment, 100% of tobacco and 51% of textiles. It is interesting to note here that, in the textile industry, only 10% was in foreign hands. Taking industry as a whole, no more than 22% of production was in the public sector, while in the rest, which was in private hands, 'no control was exercised by the workers or by the government'. As a result, 'the items which yielded higher profits were produced instead of the most necessary ones. Luxury articles were made, which gave higher returns, but not popular consumer goods, which were far more necessary'. As for distribution of industrial production, the public sector controlled no more than 30%.[20]

The lack of real control over the production process made it difficult to rapidly adjust that process to the needs of the masses while at the same time reducing the output of luxury goods. The achievement of such a goal was made even more difficult by the impossibility of legally raising or even imposing taxes on high incomes, large holdings and other forms of wealth.

The production structure is historically the result of the existent unequal income distribution, i.e. of the Chilean class structure. Any effective change in income distribution without a planned adjustment of the class structure would have caused inflation and shortages which would in turn constitute the best conditions, given the logic of an unrestricted market system, for an automatic elimination of redistribution. Consequently, control over the production process was an essential condition for effective income redistribution.

In Chile, apart from for moral reasons, control of production was justified by the need to win votes, yet its modest achievement contributed the excuse – inflation – and the means – an increase in profits not subject to taxation – for disrupting the Government policy and retarding the acquisition of a degree of economic control. Such control was not only part of the programme on the basis of which Allende had become President: more importantly it was the most decisive measure for acquiring the resources necessary for carrying out income redistribution without being forced to create greater liquidity through an abnormal increase in public deficit financing.

The difficulty the UP Government encountered in extending its real control over the production structure made it impossible to maintain the short-term income redistribution initiated by the Allende Government. The existing demand structure was the main obstacle which hindered the Government in acquiring the power needed for remolding the production structure so that it would serve a new demand pattern which was more suitable to satisfying the basic private needs and solving the most pressing social problems. As a result the UP Government did not get very far in dealing with such problems.

The use of the market to correct the disruptive effects of the measures directed at achieving short-term objectives, and some long-term changes, merely served to bring about the reduction in aggregate demand, through the increase in prices and the contraction of public expenditures. The price increase actually meant a decrease of real wages, due in part to the biased operation of the index used for computing wages which linked the cost of living to the level of wages. As a result of this mechanism[21] a regressive redistribution process was set in motion, which was accelerated in the second half of 1972.[22] The contraction of public expenditure produced a drastic reduction in investments[23] as a substantial part of public expenses had to be devoted to paying the wages of those employed in public services. As the production structure had been left quite unchanged, it could only tend to achieve the balance between demand and supply by re-establishing the original income distribution, the only one capable of guaranteeing such an equilibrium. Even rationing, which was proposed at the end of 1972, would not have been sufficient to obtain such an equilibrium without extensive control over production and distribution. The inflation process and the black market were the instruments for maintaining the existing production structure:[24] the reduction of demand was bound to have a stronger effect on the poorer classes, as indicated by a 15% drop in real salaries, which took place between July 1972 and July 1973.[25]

Yet this orthodox way of dealing with the inflation did not prevent private foreign investments from declining further. Meanwhile, hopes that the National Congress would finally pass the bill creating the *Area de Propiedad Privada* (APP) [Area of Private Property] were dashed by the already well established coalition between the PDC and the right. Furthermore, a series of well coordinated strikes by white collar workers, shopkeepers and lorry owners further contributed to the final disruption of distribution and so institutionalized the highly speculative 'parallel' market. When the manufacturing sector's idle capacity was fully used, the possibility of fostering new investment – to expand production or create new types of production – shrunk and at the same time reserves were depleted. The low copper price and the lack of foreign financing made the Chilean economic situation even more precarious, while domestic opposition and boycotts were carefully synchronized to have increasingly devastating effects. Domestic prices for capital goods[26] and durable consumer goods – the only two sectors which had been transferred entirely in the APS – especially cars and household appliances, as well as petrol (almost all of which was imported), were maintained at low levels for political reasons. This was done despite mounting costs resulting from the income redistribution policy and the rise in prices of imported inputs, the latter constituting a very large component of industrial production. Ironically, the main beneficiaries of the 'politically fixed' prices were those strata of the middle class and the military that the Allende Government wanted to gain to its cause. Furthermore, low prices and rising costs required large subsidies to public utilities companies and to nationalized industries; this in turn drained resources and so reduced the Government's capacity to invest productively.

The relatively small income redistribution during 1971 resulted in a situation in which the poorest part of the population, largely UP supporters, came to actually finance the consumption of those social groups which were most aggressively against the UP programme and Government.

The attempt to win over the middle class resulted – and it could not be otherwise – in the impossibility of carrying out even the more gradual measures which had been incorporated in the UP programme in order to reach precisely that class. Given the income distribution shown in Table 10.1, which prevailed at the end of the 1960s, and given the fact that the UP did not have a majority in the National Congress, Allende's Government had to try to increase the income of those earning the least without being really able to affect the income of those earning the most. Yet the latter income was, in theory, the only one which could be reduced because the income of half of the population included in the middle income group could hardly be changed as it was already quite low, even in absolute terms. To double the lowest income, i.e. to raise it to less than two minimum wages, would in fact have required that the middle group's income be halved. The overall result would have been to put 91% of the total population on an income of no more than two minimum wages.

Furthermore, the increase in the money wages of the lower income group made an increase of imported inputs necessary. Thus imports grew increasingly as soon as the existing industrial idle capacity was fully used and the demand for food generated by the wage increase could no longer be satisfied by domestic production.

The real problem was to expand production while adjusting it to the new income distribution and consumption pattern which had resulted from the necessary limiting of the high income group's earnings and from the simultaneous modification of the middle income group's spending habits. Foreign assistance could have been of great help during this transitional stage. Yet its drastic reduction (see section 3.1 below) had a negative effect on the economic growth rate, although it did not cause the domestic saving ratio to rise proportionally.[27] During the 1960s this ratio oscillated around 15% of national income.[28] After a rapid increase in savings in real terms by about 50% in 1971,[29] there was a sharp decline in the following two years of 27%[30] and 25%[31] respectively.

The substantial increase in savings during 1971 was certainly due to the rapid increase in liquidity. However, the decline in savings during the two following years, when liquidity was still quite high and income redistribution was largely neutralized, must be explained by psychological factors and the existence of a thriving black market into which savings could easily and profitably, politically and economically, be channeled.

Thus, in considering the relationship between income distribution, savings and economic growth on the basis of the data and targets included in the economic plan for 1971-76 prepared by the UP, it has been argued that 'a radical redistribution of income, i.e. a redistribution of the share of owners-entrepreneurs' disposable income from 18.6 to 8.3 percent in six years', would require that 'wage- and salary-earners...will have to raise its incremental saving rate from the virtual zero or negative quantity recorded in 1970 to close to 18 percent over a period of four years' if the target of a 7% growth of production is to be reached.[32] This target was in fact achieved in 1971 only, when the wage- and salary-earners' share increased over the preceding year by 12.4%;[33] it was not reached later, when income redistribution had already been completely eliminated, although some of its effects were still operative.

All this seems to indicate that, apart from the problem of remolding the production structure, the range within which income redistribution is economically feasible depends on the one hand on the extent to which the upper class's consumption can be restricted, and on the other on the national economy's growth rate.[34] However, for political reasons Allende could neither touch the consumption of the high income group nor let the economy grow faster than the availability of foreign currency permitted. In fact, as the copper price was low and foreign aid and foreign investment declined, the economy's growth rate was also bound to decrease; thus the income redistribution achieved during 1971 became untenable and consequently was very rapidly eliminated. It seems ironical that analysis of harmonizing the objectives of the development strategy guiding the 1971-76 plan, i.e. a rapid rate of economic growth, full employment, and income redistribution, seems to indicate that this strategy hinged 'essentially on the economy's ability to increase exports'.[35] As it would have been difficult to achieve such an increase without creating a conflict with the Government's goal of reducing the country's dependence, the inflow of concessional foreign resources with no political strings attached would have enhanced the possibility of the transition to at least a better income distribution and possibly to a new production pattern.

On the basis of these considerations, it seems difficult to continue arguing, in order to explain the demise, that the UP programme and its implementation were too radical. The belief that a more revolutionary approach would have been more successful also seems rather irrelevant; this would be a conclusion based on an alleged lack of mass mobilization, which is not supported by the evidence on the high level of politicization which was in fact reached in Chile before the demise.[36]

The alternative to the egalitarian or socialist approach, an approach which was more or less explicitly contained in the two programmes, was a pure capitalist growth model which could provide no more than a slow, long-term betterment of the masses' living standards. This model had been rejected by two thirds of the Chilean electorate; its application has usually coincided with the establishment of authoritarian governments.

We shall now concentrate on the economic conditions needed to bring about structural change.

2. THE TRANSFORMATION PROCESS AND THE ROLE OF FOREIGN ASSISTANCE

2.1. Analysis of the conditions necessary for successfully implementing structural changes cannot be separated from considerations on the nature of underdevelopment and on the viability of some roads to development.

The main characteristics of an underdeveloped country are as follows: (1) its internal dynamics are largely conditioned by its dependent position within a hierarchically structured international system; (2) its domestic surplus is concentrated in a very small proportion of the population; (3) this surplus is largely transferred abroad to the countries at the top of the international system's hierarchy.

The relationships through which dependence is created and maintained constitute a very complex system, the most permanent and strongest element of which remains the demand structure imposed on the underdeveloped countries.[37] As the demand structure implies a given set of priorities which contribute to establishing the use of resources, so is determined the nature and direction of economic production and consequently the overall growth of the society.

The demand structures of the developed countries adjust to or reflect the evolution of their own socioeconomic systems, the reforms of which have attempted to harmonize conflicting domestic class interests. The costs of doing this have, however, been wholly or partially passed on to the underdeveloped countries.

The adoption by, or imposition on, underdeveloped countries of a demand structure derived from that of the developed countries fosters domestic class interests in the former, contributes to underdevelopment in the latter, and still constitutes the most crucial element of the latter's dependence on the developed countries. As dependence is a crucial aspect of any analysis of underdevelopment, developmental strategies must explicitly reject the existing demand structure, as the satisfaction of such alien demand cannot but remain limited to a relatively small minority of the population and consequently reinforce inequalities and maintain dependence. Thus, the acceptance of the existing demand structure on the whole tends to result in the perpetuation of underdevelopment.

Attempts to merely widen the area which satisfies such a demand structure through, for example, limited redistributive measures, are bound to fail for purely economic reasons. Having fully used the existing production capacity they soon make it necessary to import final and/or capital goods. As a result, the worsening of the balance of payments increases the country's foreign dependence – that is, its economic vulnerability – and so make it impossible to retain income redistribution.

In other words, the fragile production structure that is geared to the needs of a small minority cannot cope with a larger and increasing demand without making the system more economically dependent. Improving the conditions of the whole population implies reducing its economic dependence, that is retaining its economic surplus domestically, and requires a structural change in demand and production. Domestic inequalities and foreign dependence must be tackled simultaneously as they are *the* two aspects of the process of underdevelopment.

Even if the redistribution of income away from owners and entrepreneurs and towards wage- and salary-earners has a negative impact on the economic growth rate and consequently makes it more difficult to change the production structure, the problem now seems to be of secondary importance. Recent studies in fact indicate that an income redistribution directed at satisfying basic needs requires a lower rate of economic growth than would otherwise be the case.[38] If this is the case, then it follows that the current assumption that income redistribution should be carried out such that it is not incompatible with greater efficiency and a more open economy hardly applies. Thus, the usual conclusion that the desired level of redistribution cannot be attained unless production grows at a minimum rate seems even less relevant. In most studies of specific countries this rate has turned out to be higher than the feasible one, as is also demonstrated by figures for the Chilean economy, which show that redistribution of less than 7% of the domestic product to labour would have required at least six years![39]

To conclude, economic growth can only be pursued in conjunction with income redistribution; development strategies must be increasingly 'concerned not with the maximization of production or output, but with the maximization of consumption of the poorest – shifting the emphasis from supply to demand'.[40] Furthermore, the growth rate no longer needs to be proportional to the higher income group's ability to oppose measures that affect their consumption and income.[41] In fact, the growth rate will tend to be inversely proportional to such resistance provided that genuine international cooperation exists which could help guarantee political pluralism, economic efficiency, and a relatively open development process.

The contradictions in the traditional approach to underdevelopment are further clarified when one considers that the reforms undertaken in most Western countries, although they have not meant any fundamental revision of the priorities that determine their demand pattern, have nonetheless been able to accommodate most of their populations. When similar measures were tried in underdeveloped countries the result was the country's increasing dependence, as in the staggering indebtedness resulting from Frei's timid reforms, or economic chaos, that is, what Western ethnocentric perception defines as chaos. Besides, 'it is not hard to guess how the same commentators would have denounced...[the UP] government, if it had succeeded in putting an end to the chaos' to which 'the government's single significant "contribution"...was its own weakness'.[42]

This inherent incapacity of dependent, underdeveloped economies to satisfy a larger demand for nonluxury goods is a very efficient protection for the higher income group's power and consumption. The main components of this mechanism are Georgescu-Roegen's structural inflation lock[43] and the negative impact that the fear of change, especially if encouraged by a well-run campaign, produces on the electorate. The structural inflation lock originates from the historical process of economic growth in dependent economies and from the recognized impossibility of diverting investments away from the productive structure based on a given income distribution and into the structure required by the changing social relations. The result of the tension between the old production structure and the emerging income distribution is very rapid inflation which, however, is not the inevitable consequence of the masses' aspiration to improve their living standards but instead 'the consequence of the upper class's desire for a more luxurious life'.[44]

Consequently, not even full control over the means of production, not to speak of the limitations which appear if a country is relatively small, is sufficient to change the country's economic dependence if the production pattern is not altered. But to do this more time is needed – and more power – than the Allendė Government ever had.

2.2. The current definition of foreign aid is 'that part of the foreign capital inflow that normal market incentives do not provide'[45] and which is assumed to contribute to increase the recipient country's GDP growth rate.[46] Thus, foreign aid, originally justified on the basis of an extraordinary situation (as with the Marshall Plan aid), has finally been connected to the failure of the market system to properly cope with development problems. It is also now recognized that to realize the maximum potential from aid 'in many poor countries it is necessary to undertake basic reforms in the land tenure systems, the tax structure, education and governmental administration'.[47]

However, implementing these reforms, aside from increasing the aid's effectiveness, will not reduce the need for aid because the necessary conditions for the normal market incentives to generate the required flow of resources can only emerge at the end of a development process. Until self-sustained growth is attained the three main phases of the development process are dominated, respectively, by a lack of absorptive capacity, a savings gap and a foreign exchange gap.[48] Each of these different types of problems are dealt with, respectively, by technical assistance, aid for specific projects, and the supply of foreign exchange. Whatever the value of such a classification, it is important to note its implication, namely that different problems must be coped with through different instruments; in other words, aid can serve different purposes.

Aside from its political significance, the international transfer of resources is thus viewed as being composed of two types of flows: (1) the transfer dictated by profit motives, i.e. largely private foreign investments; and (2) the transfer apparently not dictated by the donor's profit motives but in which the recipient country evaluates the project's rate of return in rather short-term commercial terms. This flow basically covers Government grants and some of the loans to underdeveloped countries.

The size of the second type of transfer is determined either by supply, i.e. the amount the donors want to or can give, or by the demand, i.e. the amount the recipient country needs or rather can absorb. This approach can aim either to supplement domestic savings or to enlarge the import capacity, or to do a combination of both.

The assumption underlying such an approach, namely that aid enhances the recipient country's capacity or mobilize resources, is challenged by those who stress the displacement effect, that is, that development is frustrated by the organizational changes which aid stimulates. These induced changes tend to impose alien values and alien organizational patterns which consequently prevent or retard the emergence in the recipient countries of a domestically rooted and self-reinforcing process of change.

However, both analyses of the effects of aid consider that among the needs which must be fulfilled are those which arise from the very structure of underdevelopment and those largely defined in terms of the pace at which such a structure is modified. Nonetheless, these analyses ignore the needs created by the modifications, and also ignore the changes, both quantitative as well as qualitative, that such needs undergo during a real restructuring process. The absorptive capacity is consequently determined by such static factors as the rate at which technical manpower can be increased, the installed productive capacity of certain goods and commodities, or – again – the overall expansion rate. The other factor which constrains the absorptive capacity is the positive rate of return which the use of foreign aid must show. As productivity tends necessarily to be lower in underdeveloped countries compared to when the same resources are used in developed countries,[49] this consideration encourages the use of these resources where results can be more rapidly achieved.

If, then, aid must tend basically to close the gap between exports and imports, it must not only be productive but must also be used in those sectors where it can generate or save foreign exchange.

This point, and the requirement of a positive rate of return, eliminates the possibility of the transfer of resources on purely redistributive principles, i.e. aid for consumption which would 'lead to immediate improvements in the standard of living among the poor of the poorer nations'.[50]

The transfer of resources on purely redistributive principles seems closer to the 'creative aid' given 'in anticipation of a long-range economic and political development than to the more common "acquisitive" type motivated by the hope of economic profits or some other advantages'.[51] Because of the longer time span of the first type, this type is definitely more useful than the current acquisitive aid which, intentionally or not, has a short-term perspective. However, even creative aid is given for 'a long-range economic and political development in a favoured direction', so that the assumed redistributive principles remain 'in large part the function of more pressing and compelling political military, and diplomatic strategies'.[52]

The obvious conclusion if thus that foreign aid activities in themselves are unlikely to constitute a basis of a new system of international politics. On the other hand, on the theoretical level more research and insight is needed on the relationships, which are usually assumed to be constant, between aid and domestic politics and between domestic and foreign factors.[53]

3. CHILE'S DEVELOPMENT AND FOREIGN ASSISTANCE

3.1. The net inflow of foreign resources from the Development Assistance Committee (DAC) countries and multinational agencies averaged slightly more than \$130 million per year during the 1967-70 period; bilateral Official Development Assistance (ODA) accounted for most of it, being about \$110 million.[54] As a result, at the end of 1970 Chile's external debt reached \$2.5 billion (or \$2 billion if the undisbursed portion is not included); it was the third largest in Latin America, after that of Brazil and Mexico,[55] and was more than twice the country's current export earnings. One billion dollars were due to the United States. Considering that in 1960 the external debt was only \$6 million, its annual growth rate was 15.3% during 1961-65 and 17.7% during 1965-70; in both periods the growth rate was always substantially higher than the average for Latin America, which was 11% for the first half of the 1960s and 11.5% for the second half.[56] Servicing this debt cost an average of 15.3% of the exports of goods and non-service factors during the 1966-70 period; in 1971 it reached 21%. If payments for amortization are added to the interest payments the share of commodity exports devoted to debt servicing increases from 20% in 1960 to 55% in 1969,[57] equivalent to 5% of the GNP and to almost one third of Chile's gross capital formation. Available data show that, at least since World War II, net investment income outflows have exceeded net direct investment inflows during most of the years. While net private foreign capital flows averaged $52.6 million during 1961-65 and $36 million during 1966-70, net factor payments abroad averaged $97.8 million and $198.8 million respectively,[58] and foreign aid was needed to close such a rapidly increasing gap.

However, the country's ability to absorb foreign resources seemed exhausted at the end of 1970 as the net inflow of resources from DAC countries and multinational agencies became negative in 1971 and 1972 – it was $-116.2 million in 1971 and $-64.4 million in 1972 – while it had been $113.4 million in 1970. However, in 1974 it jumped to $378.8 million.[59]

The largest share of this 'assistance' in the 1960s came from the United States and was part of a general increase in U.S. aid expenditures in Latin America which had started at the beginning of the decade. This expansion coincided with the type of political model prevailing at that time in Washington and with the increased interest shown by U.S. private business in playing the role of economic developer and replacing both local governments and even local industrialists in some of their activities, which were to be geared to an increasingly internationalized system of production and distribution. In Chile, in fact, though the foreign companies owned at the end of 1969 more than 20% of the capital in the industrial limited companies, their real control was much larger and increased with the size of the companies so that forty of the 100 larger companies were controlled from abroad.[60] Although they enjoyed a monopolistic or duopolistic position in the fastest-growing sectors,[61] between 1960 and 1969 the inflow of foreign direct private capital was only $22 million, about 3% of gross capital formation during this period, plus $118 million in foreign credits.[62] Yet the stock of private direct foreign investment was about $1 billion by 1967, more than 10% of the estimated capital stock in the country.[63]

Foreign aid proper was needed for the state to maintain the infrastructure required for expanding the activities controlled by foreign interests and providing the necessary financing of the foreign-owned or controlled industries. These industries in fact tended to use an increasing share of Chile's national credit for their investments. The real cost of this credit to the foreign operators during the 1960s was quite low, or even negative.[64]

To repeat, foreign aid is easily turned into an instrument to facilitate and finance the expansion of foreign penetration in the economic structure of the recipient country.[65] Therefore, the amount of aid received is in no significant way positively correlated to economic growth.[66] This phenomenon is also due to the substitution effect, namely the reduction of the higher income group's savings,[67] and the diversified and perverted demand structure it generates. Such a structure generates an increasing concentration on new goods or on technologically more sophisticated production[68] which are unnecessary for or unaccessible to most of the population.

It is thus not difficult to accept that

> much of the process of economic and social change in Chile...reflects the decisive influence exerted by the external sector, particularly foreign trade and investments from abroad, which have served as vehicles for obtaining the necessary technology needed at each stage of output. They have also in turn been responsible for shaping the overall consumption pattern and determining the direction of its change, the structure of production created to satisfy these changing demands and the level of techniques and skills which are used in production.[69]

If we compare this conclusion with that reached by Muñoz, namely that 'the composition of industrial goods' consumption is determined much more by production decisions than by consumers' demand',[70] then the close relationship between foreign capital, including foreign aid, and the type and distribution of consumption becomes evident.

3.2. Naturally, the question arises of why the foreign assistance that had been so abundantly supplied to the PDC Government[71] was reduced after 1970 – even denied completely by the United States as AID loans were discontinued[72] – although the new Government's programme took an approach similar to that for which Tomić had campaigned on many problems affecting Chilean development. The most plausible answers are that either these programmes did not guarantee enough continuity with the past, or that their chances of being implemented were quite varied, or were so perceived.

In other words, foreign assistance seemed to be more responsive to declarations on the reforms considered necessary for enhancing the aid's effectiveness – see the Alliance for Progress programme – than to the concrete implementation of such reforms and to the problems that implementation would create.

In Chile, given the narrow margins of manoeuvrability within which the UP Government attempted to implement its programme, the role of foreign assistance, even in its traditional form, was quite important. Its importance rested not merely in its being a source of badly needed foreign reserves – to which foreign aid in any case does not contribute much – but also in that it would provide assurance to some hesitant sectors of Chilean society and to the military that the '*via chilena*' would not result in the country's isolation.

Instead of this, the publicized reduction of foreign assistance was used to create, or reinforce, the impression that the newly elected Government constituted a drastic break with the past, and consequently fostered the outflow of resources and experts.

On top of this, the reduction of foreign assistance took place immediately after the UP Government's inauguration, when it was exceptionally difficult for that Government to create its new credit lines and its own foreign aid strategy. For this strategy was based on tapping new and more congenial sources (see Alexis Guardia's 'Structural Transformations in the Chilean Economy and the System of External Economic Relations', Chapter 3 of this volume) as well as some of the traditional ones, taking advantage of both the commercial interests and the rivalries between the Western countries, their internal divisions, and the often divergent interests of the various multinational corporations.

Finally, it seems necessary to stress that the withdrawal of aid, and especially the timing of that withdrawal, both rather neglected topics in the literature on aid, are often a very powerful weapon in the donor's hands for influencing the recipient country's domestic policies so as to maintain the *status quo*: for this is the purpose for which aid is basically meant.[73]

4. INTERNATIONAL COOPERATION FOR DEVELOPMENT

Rebuilding a productive structure according to well defined and well ordered requirements takes time. During the transitional period of rebuilding, basic needs must be satisfied just as they had to be in the past, i.e. production has to continue though the management of nationalized production may be assumed by people who do not necessarily possess the required capacities. But training abroad, in some sort of technical assistance programme, may not be the most appropriate way to satisfy more basic and general needs; and the foreign techniques acquired may also not be the most 'efficient' means for coping with these needs. Managers' training and new techniques must be created or adopted domestically through an institutionalized process which requires time to be established and time to become operative.

Reforms have two important effects: on the one hand, as we have seen, they tend to disrupt the economic system within which they are attempted and require a certain amount of time to produce the wanted results; on the other hand, they tend to alter the pre-existing balance of political forces and put a strain on the institutional framework. However, during this process the necessary sacrifice of some upper and middle class interests, which egalitarian development implies, may make it difficult to maintain formal democratic rule and may require loosening the country's ties with the international system.

Genuine international cooperation could be instrumental in overcoming these inherent imbalances and in avoiding uncoordinated political radicalization.[74] Such support for the poor countries' development would also greatly contribute to creating more realistic conditions for establishing a better international order.

Given this perspective, aid must be defined as only those foreign resources, including services, which are directed at supplementing domestic resources in coordination with the efforts which are being made to reorganize the existing production structure. Such a production structure is set up on the basis of an income distribution which must be made more egalitarian through substantial and permanent modification.

While traditional foreign aid is certainly not – and foreign investment even less so – a necessary or sufficient condition for development, the transition to independent development can be made easier, especially if formal democratic rule is to be maintained and excessive radicalization avoided, by the kind of international aid and cooperation which is qualitatively and quantitatively different from that which is current today.

This cooperation should be aimed towards (1) closing the gap between the quantity and type of goods produced and the quantity and type needed, while income is gradually redistributed and the production structure adjusted (the best example of such a gap is given by agrarian reform in its initial stage); (2) limiting or eliminating the possible negative reaction of some countries or industrial and financial circles to this process of transformation.

These two aims require both the continuous reassessment of the problems which developing countries face and the use of a more complex combination of instruments than those presently included in foreign aid. Not even the simple transfer of money could help very much, for developing countries also need relevant information on procurement, markets, etc., as well as active cooperation to obtain certain products and technological inputs.

It should also be clear that the impossibility of establishing a selective increase in production results in more strain being put on the balance of payments through increasing imported inputs, material as well as technological, thus necessitating foreign assistance in the traditional form. However, it may also implicitly reinforce unequal income distribution, strengthen uneven satisfaction of needs and worsen unbalanced allocation of resources between needs and wants and between private and public needs.

International cooperation should thus technically support the restructuring of production while helping to maintain production levels, so as to render possible a wider political participation in the development process. The more progressive sectors of the middle class would not immediately feel the threat to their standard of consumption and would consequently more easily cooperate with the transformation of the economy. This, together with the fact that 'the more time...is allowed for an economy to adjust its productive structure to the changing pattern of demand, the less likely it becomes that the rigidities...will persist',[75] strengthen the dependent countries' capacity to absorb both the foreign and the domestic reaction to their development measures.

Such an approach to foreign aid is quite different from the current one, which was summarized by Meier as the closing of the gap created by 'the claims of the development plan exceed[ing] the available domestic resources'.[76] The international cooperation sketched here is meant to make possible the largely *domestic* and *orderly* transfer of resources from one type of production structure to another, which is designed to satisfy a different pattern of consumption. In such a case the concessional transfer of resources then becomes part of a wider package and basically only a short-term measure.

The structural reforms which have been carried out in the rich or capitalist industrial countries have largely been possible because of these countries' access to the resources and markets in the underdeveloped world. However, the latter is not only denied such a solution to their reform efforts, but must also bear the brunt of certain rich countries' economic reactions as well as military opposition to these reform efforts.

Given this situation it is up to the rest of the rich countries, and some less rich countries that are able to do so, to cooperate with those underdeveloped countries which try to implement these reforms, for all these countries have, after all, committed themselves to cooperation through undersigning the UN resolutions on development.

On the other hand, it must be left to the government of each underdeveloped country to decide for itself whether it should attempt, on its own, the socioeconomic transformation which is required for its development. If international cooperation is deemed really necessary, then the search for the most appropriate partners among the rich as well as the poor countries must be conducted according to such well defined criteria as (1) the overall world situation with all its contradictions, and (2) the specific problems posed by the country's developmental goals and socioeconomic structure.

Point (1) should help to identify possible partners on the basis of political similarity or reciprocal interests. For some rich countries the latter could very likely be the result of competition among the industrial centres or of domestic political pressure and economic necessity. Point (2) should enable the underdeveloped country to establish quite precisely the type of resources or services wanted and the conditions for accepting development cooperation. As both points would necessarily tend to change with time, periodical reexamination of them is needed in order to maximize the amount and usefulness of the cooperation, and at the same time minimize the danger that cooperation would negatively effect the country's developmental goals by introducing unwanted foreign values, fostering the wrong type of consumption or production, and enhancing the use of technologies not suited to the country's conditions.

Furthermore, the developing country must diversify its sources of international cooperation so that the negative features which are necessarily implicit in such international cooperation are kept to a minimum.

While an underdeveloped country cannot reasonably expect to obtain cooperation from all the rich countries, it should be able to find some rich countries which, for one of the reasons mentioned above, are willing to help.

In the rich countries, the moral argument in favour of international cooperation should certainly appear more persuasive when it is shown that assistance will contribute towards concretely establishing minimum economical well-being for the masses, rather than abstractly 'promoting optimal economic growth of societies'. The assumption is thus that the rich countries are not afraid 'that the elimination of grinding poverty in other countries...may well decrease their own security',[77] for otherwise there is no basis for any real international cooperation.

The last point to consider is whether the kind of cooperation described here is applicable mainly to underdeveloped countries such as Chile, which have already reached a certain level of industrialization. This point is, however, one that requires an analysis which is clearly outside the scope of this chapter.

4.2. While Chile had some success in securing loans from countries other than the United States, these lines of credit were not obtained until the end of 1972 and mostly during the first half of 1973, that is after the effects of the sudden closure of the traditional credit lines had disrupted market arrangements and spare parts inflows. Furthermore, these alternative sources provided largely very short-term loans which could certainly not be any great help in coping with structural transformations.

Yet the very fact that such alternative sources, which were by no means only in the U.S.S.R., Eastern Europe and China, were found indicates that there are differences among countries which can offer useful leverage to a government attempting genuine development. This is because such differences provide a government with time to reorganize the economic system according to the equalitarian principles established in its programme, and thus it can exploit these differences for the benefit of the masses in some countries.[78] This situation may explain Allende's tolerance of domestic opposition in Chile, which started to yield results during July-August 1973, when a few European countries offered substantial credits to Chile.[79]

The fact that these efforts were successful is not contradictory to the present tendency towards verticalization of relations between a given centre and its own periphery (a verticalization which, should it become complete, would worsen the position of the periphery[80]). It shows that that principle of noninterference by one centre in another centre's sphere of influence has not yet been established among the new rules for relations between the various centres.

In examining Chile's success in obtaining loans one should not exclude the importance that domestic pressure exercised by active minorities in the rich countries which supported the Allende Government may have had in influencing the policies of those rich countries' cooperation. The domestic pressures also made possible the development of a degree of regional assistance, so that new lines of credit were opened to Chile by several Latin American countries, including Brazil, and this induced a sharp shift in Chilean trade towards the countries in the Latin American Free Trade Association (LAFTA), whose share in Chilean imports increased from 22% in 1970 to 30% in 1972 and 28% in 1973.[81]

Such pressures from active minorities can be important in counterbalancing another kind of pressure, that is, the pressure which multinationals operating in underdeveloped countries will put on the governments of their home countries if they notice that these governments intend to support such reforms in the underdeveloped countries as would imperil the multinationals' interests. Coping with the reactions of the multinationals which are negatively affected by development processes requires all the talent and imagination of these rich countries' active minorities. One possibility for placating the multinationals is that the rich countries' governments provide certain national resources.

In all of this, the crucial problem is to develop the country's awareness in order to generate the political will to act.

4.3. If all these efforts fail, a country which is struggling to develop is left alone to confront its domestic as well as its foreign enemies. As material sacrifices increase, the internal breakdown of the social structure becomes a more rapid and painful process. The possibility of a pluralistic transformation is sharply reduced and a take-over of power becomes the only solution. Regardless of who obtains power the majority of the population is bound to suffer longer, while the international order once again reveals its basic bias in favour of the present unequal order.

The UP programme, which aimed at transformation without violence, was a much more adequate answer to the tragic predicament in which the underdeveloped countries find themselves than that offered by the New International Economic Order. There are two reasons for this:

(1) The New Order neglects the crucial issue of control over the productive process during its transformation so as to implement a more equalitarian income distribution.

(2) It ignores the possible conflict between short and long-term problems and the need to harmonize the two differing sets of policies meant to deal with them. It thus ignores the fact that harmonization requires time.

The implementation of the UP programme constituted for the governments of several rich countries and many poor ones an unbearable challenge, which became more dangerous as: (1) the experiment was given a fairer chance through increasing international cooperation, which was becoming instrumental in allowing the Allende Government to move from basically short-term policies to long-term structural changes; and (2) the Chilean people clearly indicated that they understood what was at stake. Consequently they were increasingly more determined to support the UP Government and endure all sacrifices necessary to obtain not merely more goods but rather to realize a different structure of consumption and more meaningful lives.

The degree to which these two elements were interconnected is not easy to determine; however, the more certain they became during the first half of 1973, the closer the country moved to the day of the crudest military intervention, which was clearly the only way to stop such an historical process and revert the country to a time when

> 'comienza un nuevo invierno.
> No hay en esa ciudad, en donde está
> lo quo amo, no hay pan ní luz:
> un cristal frío cae sobre secos geranios'.[82]

NOTES

1. L. Pacheco, 'La inversión extranjera y las corporaçiones internationales en el desarrollo de Chile' [Foreign Investment and the International Corporations in the Development of Chile], in O. Muñoz *et al.*, *Proceso a la industrialización chilena* [Chilean Industrialization on Trial] (Santiago de Chile, Editiones Nueva Universidad, 1972), p. 115, Table 2.
2. ODEPLAN, *Antecedentes sobre el desarrollo chileno 1960-70* [Antecedents of Chilean Development from 1960 to 1970] (ODEPLAN, Series I, no. 1, *Planes semestrales, Plan de la economía nacional 1971-76* [Half-Yearly Plans, Plan of the National Economy for 1971-76]) (Santiago de Chile, 1971), p. 62, Table 48.
3. These data are from Dirección de Estadisticas y Censos [Office of Statistics and Census], *Serie de investigaciones muestrales B.5 – Encuesta nacional sobre ingresos familiares* [Series of Research Samples B.5 – National Survey of Family Incomes], March/June 1968 (Santiago de Chile, 1969), p. 15; they are also in ODEPLAN, *Antecedentes sobre el desarrollo...*, p. 16, Table 17. According to I. Heskia, *Análisis estadístico de la distribución del ingreso personal en Chile en 1967* [Statistical Analysis of Personal Income Distribution in Chile in 1967] (Santiago de Chile, Universidad de Chile, 1970), income distribution in Chile at the end of the 1960s was as follows:

	population %	income %	legal minimum wage unit
lowest	45	14	1 or less
middle	46	50	1 to 4
top	9	35	4 to 80

Such a distribution can be compared with that of Brazil (1960), where 80% of the population obtained 38.5% of the national income; Argentina (1961), with 79% and 48% respectively; Columbia (1964), with 79% and 40% respectively; and Mexico (1963), with 91% and 60% respectively. W.R. Cline, *Potential Effects of Income Redistribution on Economic Growth, Latin American Cases* (New York, Praeger, 1972), Statistical Appendix A.
4. G. Martner, 'Los aspectos económicos del Gobierno de Allende, problemas y perspectivas' [The Economic Aspects of the Allende Government, Problems and Perspectives], *Nueva Economía* [New Economy] (Sept.-Dec. 1971), 25.

5. S. Barraclough and A. Affonso, 'Diagnostico de la reforma agraria chilena' [Prognosis of Chilean Agrarian Reform], *Cuadernos de la Realidad Nacional. Revista del Centro de Estudios de la Realidad Nacional (Universidad Católica de Chile) (CEREN)* [Notebooks on the National Reality. Review of the Center for Studies of National Reality (Catholic University of Chile)] (April 1973), 21; C. Kay and P. Winn, 'La reforma agraria en el Gobierno de la Unidad Popular' [Agrarian Reform and the UP Government], *Sociedad y desarrollo* [Society and Development], 3 (July-Sept. 1973), 5.

6. During the electoral campaign this convergence was exploited by the PDC to create and defend its 'revolutionary and popular' image: J.E. Garcés, *La pugna política por la presidencia en Chile* [The Political Struggle for the Presidency in Chile] (Santiago de Chile, Editorial Universitaria, 1971), p. 102.

7. 'In the general elections of 1968, more than 70% of Chileans voted for parties, programmes and candidates which proclaimed their opposition to capitalism and to traditional structures and favoured more or less advanced socialization forms.' Since its origin the PDC had declared itself anti-capitalist and the 1969 platform included 'the substitution of capitalism by the organized workers'. See R. Tomić, 'Reflexiones sobre el golpe de estado en Chile' [Reflections on the *Coup d'état* in Chile], *IDS Bulletin* (Oct. 1975), 291.

8. The PDC's programme contemplated 'banking reform aimed at the nationalization of the whole system of banks and insurances'.

9. P. Vuskovic, 'El Gobierno Popular y el Area Privada' [The Popular Government and the Private Area], *Nueva Economía* [New Economy] (Sept.-Dec. 1971; this is a speech made in Dec. 1971), 14. O. Millas, 'Hay que ganar la batalla en el terreno de la economía' [The Struggle Must Be Won on the Economic Battlefield], *Revista de la Universidad Technica del Estado* [Review of the State Technical University] (Nov. 1972-Feb. 1973), 20.

10. The share of wages in domestic income rose from 54.9% in 1970 to 61.6% in 1971 and returned to 54.5% in 1972: Taller de Coyunctura [Economic Workshop], *Comentarios sobre la situación económica* [Statement on the Economic Situation], No. 8 (Santiago de Chile, Universidad de Chile, Sept. 1973), p. 218. The data for 1970 are accepted by A. Foxley in his recent work entitled *Estrategias de desarrollo y modelos de planificación* [Development Strategies and Planning Models] (Mexico City, Fondo Cultura Económica, 1975) in which he wrote that 'the percentage of wages in domestic income grew from 51.5% in 1960 to 55% in 1970' (p. 83). Yet Foxley and O. Muñoz ('Income Redistribution, Economic Growth and Social Structure: the Case of Chile', *Oxford Bulletin of Economics and Statistics* (Feb. 1974), 28), using nonspecified ODEPLAN data, put the 1971 increase of the wage and salary earners' share at from 55% to 66%.

11. International Development Bank, *Annual Report 1974* (Washington, D.C.), Table I-1, p. 4. Similar data for the GDP growth rate, namely 8.3% in 1971, 2.1% in 1972 and -4.1% in 1973, are presented in the United Nations, *Economic Survey of Latin America, 1973* (New York, 1975), Table 100, p. 169.

12. D. Seers, 'A Theory of Inflation and Growth in Under-Developed Economies Based on the Experience of Latin America', *Oxford Economic Papers* (June 1962), 190-193.

13. L.B. Pearson, *et al.*, *Partners in Development. Report of the Commission on International Development* (New York, London, Praeger, 1969), p. 256.

14. L.B. Pearson, *et al.*, *Partners in Development...*, p. 7: 'Change is, itself, intrinsically disruptive'.

15. 'If allowance is made for inflation, there was an actual decline in tax revenue in 1971.' See P.E. Sigmund, 'Chile, Two Years of "Popular Unity"', *Problems of Communism* (Sept.-Oct. 1972), 49.

16. In the middle of 1972 35.5% of productive agricultural land was in the reformed sector. See Barraclough and Affonso, 'Diagnostico de la reforma agraria chilena', 2.

17. Pearson, *et al.*, *Partners in Development...*, 62.

18. J. Faúndez, 'The Chilean Road to Socialism', *The Political Quarterly* (July-Sept. 1975), 316-317.

19. S. Ramos, *Chile: una economía de transición?* [Chile, A Transition Economy?] (Santiago de Chile, Editorial Prensa Latinoamericano, 1972), 225: 'It has not been possible to establish drastic changes in the functioning of the APS.' But as 'the left [had ob-

tained] access to the country's top office before equivalent power transfers had taken place at other levels...in such a situation, a continuous emphasis on legality was not just one possible option for a left-wing government; it was a condition for survival': V. Wallis, 'Imperialism and the "Via Chilena" ', *Latin American Perspectives*, 2 (1974), 50.
20. A. Salgado D., 'Scope and Limitations of the Economic Policy of the Popular Government', *Vierteljahresberichte* [Quarterly Reports] (Dec. 1974), 363.
21. U. Müller-Plantenberg and F. Hinkellamert, 'Condiciones y consecuencias de una política de redistribución de ingreses' [Conditions and Consequences of an Income Redistribution Policy], *Cuadernos de la Realidad Nacional...(CEREN)* (March 1973).
22. '...given rapid inflation of the kind that has taken place in Chile, it is very difficult, if not virtually impossible, to expect an increase in saving on the part of the wage and salary earners who would normally be in a position to save'. Foxley and Muñoz, 'Income Redistribution...', 24.
23. Data on capital formation are somewhat contradictory:

% rate of change of gross domestic investment (in 1970 escudos)

1970-71	-10.97[a]	(official -7.7[f]) and -4.9[d]
1971-72	- 5.7[b]	and +4.1[e]
1972-73	+11.6[c]	

Gross domestic investment (in 1970 escudos)

	billion[c]	index (1970=100)[c]	billion[f]
1970	17.0	100	14.5
1971	12.9	76	13.3
1972	12.1	71	-

a Taller de Coyunctura, *Comentarios...*, No. 3 (July 1972), p. 192.
b Taller de Coyunctura, *Comentarios...*, No. 4 (Jan. 1973), p. 146.
c Taller de Coyunctura, *Comentarios...*, No. 8, p. 161.
d Foxley and Muñoz, 'Income Distribution...', p. 24.
e Universidad de Chile, Facultad de Economía Politica [University of Chile, Department of Political Economy], *La economía chilena en 1972* [The Chilean Economy in 1972] (Santiago de Chile, 1973), p. 384.
f Universidad de Chile, Facultad de Economía Política, *La economía chilena...*, p. 382, Table IV-11.

24. Müller-Plantenberg and Hinkellamert, 'Condiciones y consecuencias...', 225 and 227.
25. Salgado, 'Scope and Limitations...', 379.
26. In 1970 capital goods constituted only 1.8% of the gross value of domestic industrial production.
27. D.C. Davy, 'Foreign Aid, Government Consumption, Saving and Growth in Less-Developed Countries', *Economic Journal* (Sept. 1975), 60. Given the low propensity to save in Chile during 1972 and 1973, it is possible that once aid was discontinued the growth rate fell below what it would have been without any aid at all.
28. ODEPLAN, *Antecedentes sobre el desarrollo...*, Table 19, p. 27.
29. Universidad de Chile, Facultad de Economía Política, *La economía chilena...*, p. 342.
30. Taller de Coyunctura, *Comentarios...*, No. 4, Table 6, p. 151.
31. Taller de Coyunctura, *Comentarios...*, No. 8, Table 8, p. 167.
32. Foxley and Muñoz, 'Income Redistribution...', 23-24.
33. See note 10.
34. Foxley, *Estrategias de desarrollo...*, pp. 114-115.
35. Foxley, *Estrategias de desarrollo...*, p. 88.
36. 'The Allende government is blamed for its failure to make adequate preparations (such as arming the workers), on the assumption that it had enjoyed complete freedom to carry out whatever steps were called for.... In fact, the government's conciliatory strategy can very well be accounted for without assuming either betrayal (i.e. secret loyalty to the bourgeoisie) or naiveté (i.e. illusions that the bourgeoisie might be 'won over'). Part of the problem...was the need to 'buy time', in order that real popular mobilization might catch up with the level of purely electoral support which had been built around the issue of imperialism.' Wallis, 'Imperialism...', 53-54.

37. S. Sideri, 'International Trade and Economic Power', in J. Tinbergen (ed), *Towards a New World Economy* (Rotterdam, Rotterdam University Press, 1972), pp. 345-394.
38. M.J.D. Hopkins and H. Scolnik, 'Basic Needs, Growth and Redistribution: A Quantitative Approach', *ILO Working Papers*, 29 (Dec. 1975). This paper uses the Bariloche model.
39. Foxley and Muñoz, 'Income Redistribution...', 29.
40. Hopkins and Scolnik, 'Basic Needs...', 5.
41. Foxley and Muñoz, 'Income Redistribution...', 29-30.
42. Wallis, 'Imperialism...', 51.
43. N. Georgescu-Roegen, O estrangulamento-inflação estrutural e o crescimento econômico' [Structural Strangulation-inflation and Economic Growth], *Revista Brasileira de Economía* [Brazilian Review of Economics] (March 1968).
44. N. Georgescu-Roegen, 'O impasse de inflação estrutural e o desenvolvimento equilibrade' [The Impasse of Structural Inflation and Equilibrated Development], *Revista Brasileira de Economía* (July-Sept. 1972), 134.
45. G.M. Meier, 'Foreign Aid: Economic Aspects', *International Encyclopedia of the Social Sciences* (London, MacMillan, 1968), vol. 5, p. 521.
46. As the growth rate in underdeveloped countries has increased since World War II at the record level of 5% *per annum*, it has been concluded that 'an important contribution to this overall rate of progress has been the flow of resources from the developed countries in the form of foreign aid'. C.R. Frank Jr., 'Debt and Terms of Aid', in C.R. Frank Jr., J. Bhagwati, R. d'A. Shaw, H.B. Malmgren, *Assisting Developing Countries* (New York, Praeger, 1972), p. 5.
47. Meier, 'Foreign Aid: Economic Aspects', p. 527.
48. H.B. Chenery and A.M. Strout, 'Foreign Assistance and Economic Development', *The American EconomicReview* (Sept. 1966).
49. Bhagwati *et al.*, *Assisting Developing Countries*, p. 163.
50. Bhagwati *et al.*, *Assisting Developing Countries*, p. 186.
51. G. Liska, 'Foreign Aid: Political Aspects', *International Encyclopedia of the Social Sciences*, vol. 5, pp. 516 and 519.
52. Meier, 'Foreign Aid: Economic Aspects', p. 527.
53. J. White, *The Politics of Foreign Aid* (London, The Bodley Head), pp. 131-132.
54. OECD, DAC, *1970 Report* (Paris, 1970), Table 19, pp. 194-195, and *1971 Report*, Table 16, pp. 186-187. The U.S. 'aid programs of loans' totalled $301.3 million during the 1961-69 period, representing 20% of all U.S. aid to Latin America for that period and reaching $152 *per capita*, the highest in Latin America, followed by Panama and the Dominican Republic wth $115 each. The cumulative and authorized distribution of resources by AID to Chile amounted to $541.1 million in 1969. See OAS, CIAP, *United States Cooperation with Latin America* (CIAP/438 Corr. 2, Washington, D.C., 8 January 1971), Tables IV-6, IV-11 and p. IV-47.
55. The World Bank, *Annual Report 1972* (Washington, D.C.) Table 6, pp. 82-83, and *Annual Report 1975*, Table 5, pp. 92-93, and Table 6, pp. 94-95.
56. The World Bank, *Annual Report 1974*, Table III-19, p. 111.
57. O. Muñoz, *La crisis del desarrollo económico chileno, caracteristicas principales* [The Crisis of Chilean Economic Development, Principal Characteristics] (CEPLAN No. 16, Santiago de Chile), p. 12.
58. UNCTAD, *Major Issues Arising from the Transfer of Technology, A Case Study of Chile* (TD/B/AC11/20; 17 May 1974), pp. 4, 5 and Table 16, p. 35.
59. OECD, DAC, *1975 Report* (Paris, 1975), Table 28, pp. 234-235.
60. Pacheco, 'La inversión extranjera...', p. 120.
61. Pacheco, 'La inversión extranjera...', pp. 129-130.
62. S. Bitar, *La presencia de la empresa extranjera en la industria chilena* (CEPLAN No. 21, Santiago de Chile, November 1972), pp. 26-27.
63. OECD, DAC, *Stock of Private Direct Investment by DAC Countries in Developing Countries, End 1967* (Paris, 1972), and UNCTAD, *Major Issues...*, p. 4, footnote 5.
64. Bitar, 'La presencia...', p. 31. At the end of the 1960s, for twenty-two enterprises whose capital was far more than 50% foreign, 41% of the funds used were national.

65. '...the main objective of foreign assistance, as of many of the tools of foreign policy, is to produce the kind of political and economic environment in the world in which the United States can best pursue its own social goals'. H.B. Chenery, in K.S. Griffin and J.L. Enos, 'Foreign Assistance: Objectives and Consequences', *Economic Development and Cultural Change* (April 1970), 313.
66. Meier, 'Foreign Aid: Economic Aspects', p. 527.
67. A. Raham, 'Foreign Capital and Domestic Savings...', *Review of Economics and Statistics* (1968).
68. Bitar, 'La presencia...', p. 35. 'On average for 1966-69, net imports of machinery and equipment, normally of the technology-intensive type, constituted around one-third of gross capital promotion and more than four-fifths of the capital formation in the machinery and equipment sector': UNCTAD, *Major Issues...*, p. 47.
69. UNCTAD, *Major Issues...*, p. 5.
70. O. Muñoz, 'Conocimiento industrial, estructura del consumo y distribución del ingreso', [Industrial Know-how, Consumption Structure and Income Distribution], in Foxley and Muñoz, 'Income Redistribution...', 17.
71. The official foreign assistance received by Chile during 1968-70 was $14.00 per person, the highest in Latin America with the exception of Guyana. UN, ECLA, *Latin America and the International Development Strategy* (Part Two, E/CN. 12/947/Add.1, 7 February 1973), Table 12, p. 186.
72. 'Given the willingness of Chilean authorities to cooperate in the resolution of outstanding bilateral problems of debt and compensation, the efforts underway to regularise Chile's international financial obligations and the serious Chilean stabilisation effort, reactivation of the A.J.D. loan programme is proposed for FY 1975.' This was stated in the AID presentation of its plan to Congress, published in *Inter-American Economic Affairs* (Summer 1974), 89. Only military assistance was maintained; during the 1970-74 period the U.S. Government granted Chile $44.5 million in military aid, which doubled the amount given in previous years.
73. 'The typical means to assure B's continuous dependence on A...is the 'monopolisation of needed rewards' which A can achieve by: (i) maintaining B's resources always lower than necessary for B to obtain the wanted rewards; (ii) restricting B's access to alternative sources of supply for its rewards; e.g. by avoiding competition among various A's.' Sideri, 'International Trade and Economic Power', p. 351.
74. The suggestion that foreign aid, and foreign capital, has 'to enable and to embolden a country to set out on the path of unbalanced growth' was made long ago by A.O. Hirschman in *The Strategy of Economic Development* (New Haven, Yale University Press, 1961), p. 205, but it clearly did not include the socio-political imbalances which necessarily accompany a process of egalitarian development.
75. Chenery and Strout, 'Foreign Assistance and Economic Development', 697.
76. Meier, 'Foreign Aid: Economic Aspects', p. 256.
77. S.P. Huntington, 'Foreign Aid for What and for Whom', *Foreign Policy* (Winter 1970-71), 175-177.
78. This view is not fully shared by R.E. Feinberg, who believes that 'many UP leaders were not fully aware of how crucial the role of foreign finance was in Chile's trade relations. Also, they may have underestimated the degree of interconnectedness of the U.S. business community. It was known, for example, that many of the major New York banks had helped finance the copper expansion of the Frei period; less known were the interlocking relations between Anaconda and Chase Manhattan, between Kennecott and Morgan Guaranty. Certainly the UP hoped that these relationships would not be determinant in deciding these banks' policy towards Chile. The UP underestimated the degree of class solidarity existing among their external foes, just as they underestimated the resilience, unity and determination of their internal enemies.' 'Dependency and the Defeat of Allende', *Latin-American Perspectives* (Summer 1974), 34.
79. *Le monde diplomatique* [The Diplomatic World] (October 1973).
80. S. Sideri, 'De herstructurering van het internationale systeem en de gevolgen voor de ontwikkelingslanden' [The Restructuring of the International System and the Consequences for the Developing Countries], *Internationale Spectator* (December 1972).
81. IMF, The World Bank, *Direction of Trade, 1970-74* (Washington, D.C.), p. 106. Im-

ports from the United States declined from 32% in 1970 to 17% and 22% in 1972 and 1973 respectively.

82. P. Neruda, 'Madrid' (1937), in *Obras completas* [Complete Works], Vol. I, 3rd edition (Buenos Aires, 1967), p. 292.

Table 10.1. *Income Distribution*

	Economically active population %	*Income*[a] %	*Legal minimum wage unit*	*Families*[b] %	*Income*[b] %
Lower income group	45	14	1 or less	30	8
Middle income group	46	50	1 to 4	57	50
Upper income group	9	35	4 or more	13	42

[a] I. Heskia, *Analís estadistico de la dístribución del ingreso personal* . . . .
[b] ODEPLAN, *Antecedentes sobre el desarrollo* . . . , p. 16, Table 17.

INDEX

SERIES ON THE DEVELOPMENT OF SOCIETIES

Vol. I – A. F. Leemans, editor
The Management of Change in Government
1976

Vol. II – L. Cliffe, J. S. Coleman, and M. R. Doornbos, editors
Government and Rural Development in East Africa. Essays on Political Penetration
1977

Vol. III – K. Post
Arise Ye Starvelings. The Jamaican Labour Rebellion of 1938 and its Aftermath
1978

Vol. IV – S. Sideri, editor
Chile 1970–73: Economic Development and its International Setting. Self-criticism of the Unidad Popular *Government's Policies*
1979